# QuickBooks® 2002

## THE OFFICIAL GUIDE

# QuickBooks® 2002

## THE OFFICIAL GUIDE

**Kathy Ivens**

Osborne/**McGraw-Hill**

New York   Chicago   San Francisco   Lisbon
London   Madrid   Mexico City   Milan   New Delhi
San Juan   Seoul   Singapore   Sydney   Toronto

Osborne/**McGraw-Hill**
2600 Tenth Street
Berkeley, California 94710
U.S.A.

To arrange bulk purchase discounts for sales promotions, premiums, or fund-raisers, please contact Osborne/**McGraw-Hill** at the above address.

## QuickBooks 2002: The Official Guide

34567890 FGR FGR 0198765432

ISBN 0-07-219416-2

| | | |
|---|---|---|
| **Publisher** | **Acquisitions Coordinator** | **Proofreader** |
| Brandon A. Nordin | Tana Diminyatz | Kelly Marshall |
| **Vice President & Associate Publisher** | **Project Manager** | **Indexer** |
| Scott Rogers | Deidre Dolce | Jack Lewis |
| **Editorial Director** | **Freelance Project Manager** | **Computer Designer** |
| Roger Stewart | Laurie Stewart | Maureen Forys, Happenstance Type-O-Rama |
| **Acquisitions Editor** | **Technical Editor** | **Series Design** |
| Megg Bonar | Tom Barich | Jill Weil, Peter F. Hancik |
| | **Copy Editor** | |
| | edilogica | |

This book was composed with QuarkXPress 4.11 on a Macintosh G4.

This book is dedicated to Leah Rose Telepan,
with love and awe. Welcome to our family.

# Contents at a Glance

## Part Three  Using Time and Billing

## Part Four  Managing QuickBooks

## Part Five  Appendices

# Contents

## Part One    Getting Started

## Part Two    Bookkeeping

## Part Four    Managing QuickBooks

# Part Five    Appendices

# Acknowledgments

It's always great to work with the folks who work at Osborne/McGraw-Hill, because this is the "dream team" for computer book authors. Acquisitions editor Megg Bonar is a wonderful person and a pleasure to work with. Acquisitions coordinator Tana Diminyatz juggled a zillion details expertly and cheerfully and kept us all on track. Technical editor Tom Barich provided expert insights about presenting material in addition to making sure that the facts and instructions in this book are correct. My thanks also to copy editor Kari Brooks, project manager Laurie Stewart, and to Maureen Forys for page layout.

For Intuit, here's a nod of appreciation for their support, with a special thank you to Kristy Stromberg for her help. And, my gratitude and praise for Intuit's Roger Kimble whose expertise in QuickBooks is surpassed only by his cooperative attitude and unfailing patience.

# Introduction

## How to Use this Book

While I'd like to believe that writing this book was tantamount to writing a prize-winning novel, I really know that you won't read this book by starting at page 1 and continuing to the end. However, there is a progressive logic to the way the book is organized.

You can consult the Contents, where you'll notice that the order of the chapters reflects the way you'll probably use your QuickBooks software. The tasks you perform often (and immediately upon installing the software) are covered before the tasks you perform less frequently.

The Index guides you to specific tasks and features, so when you absolutely must know immediately how to do something, it's easy to find the instructions.

However, there are some sections of this book you should read first, just because accounting software is truly more complex than most other types of software. You should read Appendix A to learn what information to have at hand in order to set up your accounting system properly. Then you should read the first two chapters so you can configure your system properly. After that, read the chapter or section you need to in order to perform the tasks that have to be accomplished immediately.

## What's Provided in this Book to Help You

There are some special elements in this book that you'll find extremely useful:

- **Tips** give you some additional insight about a subject or a task. Sometimes they're shortcuts, and sometimes they're tricks I've learned working with clients.

- **Notes** provide extra information about a topic or a task. Sometimes they provide information about what happens behind the scenes when you perform a task, and sometimes they have additional information I think you might be curious about.

- **Cautions** are presented to help you avoid the traps you can fall into if a task has a danger zone.
- **Putting QuickBooks to Work** is a device for showing you how the tasks you're learning can be used in your business. In these supplementary sections, I've illustrated ways in which various businesses have actually used QuickBooks features. Within these stories, you'll find information aimed at helping you use certain features in a more creative and robust manner.

# You and Your Accountant

One of the advantages of double-entry bookkeeping software like QuickBooks is that a great many simple bookkeeping tasks are performed automatically. If you've been keeping manual books, or using a check-writing program such as Quicken, your accountant will probably have less work to do now that you're using QuickBooks.

Many accountants visit clients regularly or ask that copies of checkbook registers be sent to the accountants' offices. Then, using the data from the transactions, a general ledger is created, along with a trial balance and other reports based on the general ledger (profit & loss statements and balance sheets).

If you've had such a relationship with your accountant, it ends with QuickBooks. Your accountant will only have to provide tax advice and business planning advice. All those bookkeeping chores are performed by QuickBooks, which keeps a general ledger and provides reports based on the data in the general ledger. However, you'll want to check with your accountant as you set up your chart of accounts (the accounts that make up the general ledger), and also as you link tax forms to the accounts that are connected to your tax reports.

Throughout this book, I've provided information about general ledger postings as you create transactions in QuickBooks, and you'll also find references from me when I think specific information is going to be important to your accountant. Accountants tend to ask questions about how software handles certain issues (especially payroll, inventory, accounts receivable, and accounts payable). I've had many years of experience working with accountants as I set up bookkeeping software. As a result, you'll see comments from me such as, "Your accountant will probably ask how QuickBooks handles this," followed by an explanation that you can give your accountant. There are also a number of places in this book in which I advise you to call your accountant before making a decision about how to handle a certain transaction.

Don't worry, your accountant won't complain about losing the bookkeeping tasks. Most accountants prefer to handle more professional chores, and they rarely protest when you tell them they no longer have to be bookkeepers. Their parents didn't spend all that money on their advanced, difficult educations for that.

## Upgrading the Information in this Book

Like most software applications, QuickBooks is updated, tweaked, and improved over the course of time. As software features change, so do the contents of this book. To keep this book up to date, you can visit this book's Web page, http://www.cpa911.com.

Besides upgraded instructions, this Web site has lots of tricks, tips, and shortcuts (hopefully, you'll add your own discoveries). There's also a lot of information for your accountant, explaining the technical accounting processes that go on behind the scenes as you use your QuickBooks software. Your accountant can also find information that helps him or her work with QuickBooks clients.

# Getting Started

*The decision to use a software application for your bookkeeping and accounting needs is a momentous one. It will change your business life—for the better.*

*However, installing QuickBooks isn't the same as installing a word processor. With a word processor you can dive right in and begin using the program—sending letters to Mom or memos to the staff or writing the great novel of the century.*

*QuickBooks, on the other hand, has to be set up, configured, built one brick at a time. Otherwise, you can't use it properly as a foundation for your business activities. In fact, the first time you use QuickBooks, you'll be asked to take part in an interview. The software has a slew of questions for you, all of them designed to help you configure your QuickBooks system properly.*

*In Part One of this book, you'll learn how to get through the interview. I'll explain what's really important, what can wait until later, and what you can do all by yourself instead of through the interview process. I'll even explain when it's okay to lie, and how to lie in a way that makes your QuickBooks database accurate. Part One also includes a chapter containing instructions and hints about putting all those boring details into your accounting system, like customers, vendors, and general ledger information. (Sorry, but these fine points are necessary; you cannot keep books without them.)*

*Before you read Part One, be sure you've looked at Appendix A, which I've titled "Do This First!" Take that title seriously; it'll make getting through all this setup stuff easier.*

Part One

# Using QuickBooks for the First Time

## Chapter 1

## In this Chapter:

- *Open QuickBooks*

- *Go through the setup interview*

- *Decide whether to continue the interview*

- *Perform a manual setup*

- *Navigate the QuickBooks window*

The first time you launch QuickBooks, you have to introduce yourself and your company to the software by means of a rather substantial setup process. This process has a lot of tasks to wade through, but it's a one-time-only job.

# Launching the Software

The QuickBooks installation program places a shortcut to the software on your desktop (unless you told the installation program not to do so), and the easiest way to open QuickBooks is to double-click that shortcut. You can also use the Start menu, where you'll find QuickBooks in the Programs menu. Place your pointer on the QuickBooks listing in the Programs menu and choose QuickBooks from the submenu.

**Tip**    *For even faster access to QuickBooks, copy or move the desktop shortcut to your Quick Launch toolbar. Right-drag the shortcut icon onto the Quick Launch toolbar, and then choose Move Here (or Copy Here, if you want a shortcut in both places).*

When QuickBooks opens for the first time, you see a QuickBooks window (called a *splash screen* in computer jargon), followed by the Welcome to QuickBooks window displaying the following icons that represent your options for using QuickBooks for the first time:

**Create a New Company**    This option begins the process of creating a company file. All of the steps involved in this task are covered in this chapter.

**Open an Existing Company**    Select this option if you're upgrading from a previous version of QuickBooks. The Open A Company dialog box appears so you can select your company file. QuickBooks offers to upgrade the file to your new version, and after you click Yes to accept the offer, QuickBooks insists on making a backup of your file first. When the backup is complete, the file is converted and you can go back to work.

**Convert from Quicken**    Select this option if you are moving to QuickBooks from Quicken. There are a number of preliminary steps to take before selecting this option, to make sure the conversion process works properly. It's beyond the scope of this book to discuss converting Quicken files to QuickBooks companies, but if you need additional help, look for articles at http://www.cpa911.com. Select the QuickBooks Tips for Businesses link, and then select the article Converting from Quicken to QuickBooks.

**Open a Sample File**   Click this option to display a list of two sample companies you can explore and play with in order to get familiar with QuickBooks. One company is designed for product-based businesses, the other for service-based businesses.

If you're not ready to start, you can exit QuickBooks by clicking the X in the top-right corner of the QuickBooks window, or by choosing File | Exit from the menu bar. The next time you open QuickBooks, all the processes described here will start again.

For now, choose Create A New Company because that's what this chapter is all about.

## Starting the Setup Interview

The EasyStep Interview window, shown in Figure 1-1, opens to begin the company creation process. Click Next to begin the interview.

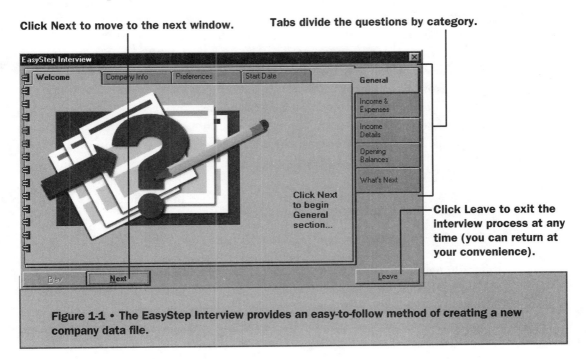

Figure 1-1 • The EasyStep Interview provides an easy-to-follow method of creating a new company data file.

## The Welcome Interview

The first section of the interview is the Welcome section. Click Next to display the first screen of the interview, which tells you about getting help with QuickBooks.

The next window offers you the opportunity to skip the interview altogether. If you do want to skip it, you can always return later. You can also enter some of the information QuickBooks needs by using the functions available on the menu bar. Chapter 2 has a great deal of information that will help you do this. Incidentally, even if you opt to skip the interview, you still have to answer several questions by filling out a dialog box with basic information about your company.

For now, however, move on with the interview so you can learn more about it before deciding whether to set up a company without the interview.

## The Company Info Interview

After you read all the information on the pages of the Welcome section, the Company Info portion of the interview begins. Remember to click Next to keep chugging along throughout the entire interview process.

The first item of information QuickBooks needs is your company name, for which two entry fields are available. The first field is for the real company name, the one you do business as. The second entry is optional and is used only if the legal name of your company differs from the company name you use for doing business. For instance, if your company does business as WeAreWidgets, but the legal name or corporate name is WAW, Inc., you should fill out both name fields.

Continue to the following windows and fill out the company address, and then the basic tax information (your federal tax ID number and the starting month of your fiscal and tax year). The federal ID number is a nine-digit number in the format *XX-YYYYYYY,* where *XX* is a number assigned to your state and *YYYYYYY* is the number assigned to your company.

You already have a federal tax ID number if you have employees, and you may have one if you have a bank account in the business name. (Many banks require this, although some banks merely ask for a copy of a fictitious name registration certificate and will accept your social security number instead of a federal ID.)

**Tip**    *If you are a sole proprietor and haven't bothered applying for a federal ID number, but instead are using your social security number for tax reporting, think again. You should separate your business and personal taxes/finances. The best way to do this is to have an EIN number and a separate bank account in your business name. Additionally, since you should be thinking in terms of business growth, you're going to need a federal ID number eventually to pay subcontractors, consultants, or employees. Get it now and avoid the rush.*

QuickBooks also asks which tax form you use for your business. The common forms for small businesses are

- 1120 for C Corporations
- 1120S for S Corporations
- 1065 for Partnerships
- 1040 for Proprietorships

Note that these are the tax forms on which income (loss) is reported, but there are lots of other tax forms you'll use in addition to these.

In the next window, tell QuickBooks the type of business you have (see Figure 1-2).

Move through the next windows (which provide information, and don't require user input) to get to the point at which QuickBooks creates the company file you'll use when you work in the software. A Save As dialog box opens, asking for a filename. QuickBooks suggests a name based on the company name you've entered, so just click Save to use that filename. It takes a few seconds for QuickBooks to save the company and set up all the files for the company.

**Tip**   *It's a good idea to use a filename that reflects your company name, instead of choosing a name such as Myfiles. Then, if you start another business, you can choose another specific filename for your new venture. Of course, you may end up using QuickBooks for your personal financial records, in which case you'll want a specific filename for that, too.*

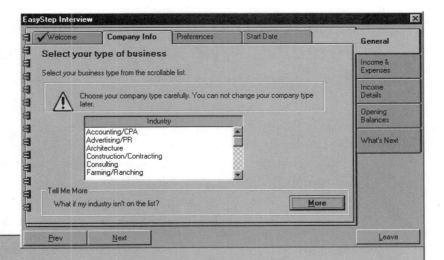

**Figure 1-2 • If you don't see an exact description of your business type, choose one that comes close.**

QuickBooks displays the Income and Expense accounts it has established for your company, based on the response you made to the interview question regarding your type of business. You can accept the chart of accounts QuickBooks shows you, or select the option to create your own chart of accounts (covered in Chapter 2). It doesn't really matter which option you select, because you and your accountant will be adding, changing, and removing accounts as you fine-tune your QuickBooks files.

Click Next to move to the next wizard window. You're asked how many people will have access to your QuickBooks file (which really means the computer on which it resides). This is not connected to running QuickBooks on a network; it refers only to this QuickBooks software on this computer. Many small businesses permit multiple users access to the computer and accounting software, and if you plan to do so, you should tell QuickBooks about it. Then, you'll be able to determine who sees which part of your accounting records. This is a good way to keep payroll records away from everyone except the person who enters payroll data, or to keep employees out of the general ledger (where the totals and profit/loss reports are).

Restrictions on users are implemented with the use of passwords that are attached to user names. The password feature is covered in Chapter 21.

**Tip** *The question about additional users is worded to mean "in addition to yourself," so if nobody but you uses your computer, zero is an appropriate answer.*

## Deciding Whether to Continue the Interview

At this point, you can continue the interview process or leave it. Everything else you do in the EasyStep Interview can be accomplished manually. To help you make the decision, this section presents some things to consider.

In the setup interview, you will be asked about the features you need (such as inventory tracking or collecting sales tax from customers). You can turn on these features manually via the menu system or take care of setting them up now. It's six of one and a half dozen of the other; there's no particular advantage to either approach.

The setup interview will ask for a starting date, which means you need to decide on the date your use of QuickBooks begins. Any activity that occurred in your system before that date is entered as a series of totals. For example, QuickBooks asks you about the amount of money owed to you by customers as of that date, and you must fill out the customer information (and the balance as of the starting date) for each of those customers. The same process occurs for vendors and, in fact, for all the totals of your accounts (banks, liabilities, and so on) as of the starting date.

QuickBooks adds up all the customer balances and uses the total as the starting accounts receivable balance. You can enter customer invoices yourself manually, pretty much in your spare time. That's because QuickBooks is date-sensitive. If you tell QuickBooks your starting date is 3/30, entering customer invoices that predate that starting date (invoices that aren't yet paid) creates the same accounts receivable balance, but you have details about the invoices.

If it's early in the year, you can tell QuickBooks that your starting date is the first day of the year and enter all the transactions for the year. You don't have to enter them before you can begin using QuickBooks for current transactions; you can make your entries in your spare time. If it's November or December, you might want to wait until January to start using QuickBooks.

A major problem with doing all of this through the interview process is that you're forced to set up accounts in your chart of accounts during the procedure, and you may want to use a different naming system than the one QuickBooks presents. Specifically, I'm talking about using numbers for your chart of accounts instead of names. Numbered accounts also have names, but the accounts are sorted by numbers. You assign the first digit to reflect the type of account; for example, assets always start with 1, liabilities with 2, and so on. After you finish the interview process and begin to use QuickBooks, you can configure the software to use numbers. However, that choice isn't offered during the interview process, so you're stuck with names instead of numbers (even though you can switch later). Check with your accountant—I think you'll find that he or she is an enthusiastic advocate of numbered accounts.

Chapter 2 explains how to enter all the information QuickBooks needs manually, from customers to the chart of accounts.

In the meantime, this section describes the interview process, so you can either follow along if you've decided to complete the interview, read this section in order to make your final decision, or read this section to get an idea of the type of information you'll need if you set up your company file manually.

# The Preferences Interview

The QuickBooks features you plan to use, and assorted other preferences, are determined in the Preferences section of the EasyStep Interview. Nothing you enter is etched in stone. After all, you'll probably change your mind about some of the responses you give here, because as you work in QuickBooks and get to know it better, you'll think of a better way to customize it for yourself.

## Inventory Feature

The first thing you're asked is whether or not you want to use inventory. Actually, you first are asked whether you maintain inventory in your business, and *then* you're asked whether you want to turn on the inventory features.

If you use inventory, answer Yes to the first question. Regarding the second question, about turning on the inventory feature, I can give you a good argument for either choice. If you do turn it on, you are walked through the process of entering all of your inventory items at the end of the interview. Personally, I think this is really onerous and I wouldn't do it. You can enter your inventory items later, perhaps one morning when your telephones aren't ringing off the hook and you've had plenty of sleep and several cups of coffee (and you haven't just gone through this long interview process). Inventory is one of those things that has to be entered accurately and precisely if the feature is going to work properly. If you stock only a few inventory items, you might want to complete this now; otherwise, wait a while, and when you're ready, start by reading Chapters 2 and 10, which cover entering inventory items.

## Sales Tax Feature

If you collect sales tax from your customers, you have to tell QuickBooks about it so it can be added to your invoices. First, answer Yes to the question about whether or not you are responsible for collecting (and remitting) sales tax. Then, specify whether or not you collect a single tax or multiple taxes. Fill in the information for the single tax, or for the most common tax if you have multiple taxes, because you cannot set up multiple taxes during the interview; you must do that later. Multiple taxes can be defined in several ways:

- You do business in more than one state and collect sales tax and remit it to the appropriate states.
- You do business in only one state, but different tax rates apply depending on the city in which your customer resides.
- You have both of the preceding situations.

If you do business in a state that has a different sales tax for one city than it does for other cities (for example, New York City has a higher tax rate than the rest of New York state, and Philadelphia has a higher tax rate than the rest of Pennsylvania), then be sure to read the tax law carefully. Some tax rates are determined by the address of the vendor (which is you), not the address of the customer. When Philadelphia raised its rate one percent higher than the rest of Pennsylvania, companies inside Philadelphia had to raise the rate for all customers (including those outside of Philadelphia), and companies outside of Philadelphia collected tax from their customers (including Philadelphia businesses) at the lower rate. Many businesses (and, sadly, many accountants) didn't understand this and spent hours changing tax rates on customer records based on customer addresses. Of course, later, when the details of the tax law became clearer, they had to change everything back again.

## Invoice Form Preference

Choose the invoice form you prefer from the formats available in QuickBooks (see Figure 1-3). The form can be modified, so pick the one that comes closest to your own taste, and then read Chapter 3 (see the section called "Customizing Forms") to learn how to tweak it to a state of perfection. When you're actually creating invoices, all the forms are available, so the decision you make here isn't irrevocable.

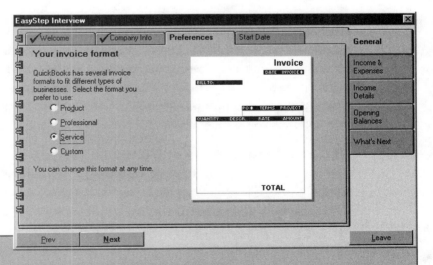

**Figure 1-3 • Choose the invoice form that best suits your needs.**

## Payroll Feature

If you have employees, and you plan to do your own payroll processing in QuickBooks, select Yes to the question about using QuickBooks payroll. If you have employees and use an outside payroll service, select No.

An employee is someone you pay for whom you withhold taxes and issue a W-2 form at the end of the year. This includes you, if that's how you pay yourself (instead of writing a check that's a draw against the business income). Subcontractors for whom you report payments on Form 1099 are not employees.

See Chapters 8 and 9 to learn everything about doing your own payroll.

## Estimating Preferences

If you provide estimates and then bill your customers according to a formula that tracks the progress of a job, QuickBooks has some features you may want to use. Answer the questions to match the way you do business.

## Time Tracking Preferences

If you bill for time and want to track the amount of time you or your employees spend on each job, an interview question is provided for that, also. See Chapters 18 through 20 for information about using this feature.

## Classes Preferences

You also are given an opportunity to turn on the classes feature, which is a way to combine categories and accounts to create reports that produce an overview. The feature can be useful for tracking types of customers, jobs, or even branch offices. More information about setting up and using classes is found in Chapter 21. If you turn on the classes feature here, you must establish the classes at some point after the interview (or answer No now and turn on the feature when you're ready to set up the classes).

## Accounts Payable Preferences

The next section in the interview process is the determination of the method for handling your bills from vendors. You have two choices and both offer advantages and disadvantages:

- Enter the checks directly.
- Enter the bills first and then enter the payments later.

If you opt to enter your checks directly, it means that as bills arrive in your office, you put them somewhere (an envelope, a folder, or a shoebox) until you're ready to pay them. Then, you just have to enter the checks in the QuickBooks check register, place the checks in the envelopes, and attach a stamp. The advantage of this method is that it takes less time and less data entry. The disadvantage is that the only way to know how much money you owe at a given moment is to take the bills out of the container and total them manually. Also, unless you specially mark and store those bills that offer a discount for timely payment, you might inadvertently miss a deadline and lose the discount.

If you decide to enter the bills first and then go through the process of paying them in QuickBooks, you can let the software remind you about due dates and simultaneously get a total for your current accounts payable. Another consideration when you opt to enter your bills into the software is that your accountant might have to make an adjustment when it's time to figure your taxes. Tracking accounts payable (and accounts receivable, for that matter) is called *accrual accounting*. If you file on a cash basis instead of an accrual basis, the accrued amount owed is not considered an expense and has to be subtracted from your total expenses. This isn't terribly unusual or difficult, but you should be aware of it. Most small businesses that don't have inventory considerations file taxes on a cash basis.

## Reminders Preferences

QuickBooks has a feature which tracks the things you need to do and shows you a To Do list when you start the software. Included in the list are any due dates that exist (as a result of your data entry) in addition to any notes you wrote yourself and opted to be reminded about.

You can continue to let QuickBooks show you the reminder list when you open the software, or opt to display it manually through the menu. Make your decision based on the way you're most comfortable working. (You can always change it later.)

## Cash or Accrual Reporting

QuickBooks has a specific interview question about the way you want to keep your books, offering cash or accrual options. Before you make the decision, check with your accountant. The smart way to do that is to ask your accountant to give a full explanation (don't just say "Which way?" and accept a one-word answer).

**Note** | *One important fact that both you and your accountant should be aware of is that when you use QuickBooks, the decision of accrual versus cash isn't as important as it is with some other accounting software programs. QuickBooks is capable of producing reports either way, regardless of the decision you make in the interview.*

Here's a quick overview of what's really involved in this decision. (For details that apply specifically to your business, you should have a fuller discussion with your accountant.) In cash-based accounting, an expense doesn't exist until you write the check. Even if you enter the bill into the software and post it to an expense account in the general ledger, it isn't really an expense until the check is written. The same is true for revenue, meaning income isn't considered to be real until payment is received from your customer. Even though you enter an invoice and post it to a revenue account in the general ledger, it isn't revenue until it's paid.

In accrual-based accounting, as soon as you incur an expense (receive a bill from a vendor) or earn income (send an invoice to a customer), it's real.

Because most accounting software is accrual-based, most businesses, especially small businesses, keep accrual books and report to the IRS on a cash basis. Most accounting software is accrual-based because business owners want to know those accrued totals: "How much did I earn (bill customers for)?" and "How much do I owe?"

**Tip**    *If you have inventory, you'll probably file your business taxes using accrual accounting.*

My own advice is you should choose accrual-based reports in the QuickBooks interview so you can obtain information about your earning and spending in greater detail.

## Start Date Interview

If today is the first day of your fiscal year (usually January 1), your accountant has just completed all the accounting stuff for last year, and your numbers are pristine and perfect, you can keep going now. It's almost impossible to believe that this scenario exists. If any other situation exists, you should stop and read the section on selecting a start date in Appendix A. (You might also want to call your accountant.)

The start date you select has an enormous impact on the amount of detail your QuickBooks reports will have. In fact, it has an enormous impact on the accuracy of the numbers QuickBooks reports.

Without repeating all the information in Appendix A, the following is a quick overview of the choices you have:

- Choose the start date that represents the first day of your fiscal year and enter every transaction.

- Choose a start date that represents some accounting period, such as the end of a specific month or a specific quarter, enter totals as of that date, and then enter all the transactions since that date.

- Choose today (or some other non-meaningful date) and enter totals.

If the start date is not the first day of your fiscal year, you will have to enter the totals for each account in your chart of accounts as of the start date. This is called an *opening trial balance.*

**Note**     *Even if today is the first day of your fiscal year, you'll need an opening trial balance, but it's a much smaller one (a balance sheet) and doesn't involve income and expenses incurred so far.*

If you enter year-to-date totals, you won't have the details about how those totals were accrued in your QuickBooks file. That's not necessarily awful; it simply means that if you want to know how you reached a total income of a gazillion dollars by June 30, you'll have to go back to your manual records (or your old software) to get the information. If a customer calls and wants details about the billings, the individual bills won't be in your QuickBooks system and you'll have to walk to the filing cabinet and pull the paperwork.

If you're starting your QuickBooks software (and reading this book) in the first half of your fiscal year, I recommend using the first day of your fiscal year and entering each historical transaction. You don't have to enter all of them today, or even tomorrow; you can take your time.

**Tip**     *If other people in your office will be using QuickBooks, having them enter the historical transactions is a terrific way to learn how to use the software. Make sure everyone participates.*

Ready? Okay, enter the date. As Figure 1-4 shows, QuickBooks provides a graphical calendar you can use to move through the months and select a date. Or you can enter a date directly.

**Figure 1-4 •** **You can use the QuickBooks calendar in any field that asks for a date.**

## The Accounts Configuration Interview

Next on your interview agenda is the configuration of your income and expense accounts. Remember that QuickBooks entered a partial chart of accounts earlier in the interview process, when you indicated the type of business you have.

### Income Accounts Configuration

At this point, the income accounts are displayed, and you're asked whether you want to add any income accounts. By default, the Yes option is selected. I suggest you switch the option to No, even if you do need more income account types; you can add those accounts later. Chapter 2 covers this process in detail. If you didn't accept the chart of accounts and therefore have no income accounts, you must enter one now. Name the account appropriately (e.g., income, revenue, fees, etc.).

### Expense Accounts Configuration

There are a large number of interview screens connected to configuring expense accounts, because QuickBooks walks you through an explanation of accounts and subaccounts. Finally, the expense accounts already entered into your chart of accounts are displayed, and you're offered the opportunity to add additional accounts. (You can skip the explanations by choosing No when you're asked if you want detailed information about expense accounts.) There's no particular reason to add accounts now. When you're ready to add accounts, refer to Chapter 2 for directions.

If you didn't accept the pre-configured chart of accounts, you'll see Payroll Expenses as an existing expense account. QuickBooks adds this account automatically if you don't use the chart of accounts suggested earlier in the interview. This Payroll Expenses account appears even if you answered No to the question of whether or not you are using QuickBooks for payroll. You can never delete this account, even if you never use it. QuickBooks does this by design. It's not a bug (it's an annoyance). You can make this account inactive if you don't want it to appear on the list of accounts during transaction entry (see Chapter 2 to learn how to make accounts inactive).

## The Income Details Interview

Here's where you set up the income and accounts receivable features you'll use in QuickBooks. Move through the questions and respond according to the way you do business. You are asked about the manner in which customer payments are made, and whether you send statements to customers. Then you're asked whether you want to set up the service items for which you invoice customers. If you select Yes to indicate that you're ready to set up your service items, QuickBooks presents a dialog box to do so, as shown in Figure 1-5.

This is another one of those tasks that you can (and should) put off until later. This interview process is long and tiresome, and there's no reason to make it worse by entering all of this information now. When you decide to put these items into your system (which you can do any time before you send your first invoice to a customer), Chapter 2 will walk you through the process.

The Items portion of the Income Details Interview continues with different types of items, starting with non-inventory Parts, and moving through Other Charges (shipping fees, postage, and other expenses you might want to charge to your customers). From there, the wizard asks if you want to enter inventory items. I advise you to respond No to each invitation to enter an item. You can do it later.

If you want to accomplish these tasks now (make that decision only if you have a small number of items you'll be using for customer invoices), answer Yes and fill out the dialog boxes with the appropriate information. Chapter 2 provides assistance.

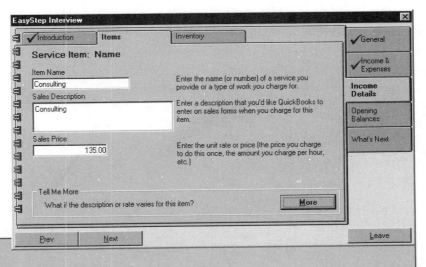

**Figure 1-5 • Services you provide for customers are called *items*.**

## The Opening Balances Interview

The next series of interview windows ask about balances—all sorts of balances.

### Customer and Vendor Balances

QuickBooks wants to know about the balances owed by your customers as of the opening date. If you fill out the interview questions, be prepared to fill out the customer information as well as the balance due (and the revenue account you posted the balance to, which you had to enter in the interview section about the chart of accounts).

The balances you owe your vendors are also requested, requiring you to fill out vendor cards and the expense accounts used for your purchases.

If you don't want to fill in these amounts now, just lie. Tell QuickBooks that none of your customers owe you money as of your start date. (I'm assuming that's a lie, unless you have a retail business, because it's normal to have customers with balances due.) Or, answer that you don't owe any money to vendors (wouldn't that be nice!).

### Balance Sheet Balances

When the interview gets to the Accounts section, you're asked whether you want to set up credit card accounts. That means QuickBooks wants to track the money you spend via plastic for business expenses. It tracks the credit card as a liability, an outstanding loan. If you pay off your credit card balances each month, there is no reason to do this. If you make partial payments on your credit cards and frequently have a running balance, you can choose to track the credit card as a liability (although you don't have to do it during the interview; you can establish it later).

Personally, I don't understand why QuickBooks makes the assumption that the only way to handle credit cards with running balances is as a liability. It means that you have to open a credit card account to record your purchases and reconcile the account (filling in the finance charges and interest charges). I hate that—I'm far too lazy for that process. I like to treat my credit card as just another vendor. I apply the appropriate amounts to the appropriate expense accounts when I enter the bill (or write a check if I don't want to enter the bill). If I don't want to pay off the whole balance, I make a partial payment. I enter any finance charges as just another expense when I enter the vendor invoice.

**Tip** *Credit card interest or finance charges you incur for a business are deductible. They are not deductible if the credit card is used for personal purchases.*

This option has no right and wrong answer. I just want to point out that QuickBooks takes the liability account connection for granted, and you don't have to do it that way if you don't want to. You might want to discuss this with your accountant before making the decision.

This is also the place to set up loans (including lines of credit) and bank accounts.

The interview process next walks through all the different types of asset accounts you might have on your balance sheet, asking for the name of the account, the type of asset, and the balance as of your start date. You'll probably have at least one bank account to set up, in addition to other important asset accounts (you don't have to enter opening balances).

Following asset accounts is an interview section for equity accounts. These are the accounts that represent the worth of your business. Generally, your current equity is the difference between your income and your expenses (your profit or loss), along with the original capital you put into the business. If your business is a proprietorship or partnership, the money you've pulled out of the business as a draw is subtracted from that number (if you take a draw instead of being on the payroll).

QuickBooks automatically provides two equity accounts:

- Opening Bal Equity, which is the worth of your business as of your opening date
- Retained Earnings, which is the difference between income and expenses for the current fiscal year

## The What's Next Interview

The last section of the interview process is called What's Next, and it begins with a list of recommended actions, as shown in Figure 1-6. The list contains items that are specific to your company set up, and the contents of the list reflect the windows you skipped, or information you decided to skip during the interview process.

As you click Next, each window displays instructions about how to accomplish the task QuickBooks is recommending. You don't perform the task in the interview; these are just recommendations and reminders.

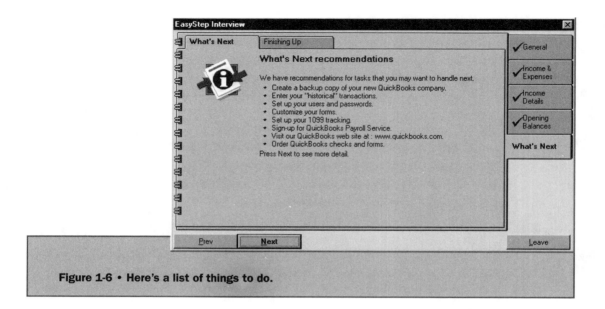

**Figure 1-6 • Here's a list of things to do.**

## Finishing Up

Guess what? You're finished. This is the last window in the EasyStep Interview. If you failed to make entries in any section of the interview, no check mark appears on the tab to the right.

You can click any side tab to return to an interview section. If you can't face that now (and I can't blame you), you can always return to the EasyStep Interview by choosing File | EasyStep Interview from the menu bar.

Choose Leave to close the EasyStep Interview and start working in the QuickBooks window. QuickBooks displays a page full of information, including links for more information about QuickBooks features and services. You can close this window by clicking the X in its top-right corner (not the top-right corner of the QuickBooks software window). See the section "The QuickBooks Software Window" later in this chapter to continue learning about using the QuickBooks window.

## Performing a Manual Setup

You can configure your QuickBooks company file manually either by choosing Leave at the point in the interview where QuickBooks saves your company file, or at any other point after that.

## Manual Company Setup

You can perform a completely manual setup that skips the EasyStep Interview altogether by choosing Skip Interview on the third window. The Creating New Company dialog opens, and you can enter the basic information quickly (see Figure 1-7).

Click Next to select a type of business so QuickBooks can install the appropriate chart of accounts. Then click Next to save the company file. Now you can use the QuickBooks menu system to turn on features and enter data.

## Manual Preferences Setup

This section reviews the method for turning on features. Then, in Chapter 2, you can learn how to enter the basic data that QuickBooks needs.

Choose Edit | Preferences from the menu bar to select the QuickBooks features you want to use. The Preferences dialog box appears with the General category selected, as shown in Figure 1-8.

Each category has two tabs: My Preferences and Company Preferences. The My Preferences tab offers options that are universally applied in QuickBooks, no matter which company you're working in. The Company Preferences tab offers options for the currently opened company. The majority of categories have no options available in the My Preferences tabs; you can only set company preferences.

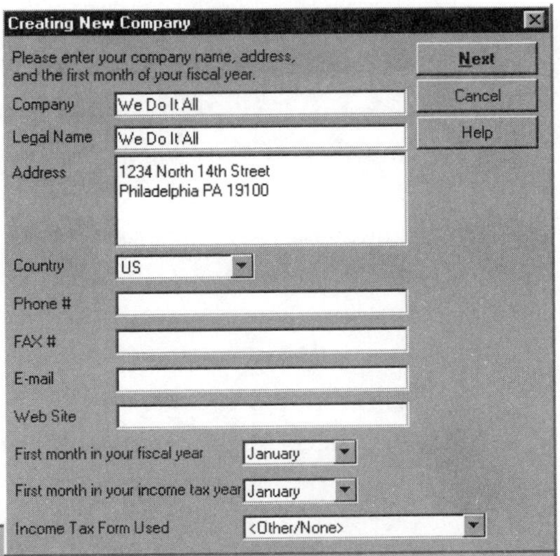

**Figure 1-7 •** **You can enter company information directly into the Creating New Company dialog box.**

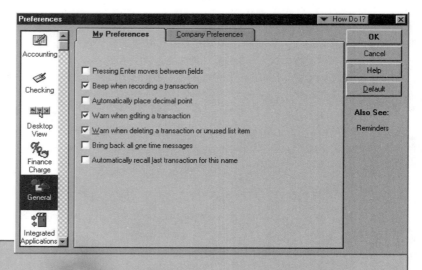

**Figure 1-8 •** Use the Preferences dialog box to select and deselect the features you want to use.

For this discussion, you won't be using the My Preferences tab, but you can read Chapter 21 to learn how to set these preferences.

Here are some guidelines for establishing the features you want to use in QuickBooks using the Company Preferences tab. In this section, I'm skipping some of the categories, concentrating only on those that are connected to basic bookkeeping tasks. The other categories are discussed throughout this book.

**Accounting Preferences**    Specify whether or not you want to use account numbers (a good idea). Also, you can indicate whether you want to use class tracking (see Chapter 21 for more information) and whether you want to keep an audit trail. An *audit trail* is a list of changes made to transactions, and if you turn this feature on, you may notice a small slowdown in the software. Despite this inconvenience, it's sometimes handy to track changes, particularly if you need to be reminded why some numbers have changed in your reports.

**Checking Preferences**    You can choose what you want to print on check vouchers (stubs), and decide the way you want to date checks (when you fill in the data or when you actually print the check). You can also choose the default bank accounts to use for payroll and payroll liabilities.

**Finance Charge Preferences**    Use this dialog box to turn on finance charges for late-paying customers. You can set a default rate and the circumstances under which finance charges are assessed.

**Integrated Applications Preferences**    Use this dialog box to allow or disallow access to the company file from other applications. See Appendix C for more information on integrating other software with QuickBooks.

**Jobs & Estimates Preferences**    This is the place to configure estimating and progress billing (billing a percentage of the price of a job as you reach a percentage of completion), if you need it. You can also configure the language you want to use for describing the status of jobs.

**Payroll & Employees Preferences**    If you're doing your own payroll processing in QuickBooks, set the preferences for creating employees and printing paychecks.

**Purchases & Vendors Preferences**    Use this dialog box to configure the way you handle bills and bill paying. You can also turn on inventory and purchase orders (you have to enable both features; you can't pick only one of them, but you don't actually have to use purchase orders).

**Sales & Customers Preferences**    Here's where you establish your shipping preferences and the default markup on inventory products. In addition, you can configure the way you want to handle reimbursed expenses. One of the important preference options on this dialog box is whether or not you want to apply customer payments automatically or manually. This really means that if the feature is turned on, customer payments are applied starting with the oldest invoice first. I've found that this frequently doesn't work well, because customers skip invoices that they want to contend (the product didn't arrive, or it arrived damaged, or they think the price is wrong). I find that if you apply the payments against the invoices manually, you have a more accurate record of payments. Most customers are applying the payment to one of your specific invoices when they cut the check, so if you follow their lead, you and your customer will have identical payment records.

**Tip**    *If you don't apply payments by invoice and use balance-forward billing, it's okay to leave the automatic application feature turned on.*

**Sales Tax Preferences**    This is the place to turn sales tax on or off. You must also specify when you have to remit the sales tax to the taxing authority, as well as whether the tax is due when it's charged or collected (check the state law).

**Tax 1099 Preferences**    If you pay subcontractors and need to send Form 1099 at the end of the year, this is the dialog box to use for configuration (see Figure 1-9).

You can attach a single account to a 1099 category by selecting that account, or you can attach several accounts to a 1099 category by clicking Selected Accounts (at the top of the drop-down list). For example, suppose you post expenses for

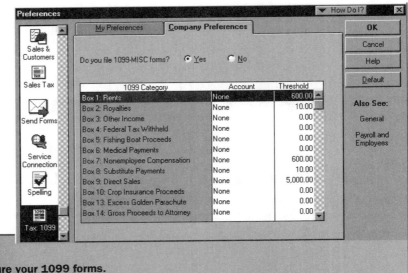

**Figure 1-9 • Configure your 1099 forms.**

subcontractors to an account named Outside Contractors, and you post expenses for freelance artists to an account named Freelancers. Vendor payments that are posted to either account could involve vendors who need Box 7 totals for 1099s.

However, once any account is posted to a category/Box #, that account cannot be attached to a different category/Box #. So, if some of your freelance artists are earning royalties, and you're posting their checks to the account named Freelancers, you can't also attach the Freelancers account to the category Royalties (Box 2).

After you configure your 1099 forms, you must remember to specify the 1099 check box in each applicable vendor card. See Chapter 2 for information on setting up vendors.

As you go through the Preferences dialog boxes, each time you make a change and move to the next category, you're asked whether you want to save the changes in the category you just completed. Answer Yes. When you're finished with all the categories, choose OK to close the Preferences dialog box.

These are the important system categories, and if you've completed them, you're ready to finish your manual setup. Chapter 2 introduces you to all the lists you need to enter.

# The QuickBooks Software Window

When the EasyStep Interview window closes, QuickBooks displays several windows: privacy information on automatic updates, a Getting Started window (read any article you wish by clicking its link), and the Company Navigator.

You can close the first two windows by clicking the X in the top-right corner. Don't click the X in the QuickBooks window, or you'll close the software.

When you close the first two windows, you see the QuickBooks software window, Company Navigator, shown in Figure 1-10.

Most people find it easier to access transaction windows and other components of the company file from the QuickBooks toolbars instead of via the Company Navigator. If you don't want to use the Company Navigator, click the X in the top-right corner of the navigator window. This changes the software window to the basic QuickBooks window, which is shown in Figure 1-11.

**Tip**     *By default, the Company Navigator appears every time you load the company file. To eliminate its appearance permanently, choose Edit | Preferences and click the Desktop View icon. On the My Preferences tab, deselect the option Show Company Navigator When Opening A Company File.*

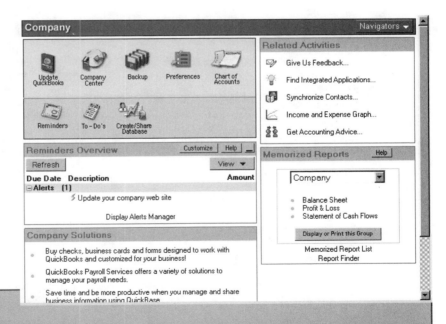

**Figure 1-10 • The Company Navigator lets you access features for the currently loaded company file.**

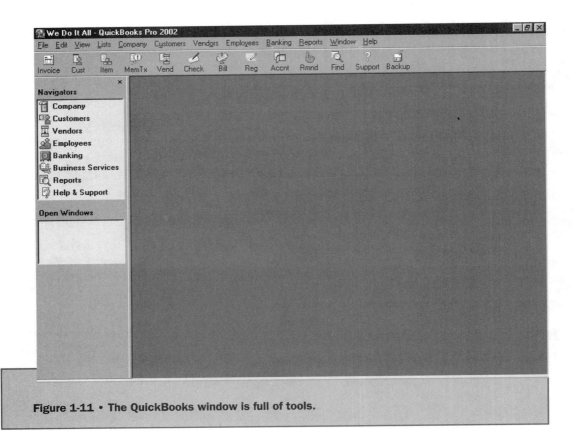

**Figure 1-11 • The QuickBooks window is full of tools.**

By default, the QuickBooks basic working window has the following elements:

- Title bar, which displays the name of your company file
- Menu bar, which contains all the commands for working in QuickBooks
- Icon bar, which contains buttons for quick access to oft-used functions (see Chapter 21 to learn how to customize the icon bar)
- Navigators list, which also contains the Open Windows list

Clicking any item on the Navigators list opens the associated Navigator window. For example, click the Company listing on the Navigators list to open the Company Navigator window you saw when you finished setting up your company. Each Navigator contains icons and links for accessing functions and information.

The Open Windows list lets you move between multiple open QuickBooks windows easily—click a window's name to put that window in the foreground of your QuickBooks window.

You can close the Navigators list by clicking the X at the top-right corner of its panel. To bring it back, choose View | Open Window List from the menu bar.

**Note**   *Even though the top of the panel says Navigators, that's not the name of this QuickBooks toolbar—the name is really Open Window List. This seems confusing to me—the name in the View menu should match the title on the panel.*

QuickBooks also offers another left-side panel for easy access to functions; it's called the Shortcut list, and you can choose it from the View menu. Like the icon bar, it provides icons for commonly used functions, but it organizes those icons by category (see Figure 1-12).

To exit QuickBooks, click the X in the top-right corner of the QuickBooks window or choose File | Exit from the menu bar.

The Shortcut list is customizable, and you can learn how to optimize it by reading Chapter 21.

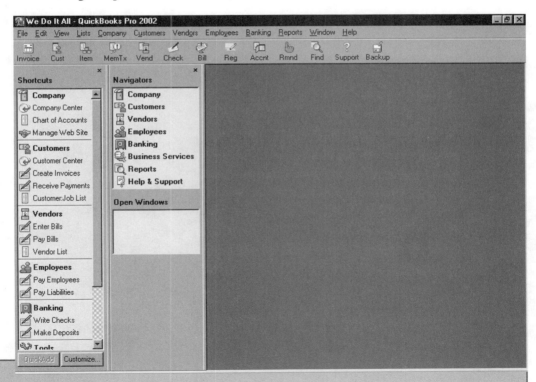

**Figure 1-12 • You can use the Shortcut list instead of, or in addition to, the Navigators list.**

# Setting Up Your Lists

## In this Chapter:

- *Create a full chart of accounts*

- *Enter all your lists*

- *Invent your own fields to make your lists more useful*

In this chapter, we're going to cover a lot of basic chores. They aren't terribly exciting or creative, but if you don't do them now, you'll regret it later. That's because every time you enter a transaction or fill out a form, you'll have to enter some basic data at the same time. Talk about annoying! So take the time now to get the basic data into the system. This is the preparation stuff, the work that makes future work faster and more efficient.

QuickBooks has a spelling checker, and some of the List windows contain a Spelling button. Click it to check the text you entered. Then you won't have to worry about spelling errors in transactions (for instance, invoices) because you've prechecked the elements.

**Tip** Each of the lists you create in QuickBooks has its own List window, and when you view the items in a list, you can sort the list by any column in the window. Just click the column heading to sort the list by the category of that column.

## Creating a Full Chart of Accounts

The first priority is your chart of accounts. QuickBooks created some accounts for you during the initial setup of your company, but most people need lots of additional accounts in order to keep books accurately. The reason you do the chart of accounts first is that some of the other lists you create require you to link items in the list to accounts. For example, service items are linked to income accounts.

### Using Numbers for Accounts

As we go through the entry of accounts, remember that I'm using numbers as the primary element in my chart of accounts. There's a title attached to the number, but the primary method of sorting my account list is by number. Even though the QuickBooks default is to use names, it's a simple matter to change the default and use numbers. Your accountant will be grateful, and you'll find you have far fewer mistakes in posting to the general ledger. If you prefer to stick to names, see the next section for some hints about creating account names.

To switch to a number format for your accounts, you just need to spend a couple of seconds changing the QuickBooks preferences:

1. Choose Edit | Preferences from the menu bar to bring up the Preferences dialog box.

2. Select the Accounting icon from the scroll box.
3. Click the Company Preferences tab, shown in Figure 2-1.
4. Select the Use Account Numbers check box.

If you chose a pre-built chart of accounts during the EasyStep Interview, those accounts will switch to numbered accounts automatically. You may want to change some of the numbers, and you can do so by editing the accounts (which is covered in this chapter). Any accounts you added yourself during the interview (or after the interview) will have to be edited manually to turn them into numbered accounts.

When you select the option to use account numbers, the option Show Lowest Subaccount Only becomes accessible (it's grayed out if you haven't opted for account numbers). This option tells QuickBooks to display only the subaccount on transaction windows instead of both the parent account and the subaccount, making it easier to see precisely which account is receiving the posting. (Subaccounts are discussed later in this section.)

If all your accounts aren't numbered, and you select Show Lowest Subaccount Only, when you click OK, QuickBooks displays an error message that you cannot enable this option until all your accounts have numbers assigned. After you've edited existing accounts that need numbers (any accounts that QuickBooks didn't automatically number for you), you can return to this preferences window and enable the subaccount option.

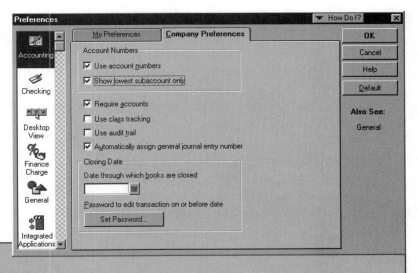

**Figure 2-1 • Change the accounting options to enable numbers for your chart of accounts.**

After you've set up numbered accounts, you have a more efficient chart of accounts; now you, your bookkeeper, and your accountant will have an easier time.

Numbers give you a quick clue about the type of account you're working with. As you enter the accounts, you must use the numbers intelligently, assigning ranges of numbers to account types. You should check with your accountant before finalizing the way you use the numbers, but there's a common approach you might find helpful. You can have as many as seven numbers (plus the account name) for each account. In this example, I'll use four numbers (the starting number represents the beginning of a range):

- 1xxx Assets
- 2xxx Liabilities
- 3xxx Equity
- 4xxx Revenue
- 5xxx Expenses
- 6xxx Expenses
- 7xxx Expenses
- 8xxx Expenses
- 9xxx Other Revenue and Expenses

Notice the amount of room for further breakdowns, especially in the expenses. (You always need more expense categories than revenue categories.)

You can, if you wish, have a variety of expense types and reserve the starting number for specific types. Many companies, for example, use 5xxx for sales expenses (they even separate the payroll postings between the sales people and the rest of the employees), then use 6000 through 7999 for general operating expenses, and 8xxx for other specific expenses that should appear together in reports (perhaps taxes or licensing). Some companies use one range of expense accounts, such as 7000 through 7500 or 7999 for expenses that fall into the "overhead" category. This is useful if you bid on work and need to know the total overhead expenses so you can apportion them to appropriate categories in your bid.

Also, as an example, think about the breakdown of assets. You might use 1000 through 1099 for cash accounts, 1100 through 1199 for receivables and other current assets, then use 1200 through 1299 for tracking fixed assets such as equipment, furniture, and so on. Follow the same pattern for liabilities, starting with current liabilities, and moving to long term. (It's also a good idea to keep all the payroll withholding liabilities together.)

Usually, you should add accounts by increasing the previous account number by ten, so that if your first bank account is 1000, the next bank account is 1010, and so on. For expenses (where you'll have many accounts), you might want to enter the accounts in intervals of five. This gives you room to squeeze in additional accounts that belong in the same general area of your chart of accounts when they need to be added later.

## Using Names for Accounts

Okay, I didn't convince you, or your accountant is just as happy with names for accounts. Or you've imported your accounts from another software application and you cannot bear the thought of changing all that data. Here's how to avoid the pitfalls that named accounts throw in your path: Make rules about naming and using accounts, and then stick to those rules.

This means that when you name an account, you keep the naming convention consistent, and you use the same abbreviations and shortcuts all the time. I have been in too many offices where I found accounts with names such as these in one chart of accounts:

- Telephone Exp
- Exps-Telephone
- Tele Expense
- Telephone & Answering Serv
- Tele and Ans Service

You get the idea, and I'll bet you're not shocked to hear that every one of those accounts had amounts posted to them. That's because users "guess" at account names and point and click on whatever they see that seems remotely related. If they don't find the account the way they would have entered the name, they invent a new one. Avoid all of those errors by establishing rules about searching the account list before applying a transaction.

## Using Subaccounts

Subaccounts provide a way to post transactions more precisely using subcategories for main account categories. For example, if you create an expense account for insurance expenses, you may want to have subaccounts for vehicle insurance, liability insurance, equipment insurance, and so on. For best results, post transactions only to the subaccounts, never to the parent account. When you create reports, QuickBooks will display the individual totals for the subaccounts, along with the grand total for the parent account. To create a subaccount, you must first create the parent account, as described in the next section, "Adding Accounts."

If you're using numbered accounts, when you set up your main (parent) accounts, be sure to leave enough open numbers to be able to fit in all the subaccounts you'll need. If necessary, use more than four digits to make sure you have a logical hierarchy for your account structure. For example, suppose you have the following parent accounts:

- 6010 Insurance
- 6020 Utilities
- 6030 Travel

You can create the following subaccounts:

- 6011 Insurance:Vehicles
- 6012 Insurance:Liability
- 6013 Insurance:Equipment
- 6021 Utilities:Heat
- 6022 Utilities:Electric
- 6031 Travel:Sales
- 6032 Travel:Seminars and Meetings

## Adding Accounts

After you've done your homework, made your decisions, and checked with your accountant, adding accounts is a piece of cake:

1. Press CTRL-A to open the Chart of Accounts window.

**Note**   *QuickBooks provides various ways to get to the Chart of Accounts list. Click the Accnt icon on the icon bar, select Company in the Navigators list, and then click the Chart of Accounts icon in the Company Navigator window, or choose Lists | Chart of Accounts from the menu bar.*

2. Press CTRL-N to enter a new account. The New Account dialog box opens so you can begin entering information.
3. Click the down arrow to the right of the Type box and select an account type from the drop-down list.

The dialog box for entering a new account changes its appearance depending on the account type, because different types of accounts require different information. In addition, if you've opted to use numbers for your accounts, there's a field for the account number. Figure 2-2 shows a blank New Account dialog box for an Expense account.

Here are some guidelines for entering account information:

- Use consistent protocols for the account name, abbreviating words in the same manner throughout the entire list of accounts.
- If you are using subaccounts, you can assign the subaccount to an existing account, or create a new parent account while you're configuring the subaccount.
- The Description field is optional. I've found that unless there's a compelling reason to explain the account, descriptions only make your account lists busier and harder to read.

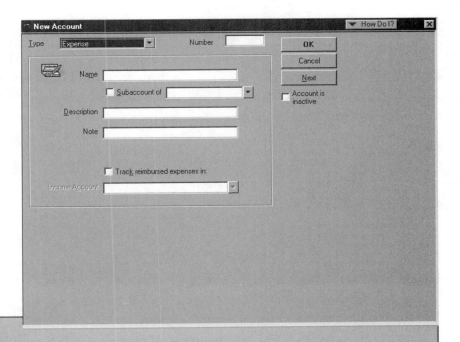

**Figure 2-2 •** **The only required entries for a new account are a number (if you're using numbers) and a name.**

If you're not currently using an account, you can select the Account Is Inactive option, which means the account won't be available for posting amounts while you're entering transactions. Entering a new account and marking it inactive immediately means you're really good at planning ahead. (Okay, I really wanted to say, "you're compulsive.")

Some account types (those connected to banks) have a field for an opening balance. Don't worry about it during this initial entry of new accounts. The priority is to get all of your accounts into the system; you don't have to worry about balances now. In fact, the fastest and easiest way to put the account balances into the system is to enter an opening trial balance as a journal entry (see Appendix A).

As you finish entering each account, choose Next to move to another blank New Account dialog box. When you're finished entering accounts, click OK and then close the Chart of Accounts list by clicking the X in the top-right corner.

## Editing Accounts

If you need to make changes to any of the account information, select the account and press CTRL-E. The Edit Account dialog box appears, which looks just like the account card you filled out. Just make your changes and click OK to save them.

To add a number to an account that wasn't automatically numbered when you changed your preferences to indicate numbered accounts, follow these steps:

1. Open the Chart of Accounts list.
2. Select an account that lacks a number.
3. Press CTRL-E to open the Edit Account dialog box.
4. Enter the account number.
5. Click OK.

## Creating Subaccounts

In order to create a subaccount, you must have already created the parent account. Then take these steps:

1. Open the Chart of Accounts list.
2. Press CTRL-N to create a new account.
3. Select the appropriate account type.

**4.** Click the Subaccount check box to place a check mark in it.

**5.** In the drop-down box next to the check box, select the parent account. (This gives you access to the parent account number if you're using numbered accounts—otherwise you'd have to memorize them.)

**6.** If you're using numbered accounts, enter the appropriate number.

**7.** Enter the account name.

**8.** Click OK.

You can have multiple levels of subaccounts. For example, you may want to track revenue in the following manner:

- Revenue
  - Revenue:Consulting
    - Revenue:Consulting:Engineering
    - Revenue:Consulting:Training
  - Revenue:Products
    - Revenue:Products:Technical
    - Revenue:Products:Accessories

Creating the sub-subaccounts is as easy as creating the first level; just make sure you've already created the first-level accounts (which become the parents of the sub-subaccounts). When you fill in the New Account dialog box, after you check the Subaccount check box, select the appropriate subaccount to act as the parent account.

When you view the Chart of Accounts list, subaccounts appear under their parent accounts, and they're indented. When you view a subaccount in a transaction window, it appears in the format: *ParentAccount:Subaccount*. For example, if you create a parent account named Revenue with a subaccount Consulting, the Account field in transaction windows shows Revenue:Consulting. If you've used numbers, the Account field shows 4000-Revenue:4001-Consulting. Because many of the fields in transaction windows are small, you may not be able to see the subaccount names without scrolling through each account. This can be annoying. It would be much easier if only the subaccount name were displayed. That's the point of enabling the preference Show Lowest Subaccount Only, discussed earlier in this section. When you enable that option, you see only the accounts you need.

## Entering Your Customer List

In QuickBooks, customers and jobs are handled together. In fact, QuickBooks doesn't call the list a Customer List, it calls it a Customer:Job List. You can create a customer and consider anything and everything you invoice to that customer a single job, or you can have multiple jobs for the same customer.

The truth is that most small businesses don't have to worry about jobs; it's just the customer that's tracked. But if you're a building contractor or subcontractor, an interior decorator, or some other kind of service provider who usually bills by the job instead of at an hourly rate for an ongoing service, you might want to try tracking jobs. For example, I find it useful and informative to track income by jobs (books) instead of customers (publishers).

Jobs don't stand alone as an entity in QuickBooks; they are attached to customers, and you can attach as many jobs to a single customer as you need to. If you are going to track jobs, it's a good idea to enter all the customers first (now), and then attach the jobs second (later).

If you enter your existing customers now, when you're first starting to use QuickBooks, all the other work connected to the customer is much easier. It's bothersome to have to stop in the middle of every invoice you enter to create a new customer record.

## Entering a New Customer

Putting all your existing customers into the system takes very little effort:

1. Press CTRL-J to open the Customer:Job List window. (Alternatively, you can click the Cust icon on the icon bar, or click the Customers listing in the Navigator list and then click the Customers icon in the Customers Navigator window.)

2. Press CTRL-N to open a blank customer card and fill in the information for the customer (see Figure 2-3).

Consider the Customer Name field a code rather than just the billing name. It doesn't appear on your invoices. (The invoices print the company name, the primary contact name, and the address you enter on this customer card.)

You must invent a protocol for this Customer Name field so that you'll enter every customer in the same manner. Notice the Customer Name field in Figure 2-3. This customer code entry has no apostrophe or space, even though the client name contains both. Avoiding punctuation and spaces in codes is a good protocol for filling in code fields.

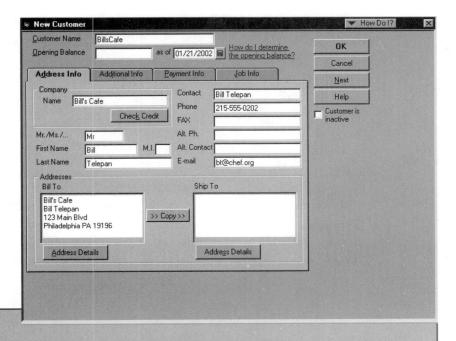

**Figure 2-3 • The customer card has plenty of fields for detailed information.**

Your lists and reports use this field to sort your customer list, so if you want it alphabetized, you must make sure you use the last name if there's no company name. Each customer must have a unique entry in this field, so if you have a lot of customers named Jack Johnson, you may want to enter them as JohnsonJack001, JohnsonJack002, and so on.

QuickBooks makes an Opening Balance field available, along with the date for which this balance applies (by default, the current date is inserted). You may want to use this if you're just setting up your company files, but don't use it if you're adding a customer after you've begun using QuickBooks. The amount you enter in this field is the total amount owed by this customer as of the date you specify. If you enter that amount, you'll have no detailed records on how the customer arrived at this balance, which makes it difficult to accept payments against specific invoices. It's better to skip this field and then enter an invoice, or multiple invoices, to post this customer's balance to your books. However, if the customer has a large quantity of outstanding invoices, you could consider using this field to avoid the need to enter each invoice separately.

## Address Info Tab

In the Name and Address section of the window, enter the company name, optionally enter a contact, and enter the billing address. When you enter the company name and the contact name, that information is automatically transferred to the address field, so all you have to do is add the street address.

Enter a shipping address if it's different from the billing address. If the shipping address isn't different (or if you have a service business and don't ship products), you can ignore the shipping address field or click Copy to duplicate the billing address.

If you've subscribed to the QuickBooks Credit Check Services, you can check the customer's Dun & Bradstreet credit rating by clicking the Check Credit button. See Appendix D for information about this service.

Click Address Details to enter or view the address as a series of fields, including fields for additional information.

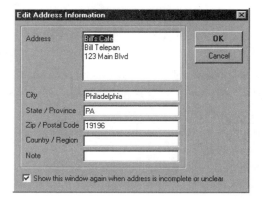

Use the check box to tell QuickBooks to display this window whenever you enter an incorrectly formatted address in a transaction window. For example, if you enter an address in the wrong place, after you click OK on the transaction window, this address window opens. On the transaction window, your cursor flashes in the field where you made the mistake.

## Additional Info Tab

The information you enter in the Additional Info tab of a customer card (see Figure 2-4) ranges from essential to convenient. It's worth spending the time to design some rules for the way data is entered. (Remember, making rules ensures consistency, without which you'll have difficulty getting the reports you want.)

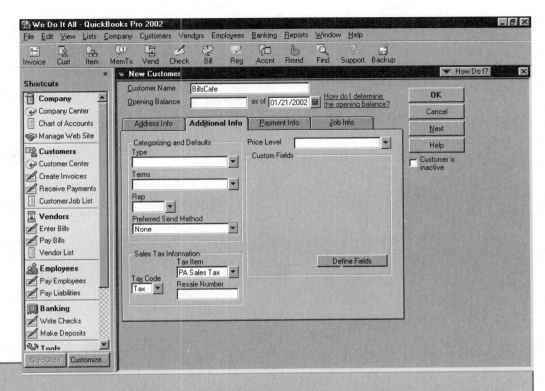

**Figure 2-4 • Entering additional information can make reports and analysis more accurate.**

Let's spend a minute going over the fields in this tab. Most of the fields are also QuickBooks lists, and if you haven't already entered items in those lists you can do so as you fill out the fields in the Customer card. Each field that is also a list has an entry named <Add New>, and selecting that entry opens the appropriate new blank entry window.

- **Type** is a field you can use to sort your customers, and there's a Type List (see the section "Customer Type List" later in this chapter). For example, you may want to consider wholesale and retail customers as your customer types. To use the field, click the arrow to select a type that you already entered, or create a new type.

- **Terms** is, of course, payment terms. Click the arrow to the right of the text box to see the terms that are already defined, or define a new one.
- **Rep** means sales representative. If you pay commissions (or just want to know who is in charge of this customer), you can use the field. Sales reps can be employees, or vendors, or "other" (usually applied to owners who don't receive commissions). Select a rep from the list of reps or add a new rep.

> **Note** | *If you're upgrading from QuickBooks 99 or earlier, note that the Rep field is no longer limited to employees.*

- **Preferred Send Method** is the way you want to send invoices to this customer. The choices are None (which means use regular mail), E-Mail, and Fax.
- **Sales Tax Information** uses several fields in this tab. If the customer is liable for sales tax, select the appropriate sales tax item for this customer, or create a new sales tax item. If the customer does not pay sales tax, select Non and enter the Resale Number provided by the customer (handy to have when the state tax investigators pop in for a surprise audit).
- **Price Level** is a pricing scheme, usually involving special discounts, that you want to use for this customer's purchases. Select an existing price level or create a new one.
- **Custom Fields** are your opportunity to invent fields for sorting and arranging your QuickBooks lists. (See the section "Using Custom Fields" at the end of this chapter.)

## Payment Info Tab

This tab puts all the important information about customer finances in one place.

- **Account** is an optional field you can use if you assign account numbers to your customers.
- **Credit Limit** is a way to establish a number that works as a threshold. If a customer places an order, and the new order combined with any unpaid invoices exceeds the threshold, you should reject the order (or ship it COD).

> **Tip** | *If you aren't going to enforce the credit limit, don't bother to use the field.*

- **Preferred Payment Method**, which is really "expected payment method," is a list of payment methods. You can select the appropriate item from the list

(QuickBooks preloads two payment methods: Cash and Check) or add a new one by selecting <Add New>. See the section "Payment Method List" later in this chapter for more information.

**Tip**     *The payment method you select automatically appears on the Receive Payments window when you are using this customer (you can change the payment method at that time if necessary).*

- **Credit Card Information** is the place to fill in the necessary data for this customer's credit card if that's the customer's preferred payment method.

When you have finished filling out the fields (we're skipping the Job Info tab for now), choose Next to move to another blank customer card so you can enter the next customer. When you have finished entering all of your customers, click OK.

## Editing Customer Records

You can make changes to the information in a customer record quite easily. Open the Customer:Job List and select the customer record you want to change. Double-click the customer's listing or select the customer listing and press CTRL-E to open the customer card.

When you open the customer card, you can change any information, or fill in data you didn't have when you first created the customer entry. In fact, you can fill in data you *did* have but didn't bother to enter. (Some people find it's faster to enter just the customer name and company name when they're creating their customer lists, and then fill in the rest at their leisure or the first time they invoice the customer.)

However, there are several things I want you to note about editing the customer card:

- Don't mess with the Customer Name field.
- There's a button named Notes on the right side of the customer card.
- You can't enter an opening balance.

Unless you've reinvented the protocol you're using to enter data in the Customer Name field, don't change this data. Many high-end (translate that as "expensive and incredibly powerful") accounting software applications lock this field and never permit changes. QuickBooks lets you change it, so you have to impose controls on yourself.

Click the Notes icon to open a Notepad window that's dedicated to this customer, as shown in Figure 2-5. This is a useful feature, and I bet you'll use it frequently.

The Notepad is a great marketing tool, because you can use it to follow up on a promised order, track a customer's special preferences, and notify the customer when something special is available. When you view the Customer:Job List, an icon appears in the Notes column for each customer that has a note in its record.

**Tip**    *Don't forget to use the To Do list to remind yourself to nag about unpaid invoices.*

You can click New To Do to open a To Do window where you can enter a reminder and a reminder date. The information appears on the QuickBooks Reminder window.

You can click Date Stamp to enter the date followed by a colon in the note area.

Enter your note here; you can enter additional notes later and scroll through them (which is why the Date Stamp is a good idea).

You can click Print to print a copy of the note.

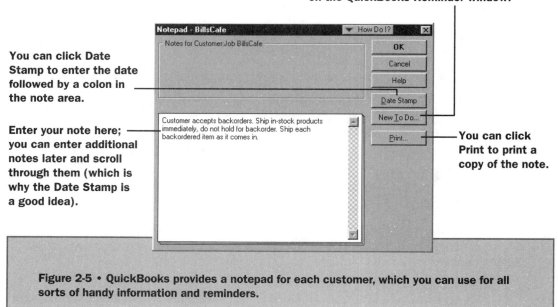

**Figure 2-5** • QuickBooks provides a notepad for each customer, which you can use for all sorts of handy information and reminders.

## Configuring Protocols for Customer Records

WeRWound is a manufacturer of videotape-rewinding machines. The people at WeRWound sell their products all over the country, and most of their customers are video stores. When they began planning their QuickBooks installation, there was major concern about tracking their customers accurately and easily.

The big problem was that they have thousands of customers, and 80 percent of them are named Video*SomethingOrOther*—there are lots of VideoHuts, VideoPalaces, and other similar incarnations.

WeRWound's manual invoicing system required lots of double-checking, which was time-consuming and frequently failed. Orders were taken over the phone by telemarketers, and then the orders had to be passed around the office, through the accounts receivable department, the sales department, and anyone else who could say "yes, that's the right VideoHut store." The telemarketers pulled an index card when the order came in, but the system's frequent failures resulted from the fact that sometimes the wrong card was pulled. Also, if the card couldn't be located quickly, telemarketers assumed that the customer didn't exist in the system, and a new index card was created. Now there were two sets of cards for the same customer, and the accounts receivable people went crazy trying to send invoices and statements, apply payments, and track credit limits.

The solution this company devised for using the customer code to assure accurate records is quite inventive. It's also foolproof. They use the customer's telephone number, including the area code. This is an absolutely unique identifier for any business (or for any individual). For example, a VideoHut in Philadelphia has a customer code 2155551234, a VideoHut in Berkeley has the customer code 5105559876, and so on.

No matter who calls to place the order, that person knows his or her company telephone number. (Have you ever asked a customer if they know their customer number with your company?) If an order arrives by mail, the WeRWound order form (which is mailed out as part of their marketing mailings and also appears in trade magazine ads) has a line for the telephone number that is marked "required information."

# Entering Your Vendor List

The vendors you purchase goods and services from have to be entered into your QuickBooks system, and it's far easier to do it now. Otherwise, when you want to enter a vendor bill or write a check, you'll have to go through the process of establishing the vendor and entering all the important information.

To open the Vendor List, click the Vend icon on the icon bar. (You can also select Vendors from the Navigators list, and then click the Vendors icon on the Vendors Navigator window, or choose Lists | Vendor List from the menu bar.)

When the Vendor List window opens, press CTRL-N to open a New Vendor card and fill out the fields (see Figure 2-6).

If you wish, you can enter the opening balance for this vendor, along with the date on which that balance exists. However, it's better to skip this field and enter an invoice to represent that balance so you have details about the transaction(s).

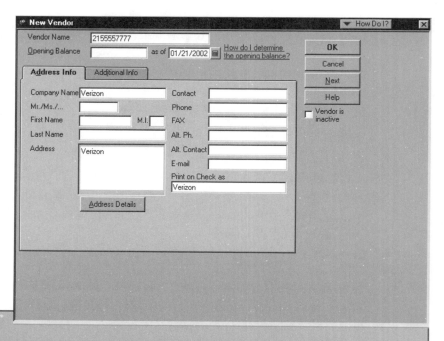

**Figure 2-6 • Vendor cards are less complicated than customer cards.**

As with customers, you should have a set of rules about entering the information in the Vendor Name field. This field doesn't appear on checks or purchase orders; it's used to sort and select vendors when you need a list or a report. Think of it as a code. Notice that in Figure 2-6, the code is a telephone number, but the vendor is the telephone company. This is how I create separate checks for each telephone bill I receive.

The Address field is important if you're planning to print checks, and the vendor doesn't enclose a return envelope. You can purchase window envelopes, and when you insert the check in the envelope, the vendor name and address is in the right spot.

The Additional Info tab for vendors has several important categories:

**Account**   Enter your account number with this vendor (to the vendor, it's your customer number) and the number will appear in the memo field of printed checks.

**Type**   Select a type or create one. This optional field is handy if you want to sort vendors by type, which makes reports more efficient. For example, you can create vendor types for inventory suppliers, 1099 recipients, tax authorities, and so on.

**Terms**   Enter the terms for payment this vendor has assigned to you.

**Credit Limit**   Enter the credit limit this vendor has given you.

**Tax ID**   Use this field to enter the social security number or EIN number if this vendor receives Form 1099.

**1099 status**   If appropriate, select the check box for Vendor Eligible For 1099.

**Custom Fields**   As described earlier for customers, you can create custom fields for vendors.

After you fill in the information, choose Next to move to the next blank card and enter the next vendor. When you're finished, click OK. Later, when you view or edit a vendor card, you'll find a Notes button just like the one in the customer card.

# Entering the Payroll Lists

If you plan to use QuickBooks for payroll, you must enter all of your employees, including their pertinent tax information. In order to do that, you have to define the tax information, which requires you to define the items that make up the payroll check. This means you have two lists to create—the payroll items and the employees. I'm assuming all the vendors who receive checks from the payroll system have been entered into your Vendor List (the IRS, the state and local tax authorities, the medical insurance companies, and so on). And your chart of accounts should have all the accounts you need in order to post payroll items.

## Entering Payroll Items

The number of individual elements that go into a paycheck may be more than you thought. Consider this list, which is typical of many businesses:

- Salaries
- Wages (hourly)
- Overtime
- Doubletime
- Federal tax withholdings (including FIT, FICA, and Medicare)
- State tax withholdings
- State unemployment and disability withholdings
- State unemployment and disability payments from employers
- Local tax withholdings
- Pension plan deductions
- Medical insurance deductions
- Life insurance deductions
- Garnishes
- Union dues
- Reimbursement for auto expenses
- Bonuses
- Commissions
- Vacation pay
- Sick pay
- Advanced Earned Income Credit

Whew! And you may have some other elements that I haven't listed.

Each payroll item has to be defined and linked to the chart of accounts. The vendors who receive payments (for example, the government and insurance companies) have to be entered and linked to the payroll item. Oh yes, don't forget about employer payments (FICA, Medicare, SUTA, and FUTA).

To create or add to your list of payroll items (you may have some items listed as a result of your EasyStep Interview), select Employees from the Navigators list and then click the Payroll Items icon on the Employees Navigator window. (Or, choose Lists | Payroll Item List from the menu bar.)

Scroll through the list, and if anything is missing, add it now by pressing CTRL-N to open the Add New Payroll Item Wizard shown in Figure 2-7.

One common payroll item that users need is a local sales tax. If you have a local sales tax, you'll have to choose a Custom Setup. For Custom Setup items, step through the wizard by clicking Next and then answering all the questions and filling in all the information.

For Easy Setup items (wages, tips, and taxable benefits), the wizard closes and the Payroll Setup window opens. Select the items you need, and click Create. Then fill in the details and follow the prompts on the screen.

More information about setting up payroll is in Chapter 8. Here are some tricks and tips you should be aware of as you enter payroll items:

- Check everything with your accountant.
- QuickBooks already has information on many state taxes, so check for your state before you add the information manually.
- You'll have to enter your local (city or township) taxes manually.

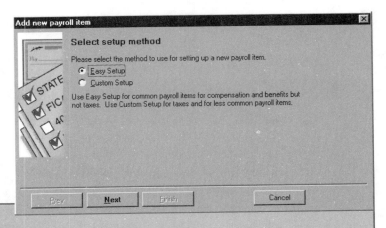

**Figure 2-7 • The first step is to select the method for setting up the payroll item (which depends on the type of payroll item you want to add).**

- For deductions, the wizard will ask about the vendor who receives this money. (It's called an *agency*, but it's a vendor.)

- If you want the employer contributions to pension, health insurance, life insurance, and so on to appear on the payroll check stubs, you must enter those items as payroll items.

- When you enter a pension deduction, you must make sure to specify the taxes that are *not* calculated (I said *calculated*, not *deducted*) before you deduct the new payroll item. If you forget one, the paychecks and deductions may be incorrect. Some plans permit employees to choose between pre- and post-tax deductions. Some states have pre-tax deduction allowances.

When you have entered all your payroll items, you're ready to move on to the next step in entering your payroll information—employees.

## Create an Employee Template

There is a great deal of information to fill out for each employee, and some of it is probably the same for all or most of your employees. You may have many employees who share the same hourly wage or the same deductions for medical insurance.

To avoid entering the same information over and over, you can create a template and then apply the information to all the employees who match that data. You'll save yourself lots of time, even if some employees require one or two entries that differ from the template.

To get to the template, you have to start with the Employee List. To do so, click Employees on the Navigators list and then click the Employees icon on the Employees Navigator window. Or, choose Lists | Employee List from the menu bar.

**Note**    *The first time you access the Employee List, a message appears asking if you want help setting up payroll. If you answer yes, the Payroll Setup window opens. If you answer no, the Employee List opens.*

In the Employee List window, click the Employee button at the bottom of the window and choose Employee Defaults. This opens the Employee Defaults window (see Figure 2-8), where you can enter the data that applies to most or all of your employees. The information you put into the template is used on the Payroll Info tab for each employee (discussed in the next section).

- In the Item Name column of the Earnings box, click the arrow to see a list of earnings types that have been defined in your Payroll Items, and choose the one that is suitable for a template.

- In the Hour/Annual Rate column, enter a wage or salary figure if there's one that applies to most of your employees. If there's not, just skip it and enter each employee's rate on the individual employee card.
- Use the arrow to the right of the Pay Period field to see a list of choices and select your payroll frequency. The available choices are Daily, Weekly, Biweekly, Semimonthly, Monthly, Quarterly, and Yearly. That should suffice, but if you're planning to pay your employees with some unusual scheme, you're out of luck, because you cannot create a new choice for this field.
- Use the Class field if you've created classes for tracking your QuickBooks data. (See Chapter 21 for information on using classes.)
- If you're using QuickBooks' time-tracking features to pay your employees, check the box Use Time Data To Create Paychecks. See Chapter 19 to learn how to transfer time tracking into your payroll records.
- If all or most of your employees have the same additional adjustments (such as insurance deductions, 401(k) deductions, or reimbursement for car expenses), click the arrow in the Item Name column in the Additions, Deductions, And Company Contributions box to select the appropriate adjustments.
- Click the Taxes button to see a list of taxes and select those that are common and therefore suited for the template (usually all or most of them).
- Click the Sick/Vacation button to set the terms for accruing sick time and vacation time if your policy is similar enough among employees to include it in the template.

When you are finished filling out the template, click OK to save it.

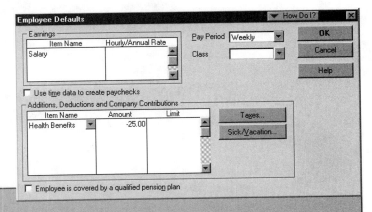

**Figure 2-8 • Use the Employee Defaults template to avoid the boredom of entering the same information over and over.**

# Entering Employees

Finally, you're ready to tell QuickBooks about your list of employees. In the Employee List window, press CTRL-N to bring up a New Employee form (see Figure 2-9).

## Address Info Tab

The Address Info tab on the employee card has many fields, not all of which are necessary. Use the following list of guidelines to fill out this dialog box (I'm skipping the fields that are self-explanatory):

- QuickBooks does not give you a field for an employee code; however, the payroll list is kept by social security number (which is, of course, totally unique).

- When you need reports about employees, you can sort by either the first or last name—use the Employee and Payroll preferences section of the Preferences dialog box (Edit | Preferences) to make that determination.

- Enter the social security number without typing the dashes; QuickBooks will add the dashes as soon as you move to another field.

- The Type field is very important; see the section "Understanding Employee Types" later in this chapter.

- The Gender field exists because some states require employers to keep track of hiring by gender.

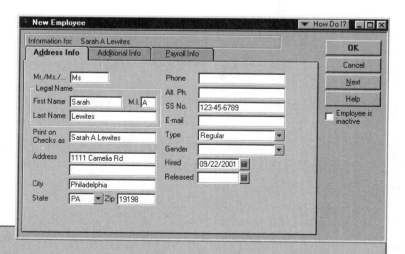

**Figure 2-9 • Enter employee information carefully, because there's no room for error here.**

## Additional Info Tab

The Additional Info tab is sparse, and the only existing field is Account. You can use the Account field if you issue employee numbers, or badge numbers. You can also add custom fields to the employee records on this tab. See the section "Using Custom Fields" later in this chapter.

## Payroll Info Tab

The Payroll Info tab contains the information QuickBooks needs to pay employees (see Figure 2-10). If the employee's pay matches the information already filled in from the template, you can skip the earnings and deductions columns. However, if the employee has a different pay category (for instance, hourly instead of salary), additional compensation or deductions on his or her paycheck, fill them in now. For example, there may be a commission due every week, or there may be a deduction for a garnish or a loan from the company.

If the amount of the additional income or the deduction is the same every week, enter an amount. If it differs from week to week, don't enter an amount on the employee card. (You'll enter it when you create the payroll check.)

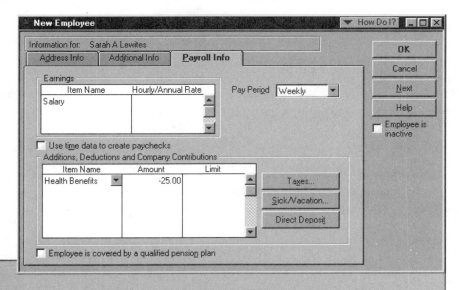

**Figure 2-10 • The stuff from my template is already filled in, making this step a snap.**

## Configuring Employee Tax Status

If the employee tax status matches the template you created, you don't have to reenter the data, but you should check the data to make sure.

1. Click the Taxes button to open the Taxes dialog box, which starts with Federal tax information, as shown here.

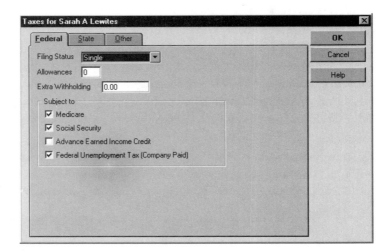

2. Move to the State tab and configure the employee's status for the state. This varies from state to state, of course, and you should check with your accountant if you aren't sure of something you find there.

**Note** *QuickBooks has built in a great deal of state information. Depending on the state, you should see the appropriate withholdings and company-paid items. For example, states that don't deduct SUI from employees have a check box for SUI (Company Paid); states that collect disability funds will display the appropriate check box.*

3. In the Other tab, apply any local payroll tax that applies to this employee. If you haven't already configured that tax in the Payroll Items List, you can click <Add New> to enter it now.

4. Click OK to save the tax status information and return to the employee card.

### Configuring Sick and Vacation Pay Information

If this employee matches the template information, you can skip this section. Otherwise, click the Sick/Vacation button and enter the configuration for this employee. When you are finished, click OK to return to the employee card.

### Configuring Direct Deposit

The employee card has a Direct Deposit button, which you can use to establish direct deposit of the employee's paycheck to his or her bank account. The button won't work until you've set up direct deposit as an online feature. See Chapter 8 to learn how to use direct deposit.

## Understanding Employee Types

The Type field on the Address Info tab of the Employee card offers four choices, which are explained in this section. The selection you make has an impact on the way your tax returns are prepared. You must check with your accountant if you have any question about the Type you should assign to any employee.

### Regular Employee Type

A Regular employee is exactly what it seems to be: a person you hired, for whom you deduct withholdings, issue a W-2, etc. It's important to have every employee fill out a W-4 form every year (don't accept "I did that last year, nothing has changed").

**Tip** *If you need extra W-4 forms, you can download them from the IRS at http://www.irs.ustreas.gov. Go to the forms section, select W-4, and print or download the form. Then make as many copies as you need.*

### Officer Employee Type

An Officer is someone who is an officer of a corporation. If your business isn't incorporated, you have no officers. Corporate tax returns require you to report payroll for officers of the corporation separately from the regular payroll amounts. Selecting Officer as the type has no impact on running your payroll (calculations, check printing, etc); it only affects reports.

### Statutory Employee Type

A Statutory employee is someone who works for you that the IRS has decided qualifies as an employee instead of as an independent contractor. The list of the job types that the rules cover isn't very long, and the definition of *independent contractor* is the subject of much debate (especially in IRS audit hearings). The IRS has a list of criteria that must be met in order to qualify as an independent contractor (which means you don't have to put that person on your payroll, you don't have to withhold taxes, and you don't have to pay employer taxes). The rules that govern this change frequently, so it's important to check the rules in Circular E or with your accountant.

The IRS has issued a list, which is not at all comprehensive, because under the right conditions, many independent contractors could be considered employees. However, here's a quote from the IRS. If any independent contractors are performing these duties for you, you must put them on your payroll and configure them as Statutory Employee Types:

- An agent (or commission) driver who delivers food, beverages (other than milk), laundry, or dry cleaning for someone else.
- A full-time life insurance salesperson.
- A traveling or city salesperson (other than an agent driver or commission driver) who works full time (except for sideline sales activities) for one firm or person getting orders from customers. The orders must be for items for resale or use as supplies in the customer's business. The customers must be retailers, wholesalers, contractors, or operators of hotels, restaurants, or other businesses dealing with food or lodging.
- A home worker who works by guidelines of the person for whom the work is done, with materials furnished by and returned to that person or to someone that person designates.

While I'm amused by the exception of milk delivery agents (which probably means the milk delivery folks hired a good lobbyist to go to Washington D.C. to plead their case), the important item is the last one. Someone who works for you at home (usually in a home office) as a freelance professional could be deemed an employee, which increases your expenses. For example, if you hire a consultant, make sure that person doesn't use (or charge to you) materials; doesn't follow your orders about the days and hours for working; and generally works totally independently. Many computer consultants who worked long term for a single company got caught in this bind.

### Owner Employee Type

Owner and Employee are mutually exclusive terms to the IRS. If you own a company, that means the company is a proprietorship; it's not a corporation (a corporation doesn't have owners, it has officers and directors). The same thing is true of a partnership, which has multiple owners. You cannot put yourself on the payroll; you must draw regular checks and post the amounts against a Draw account in the Equity section of your accounts.

QuickBooks puts this type in the list in case it's too late and you have already listed yourself or a partner in the Employee List. The QuickBooks payroll program won't perform payroll tasks for any employee of this type. If you did add your name to the Employee List, delete it rather than assign this type.

# Entering Items

If you are a service business, this is going to be a snap. If you sell a few items, it'll still be pretty easy. But if you have a large inventory, get a cup of coffee or a soda or take a bathroom break, because this is going to take some time.

## Understanding Items

Items are the things that appear on your invoices when you send an invoice to a customer. If you think about it, that's a bit more complicated than it might appear. Do you charge sales tax? If you do, that's an item. Do you subtotal sections of your invoices? That subtotal is an item. Do you show prepayments or discounts? They're items, too.

While you can issue an invoice that says "Net amount due for services rendered" or "Net amount due for items delivered" and enter one total in the invoice, your customers aren't going to be very happy with the lack of detail. More important, when you try to analyze your business in order to see where you're making lots of money and where you're making less money, you won't have enough information to determine the facts.

This is another setup chore that requires some planning. Each of your items must have a code, a unique identification (QuickBooks calls that the Item Name or Number). Try to create a system that has some logic to it so your codes are recognizable when you see them listed.

## Understanding Item Types

It isn't always clear how and when some of the item types are used (or why you must define them). Here are some guidelines you can use as you plan to enter your items:

**Service** A service you provide to a customer. You can create services that are charged by the job or by the hour.

**Inventory Part** A product you buy for the purpose of reselling.

**Non-inventory Part** A product you don't stock in inventory or don't track even though it's in your inventory warehouse. Most of the time, you use this item type to buy products that you don't resell, such as office supplies. You generally only need to enter non-inventory parts if you use purchase orders when you order these items, and if you only use purchase orders for inventory items, you don't have to create any items of this type.

> **Tip** *You should use purchase orders only for inventory items, which are those things you buy in order to resell. It's an unnecessary complication to use purchase orders for your own purchases, such as office supplies.*

**Other Charge** You'll need this item type for things like shipping charges, or other line items that appear on your invoices. In fact, some people create one for each method of shipping.

**Subtotal** This item type adds up everything that comes before it. It's used to give a subtotal before you add shipping charges, or subtract any discounts or prepayments.

**Group** This item type is a clever device. You can use it to enter a group of items (all of which must exist in your Item List) at once. For example, if you frequently have a shipping charge and sales tax on the same invoice, you can create a group item that includes those two items.

**Discount** You can't give a customer a discount as a line item if the item type doesn't exist. You may have more than one item that falls within this item type—for example, a discount for wholesale customers and a discount for a volume purchase. When you enter the item, you can indicate a percentage as the rate.

> **Tip** *I have an income item in my chart of accounts called "customer discounts," and items are posted there as discounts (reverse income) instead of as expenses. (This system gives me a better picture of my revenue.) Check with your accountant about the best method for posting discounts; you can use income or expense accounts.*

**Payment**   If you receive a prepayment (either a total payment or a deposit), you must indicate it as a line item. You can use this item type to do that (or you can create a discount item to cover prepayments if you prefer).

**Sales Tax Item**   Create one of these item types for each sales tax authority for which you collect.

**Sales Tax Group**   This is for multiple sales taxes that appear on the same invoice.

**Tip** *Even though I've described all of the item types in terms of their use on your invoices, many of them are used on your purchase orders, too.*

## Entering the Data for Items

To put your items into the system, click the Item icon on the icon bar, or choose Lists | Item List from the menu bar. When the Item List window opens, any items that were created during your EasyStep Interview are listed. To create a new item, press CTRL-N. The New Item window opens, displaying a list of item types, as described in the previous paragraphs. Select an item type to display the appropriate fields in the blank New Item window. Figure 2-11 shows a blank New Item window for an Inventory Part. Other item types (such as Service items) have fewer fields.

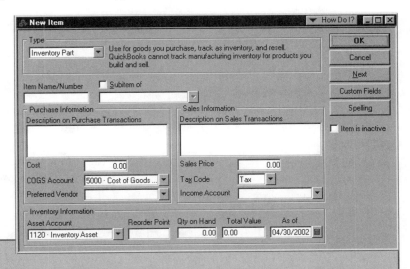

**Figure 2-11 • The fields in the New Item window cover all the data you need to use the item in transactions and to generate reports.**

The Item Name/Number field is the place to insert a unique identifying code for the item. When you are filling out invoices (or purchase orders), this is the listing you see in the drop-down list.

**Note** *After you've created an item, you can create subitems. For example, if you sell shoes as an item, you can create subitems for dress shoes, sneakers, boots, and so on. Or use subitems for a parent item that comes in a variety of colors. Not all Item types provide subitems.*

Many of the rest of the fields in the New Item window change depending on the item type you select. Most of them are self-explanatory, but some are important enough to merit discussion:

- If you're entering an inventory item, fill in the cost of the item and enter the account to which you post Cost of Goods. Optionally, fill in the name of the vendor from whom you purchase the item.
- In the Sales Price field, you can enter a rate for those items that you've priced; leave the rate at zero for the items you want to price when you are preparing the invoice. Don't worry—nothing is etched in stone. You can change any rate that appears automatically when you're filling out an invoice. Link the price to an income account in your chart of accounts and indicate whether the item is taxable (choose Tax) or not taxable (choose Non).

When you complete the window, choose Next to move to the next blank New Item window. When you finish entering items, click OK.

# Entering Jobs

If you plan to track jobs, you can enter the ones you know about during this setup phase or enter them as they come up.

Jobs are attached to customers; they can't stand alone. To create a job, press CTRL-J to open the Customer:Job List and select the customer for whom you're creating a job. Right-click the customer listing (or select the customer listing and then click the Customer:Job button at the bottom of the Customer:Job List window) and choose Add Job from the drop-down menu. This opens the New Job window, shown in Figure 2-12.

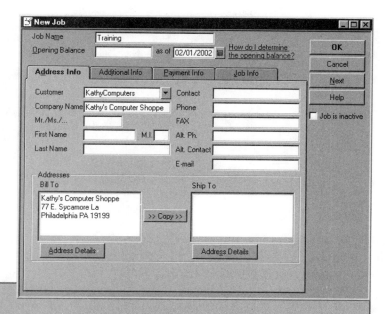

**Figure 2-12 •** **You're only required to enter the job name; everything else that's important is already filled in from the customer card.**

Create a name for the job (you can use up to 41 characters) and make it descriptive enough for both you and your customer to understand.

The Additional Info tab is related to the customer (in fact, it *is* the Additional Info tab for the customer card), so you can skip it. Move to the Job Info tab (see Figure 2-13) to begin configuring this job. All of the information on the Job Info tab is optional. For example, I track book royalties as jobs, and never have to use the Job Info tab at all.

When you finish entering all the data, choose Next if you want to create another job for the same customer. Otherwise, click OK to close the New Job window and return to the Customer:Job List window. The jobs you create for a customer become part of the customer listing.

Enter a start date for this job

Enter the projected completion date for this job

When the job is completed, you can note the end date

Choose a job status from the drop-down list

Enter an optional description of this job

Select or create a job type if you want to categorize jobs (only available in QuickBooks Pro)

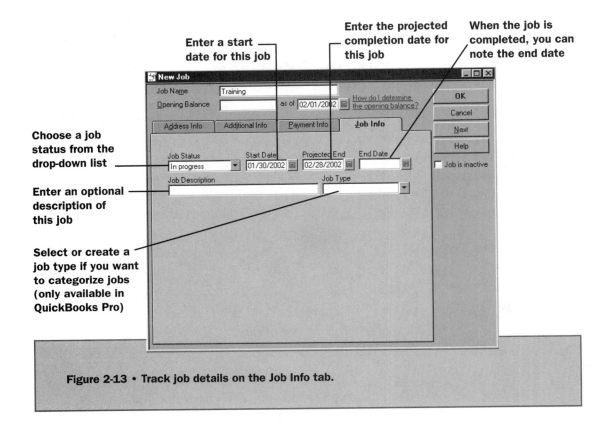

Figure 2-13 • Track job details on the Job Info tab.

# Entering Other Lists

There are a few items in the Lists menu that I haven't covered in detail. They don't require extensive amounts of data, and you may or may not choose to use them. If you do plan to use them, here's an overview of the things you need to know.

Some of these items are in the Lists menu and some of them are in a submenu called Customer & Vendor Profile Lists (in the Lists menu). I'll cover all of them, and you'll know you can find the items in one place or another.

**Note** *One item in the Lists menu, Templates, isn't covered here. These are the lists of invoice, purchase order, sales receipt, and other forms you use in transactions. Working with those templates, and customizing them, is discussed throughout this book, in the appropriate chapters.*

## Price Level List

This List is only available if you've enabled Price Levels in the Sales & Customers section of your Preferences (choose Edit | Preferences). The Price Level list is a nifty, easy way to connect special pricing to customers and jobs. Each price level has two components: a name and a formula. The name can be anything you wish, and the formula is based on the price of items (increase or reduce the price by a percentage).

For example, you may want to give your favorite customers an excellent discount. Name the price level something like "Special" or "StarCustomer." Then enter a healthy percentage by which to reduce the price of items purchased by this customer. Or you may want to create a discount price level for non-profit organizations in your Customer List.

You may want to keep your regular prices competitive and increase them for certain customers (perhaps customers who don't pay in a timely fashion). It's probably politically incorrect to name the price level "Deadbeat," so choose something innocuous such as "DB." You could also use numbers for the price-level names, perhaps making the highest numbers the highest prices.

To apply price levels to customers, open the Customer List and select a customer. Press CTRL-E to edit the customer card and select a price level on the Additional Info tab.

## Sales Tax Code List

This list is available if you configured your business to collect sales tax. If you only collect tax for one taxing authority, you don't have to add another tax code item. If you collect tax for multiple authorities, enter a code for that tax, using a 3-letter abbreviation.

## Class List

The Class List command appears in the Lists menu only if you've enabled the classes feature. Classes provide a method of organizing your activities (income and disbursement activities) to produce reports that you need. Many times, a well-designed chart of accounts will eliminate the need for classes, but if you do want to use them, you can create them ahead of time through the Lists menu.

It's a better idea to work with QuickBooks for a while and then, if you feel you need a report that can only be produced with the use of classes, create the class at that point. Chapter 21 covers the use of classes.

## Other Names List

QuickBooks provides a list called Other Names, which is the list of people whose names come up but whose activity you don't want to track. This list will appear when you write checks, but the names are unavailable for invoices, purchase orders, and any other QuickBooks transaction type.

If there are several partners in your business, use this list for the checks you write to the partners' draw. If your business is a proprietorship, put yourself on the list to make sure your name is listed when you write your draw check.

When you open a New Name window, there are fields for the address (handy for printing checks), telephone numbers, and other contact information.

> **Tip** *Many people overuse this category and end up having to move these names to the Vendor List because they do need to track the activity. Unless you're a proprietor or partner, it's totally possible to use QuickBooks efficiently for years without using this list.*

## Memorized Transaction List

This list (which isn't really a list, but rather a collection of transactions) should be built as you go, instead of creating it as a list. QuickBooks has a clever feature that memorizes a transaction you want to use again and again. Paying your rent is a good example. You can tell QuickBooks to memorize the transaction at the time you create it, instead of filling out this list in advance.

## Customer Type List

(This list appears in the submenu of Customer & Vendor Profile Lists.) When you created your customer list, you may have used the Customer Type field as a way to categorize the customer. This gives you the opportunity to sort and select customers in reports, perhaps to view the total income from specific types of customers.

You can predetermine the customer types you want to track by opening this list item and creating the types you need during setup. (Oops, it's too late if you've followed this chapter in order.) Or you can create them as you enter customers.

## Vendor Type List

(This list appears in the submenu of Customer & Vendor Profile Lists.) See the previous two paragraphs, substituting the word "vendor" for the word "customer."

## Job Type List

(This list appears in the submenu of Customer & Vendor Profile Lists.) If you're using QuickBooks Pro, you can set up categories for jobs by creating job types. For example, if you're a plumber, you may want to separate new construction from repairs.

## Terms List

(This list appears in the submenu of Customer & Vendor Profile Lists.) QuickBooks keeps both customer and vendor payment terms in one list, so the terms you need are all available whether you're creating an invoice or a purchase order. To create a terms listing, press CTRL-N to open the New Terms window, shown in Figure 2-14.

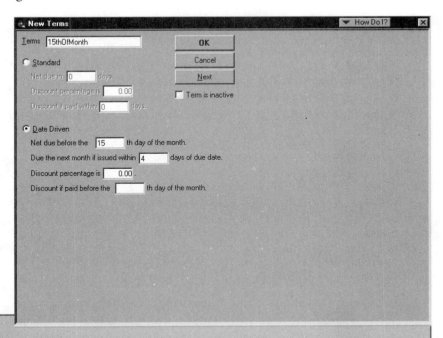

**Figure 2-14 • Name the new terms item and then configure it so QuickBooks can calculate it.**

Use the Standard section to create terms that are due at some elapsed time after the invoice date:

- *Net due* is the number of days you allow for payment after the invoice date.
- To give customers a discount for early payment, enter the discount percentage and the number of days after the invoice date that the discount is in effect. For example, if you allow 30 days for payment, but want to encourage customers to pay early, enter a discount percentage that is in effect for 10 days after the invoice date.

Use the Date Driven section to describe terms that are due on a particular date, regardless of the invoice date:

- Enter the day of the month the invoice payment is due.
- Enter the number of days before the due date that invoices are considered payable on the following month (it's not fair to insist that invoices be paid on the 10th of the month if you mail them to customers on the 8th of the month).

To give customers a discount for early payment, enter the discount percentage and the day of the month at which the discount period ends. For example, if the standard due date is the 15th of the month, you may want to extend a discount to any customer who pays by the 8th of the month.

**Tip** *Date-driven terms are commonly used by companies that send invoices monthly, usually on the last day of the month. If you send invoices constantly, as soon as a sale is completed, it's very difficult to track and enforce date-driven terms.*

## Customer Message List

(This list appears in the submenu of Customer & Vendor Profile Lists.) If you like to write messages to your customers when you're creating an invoice, you can enter a bunch of appropriate messages ahead of time and then just select the one you want to use. For example, you may want to insert the messages "Thanks for doing business with us," or "Pay on time or else."

Press CTRL-N to enter a new message to add to the list. You just have to write the sentence—this is one of the easier lists to create.

## Payment Method List

(This list appears in the submenu of Customer & Vendor Profile Lists.) You can track the way payments arrive from customers. This not only provides some detail (in case you're having a conversation with a customer about invoices and payments), but also allows you to print reports on payments that are subtotaled by the method of payment, such as credit card, check, cash, and so on. (Your bank may use the same subtotaling method, and that makes it easier to reconcile the account.)

QuickBooks provides two payment methods for you: Cash and Check. You probably want to add the credit cards you accept as new payment methods. To do so, press CTRL-N to open the New Payment Method window, and then name the payment method (Visa, Amex, etc.).

## Ship Via List

(This list appears in the submenu of Customer & Vendor Profile Lists.) You can describe the way you ship goods on your invoices (in the field named Via), which many customers appreciate. Press CTRL-N to add a new Ship Via entry to the list. All you need to do is enter the name (UPS, USPS, FedEx, OurTruck, etc.).

If you use one shipping method more than any other, you can select a default Ship Via entry, which appears automatically on your invoices (you can change it when the shipping method is different). In addition, if you charge clients for shipping, you can specify a default markup for shipping costs. To perform these tasks, follow these steps:

1. Choose Edit | Preferences.
2. Select the Sales & Customers icon.
3. Select the Company Preferences tab.
4. In the Usual Shipping Method field, click the drop-down list and select the Ship Via entry you want to make the default. (If you haven't entered anything in the Ship Via list, select <Add New> to enter these items here.)
5. Enter a default markup percentage.
6. Enter the FOB site you want to appear on invoices, if you wish to display this information. FOB (Free On Board) is the site from which an order is shipped and is also the point at which transportation costs are the buyer's responsibility. (There are no accounting implications for FOB—it's a customer service.)

## Sales Rep List

(This list appears in the submenu of Customer & Vendor Profile Lists.) A sales rep is a person who is connected to a customer, usually because he or she receives a commission on sales to that customer. However, you can also track sales reps just to know which non-commissioned person is attached to a customer (some people call this a service rep).

To enter a new sales rep, enter the person's name. If that name doesn't already exist as an employee, vendor, or other name, QuickBooks asks you to add the name to one of those lists.

# Using Custom Fields

If you're brave, adventurous, and comfortable with computers, you can add fields to the customer, vendor, employee, and item records. In fact, even if you're not any of those things, you can add your own fields, because it isn't very difficult. You can create custom fields for names (customers, vendors, and employees) and for items.

Custom fields are useful if there's information you just have to track, but QuickBooks doesn't provide a field for it. For example, if it's imperative for you to know what color eyes your employees have, add an Eye Color field. Or perhaps you have two offices and you want to attach your customers to the office that services them. Add an Office field to the customer card. If you maintain multiple warehouses, you can create a field for items to indicate which warehouse stocks any particular item (you can do the same thing for bins).

## Adding a Custom Field for Names

To add one or more custom fields to names, open one of the names lists (Customer:Job, Vendor, or Employee) and then follow these steps:

1. Select any name on the list.
2. Press CTRL-E to edit the name.
3. Move to the Additional Info tab.
4. Click the Define Fields button.
5. When the Define Fields dialog box opens, name the field and indicate which list you want to use the new field with (see Figure 2-15).

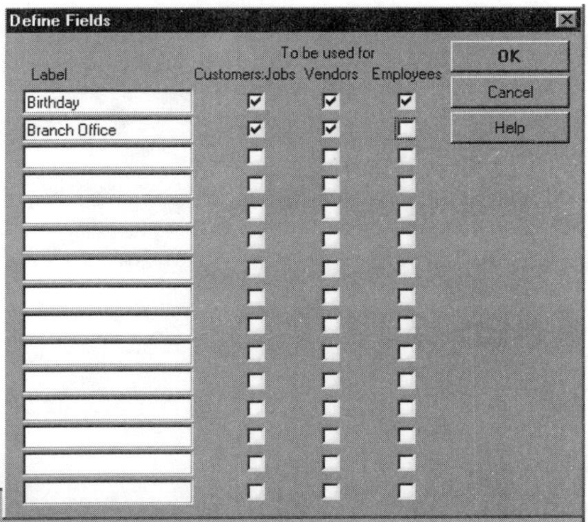

**Figure 2-15 • You can track any information you need (or are curious about) with custom fields.**

That's all there is to it, except you must click OK to save the information. When you do, QuickBooks flashes a message reminding you that if you customize your templates (forms for transactions such as invoices), you can add these fields. Click OK to make the message disappear (and select the option to stop showing you the message, if you wish). The Additional Info tab on the card for each name to which you attached the fields now shows those fields (see Figure 2-16).

To fill in the custom fields for each name, select the name and press CTRL-E to edit the name and add the appropriate data to the field.

## Adding a Custom Field for Items

You can add custom fields to your items in much the same manner as you do for names:

1. Click the Item icon on the toolbar to open the Item List.
2. Select any item.
3. Press CTRL-E.
4. Click the Custom Fields button.
5. When a message appears telling you that there are no custom fields yet defined, click OK.

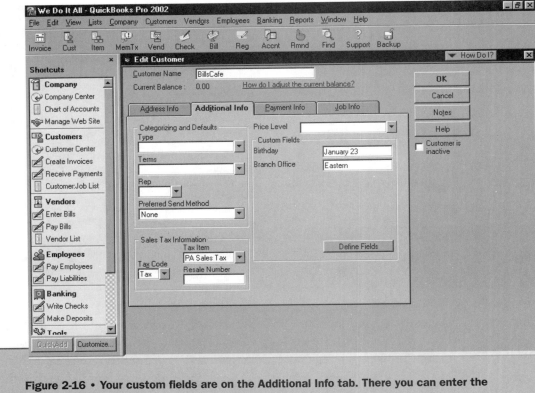

**Figure 2-16 • Your custom fields are on the Additional Info tab. There you can enter the appropriate data.**

6. When the Custom Fields dialog box appears, it has no fields on it (yet). Choose Define Fields.

7. When the Define Custom Fields for Items dialog box opens, enter a name for each field you want to add. You can add fields that fit services, inventory items, etc., and use the appropriate field for the item type to enter data.

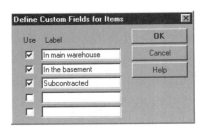

**8.** Click the Use box to use the field. (You can deselect the box later if you don't want to use the field any more.)

**9.** Click OK.

The first time you enter a custom field on an item, a dialog box appears to tell you that you can use these fields on templates (forms such as Invoices and Purchase Orders). Click OK and select the option to stop displaying this message in the future.

When you click Custom Fields on the Edit Item dialog box, your existing custom fields appear. If you want to add more custom fields, click the Define Fields button to open the Define Custom Fields for Items dialog box and add the additional custom field. You can create up to five custom fields for items.

To view or enter data for the custom fields in an item, select the item in the Items list and click the Custom Fields button on the Edit Item window.

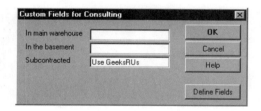

Your QuickBooks setup is complete, and now it's time to start entering transactions. The following chapters cover all the things you'll be doing in QuickBooks.

# Bookkeeping

**Part Two**

*Now we're getting into the good stuff. Part Two is a series of chapters about the day-to-day bookkeeping chores you'll be performing in QuickBooks. The chapters are filled with instructions, tips, and explanations. There's even a lot of information that you can pass along to your accountant, who will want to know about these things.*

*The chapters in Part Two take you through everything you need to know about sending invoices to your customers and collecting the money they send back as a result. You'll learn how to track and pay the bills you receive from vendors. There's plenty of information about dealing with inventory—buying it, selling it, and counting it—and keeping QuickBooks up-to-date on those figures. Payroll is discussed, both for in-house payroll systems and outside services.*

*All the reports you can generate to analyze the state of your business are covered in Part Two. So are the reports you run for your accountant—and for the government (tax time is less of a nightmare with QuickBooks).*

*Finally, you'll learn about budgets, general ledger adjustments, and all the other once-in-a-while tasks you need to know how to accomplish to keep your accounting records finely tuned.*

# Invoicing

## In this Chapter:

- *Create and edit invoices*

- *Create and edit credit memos*

- *Print invoices and credit memos*

- *Use invoices for sales orders*

- *Create pick lists and packing slips*

- *Customize your invoices*

For many businesses, the way to get money is to send an invoice to a customer (the exception is retail, of course). Creating an invoice in QuickBooks is easy once you understand what all the parts of the invoice do and why they're there.

## Creating Standard Invoices

To create an invoice, click the Invoice icon on the icon bar. Alternatively you can press CTRL-I or select Customers on the Navigator list and then click Invoices. Either action opens the Create Invoices window, which is really a blank invoice form (see Figure 3-1).

**Note**    *When you open a transaction form, QuickBooks asks if you want help in choosing a sales form. Click the option Do Not Display This Message In The Future, and then click No. It would be hard to believe that you need to take the time to answer a bunch of questions in order to be sure that when you're invoicing a customer you want an Invoice form, and when you're entering a bill from a vendor you'd need a different form.*

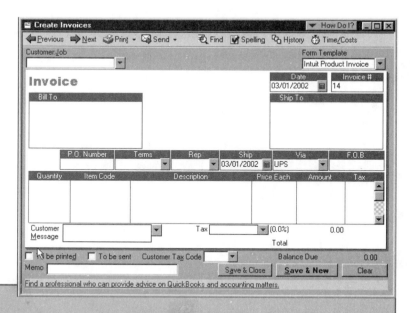

**Figure 3-1** • **The invoice template you chose during the EasyStep Interview is presented when you first open the Create Invoices window.**

There are several invoice templates built into QuickBooks, and you can use any of them (as well as create your own, which is covered later in this chapter in the section "Customizing Forms"). The first thing to do is decide whether or not the displayed template suits you, and you should probably look at the other templates before settling on the one you want to use. To do that, click the arrow next to the Form Template box and select another invoice template.

- The Professional and Service templates are almost identical. There's a difference in the order of the columns, and the Service template has a field for a purchase order number.
- The Product template has more fields and columns because it contains information about the items in your inventory.
- The Progress template, which is covered later in this chapter, is designed specifically for progress billing against a job estimate. It doesn't appear in the Template list unless you have specified Progress Invoicing in the Company Preferences tab of the Jobs & Estimates category of the Preferences dialog. Estimates are only available in QuickBooks Pro.

For this discussion, I'll use the Product template, because it's the most complicated. If you're using any other template you'll still be able to follow along, even though your invoice form lacks some of the fields related to products.

The top portion of the invoice is for the basic information (this is called the *invoice heading*), the middle section is where the billing items (called *line items*) are placed, and the bottom contains the totals (called *totals*). Each section of the invoice has fields into which you must enter data.

## Entering Heading Information

Start with the customer, or the customer and job. Click the arrow to the right of the Customer:Job field to see a list of all your customers. If you've attached jobs to any customers, those jobs are listed under the customer name. Select the customer or job for this invoice.

**Tip** *If the customer isn't in the system, choose <Add New> to open a new customer window and enter all the data required for setting up a customer. Read Chapter 2 for information on adding new customers.*

In the Date field, the current date is showing, which usually suffices. If you want to change the date, you can either type in a new date, use the calendar icon, or employ one of the nifty date-entry shortcuts built into QuickBooks. (Just inside the front cover of this book, you'll find all the shortcuts for entering dates.)

**Tip**   *For service businesses, it's a common practice to send invoices on the last day of the week or month. If you have such a regular invoicing date, you can start preparing your invoices ahead of time and set the invoice date for the scheduled date. That way, the actual billing day isn't a zoo as you scramble to put together your information and enter the invoices.*

The first time you enter an invoice, fill in the invoice number you want to use as a starting point. Hereafter, QuickBooks will increment that number for each ensuing invoice.

The Bill To address is taken from the customer card, as is the Ship To address. Only the Product invoice template has a Ship To field.

If you have a purchase order from this customer, enter it into the P.O. Number field.

The Terms field is filled in automatically with the terms you entered for this customer when you created the customer. You can change the terms for this invoice if you wish. If terms don't automatically appear, it means you didn't enter that information in the customer record. If you enter it now, when you finish the invoice, QuickBooks offers to make the entry the new default for this customer by adding it to the customer card.

**Tip**   *In fact, if you enter any information about the customer such as a new address or a shipping address, QuickBooks offers to add the information to the customer card. Just click the Yes button in the dialog box that displays the message. This saves you the trouble of going back to the customer record to make the changes.*

- The Rep field is for the salesperson attached to this customer. If you didn't indicate a salesperson when you filled out the customer card, you can click the arrow next to the field and choose a salesperson from the list of employees that appears.
- The Ship field is for the ship date (which also defaults to the current date).
- The Via field is for the shipper. Click the arrow next to the field to see the carriers you entered in your Ship Via list. (See Chapter 2 for information about creating this list.)

- The FOB field is used by some companies to indicate the point at which the shipping costs are transferred to the buyer, and the assumption of a completed sale takes place. (That means, if it breaks or gets lost, the customer owns it.) If you use FOB terms, you can insert the applicable data in the field; it has no impact on your QuickBooks financial records and is there for your convenience only.

## Entering Line Items

Now you can begin to enter the items for which you are billing this customer. Click in the first column of the line item section.

If you're using the Product invoice template, that column is Quantity. (If you're using the Professional or Service invoice template, the first column is Item). Enter the quantity of the first item you're billing for.

Press TAB to move to the Item Code column. An arrow appears on the right edge of the column—click it to see a list of the items in your inventory. (See Chapter 2 to learn how to enter items.) Select the item you need. The description and price are filled in automatically, using the information you provided when you created the item.

QuickBooks does the math, and the Amount column displays the total of the quantity times the price. If the item and the customer are both liable for tax, the Tax column displays a "T."

Repeat this process to add all the items that should be on this invoice. You can add as many rows of items as you need; if you run out of room, QuickBooks automatically adds additional pages to your invoice.

You can make adjustments to the total with discounts or credits due this customer. These are entered as line items. Before you enter a discount, use a line to enter a subtotal item (which you should have created when you created your items). Then add the discount line items section, and the discount will be applied to the subtotal. Doing it this way makes all discounts very clear to the customer.

## Checking the Invoice

When you're finished entering all the line items, you'll see that QuickBooks has kept a running total, including taxes (see Figure 3-2).

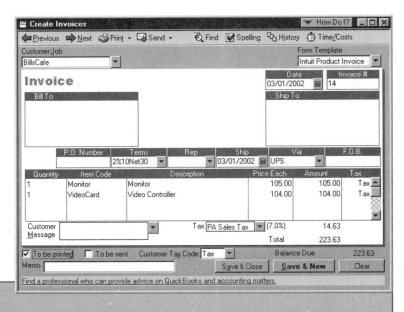

**Figure 3-2 •** The invoice is complete, and there are no math errors because QuickBooks does the addition.

## Add a Message to the Invoice

If you want to add a message, click the arrow in the Customer Message field to see all the available messages. You can create a new message if you don't want to use any of the existing notes. To do so, choose <Add New> from the message drop-down list and enter your text in the New Customer Message window. Click OK to enter the message in the invoice and save the message in the Message list so you can use it again.

## Check Spelling

Click the Spelling icon on the toolbar of the Create Invoices window to run the QuickBooks spelling checker. If the spelling checker finds any word in your invoice form that isn't in the QuickBooks dictionary, that word is displayed. You can change the word, add it to the QuickBooks dictionary, or tell the spelling checker to ignore the word. Information on customizing and using the spelling checker is in Chapter 21.

**Tip**   *If you check the spelling each time you create a customer or an item, you eliminate the need to worry about spelling on an invoice—everything is pre-checked before you insert the items in the invoice form.*

## Delivering Invoices

QuickBooks offers several options for delivering invoices to customers (click the arrow next to the Send icon at the top of the Create Invoices number to see them):

- Print (and mail)
- Fax
- E-mail

See the section "Sending Invoices and Credit Memos" later in this chapter for detailed information about printing invoices or using any of the other invoice delivery options.

### Saving the Invoice

Choose Save & New to save this invoice and move on to the next blank invoice form. If this is the last invoice you're creating, click Save & Close to save this invoice and close the Create Invoices window. In either case, if your computer has a sound card, you'll hear the sound of a cash register ringing.

# Creating Progress Billing Invoices

If you work with estimates and job tracking in QuickBooks, you can use the Progress invoice template to invoice your customers as each invoicing plateau arrives. This feature is only available in QuickBooks Pro. See the section "Creating Estimates" later in this chapter to learn how to use estimates.

## Choosing the Job

Progress invoices are connected to jobs. Choose the job for which you're creating the progress invoice. QuickBooks checks to see if you've recorded any estimates for this job, and if so, presents them.

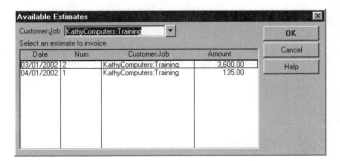

Select the estimate you're invoicing against and click OK. QuickBooks then asks you to specify what to include on the invoice.

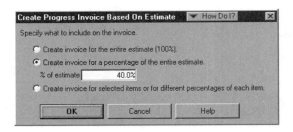

Fill out the dialog box, using the following guidelines:

You can bill for the whole job, 100% of the estimate. When the line items appear, you can edit any individual items. In fact, you can bill for a higher amount than the original invoice (you should have an agreement with your customer regarding overruns).

You can create an invoice for a specific percentage of the estimate. The percentage usually depends upon the agreement you have with your customer. For example, you could have an agreement that you'll invoice the job in a certain number of equal installments, or you could invoice a percentage that's equal to the percentage of the work that's been finished.

You can create an invoice that covers only certain items on the estimate, or you can create an invoice that has a different percentage for each item on the estimate. This is the approach to use if you're billing for completed work on a job that has a number of distinct tasks. Some of the work listed on the estimate may be finished, other work not started, and the various items listed on the estimate may be at different points of completion.

After you've created the first invoice for an estimate, a new option appears on subsequent invoices. That option is to bill for all remaining amounts in the estimate. This is generally reserved for your last invoice, and it saves you the trouble of figuring out which percentages of which items have been invoiced previously.

As far as QuickBooks is concerned, the estimate is not etched in cement; you can change any amounts or quantities you wish while you're creating the invoice.

Your customer, however, may not be quite so lenient, and your ability to invoice for amounts that differ from the estimate depends on your agreement with the customer.

## Entering Line Items

Choose your method and click OK to begin creating the invoice. QuickBooks automatically fills in the line item section of the invoice based on the approach you've selected (see Figure 3-3).

## Changing Line Items

Sometimes some of the line items contain work orders that aren't at the same percentage of completion as others. To change the percentages or amounts of a line item on this invoice, click the Progress icon at the top of the Create Invoices window to open a dialog box that allows configuration of the line items, as shown in Figure 3-4.

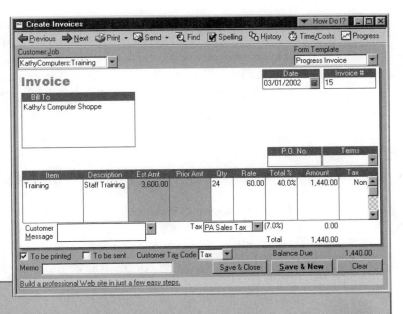

**Figure 3-3 • Progress invoices are filled in automatically.**

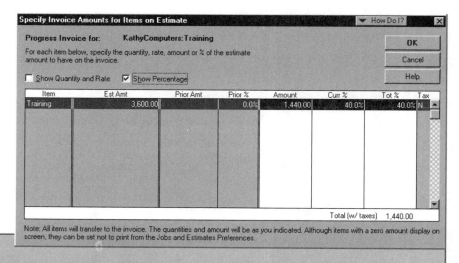

**Figure 3-4 •** You can alter the amounts that are automatically entered in the line items on the invoice.

Using this method to change a line item keeps the history of your estimate and invoices intact (as opposed to making changes directly on the invoice form, which does not link back to your estimate history). You can change the quantity, rate, or percentage of completion. The changes you make on any line item are written back to the Progress invoice. Here's how to make changes:

- Select Show Quantity and Rate to display those columns from the estimate. The quantity and rate for previously billed items are also displayed. Then click the QTY column for any line item to highlight the default number that's been used to calculate the invoice. Replace the number with the amount you want to use for the invoice. You can also change the rate, but generally that's not cricket unless there are some circumstances that warrant it (which you and the customer have agreed upon).

- Select Show Percentage to display the column that has the percentage of completion for this and previous billings. The percentages compare the dollar amounts for invoices against the estimated total. Click the Curr% column to change the percentage for any line item.

- Select both options if you need to make changes to one type of progress on one line item, and another type of progress on another line item. All the columns (and all the history from previous billings, if any exists) appear in the window.

Click OK when you have finished making your adjustments. You return to the invoice form where the amounts on the line items have changed to match the adjustments you made.

Click Save & New to save this invoice and move on to the next invoice, or click Save & Close to save this invoice and finish your invoicing chores.

# Editing Invoices

If you want to correct an invoice (perhaps you charged the wrong amount or forgot you'd promised a different amount to a particular customer), you can do so quite easily.

## Editing the Current Invoice

Editing the invoice that's currently on the screen is quite easy. Click in the field or column that requires changing and make the changes (you've probably already figured this out).

## Editing a Previously Entered Invoice

You can open the Create Invoices window (or perhaps you're still working there) and click the Prev (which stands for Previous) button to move through all the invoices in your system. However, if you have a great many invoices it might be faster to take a different road:

1. Press CTRL-A or click Accnt on the icon bar to bring up the Chart of Accounts list.
2. Double-click the Accounts Receivable account (that's where invoices are posted).
3. When the A/R account register opens, find the row that has the invoice you want to edit and double-click anywhere on the row to open the Create Invoices window with the selected invoice displayed.
4. Make your changes and click OK. Then close the A/R register.

If you've printed the invoices, when you finish editing be sure to check the To Be Printed box so you can reprint it with the correct information.

## Voiding and Deleting Invoices

There's an enormous difference between voiding and deleting an invoice. Voiding an invoice makes the invoice nonexistent to your accounting and the customer balance. However, the invoice number continues to exist so you can account for it (missing invoice numbers are just as frustrating as missing check numbers).

Deleting an invoice removes all traces of it—it never existed, you never did it, the number is gone, and a couple of months later you probably won't remember why the number is gone. You have no audit trail, no way to tell yourself (or your accountant) why the number is missing. Never delete an invoice.

**Caution** *If you choose to ignore my advice (perhaps you have the memory of an elephant, and when someone questions the missing number you'll be able to explain no matter how much time has passed), do not ever delete an invoice to which a customer payment has been attached. Straightening out that mess is a nightmare.*

Voiding an invoice isn't difficult:

1. Press CTRL-A or click the Accnt button on the icon bar to bring up the Chart of Accounts list.
2. Select the Accounts Receivable account and double-click.
3. When the A/R account register opens, find the row that has the invoice you want to edit and click anywhere on the row to select it.
4. Right-click and choose Void Invoice from the shortcut menu. The word "VOID" appears in the memo field. (If you've entered a memo, the word "VOID" is placed in front of your text.)
5. Click Record to save your action.
6. Close the register by clicking the X in the top-right corner.

If you want to delete an invoice, follow steps 1 through 3 above, then press CTRL-D. You'll have to confirm the deletion.

## Understanding the Postings for Invoices

It's important to understand what QuickBooks is doing behind the scenes, because everything you do has an impact on your financial reports. Let's look at the postings for an imaginary invoice that has several line items:

- $500.00 for services rendered
- $30.00 for sales tax

Since QuickBooks is a full, double-entry bookkeeping program, there is a balanced posting made to the general ledger. For this invoice, the following postings are made to the general ledger:

| Account | Debit | Credit |
|---|---|---|
| Accounts Receivable | 530.00 | |
| Sales Tax | | 30.00 |
| Revenue—Services | | 500.00 |

If the invoice includes inventory items, the postings are a bit more complicated. Let's post an invoice that sold ten widgets to a customer. The widgets cost you $50.00 each, and you sold them for $100.00 each. This customer was shipped ten widgets and also paid tax and shipping.

| Account | Debit | Credit |
|---|---|---|
| Accounts Receivable | 1077.00 | |
| Revenue—Sales of Items | | 1000.00 |
| Sales Tax | | 70.00 |
| Shipping | | 7.00 |
| Cost of Sales | 500.00 | |
| Inventory | | 500.00 |

There are some things to think about as you look at these postings. To keep accurate books, you should fill out the cost of your inventory items when you create the items. As you purchase replacement items, QuickBooks updates the cost (from the vendor bill). This is the only way to get a correct posting to the cost of sales and the balancing decrement in the value of your inventory.

You don't have to separate your revenue accounts (one for services, one for inventory items, and so on) to have accurate books. In the bottom line, revenue is revenue. However, you may decide to create accounts for each type of revenue so you can analyze where your revenue is coming from.

> **Tip** *Some people think it's a good idea to have two revenue items, one for revenue liable for sales tax, and one for revenue that's not taxable. They find it easier to audit the sales tax figures that way.*

There are two theories on posting shipping: Separate your shipping costs from the shipping you collect from your customers or post everything to the shipping expense. To use the first method, in addition to the shipping expense, create a revenue account for shipping and attach that account to the shipping item you insert in invoices. If you use the latter method, don't be surprised at the end of the year if you find your shipping expense is reported as a negative number, meaning that you collected more than you spent for shipping. You won't have a shipping expense to deduct from your revenue at tax time, but who cares—you made money.

# Issuing Credits and Refunds

Sometimes you have to give money to a customer. You can do this in the form of a credit against current or future balances, or you can write a check and refund money you received from the customer. Neither is a lot of fun, but it's a fact of business life.

## Creating Credit Memos

A credit memo reduces a customer balance. This is necessary if a customer returns goods, has been billed for goods that were lost or damaged in shipment, or wins an argument about the price of a service you provided.

The credit memo itself is printed to let the customer know the details about the credit that's being applied. The totals are posted to your accounting records just as the invoice totals are posted, except there's an inherent minus sign next to the number.

Creating a credit memo is similar to creating an invoice:

1. Choose Customers | Create Credit Memos/Refunds from the menu bar to open a blank form (see Figure 3-5).
2. Select a customer or job, and then fill out the rest of the heading.
3. Move to the line item section and enter the quantity and rate of the items for which you're issuing this credit memo. Don't use a minus sign—QuickBooks knows what a credit is.

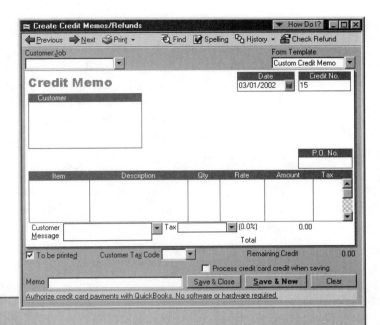

**Figure 3-5** • **The Credit Memo form has all the fields you need to provide information to the customer about a credit.**

**Tip**    *By default, the credit memo number is the next available invoice number. If you change the number because you want a different numbering system for credit memos, you'll have to keep track of numbers manually. QuickBooks will use the next number (the one after this credit memo) for your next invoice. Therefore, it's easier to use the default procedure of having one set of continuous numbers for invoices and credit memos.*

4. Remember to insert all the special items you need to give credit for such as taxes, shipping, and so on.

5. You can use the Customer Message field to add any short explanation that's necessary.

6. Click Save & Close to save the credit memo (unless you have more credit memos to create—in which case, click Save & Next).

See the section on printing later in this chapter to learn about printing credit memos.

## Issuing Refund Checks

If a customer has paid up and has no existing invoices against which a credit is desired (and has indicated no interest in having a floating credit against future purchases), you'll have to send that customer a refund.

Refunds start as credit memos, then they keep going, requiring a few extra steps to write the check and post the totals to your general ledger properly.

Follow steps 1 through 5 for creating a credit memo. Then click the Check Refund button at the top of the Credit Memo window. This opens a Write Checks window, as shown in Figure 3-6.

Make sure that everything on the check is the way it should be. (The only items you may want to change are the date and the bank account you're using for this check; everything else should be accurate.) Then either print the check or click Save & Close to save it. If you're not printing the check now, make sure the To Be Printed check box is checked so you can print it later. Information about check printing is in Chapter 7.

You're returned to the Credit Memo window where you should either print the credit memo or click Save & Close to save it for later printing.

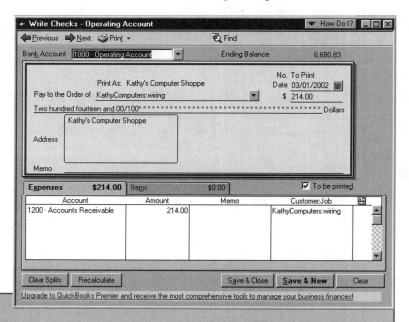

**Figure 3-6 • The check takes the information from the credit memo, so there's nothing for you to fill out.**

QuickBooks automatically links the check to the credit memo. This means the credit memo is no longer in the customer record, decrementing the balance. If you've updated to QuickBooks 2002 from QuickBooks 99 or earlier, you'll appreciate the fact that you don't have to go through all the steps to link the check to the credit manually as you did before.

# Sending Invoices and Credit Memos

You have all sorts of choices about sending invoices and credit memos. You can print them and mail them (or fax the printed copy), or send them electronically (via e-mail or by faxing directly from QuickBooks).

## Printing Invoices and Credit Memos

You can print on blank paper, preprinted forms on a single sheet of paper, preprinted multipart forms, or your company letterhead. You have to set up your printer for invoices and credit memos, but once you complete this task you don't have to do it again. There are several steps involved in setting up a printer, but they're not terribly difficult.

### Selecting the Printer and Form

If you have multiple printers attached to your computer or accessible through a network, you have to designate one of them as the invoice printer. If you use multipart forms, you should have a dot matrix printer. Your printers are already set up in Windows (or should be), so QuickBooks, like all Windows software, has access to them. Now you have to tell QuickBooks about the printer and the way you want to print invoices:

1. Choose File | Printer Setup from the menu bar to open the Printer Setup dialog box and select Invoice from the forms drop-down list (you'll have to perform these steps again for credit memos).

2. In the Printer Setup dialog box (see Figure 3-7), click the arrow next to the Printer name box to choose a printer if you have multiple printers available. This printer becomes the default printer for Invoice forms (you can assign different printers to different forms).

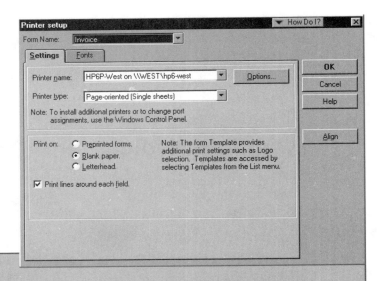

**Figure 3-7 •** **This QuickBooks system uses a network printer; if your printer is attached to your computer, you won't see a network path in the Printer Name box.**

3. In the bottom of the dialog box, select the type of form you're planning to use for invoices:

- **Preprinted forms** are templates with all your company information, field names, and row and column dividers already printed. These forms need to be aligned to match the way your invoice prints. If you purchase the forms from a company that knows about QuickBooks' invoice printing formats, everything should match just fine. Selecting this option tells QuickBooks that only the data needs to be sent to the printer because the fields are already printed.

- **Blank paper** is easiest, but it may not look as pretty as a printed form. Some of us don't care about pretty—we just want to ship invoices and collect the payments. But if you care about image this may not be a great choice. On the other hand, if you don't need multipart printing (which requires a dot matrix printer), you can use the fonts and graphic capabilities of your laser printer to design a professional-looking invoice that prints to blank paper. Selecting this option tells QuickBooks that everything, including field names, must be sent to the printer.

**Tip**     *Select the option to print lines around each field to make sure the information is printed in a way that's easy to read.*

- **Letterhead** is another option, and it means your company name and address are preprinted on paper that matches your company's "look." Selecting this option tells QuickBooks not to print the company information when it prints the invoice.

## Setting Up Form Alignment

You have to test the QuickBooks output against the paper in your printer to make sure everything prints in the right place. To accomplish this, click the Align button in the Printer Setup dialog box and select the invoice template you're using (e.g., Service, Product, etc.), then click OK. The Alignment dialog box you see differs depending on the type of printer you've selected.

### Aligning Dot Matrix Printers

If you're using a continuous feed printer (dot matrix using paper with sprocket holes), you'll see the dialog box shown here.

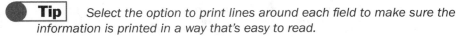

Start by clicking the Coarse button. A dialog box appears telling you that a sample form is about to be printed and warning you not to make any physical adjustments to your printer after the sample has printed. QuickBooks provides a dialog box where you can make any necessary adjustments. Make sure the appropriate preprinted form, letterhead, or blank paper is loaded in the printer. Click OK.

The sample form prints to your dot matrix printer and QuickBooks displays a dialog box asking you to enter pointer line position. You can see the pointer line at the top of the printed sample. Enter the line it's on in the dialog box and click OK (the printout numbers the lines). Continue to follow the instructions as QuickBooks takes you through any adjustments that might be needed. (I can't give specific instructions because I can't see what your sample output looks like.)

If you want to tweak the alignment a bit further, choose Fine. (See the information on using the Fine Alignment dialog box in the section "Aligning Laser and Inkjet Printers" that follows this section.) Otherwise, choose OK.

When the form is printing correctly, QuickBooks displays a message telling you to note the position of the form now that it's printing correctly. That means you should note exactly where the top of the page is in relation to the print head and the bar that leans against the paper.

**Tip** *Here's the best way to note the position of the forms in your dot matrix printer: Get a magic marker and draw an arrow with the word "invoice" at the spot on the printer where the top of the form should be. I have mine marked on the piece of plastic that sits above the roller.*

### Aligning Laser and Inkjet Printers

If you're using a page printer, you'll see only this Fine Alignment dialog box.

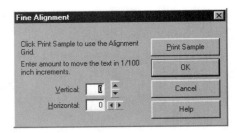

Click Print Sample to send output to your printer. Then, with the printed page in your hand, make adjustments to the alignment in the dialog box. Use the arrows next to the Vertical and Horizontal boxes to move the positions at which printing occurs.

Click OK, and then click OK in the Printer Setup dialog box. Your settings are saved, and you don't have to go through this again (except to create settings for Credit Memos).

## Batch Printing

If you didn't click the Print button to print each invoice or credit memo as you created them, and you made sure that the To Be Printed check box was selected on each of them, you're ready to start a print run:

1. Place the correct paper in your printer and, if it's continuous paper in a dot matrix printer, position it properly.

2. Choose File | Print Forms | Invoices.
3. In the Select Invoices To Print window (see Figure 3-8), all your unprinted invoices are selected with a check mark. If there are any you don't want to print at this time, click the check mark to remove it.
4. If you need to print mailing labels for these invoices, you must print them first (see the next section).
5. Click OK to print your invoices

Repeat the steps to print credit memos.

## Printing Mailing Labels

If you need mailing labels, QuickBooks will print them for you. In the Select Invoices To Print window, click the Print Mailing Labels button to bring up the Select Mailing Labels To Print dialog box, seen here.

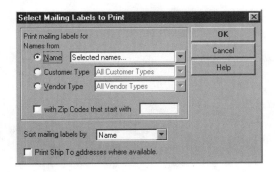

Fill out the fields to match your needs, and click OK.

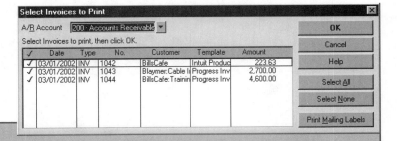

**Figure 3-8 • Batch printing is quick—you can print all or some of the invoices you created.**

The Print Labels dialog box appears (see Figure 3-9), assuming that you've loaded Avery labels into your printer. Select the appropriate printer and specify the Avery label format you use and choose Print.

After the labels are printed, you're returned to the Select Invoices To Print dialog box. Choose OK to begin printing your invoices. Then check the print job to make sure nothing went wrong (the printer jammed, you had the wrong paper in the printer, whatever). If anything went amiss, you can reprint the forms you need when the following dialog box appears. (Use the invoice number as the form number.)

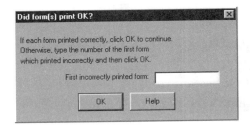

If everything is hunky-dory, click OK.

**Tip**    *You can also use the label-printing function to print Rolodex cards. Just select the appropriate card from the drop-down list in the Label Format box.*

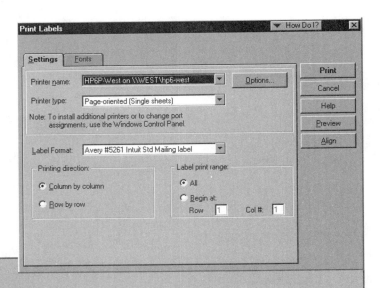

**Figure 3-9 • Set up your label printing options, including the type of label you're using.**

# E-mailing Invoices

If you have an e-mail account, you can e-mail invoices to customers (of course, the customer must also have an e-mail account). You perform this task while you're creating invoices. To send an invoice via e-mail, click the arrow to the right of the Send icon at the top of the Invoice form. Select E-mail to open the Edit E-mail Information window shown in Figure 3-10.

**Note** *If you're using QuickBooks Pro, you can also e-mail estimates.*

QuickBooks automatically inserts the e-mail addresses in the header part of the e-mail form if the information is available. The From field entry is obtained from your company information (choose Company | Company Information to view and edit your company information), and the To field entry is obtained from the e-mail address field in the customer file.

QuickBooks also automatically inserts the customer's name in the cover letter, using the name fields in the customer file. If any data fails to appear automatically, enter it manually on the E-mail Information window. When you're finished with the window, QuickBooks offers to save it in the customer's card. The invoice itself is automatically placed below the cover letter (you can't see it in the template).

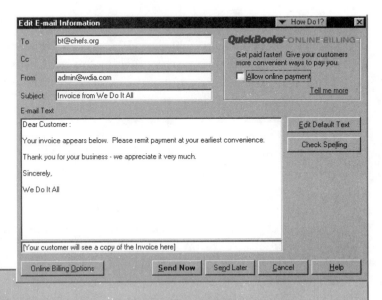

**Figure 3-10 • The e-mail template has a header, a cover letter, and the invoice.**

If you want other people to receive a copy of the invoice, enter their e-mail addresses in the CC field. For example, you might want to copy your own company bookkeeper, and the purchasing agent you work with at the customer (assuming the invoice is being sent to the customer's Accounts Payable person). Separate multiple e-mail addresses with commas.

To change the text of the cover letter, click anywhere in the text box and make your changes. You can make permanent changes to the cover letter (that topic is covered later in this chapter—see "Designing the Cover Letter").

To send the e-mail immediately, click Send Now. If you want to send the e-mail later (you can send multiple invoices as a batch process), click Send Later. When you're ready to send the e-mail, choose File | Send Forms | Send Batch. A dialog box displays the e-mail that's waiting; select the recipients you want to send to (usually all of them).

To use the QuickBooks online billing service, select Enable Invoice For Online Billing before you select Send Now or Send Later. The QuickBooks online billing service provides a URL in the e-mail invoice that your customers can click to travel to a secure Web site and pay your bill via credit card. See Chapter 16 to learn about signing up for and using the QuickBooks Online Billing Service.

## Faxing Invoices

If you have a fax-enabled modem, and you've installed faxing software (either via your operating system or with a third-party fax application), you can fax invoices to your customers. Click the arrow to the right of the Send button on the invoice form and choose Fax to open the Edit Fax Information window shown in Figure 3-11.

Faxing invoices from your computer works exactly like the e-mail invoices feature. The header information and the cover letter are automatically filled with data from your company information and the customer files. All the same functions for sending now or later are available. If you don't have faxing software, but you have e-mail, you can use eFax to send and receive faxes online. This is useful if your customers don't want to receive e-mail invoices. To learn more about eFax, click the button labeled Tell Me More on the Edit Fax Information window.

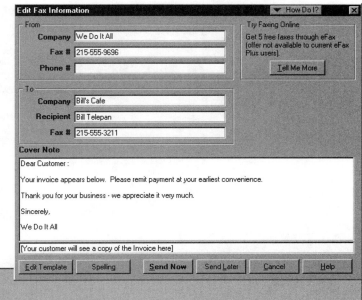

**Figure 3-11 • Send your customers invoices by fax.**

## Designing the Cover Letter

The cover letter for e-mail and faxes is a combination of a database form (for data that's filled in automatically) and a text message. You can customize the cover letter to suit your own needs and taste, and you can get to the customizing window in either of two ways:

- Choose Edit | Preferences, click the Send Forms icon, and choose the Company Preferences tab.
- If you are working in an e-mail or fax template, click the Edit Template button (which opens the Company Preferences tab of the Send Forms preferences).

In the window that appears (see Figure 3-12), you can make the following permanent changes:

- Use the drop-down list to select Dear or To as the salutation.

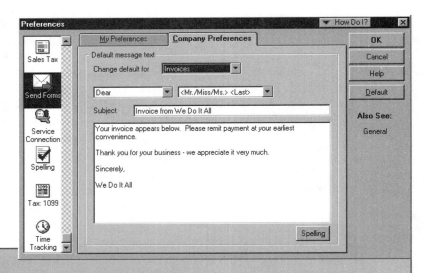

**Figure 3-12 • Redesign the cover letter that accompanies your e-mail and fax invoices.**

- Use the next drop-down list to select a format for the name that follows the salutation, choosing one of the following formats (the data within the brackets is filled with data from the customer file):
  - <First>
  - <First> <Last>
  - <Mr./Miss/Ms.> <Last>
- Change the text of the subject line.
- Change the text of the cover letter.

**Note** *If you're using QuickBooks Pro, you can customize separate cover letters for invoices, estimates, and statements. Use the Change Default For drop-down list to select the cover letter you want to work on.*

## Creating Sales Orders

Many inventory-based businesses use sales orders as the first step in selling products to a customer. A *sales order* is a tentative document, on hold until there is sufficient inventory to fill it or until prices and discounts are approved. Some companies don't want to consider a sale as a final step until the items are packed, weighed, and on the truck. Other companies don't want an invoice processed until a sales manager approves the prices (especially if the sales person has the right to give discounts to favorite customers). Nothing on a sales order is posted to the general ledger.

QuickBooks does not have a sales order form, nor does it really have a sales order concept. However, you can imitate this protocol if you need it. I discovered I could set up sales order processing in QuickBooks by using a little imagination and a couple of keystrokes.

In more robust (and more expensive) accounting software, the sales order is a separate form and a separate menu choice. It's printed along with a *pick list* (a document that's printed for the warehouse personnel, listing the items in bin order, and omitting prices); then there's a menu item that converts sales orders to invoices. When the sales order is converted, shipping costs are added (because the shipment has been packed and weighed by now) and a packing slip is printed. Packing slips do not display prices because it's none of the warehouse personnel's business what an owner pays for goods that are received.

I found it easy to duplicate all the steps I needed for small businesses that wanted sales order and pick list functions in their QuickBooks software.

Creating a sales order is just a matter of creating an invoice and then taking the additional step of marking the invoice as pending. Here's how:

1. Create an invoice as described earlier in this chapter.
2. Choose Edit | Mark Invoice As Pending from the QuickBooks menu bar (or right-click anywhere in the Invoice window and choose Mark Invoice As Pending from the shortcut menu). The Pending notice is placed on the invoice (see Figure 3-13).
3. Print the invoice and send it to the warehouse as a pick list, or send it to a supervisor to approve the pricing (or both).

**Tip**    *Some of my clients purchase multipart invoice forms that have areas of black on the last form, covering the columns that hold the pricing information. They use this copy as the pick list and the packing slip. Other clients have created pick lists and packing slips by customizing the invoice template. See information on customizing later in this chapter.*

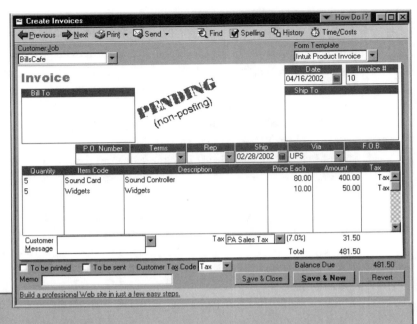

**Figure 3-13 • There's no mistaking that this invoice isn't ready to ship.**

4. When the order is through the system, bring the invoice back to the window and add the shipping costs.

5. Choose Edit | Mark Invoice As Final. Now you have a regular invoice and you can proceed accordingly.

If you have a service business, the sales order protocol can be handy for noting specific jobs or tasks that customers request. It's a good first step, even before the estimating process (if you use estimates).

# Creating Backorders

If you're selling inventory, there's nothing more frustrating than getting a big order when you're out of some or all of the products being ordered. You can ship the items you do have in stock and consider the rest of the items a backorder. The problem is that there's no backorder button on a QuickBooks invoice, nor is there a backorder form.

Instead of a backorder form, use the Pending Invoice feature described in the previous section. Here are some guidelines for making that feature work for backorders:

- As the items arrive in your warehouse, remove them from the pending invoice (and save the invoice again) and place them on a regular invoice form.
- Use the Notes feature on customer cards to indicate whether this customer accepts backorders, automatically cancels the portion of the order that must be backordered, or wants you to hold the shipment until the entire order can be sent.
- Check with the vendor of a backordered item regarding delivery date, and then create a QuickBooks reminder. The reminder is really a reminder that when those items arrive, they're backordered (otherwise somebody might just put them onto the shelves without remembering to fill the backorder).

# Customizing Forms

QuickBooks makes it incredibly easy to customize your invoices. All the existing templates can be used as the basis of a new template, copying what you like, changing what you don't like, and eliminating what you don't need.

Since the existing forms are the basis of your customization, you need to start in an invoice window:

1. Click the Invoice button on the icon bar.
2. When the Create Invoices window opens, click the arrow to the right of the Form Template box to display the drop-down list. Instead of choosing one of the invoice templates, choose Customize to open the Customize Template dialog box.

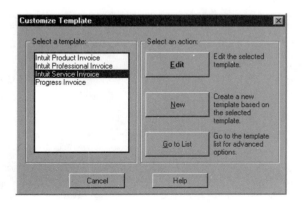

3. Choose the QuickBooks template that comes closest to the form you want to end up with.

4. Choose the action you want to use to customize your form (details are in the following section).

## Editing an Existing Form

You can make minor changes to an existing form by choosing Edit in the Customize Template dialog box. This is commonly done to make a small change in one of the existing QuickBooks templates in order to match your company's needs or your own taste. After a message appears telling you that this Edit process has limited features (remember, I said it was for minor adjustments), the Customize Invoice dialog box appears.

The Format tab (see Figure 3-14) lets you change the font for the various parts of your invoice form. Select the part of the invoice you want to change and click the Change button. (If your printer setup indicated you were using blank paper, the options to change the font you use to print the company name and address are available). You can change the font, the font style (bold, italic, etc.), the size, the color, and the special effects (such as underline).

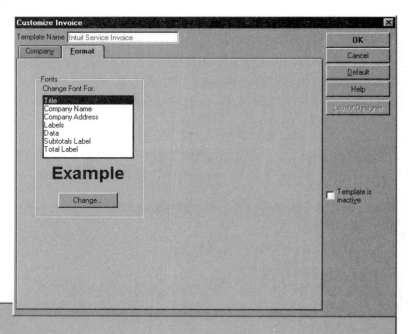

**Figure 3-14 • Alter the look of your invoice by changing the fonts.**

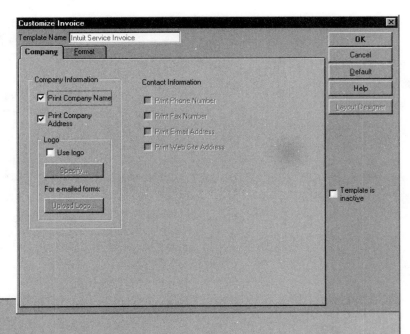

**Figure 3-15 • Modify the elements you're printing.**

On the Company tab (see Figure 3-15), you can change some of the elements on your invoice.

If you're switching from blank paper to preprinted forms, deselect the check boxes that enable printing of company information. Don't forget to go through a new printer setup, including alignment, when you use this edited template.

If you want to add a logo to your printed form, select the Use Logo option. In the Logo dialog box that appears, click File. Locate your logo file, select it, and click Open. Click OK to confirm the use of this file. Your logo file must have the following characteristics:

- A filename extension of .bmp (a bitmapped file)
- The file cannot exceed 200KB in size

The logo is positioned in the upper-left corner of your invoice form. You cannot change the positioning of the logo in this Customize Invoice dialog box. See the section "Designing a New Form" to learn how to change the location of your logo on your invoices.

If you want to change the file you're using for your logo, return to this Customize Invoice dialog box and click Specify to tell QuickBooks where to locate the new file.

**Tip** *By default, QuickBooks assumes your logo file is in the same folder in which you've installed QuickBooks. It's a good idea to put a copy of your company logo there, so you don't have to search for it.*

If you're using QuickBooks Online Billing Services to e-mail your invoices (and receive online payments), you can add the logo to your electronic documents, as follows:

1. Click Upload Logo in the Company tab of the Customize Invoice dialog box.
2. Log in to your QBN account.
3. Follow the instructions to upload your logo file.

**Note** *Logo files for QuickBooks Online Billing Services can be .bmp, .gif, or .jpg formats.*

When you've finished customizing your invoice template, click OK in the Customize Invoice dialog box to return to the Customize Invoice dialog box. Then click OK to save your customized template. You have changed the template—you are not creating a new template.

## Designing a New Form

If you want add, remove, or reposition elements in your invoice, you have to design a new form. To design a form of your own, select Customize as the Invoice form, and choose New in the first Customize Template dialog box. The Customize Invoice dialog box opens with a whole raft of choices (see Figure 3-16).

Notice that unlike the dialog box you see when you merely edit a template, QuickBooks doesn't enter the name of the template you're using as a model in the Template Name box. That's because the changes you make here are more sweeping than a minor edit, and you must give the template a name to create a new form (you cannot use your new design to replace a QuickBooks form). Enter a name for the form—something that reminds you of the format (such as "bigtypeface" or "FootersAdded") or just call it "ProductInvoice2."

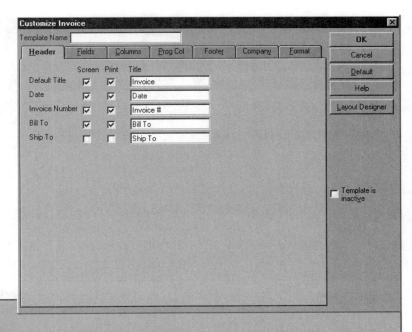

**Figure 3-16 • Each tab has specific customization options.**

Move through the tabs to make changes, deletions, or additions to the various parts of the form.

**Tip** *Many of the various tabs include an option to remove an element from both the screen display and the printed version, but some elements can only be removed from the printed version of the form.*

If you're comfortable with designing forms (or if you like to live on the edge), click the Layout Designer button on the Customize window. The Layout Designer window opens (see Figure 3-17) and you can plunge right in, moving elements around, changing margins, and building your own layout.

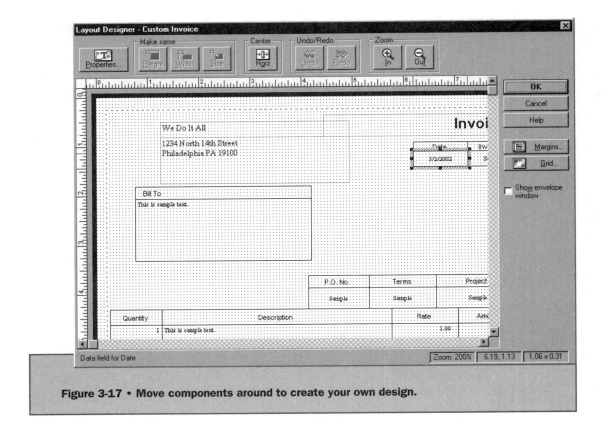

**Figure 3-17 • Move components around to create your own design.**

Before you start, select the Show envelope window option if you use window envelopes to mail your invoices. This prevents you from accidentally moving any fields into that area. Then select any element to put a frame around it; now you can perform an action on the frame, as follows:

1. Position your pointer on one of the sizing handles on the frame, then drag the handle to change the size of the element.

2. Position your pointer inside the frame and, when your pointer turns into a four-headed arrow, drag the frame to move the element to a different position on the form.

3. Double-click the frame to see a dialog box that permits all sorts of option changes for the selected element.

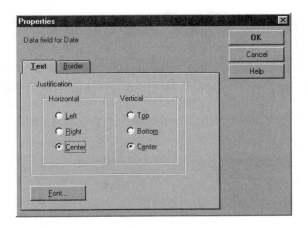

4. Click the Margins button to change the margin measurements.
5. Click the Grid button to eliminate the dotted line grid from the screen or to change the spacing between grid lines.
6. Use the toolbar buttons to align, resize, and zoom into the selected elements. There's also an Undo/Redo choice, thank goodness.

When you finish with the Layout Designer, click OK to move back to the Customize Invoice window. Once everything is just the way you want it, save your new template by clicking OK. This new template name appears on the drop-down list when you create invoices.

**Tip**   *You can also use this new template as the basis for other customizations.*

## Using the Template List

If you choose Go To List in the original Customize Template dialog box, a Templates window opens listing all the forms in your system. You can also open this listing by selecting Lists | Templates from the QuickBooks menu bar.

Select the form you want to work with, and then click the Templates button at the bottom of the window to see the available options. You can edit the selected template or build a new form based on the selected template. In addition, you can duplicate or remove a form.

# Creating Pick Lists and Packing Slips

Marty Mogul's business is growing fast—it seems the whole world wants his special-occasion balloons. He decided he needs pick lists for the warehouse staff and packing slips for the boxes, instead of having his salespeople create a list in a word processor (which takes far too much time) or write the list by hand (which nobody can read). He designed the pick lists, which also function as packing slips.

Marty opened the Create Invoices window and selected Customize as the template to use. When the Customize Template dialog box appeared, he selected the Intuit Product Invoice as the template, and then he clicked New to create a new template based on the product invoice template.

He named the new template Pick/Packing Slip. On the Columns tab he eliminated the Rate and Amount columns from the printed version. Then he clicked OK to save the new template.

Now, when an order is taken, this template is used. The Rate and Amount columns are on the screen so the order can be filled out accurately, but they don't print. The invoice is marked "Pending" (choose Edit | Mark Invoice As Pending) and is then sent to a dot matrix printer with multipart paper.

When the warehouse workers have filled the order, boxed it (with the packing slip inside), and weighed it, they call the Accounts Receivable office to tell them the shipping cost. By the way, next year, when Marty installs a network, the warehouse workers will be able to bring the invoice up on their own computer screens and fill in the shipping-cost line item.

The A/R person does the following things:

1. Brings the pending invoice onto the screen and adds the shipping cost as a line item
2. Clicks the arrow to the right of the Custom Template box and switches to the standard Product Invoice template (thus creating an invoice form while all the items remain the same)
3. Selects Edit | Mark Invoice As Final to get rid of the pending status
4. Saves, prints, and mails the invoice to the customer

The ability to switch templates without disturbing the contents of the invoice is the secret behind Marty's ingenious plan.

# Using Memorized Invoices

If you have a recurring invoice (most common if you have a retainer agreement with a customer), you can automate the process of creating it. Recurring invoices are those that are sent out at regular intervals, usually for the same amount.

Create the first invoice, filling out all the fields. If there are any fields that will change each time you send the invoice, leave those fields blank and fill them out each time you send the invoice. Then press CTRL-M to open the Memorize Transaction dialog box. Fill in the dialog box using these guidelines:

- Change the title in the Name box to reflect what you've done. It's easiest to add a word or phrase to the default title (the customer name or job), such as "Retainer."
- Choose Remind Me and specify how and when you want to be reminded in the How Often and Next Date fields. The reminder will appear in the automatic QuickBooks Reminder window.
- Choose Don't Remind Me if you have a great memory.
- Choose Automatically Enter if you want QuickBooks to issue this invoice automatically. If you opt for automatic issuing of this invoice, you must fill in the fields so that QuickBooks performs the task accurately.
- The How Often field is where you specify the interval for this invoice, such as monthly, weekly, or so on. Click the arrow to see the drop-down list and choose the option you need.
- The Next Date field is the place to note the next instance of this invoice.
- The Number Remaining field is a place to start a countdown for a specified number of invoices. This is useful if you're billing a customer for a finite number of months because you only have a one-year contract.
- The Days In Advance To Enter field is for specifying the number of days in advance of the next date you want QuickBooks to create the invoice.

Click OK when you have finished filling out the dialog box. Then click Save & Close in the Invoice window to save the transaction. Later, if you want to view, edit, or remove the transaction, you can select it from the Memorized Transaction List by clicking the MemTx icon on the QuickBooks toolbar.

# Using Estimates

If you're using QuickBooks Pro, you have the ability to create estimates. An estimate isn't an invoice, but it can be the basis of an invoice (you can create multiple invoices to reflect the progression of the job).

## Creating an Estimate

Creating an estimate doesn't impact your financial condition. When you indicate that you use estimates in your QuickBooks preferences, a non-posting account named Estimates is added to your chart of accounts. The amount of the estimate is posted to this account (invoices, on the other hand, are posted to the Accounts Receivable account).

To create an estimate, choose Customers | Create Estimates from the menu bar, which opens an Estimate form. As you can see in Figure 3-18, the form is very much like an invoice form. Fill out the fields in the same manner you use for invoices.

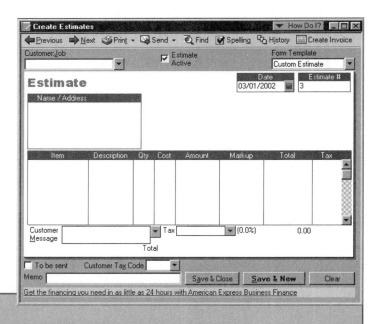

**Figure 3-18 • Estimates provide a way to track and invoice a project.**

Estimates permit you to invoice customers with a markup over cost. This is often the approach used for time and materials on bids. Just enter the cost and indicate the markup in dollars or percentage. Incidentally, if you decide to change the total of the item, QuickBooks will change the markup so your math is correct.

## Creating Multiple Estimates for a Job

New to QuickBooks 2002 is the ability to create multiple estimates for a customer or a job. This is an extremely handy feature. You can now create an estimate for each phase of the job or create multiple estimates with different prices. Of course, that means each estimate has different contents; you never want to let customers know you could do exactly the same job for less money.

When you create multiple estimates for the same job, each estimate is marked Active. If a customer rejects any estimates, you can either delete them or change the status to Closed in order to have a permanent record.

## Duplicating Estimates

Another feature new to QuickBooks 2002 Pro is the ability to duplicate an estimate. This provides a quick way to create multiple estimates with slightly different contents. Choose Edit | Duplicate Estimate while the estimate is displayed in your QuickBooks window. The Estimate Number field changes to the next number, while everything else remains the same. Make your changes, and then click Save & Close.

If the estimate isn't currently displayed, open the Chart of Accounts list and double-click the Estimates account; then double-click the listing for the estimate you want to display.

## Memorizing Estimates

If you frequently present the same estimated items to multiple customers, you can use the Memorize Estimates feature to create boilerplate estimates for future use. Memorized estimates do not contain the customer name (QuickBooks removes the name when memorizing the document).

1. Create an estimate, but don't fill in amounts (quantities, prices, or both) that usually change.
2. Press CTRL-M to memorize the estimate.
3. Give the estimate a name that reminds you of its contents.

4. Select the option Don't Remind Me.

5. Click OK.

To use the boilerplate estimate, press CTRL-T, or choose Lists | Memorized Transaction List. Select the estimate, fill in the Customer:Job information, and save it. The memorized estimate isn't changed.

This chapter covered a great deal of information about invoices, and that reflects the importance of your invoicing procedures. The more accurate your invoices are, the fewer questions you'll have from your customers. This increases the likelihood that your customers will send checks right away.

# Receiving Payments

## In this Chapter:

- *Handle payments on customer invoices*

- *Handle cash sales*

- *Issue receipts for cash sales*

- *Deposit payments and cash sales into your bank account*

- *Apply credits and discounts to invoices*

- *Customize the cash sales receipt*

The best part of Accounts Receivable chores is receiving the payments. However, you need to make sure you apply customer payments correctly, so that you and your customers have the same information in your records.

# Receiving Invoice Payments

As you create invoices and send them to your customers, there's an expectation that money will eventually arrive to pay off those invoices. And, in fact, it almost always works that way. In accounting, there are two ways to think about the cash receipts that pay off invoices:

**Balance forward**   This is a system in which you consider the total of all the outstanding invoices as the amount due from the customer, and you apply payments against that total. It doesn't matter which particular invoice is being paid, because it's a running total of payments against a running total of invoices.

**Open item**   This is a system in which payments you receive are applied to specific invoices. Most of the time, the customer either sends a copy of the invoice along with the check, or notes the invoice number that is being paid on the check stub to make sure your records agree with the customer's records.

QuickBooks assumes you're using a balance forward system, but you can override that default easily. In fact, applying payments directly to specific invoices is just a matter of a mouse click or two.

**Note**   *QuickBooks refers to the process of handling invoice payments from customers as "Receive Payments." The common bookkeeping jargon for this process is "cash receipts." You'll find I use that term frequently throughout this chapter (it's just habit).*

## Recording the Payment

When a check arrives from a customer, follow these steps to apply the payment:

1. Choose Customers | Receive Payments from the menu bar to bring up a blank Receive Payments window, as shown in Figure 4-1.

2. Click the arrow to the right of the Received From field to display a list of customers and select the customer who sent the check. If the check is for a job, select the job. The current balance for this customer or job automatically appears in the Customer Balance field.

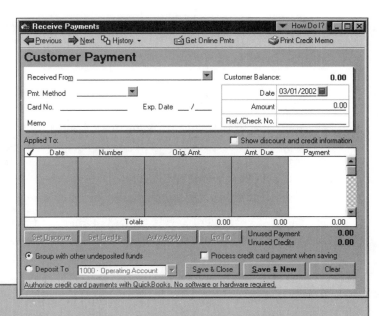

**Figure 4-1 • All sorts of details have to be filled in when you receive a customer payment.**

**Note**     *If you invoice by job, you can select the customer instead of the job and see all invoices for all jobs. This feature, which is new in QuickBooks 2002, makes it easier to apply payments across jobs.*

3. In the Amount field, enter the amount of this payment.

4. Click the arrow to the right of the Pmt. Method field and select the payment method.

5. If the payment method is a credit card, complete the Card No. and Exp. Date fields. If you have a merchant account with the QuickBooks Merchant Account Service, click the option Process Credit Card Payment When Saving to automatically put the credit card payment into your bank account. (See Appendix D for information about the QuickBooks Merchant Account Service.)

6. If the payment method is a check, enter the check number in the Ref./Check No. field.

The Memo field is optional, and I've never come across a reason to use it, but if there's some important memorandum you feel you must attach to this payment record, feel free.

## Applying Payments to Invoices

Now you have to apply the payment against the customer invoices. As you can see in Figure 4-2, QuickBooks automatically applies the payment to the oldest invoice. However, if the payment exactly matches the amount of another invoice, QuickBooks applies it correctly.

You could face several scenarios when receiving customer payments:

- The customer has one unpaid invoice, and the payment is for the same amount as that invoice.
- The customer has several unpaid invoices, and the payment is for the amount of one of those invoices.
- The customer has one or more unpaid invoices, and the payment is for an amount lower than any single invoice.

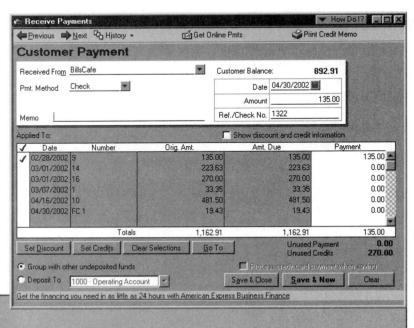

**Figure 4-2 • QuickBooks automatically applies payments to the oldest invoices.**

- The customer has several unpaid invoices, and the payment is for an amount greater than any one invoice but not large enough to cover two invoices.
- The customer has one or more unpaid invoices, and the payment is for a lesser amount than the current balance. However, the customer has a credit equal to the difference between the payment and the customer balance.

You have a variety of choices for handling any of these scenarios, but for situations in which the customer's intention isn't clear, the smart thing to do is call the customer and ask how the payment should be applied. You can manually enter the amount you're applying against an invoice in the Payment column. You must, of course, apply the entire amount of the payment.

If you are not tracking invoices, instead using a balance forward system, just let QuickBooks continue to apply payments to the oldest invoices (or a portion of the oldest invoice).

If the customer sent a copy of the invoice with the payment, or indicated the invoice number on the check or stub, always apply the payment to that invoice, even if it means an older invoice remains unpaid. Customers do this deliberately, usually because there's a problem with the older invoice. The rule of thumb is "apply payments according to the customers' wishes." Otherwise, when you and the customer have a conversation about the current open balance, your bookkeeping records won't match.

If the customer payment doesn't match the amount of any invoice (it's a partial payment), check to see whether the customer indicated a specific invoice number for the payment. If so, apply the payment against that invoice; if not, let the automatic selection of the oldest invoice stand.

If the check is for the same amount as a later invoice, QuickBooks should automatically select that invoice. If that doesn't happen, click the check mark next to the one that QuickBooks automatically selected incorrectly to remove the check mark. Then click the check mark column next to the invoice that's being paid with this payment.

## Applying Credits to Invoices

You can apply any existing credit to an invoice in addition to this payment. If credits exist for the job, QuickBooks displays the amount of credit due on the Receive Payments window (refer to the item Unused Credits shown in Figure 4-2). Usually, customers let you know how they want credits applied, and it's not unusual to find a note written on the copy of the invoice that the customer sent along with the check.

Click the Set Credits button to apply existing credits via the Discount And Credits dialog box.

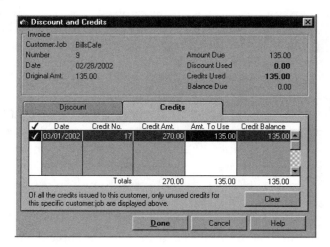

Depending on the circumstances, here's how QuickBooks automatically handles the credits:

### The Credit Total Is Equal to or Less than the Unpaid Amount of the Oldest Invoice.

This reduces the balance due on that invoice. If the customer sent a payment that reflects a deduction for the amount of his credits (a common scenario), so that the credit total is equal to the unpaid amount, the invoice has no remaining balance.

If applying the existing credit along with the payment doesn't pay off the invoice, the balance due on the invoice is reduced by the total of the payment and the credit.

The amount of the credit is added to the Payment column for the invoice. Don't worry—even though the payment amount has changed, this change only affects the invoice balance and the Accounts Receivable posting; it doesn't change the amount of the customer payment that's posted to your bank account.

### The Credit Total Is Larger than the Amount Required to Pay Off an Invoice.

If the customer payment is smaller than the amount of the invoice, but the amount of credit is larger than the amount needed to pay off the invoice, the balance of the credit is applied to the next oldest unpaid invoice. A check mark appears in the leftmost column next to that invoice to indicate that a payment (in the form of a credit) is being applied against the invoice.

To apply the unapplied credit balance to another invoice, click Done and select the next invoice in the Receive Payments window. Then click Set Credits and apply the credit balance (or as much of it as you need) against the invoice. Any unused credits remain for the future.

You should send a statement to the customer to reflect the current, new invoice balances as a result of applying the payments and the credits (even though the customer's accounting software probably reflects the facts accurately).

**Tip**    *It's easier to track what you're doing for customers with credits if you select the option Show Discount And Credit Information on the Receive Payments window.*

## Applying Credits to a Different Job

You may have a situation in which a customer has already paid the invoices for a job when the credit is created, or has paid for part of the job, exceeding the amount of the credit. If the customer tells you to apply the credit balance to another job, or to float the credit and apply it against the next job, you have a problem.

QuickBooks does not permit you to apply a credit from one job to another job. You have the same problem if you created a credit for a customer that has one or more jobs, but you applied the credit directly to the customer instead of a job. You can't use the credit amount against an invoice payment for one of that customer's jobs.

However, as a workaround, you can unapply and reapply credits, and you have a couple of methods to choose from, as described here.

Wash (zero out) the original credit with an invoice against the same job (or the same customer if you mistakenly applied a credit to the customer name instead of the job name). If the credit is a partial credit (you applied some of it against its job), make the invoice amount equal to the credit balance. In the Description column, enter **Offset to CM xxx**, where *xxx* is the original credit memo number, so you can mail the invoice to the customer to explain what you're doing. Then create a new credit for an equal amount and apply it to the other job.

There are some minor problems (well, *irritations…*) with this approach, due to the fact that QuickBooks does not have an element called a debit memo (traditionally used to offset and correct credit memos). Therefore, when your customer gets a statement at the end of the month, an invoice is listed that makes no sense to the customer. I solved this for my clients by instructing them to use the letters "DM" in front of the invoice number in the Invoice # field. Then they customized their Statement template to add a footer that explained the DM invoices. (See Chapter 5 to learn how to customize

Statement forms.) Of course, if you use this approach, you have to remember to remove the DM from the Invoice # field when you next open the Create Invoices window.

Another technique is to wash the credit with a debit via a journal entry. To do this, you need to have a "wash" account. For my clients, I create an account named "Exchanges" with an account type of Other Expense. Then I take the following steps:

1. Choose Banking | Make Journal Entry to open the General Journal Entry window.

**Note** *You'll see a message from QuickBooks telling you that journal entries are now automatically assigned numbers. Read Chapter 14 to learn all about journal entries, including the significance of this new feature.*

2. In the Account column, select the Accounts Receivable account and press TAB.
3. In the Debit column, enter the amount of the credit.
4. Optionally, enter a note to yourself in the Memo column (e.g., "Moving CM # *xxx*") and press TAB.
5. In the Name column, select the Customer:Job listing from which you are *removing* the credit and press TAB.
6. In the Account column, select the "wash" account.
7. QuickBooks automatically puts the correct amount in the Credit column.
8. Click Save & New to open a new, blank General Journal Entry window.
9. In the Account column, select the Accounts Receivable account and press TAB twice to move to the Credit column.
10. In the Credit column, enter the amount of the credit and press TAB.
11. Optionally, write a note to yourself in the Memo column (e.g., "Moving CM # *xxx*") and press TAB.
12. In the Name column, select the Customer:Job listing to which you are *applying* the credit and press TAB.
13. In the Account column, enter the "wash" account.
14. QuickBooks automatically puts the correct amount in the Debit column.
15. Click Save & Close.

Now, before you send me an e-mail to ask (sarcastically) why I didn't put all four lines on the same journal entry, I'll explain. QuickBooks, unlike other accounting software programs, does not permit you to use the A/R or A/P account multiple times in the same journal entry. There are lots of situations that arise during the course of business bookkeeping activities that would be much easier if you could have multiple entries to A/R or A/P, but QuickBooks has had this restriction forever. Also annoying is the fact that QuickBooks doesn't permit you to put both an A/R and A/P entry on the same journal entry (making entering opening trial balances a real pain). Further, you can't post anything to A/R or A/P in a journal entry without charging the amount to a customer or a vendor, which is frequently a bother. I can't explain their reasons for these restrictions, I can only explain the ramifications.

Both of these solutions create an audit trail that you can understand in the future, and that your accountant will approve of. However, even though I continuously rail against the practice of deleting transactions, I know that many of you will have figured out that merely deleting the credit memo and creating a new one for the right job will be easy (and that's what you'll do). The math works, but you're not following good accounting/bookkeeping practices. The ability to delete a transaction is another feature QuickBooks offers that most, if not all, other accounting software companies shun. As a result, if I ever decide to stop writing books and become a professional embezzler, I'll only work at companies that use QuickBooks because otherwise I won't be able to hide (delete) my devious transactions.

## Applying Discounts for Timely Payments

If you offer your customers terms that include a discount if they pay their bills promptly (for instance, 2% 10 net 30), you must apply the discount to the payment if it's applicable. You must also select the option Show Discount And Credit Information on the Receive Payments window.

Figure 4-3 shows the Receive Payments window for a customer who has been offered a discount for timely payment and has taken it by reducing the amount of the payment. The only clue you have to explain the difference between the payment amount and the invoice amount is the fact that the Disc Date column shows a date. For customers or invoices without discount terms, that column is blank in the Receive Payments window.

QuickBooks doesn't apply the discount automatically, for instance by offering a column with the discount amount and selecting that amount as part of the payment. Instead, you must click the Set Discount button to see the discount information for this invoice.

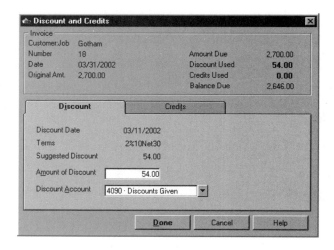

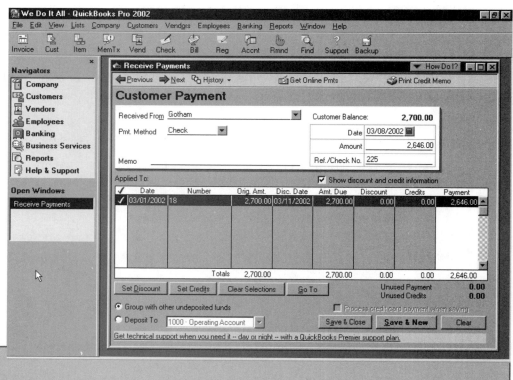

**Figure 4-3 • A discount date appears for an invoice that offers discounts.**

A summary of the invoice and discount terms appears and QuickBooks inserts the amount of the discount to use, based on the information in the invoice. Accept the amount of discount, enter a Discount Account (see "Posting Discounts" later in this section), and then click Done. You can change the amount of the discount, which you may want to do if the customer only made a partial payment (less than is required to pay off the invoice after the discount is applied) and you want to give a proportionately smaller discount.

When you return to the Receive Payments window, you'll see that QuickBooks has changed the Amt. Due column to reflect the discount. Most of the time, the Amt. Due and the customer payment amount are the same, so the invoice is now paid off.

## Applying Discounts for Untimely Payments

Sometimes customers take the discount even if the payment arrives after the discount date. (It's probably more accurate to say that customers *always* take the discount even if the payment arrives later than the terms permit.) You can apply the payment to the invoice and leave a balance due for the discount amount that was deducted by the customer, if you wish. However, most companies give the customer the discount even if the payment is late, as part of "good will."

When you click the Discount Info button in that case, QuickBooks does not automatically fill in the discount amount—it's too late, and QuickBooks is not forgiving, generous, or aware of the need to humor customers to preserve good will. Simply enter the amount manually and then click Done to apply the discount to the invoice.

## Posting Discounts

To track the amount of money you've given away with discounts, you can create a specific account in your chart of accounts. You could post discounts to your standard income account(s), which will be reduced every time you apply a discount. The math is right, but the absence of an audit trail bothers me (and bothers many accountants). It's better to create an Income account (I call mine "Discounts Given").

**Caution** *If there's an account named "Discounts" in the part of your chart of accounts that's devoted to expenses, don't use that account for your customer discounts, because it's there to track the discounts you take with your vendors.*

## Turning Payments into Bank Deposits

QuickBooks offers two options for depositing your payment on the Receive Payments window: Group With Other Undeposited Funds, and Deposit To (which you use to name a specific bank account). By default, the first option is selected. This section explains the choices so you can decide how to handle deposits.

### Group with Other Undeposited Funds

Each payment you receive is entered into an account named Undeposited Funds (QuickBooks establishes this account automatically). It's an account type of Other Current Asset. When you finish applying customer payments in QuickBooks and are ready to make your bank deposit, you move the money from the Undeposited Funds account into the bank account by choosing Banking | Make Deposits from the menu bar. (See the section "Depositing Cash Receipts" later in this chapter for details.)

While the Undeposited Funds account shows each individual payment you received, the bank account shows only the total amount of each bank deposit. This matches the bank statement that shows up each month, making it easier to reconcile the account.

### Deposit to Bank Account

Depositing each payment directly to the bank means you don't have to take the extra step involved in using the Make Deposits window. However, each payment you receive appears as a separate entry when you reconcile your bank account. If you received six payments totaling $10,450.25 and took the checks to the bank that day, your bank statement shows that amount as the deposit. You'll have to select each payment individually to mark them as cleared, which requires some calculations at the time you perform the reconciliation. (See Chapter 12 for detailed instructions on reconciling bank accounts.)

## Understanding Customer Payment Postings

When you receive money in payment for customer invoices, QuickBooks automatically posts all the amounts to your general ledger. Following are the postings if you select the option Group With Other Deposits and make the deposit separately.

| Account | Debit | Credit |
|---|---|---|
| Undeposited Funds | Total of cash receipts | |
| Accounts Receivable | | Total of cash receipts |

When you make the actual deposit, using the Make Deposit feature, QuickBooks automatically posts the following transaction:

| Account | Debit | Credit |
|---|---|---|
| Bank | Total of deposit | |
| Undeposited Funds | | Total of deposit |

Here are the postings for a customer who takes a discount. Let's assume the sale was for $100.00. The original sale posted the following amounts:

| Account | Debit | Credit |
|---|---|---|
| Accounts Receivable | $100.00 | |
| Income | | $100.00 |

The customer was entitled to (and took) a 1% discount. When you enter the customer payment, which is in the amount of $99.00, the following postings occur:

| Account | Debit | Credit |
|---|---|---|
| Undeposited Funds | $99.00 | |
| Accounts Receivable | | $100.00 |
| Discounts Given | $1.00 | |

# Handling Cash Sales

A cash sale is a sale for which you haven't created an invoice. Cash sales are the same as invoiced sales insofar as an exchange of money for goods or services occurs. The difference is that there's no period of time during which you have money "on the street." You can have a cash sale for either a service or a product, although it's far more common to sell products for cash. Most service companies use invoices.

> **Note**    *QuickBooks uses the term "sales receipt" instead of "cash sale." However, the term "cash sale" is the common jargon (a sales receipt is a piece of paper), so I'm continuing to use it.*

I'm assuming that a cash sale is not your normal method of doing business (you're not running a candy store). If you *are* running a retail store, the cash sale feature in QuickBooks isn't an efficient way to handle your cash flow. You should either have specialized retail software (that even takes care of opening the cash register drawer automatically, and also tracks inventory) or use QuickBooks only to record your daily totals of bank deposits as a journal entry.

> **Note**    *Don't take the word "cash" literally, because a cash sale can involve a check or a credit card.*

There are two methods for handling cash sales in QuickBooks:

- Record each cash sale as a discrete record. This is useful for tracking sales of products or services to customers. It provides a way to maintain records about those customers in addition to tracking income and inventory.
- Record sales in batches (usually one batch for each business day). This method tracks income and inventory when you have no desire to maintain customer information.

To record a cash sale, choose Customers | Enter Sales Receipts from the menu bar to open the Enter Sales Receipts window, shown in Figure 4-4.

## Entering Cash Sale Data

If you want to track customer information, enter a name in the Customer:Job field or select the name from the drop-down list. If the customer doesn't exist, you can add a new customer by choosing <Add New>.

If you're not tracking customers, invent a customer for cash sales (I named the customer "Cash Sale," which seemed appropriate).

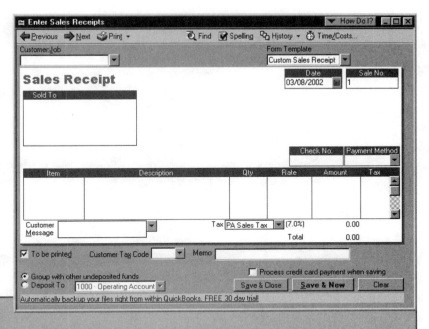

**Figure 4-4 •** The Sales Receipt window is an invoice, a payment form, and a receipt.

**Tip**    *If you have customers who always pay at the time of the sale, you might want to consider creating a customer type for this group ("Cash" seems an appropriate name for the type). You can separate this group for reports or for marketing and advertising campaigns.*

Every field in the Enter Sales Receipts window works exactly the way it works for invoices and payments—just fill in the information. To save the record, click Save & New to bring up a new blank record, or click Save & Close to stop using the Enter Sales Receipts window.

## Printing a Receipt for a Cash Sale

Many cash customers want a receipt. Click the Print button in the Enter Sales Receipts window to display the Print One Sales Receipt window, shown in Figure 4-5. If you're not printing to a dot-matrix printer with multipart paper and you want a copy of the receipt for your files, be sure you change the specification in the Number Of Copies check box.

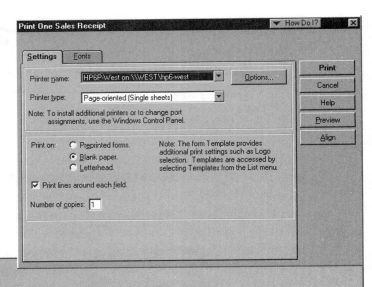

**Figure 4-5 • Choose the options you need to print a receipt.**

## Customizing the Cash Sales Form

I think a lot is missing from the form QuickBooks presents for cash sales.
For example, there's no place for a sales rep, which is needed if you're paying
commissions on cash sales. There's no Ship To address if the customer pays cash
and wants delivery, nor is there a Ship Via field.

The solution is to customize the Custom Sales Receipts form. Here's how to
do that:

1. Click the arrow next to the Form Template box in the upper-right corner
   of the form and choose Customize from the drop-down list to open the
   Customize Template dialog box. There aren't multiple forms to use as a basis
   for the new form, so Custom Sales Receipts is selected.

2. Click New to open the Customize Sales Receipt window, shown in
   Figure 4-6.

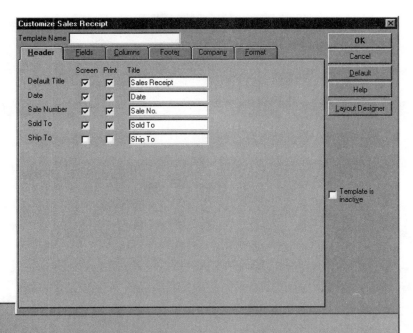

**Figure 4-6 • Build your own, more useful form for cash sales.**

3. Give the form a name in the Template Name box.
4. On the Header tab, select the Ship To field for both the Screen and the Print forms.
5. Move to the Fields tab and add any fields you need. It's common to need Rep, Ship Date, and Ship Via. (You may want to omit the Rep field from the print version).
6. Use the Columns tab to add or remove columns in the line item section of the form. You can also change the order in which the columns appear. (For instance, perhaps you'd rather have Qty in the first column instead of the Item number.)

After you finish making the changes you need, click OK. You're returned to the Enter Sales Receipts window, and your new form is ready to use (see Figure 4-7).

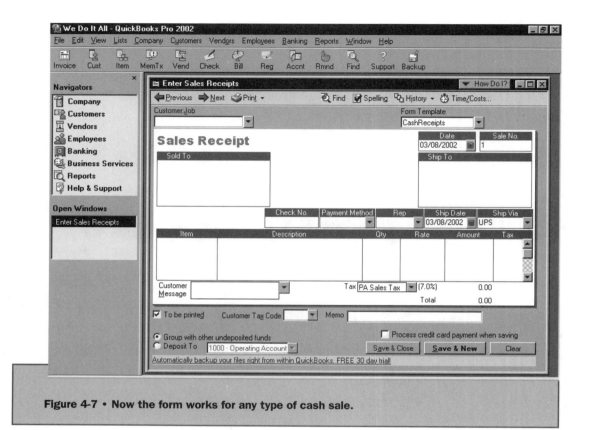

**Figure 4-7 • Now the form works for any type of cash sale.**

# Handling Batches of Cash Sales

If you sell products or services and receive instant payment on a more frequent basis, you might want to consider batching the transactions. This works only if you don't care about maintaining information about the customers, and no customer expects a receipt. This technique also works if you have a business in which sales and service personnel return to the office each day with customer payments in hand.

Create a customized form, using the steps described in the previous section, with the following guidelines:

- Name the form appropriately (for example, "Batch Sales" or "Sales Batch").
- On the Header tab, keep only the Date and Sale Number fields in the heading.
- On the Fields tab, deselect all the optional fields.
- On the Footer tab, remove the Message field.

To batch-process cash sales, use the Enter Sales Receipts window with the following procedures:

- Use a customer named "Cash" or "CashSale," or skip the Customer:Job field.
- In the line item section, use a new line for each sale, regardless of whether the same customer is purchasing each item, each item is purchased by a different customer, or there's a combination of both events.
- Use the Save & Close button at the end of the day. If you need to close the window during the day (perhaps you'd like to get some work done), open the bank account to which you're posting the income (or the Undeposited Funds account if you're using that account). Double-click the listing to re-open the window.

If you use this technique, you cannot track the method of payment, and all receipts are treated as "money in." You can create a money-in item in the Customer Payment Method list (see Chapter 2 for information about creating list items).

## Understanding the Cash Sale Postings

QuickBooks treats cash sales in the simplest, most logical manner. If you've sold a service instead of an inventory item for cash (perhaps a service call for a one-time customer you don't want to invoice), the postings are very straightforward:

| Account | Debit | Credit |
|---|---|---|
| Undeposited Funds | Total cash sales | |
| Revenue | | Total cash sales |

If the cash sale involved inventory items, here are the postings:

| Account | Debit | Credit |
|---|---|---|
| Undeposited Funds | Total cash sales | |
| Income | | Total cash sales |
| Cost of Sales | Total cost of items sold | |
| Inventory | | Total cost of items sold |

Now I'm going to suggest you make it a bit more complicated, but don't panic, because it's not difficult. In the long run, these suggestions will make your bookkeeping chores easier. There's also a chance you'll make your accountant happier.

The Enter Sales Receipts window provides two accounts choices for posting the cash you receive:

- Group With Other Undeposited Funds
- Deposit To (you're expected to enter the bank account into which you place your cash receipts)

If you use the Deposit To option, your sales won't appear in the Payments to Deposit window when you tell QuickBooks you're taking your cash receipts to the bank. (See the section "Depositing Cash Receipts" later in this chapter.) In fact, your bank account will be incremented by the amount of cash you post to it from cash sales, even though the money isn't really there until you make the trip to the bank.

There are two other ways to track receipts from cash sales separate from customer payments; pick the one that appeals to you:

- Opt to post the receipts to the Undeposited Funds account, but make those deposits separately when you work in the QuickBooks Payments To Deposit window.
- Opt to post the receipts to a new account called "Undeposited Till" (or something similar) and manually deposit the money into your bank account via a journal entry.

If you want to use the Undeposited Funds account, when you use the Make Deposits window, select only the cash receipts for deposit and then return to the Make Deposits window to deposit the remaining invoice payments in a separate transaction. Details on the procedures are found in the "Depositing Cash Receipts" section later in this chapter.

If you want to create an account to represent the cash till, to which you post cash in the Enter Sales Receipts window, make the new account a type Other Current Asset.

If you deal in real cash and have a cash register, you need to fill the till to make change. Write a check from your operating account (the payee should be Cash) and post the amount to the new account (which I call "Undeposited Till"). This produces the following posting (assuming $100.00 is allocated for change).

| Account | Debit | Credit |
|---------|-------|--------|
| Checking |  | $100.00 |
| Undeposited Till | $100.00 |  |

When it's time to go to the bank, leave the original startup money (in this example, $100.00) in the till, count the rest of the money, and deposit that money into your checking account. When you return from the bank, make the following journal entry:

| Account | Debit | Credit |
|---------|-------|--------|
| Checking | Amt of deposit |  |
| Undeposited Till |  | Amt of deposit |

In a perfect world, after you make the deposit and the journal entry, you can open the register for the Undeposited Till account and see a balance equal to your original startup cash. The world isn't perfect, however, and sometimes the actual amount you were able to deposit doesn't equal the amount collected in the Enter Sales Receipts transaction window. To resolve this, see the section "Handling the Over and Short Problem" later in this chapter.

Incidentally, if you want to raise or lower the amount you leave in the till for change, you don't have to do anything special. Just deposit less or more money, and the remainder (in the register for the Undeposited Till account and also in the physical till) just becomes the new base.

# Depositing Cash Receipts

With all of those checks you've received for invoice payments, and the cash hanging around from the cash sales, it's time to go to the bank. Wait, don't grab those car keys yet! You have to tell QuickBooks about your bank deposit. Otherwise, when it's time to reconcile your checkbook, you'll have a nervous breakdown.

## Choosing the Payments to Deposit

As you've been filling out the payment and cash sales forms, QuickBooks has been keeping a list it calls Undeposited Funds. That list remains designated as Undeposited Funds until you clear it by depositing them. (If you've been depositing every payment and cash receipt to the bank, this section doesn't apply.)

To tell QuickBooks to make a deposit, choose Banking | Make Deposits from the QuickBooks menu bar, which brings up the Payments To Deposit window, shown in Figure 4-8.

Notice that the Payments To Deposit window displays information about the items in the Type column: Customer payments are indicated by PMT, and cash sales receipts are indicated by RCPT.

You may have other deposits to make, perhaps refund checks from vendors, checks representing loans you've been approved for, checks representing a capital infusion from you, or some other type of deposit. Don't worry—you can tell QuickBooks about them in the next transaction window. This window is only displaying the cash receipts you've entered into QuickBooks through the Payments and Sales Receipts transaction windows.

Click Select All to select all the payments for deposit. If you want to hold back the deposit of any item, deselect it by clicking in the check mark column. Only the items that have a check mark will be cleared from the undeposited payments list. There are several reasons to deselect deposit items:

- You received a payment in advance from a customer and don't want to deposit it until you're sure you can fill the order.
- You've accepted a post-dated check and it cannot yet be deposited.
- You want to separate the transactions for depositing customer payments and cash sales.
- You want to deposit certain payments into one bank account, and other payments into another bank account (necessary if you hold escrow funds in an escrow account).

After you make your selections, click OK.

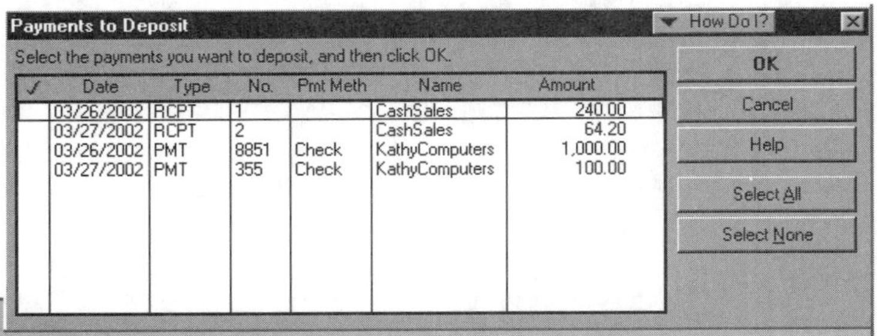

**Figure 4-8 • All the money you've received since your last bank deposit is listed in the Payments To Deposit window.**

## Filling Out the Deposit Slip

Clicking OK in the Payments To Deposit window brings up the Make Deposits window, shown in Figure 4-9.

If you were paying attention when you looked at Figure 4-8, you'll notice that in Figure 4-9 I'm making only half the deposits that appeared in the Payments To Deposit window. I'm separating the deposit of customer payments from the deposit of receipts from cash sales. This is a common practice when depositing cash, because sometimes the bank notifies you that their automatic counting machine produced a different total from the total on your deposit slip (you probably counted the cash by hand instead of purchasing counting machines for coins and paper money). If that happens, you can edit the cash sales deposit item in your bank register, and the cause of the edit will be obvious. (I'm a stickler for good audit trails.)

Select the bank account you're using for this deposit. Then make sure the date matches the day you're physically depositing the money. (If you're doing this at night, use tomorrow's date so your records match the bank statement.)

### Adding Items to the Deposit

If you decide to put back a payment you deselected in the previous window, click the Payments button at the top of the window to return to the Make Deposits window and select it.

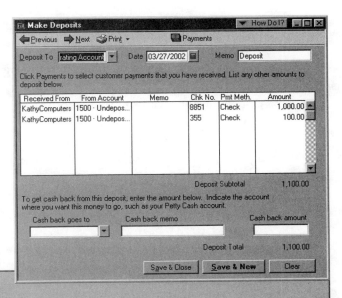

**Figure 4-9 • The Make Deposits window is a virtual bank deposit slip.**

If you want to add deposit items that weren't in the Make Deposits window, click anywhere in the Received From column to make it accessible, and select an existing name by clicking the arrow, or click <Add New> to enter a name that isn't in your system. If the source of the check is a bank, or yourself, or any other entity that isn't a customer or vendor, use the Other Name classification for the type of name.

Press TAB to move to the From Account column and enter the account to which you're posting this transaction. For example, if the check you're depositing represents a bank loan, use the liability account for that bank loan (you can create it here by choosing <Add New> if you didn't think to set up the account earlier). If the check you're depositing represents an infusion of capital from you, use the owner's capital account in the Equity section of your chart of accounts. If the check is a refund for an expense (perhaps you overpaid someone, and they're returning money to you), post the deposit to that expense. Use the TAB key to move through the rest of the columns, which are self-explanatory.

### Getting Cash Back from Deposits

If you're getting cash back from your deposit, you can tell QuickBooks about it right on the virtual deposit slip, instead of making a journal entry to adjust the total of collected payments against the total of the bank deposit.

**Note** *If you're keeping the money for yourself, and your business isn't a corporation, use the Draw account to post the cash back. If your business is a corporation, you can't keep the money for yourself.*

Enter the account to which you're posting the cash (usually a petty-cash account); optionally, enter a memo as a note to yourself, and enter the amount of cash you want back from this deposit (use a negative number). Even though you can put the cash in your pocket, you must account for it, because these are business funds. As you spend the cash for business expenses, post the expense against a petty-cash account with a journal entry.

**Caution** *Many banks will not cash checks made out to a company, so your ability to get cash back may be limited to checks made out to you, personally.*

# Printing Deposit Slips

If you want to print a deposit slip or a deposit summary, click the Print button in the Make Deposits window. QuickBooks asks whether you want to print a deposit slip and summary, or just a deposit summary.

If you want to print a deposit slip that your bank will accept, you must order printable deposit slips from Intuit. Call 800-433-8810 to order personalized deposit slips that have your name, address, and bank information, or visit their Web site at www.intuitmarket.com.

The deposit slips from Intuit are guaranteed to be acceptable to your bank. You must have a laser printer or inkjet printer to use them. When you print the deposit slip, there's a tear-off section at the bottom of the page that has a deposit summary. Keep that section for your own records and take the rest of the page to the bank along with your money.

If you don't have Intuit deposit slips, select Deposit Summary and fill out your bank deposit slip manually. Be sure to fill out the payment method field (cash or check), or QuickBooks won't print the deposit slip. A Print dialog box appears so you can change printers, adjust margins, or even print in color. Choose Print to send the deposit information to the printer. When you return to the Make Deposits window, click OK to save the deposit.

**Tip** | *If you're printing real deposit slips and your bank requires multiple copies, change the Number of Copies specification in the Print dialog box.*

# Handling the Over and Short Problem

If you literally take cash for cash sales, when you count the money in the till at the end of the day, you may find that the recorded income doesn't match the cash you expected to find in the till. Or you may find that the money you posted to deposit to the bank doesn't match the amount of money you put into the little brown bag you took to the bank. This is a common problem with cash, and, in fact, it's an occasional problem in regular accrual bookkeeping. One of the ensuing problems you face is how to handle this in your bookkeeping system. QuickBooks is a double-entry bookkeeping system, which means the left side of the ledger has to be equal to the right side of the ledger. If you post $100.00 in cash sales, but only have $99.50 to take to the bank, how do you handle the missing 50 cents? You can't just post $100.00 to your bank account (well, you could, but your bank reconciliation won't work and, more importantly, you're not practicing good bookkeeping).

The solution to the Over/Short dilemma is to acknowledge it in your bookkeeping procedures. Track it. You'll be amazed by how much it balances itself out—short one day, over another. (Of course, if you're short every day, and the shortages are growing, you have an entirely different problem, and the first place to look is at the person who stands in front of the cash register.) To track Over/Short, you need to have some place to post the discrepancies, which means you have to create some new accounts in your chart of accounts.

Create two new accounts as follows:

1. Click the Accnt button on the icon bar to open the Chart of Accounts list.
2. Press CTRL-N to create a new account.
3. In the New Account window, select an account type of Income.
4. If you're using numbered accounts, choose a number that's on the next level from your regular Income accounts; for example, choose 4290 if your regular Income accounts are 4000, 4010, and so on.
5. Name the account "Over."
6. Click Next and repeat the processes, using the next number and naming the account "Short."

If you want to see a net number for Over/Short (a good idea), create three accounts: Name the first account (the parent account) "Over-Short," and then make the Over and Short accounts subaccounts of Over-Short.

In addition, you need items to use for your overages and shortages (remember, you need items for everything that's connected with entering invoices and cash sales). Create these new items as follows:

1. Click the Item button on the icon bar to open the Items list.
2. Press CTRL-N to create a new item.
3. Create a non-inventory part item named "Overage."
4. Don't assign a price.
5. Make it non-taxable.
6. Link it to the account (or subaccount) named Over that you just created.
7. Click Next to create another new, non-inventory part item.
8. Name this item "Short" and link it to the account (or subaccount) named Short.
9. Click OK to close the Item List window.

Now that you have the necessary accounts and items, use the Over and Short items right in the Sales Receipts window to adjust the difference between the amount of money you've accumulated in the cash-sale transactions and the amount of money you're actually depositing to the bank. Remember to use a minus sign before the figure if you're using the Short item.

# Tracking Accounts Receivable

## In this Chapter:

- *Set up finance charges*

- *Send customer payment reminders*

- *Print customer statements*

- *Run A/R aging reports*

**Chapter 5**

**C**ollecting your money is one of the largest headaches in running a business. You have to track what's owed and who owes it, and then expend time and effort to collect it. All of the effort you spend on the money your customers owe you is called *tracking Accounts Receivable (A/R)*.

# Using Finance Charges

One way to speed up collections is to impose finance charges for late payments. Incidentally, this isn't "found money"; it probably doesn't cover its own cost. The amount of time spent tracking, analyzing, and chasing receivables is substantial. To use finance charges, you have to establish the rate and circumstances under which they're assessed.

## Configuring Finance Charges

Your company's finance charges are configured as part of your company preferences. Choose Edit | Preferences to open the Preferences window. Then click the Finance Charge icon in the left pane and select the Company Preferences tab (see Figure 5-1).

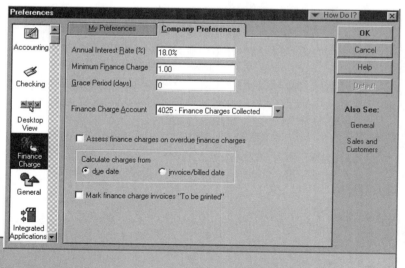

**Figure 5-1 • Configure your finance charges.**

Here are some guidelines for filling out this window:

- Notice that the interest rate is annual. If you want to charge 1.5 percent a month, enter **18%** in the Annual Interest Rate field.
- You can assess a minimum finance charge for overdue balances. QuickBooks will calculate the finance charge; if it's less than the minimum, the minimum charge is assessed.
- Use the Grace Period field to enter the number of days of lateness you permit before finance charges are assessed.
- During setup, QuickBooks probably created an account for finance charges. If so, it's displayed in this window. If not, enter (or create) the account you want to use to post finance charges.
- The issue of assessing finance charges on overdue finance charges is a sticky one. The practice is illegal in many states. Selecting this option means that a customer who owed $100.00 last month and had a finance charge assessed of $2.00 now owes $102.00. Now, the next finance charge is assessed on a balance of $102.00 (instead of on the original overdue balance of $100.00). Regardless of state law, the fact is that very few businesses opt to use this calculation method.
- Specify whether to calculate the finance charge from the due date or the invoice date.
- QuickBooks creates an invoice when finance charges are assessed in order to have a permanent record of the transaction. By default, these invoices aren't printed; they're just accumulated along with the overdue invoices so they'll print out on a monthly statement. You can opt to have the finance charge invoices printed, which you should do only if you're planning to mail them as a reminder.

Click OK to save your settings after you've filled out the window.

## Assessing Finance Charges

You should assess finance charges just before you calculate and print customer statements. Choose Customers | Assess Finance Charges from the menu bar. The Assess Finance Charges window opens, with a list of all the customers with overdue balances.

> **Note**   *If any customers have made payments that you haven't yet applied to an invoice, or if any customers have credits that you haven't yet applied to an invoice, QuickBooks issues a warning. Click OK on the message dialog box. Then if you want to apply payments and credits before creating statements, close the Assess Finance Charges windows and use the Customers | Receive Payments command to accomplish the task.*

There are some things you should know about the figures you see in the Assess Finance Charges window, shown in Figure 5-2.

## Choosing the Assessment Date

Change the Assessment Date field to the date on which you want the finance charge to appear on customer statements. It's common to assess finance charges on the last day of the month. When you press the TAB key to move out of the date field, the finance charges are recalculated to reflect the new date.

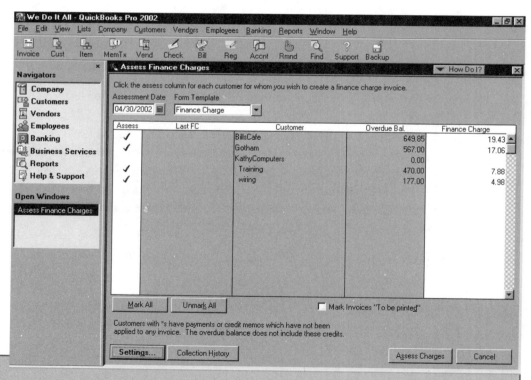

**Figure 5-2 • QuickBooks automatically calculates the finance charges as of the assessment date.**

## Selecting the Customers

You can eliminate a customer from the process by clicking in the Assess column to remove the check mark. QuickBooks, unlike many other accounting software packages, does not have a finance charge assessment option on each customer card. Therefore, all customers with overdue balances are included when you assess finance charges. It can be time consuming to deselect each customer, so if you have only a few customers for whom you reserve this process, choose Unmark All, then reselect the customers you want to include.

## Changing the Amounts

You can change the calculated total if you wish (a good idea if there are credit memos floating around). Just click on the amount displayed in the Finance Charge column to activate that column for that customer. Then enter a new finance charge amount. If you need to calculate the new figure (perhaps you're giving credit for any floating credit memos), press the equal symbol (=) to use the built-in QuickMath calculator.

## Checking the History

Select a customer and click the Collection History button to see the selected customer's history in a Collections Report. As you can see in the following illustration, your mouse pointer turns into a magnifying glass with the letter "z" (for "zoom") in it when you position it over a line item. Double-click the line item to display the original transaction window if you need to examine the details.

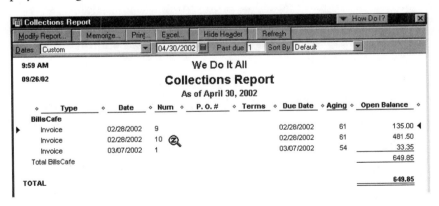

## Saving the Finance Charge Invoices

Click Assess Charges in the Assess Finance Charges window when all the figures are correct. If you've opted to skip printing, there's nothing more to do. (If you chose to print the finance charges, see the next paragraph). When you create your customer statements, these charges will appear.

### Selecting Printing Options

If you want to print the finance charge invoices (they really are invoices since they add charges to the customer balance), be sure to select the Mark Invoices To Be Printed check box. You can send the printed copies to your customers as a nagging reminder. If you just want the customer to see the finance charge on the monthly statement, deselect that option.

To print the finance charge invoices, choose File | Print Forms | Invoices. The list of unprinted invoices appears, and unless you have regular invoices you didn't print yet, the list includes only the finance charge invoices. If the list is correct, click OK to continue on to the printing process. Chapter 3 has detailed information about printing invoices.

# Sending Statements

On a periodic basis you should send statements to your customers. (Most businesses send statements monthly.) They serve a couple of purposes: They remind customers of outstanding balances, and they ensure that your records and your customers' records reflect the same information.

If you're coming to QuickBooks from a manual system, statements will seem like a miraculous tool, because creating statements from manual customer cards is a nightmare. As a result, companies without accounting software generally don't even bother to try.

## Entering Statement Charges

A *statement charge* is a charge you want to pass to a customer, for which you don't create an invoice. You can use statement charges for special charges for certain customers, such as a general overhead charge or handing charge instead of using reimbursements for your expenses. You can also use statement charges for discounts for certain customers, such as reducing the total due by a specific amount instead of creating and applying discount rates or price levels. For instance, some companies use statement charges instead of invoices for invoicing regular retainer payments. You must add statement charges before you create the statements (or else the charges won't show up on the statements).

You use items from your Item List when you enter a statement charge, and you cannot use any of the following types of items:

- Items that are taxable
- Items that have percentage discounts
- Items that represent a payment transaction

Statement charges are recorded directly in a customer's register, or in the register for a specific job. You can reach the register in order to enter a statement charge in either of two ways:

- Choose Customers | Enter Statement Charges and then select the customer or job in the Customer:Job field at the top of the register that opens (by default, QuickBooks chooses the first customer in your Customer:Job List).
- Press CTRL-J to open the Customer:Job List, and then select the appropriate listing. Click the Activities button at the bottom of the list and select Enter Statement Charges.

The Customer:Job register opens, shown in Figure 5-3.

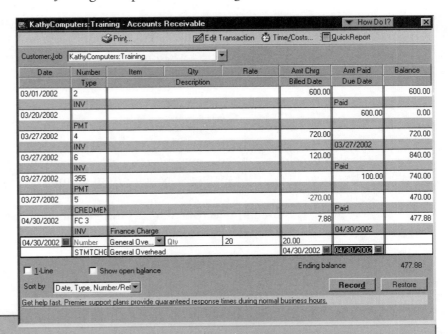

**Figure 5-3 •** Using a statement charge is like entering a simple, one-line invoice.

Use the TAB key to move through the register lines:

1. Select the item from the drop-down list (or use <Add New> to create a new item).
2. Enter a quantity in the Qty field if the item is invoiced by quantity.
3. Enter a rate if you're using the Qty field.
4. Enter the amount charged if the Qty and Rate fields aren't used (if they are, the total amount is entered automatically).
5. Optionally, edit the item description.
6. Enter the billed date, which does not have to match the transaction date in the first column of the register. Post-dating or pre-dating this field determines which statement it appears on.
7. Enter the Due Date, which affects your aging reports and your finance charge calculations.
8. Click Record to save the transaction.

If you have another statement charge to enter, select the appropriate customer or job from the Customer:Job field at the top of the register, and repeat these steps. When you are finished, close the register.

If your statement charges are recurring charges, you can memorize them to have QuickBooks automatically create them. After you create each charge, right-click its listing in the register and select Memorize Stmt Charge from the menu. This works exactly like memorized invoices (covered in Chapter 3).

# Creating the Statements

Before you start creating your statements, be sure that all the transactions that should be included on the statements have been entered into the system. Did you forget anything? Credit memos? Payments from customers? Finance charges? Statement charges?

Choose Customers | Create Statements from the menu bar to open the Create Statements window, shown in Figure 5-4.

## Selecting the Date Range

The statement date range determines which transactions appear on the statement. The statement displays the previous balance (the total due before the starting date) and includes all transactions that were created within the date range. Your opening date should be the day after the last date of your last statement run. Most companies choose the first and last days of the current month.

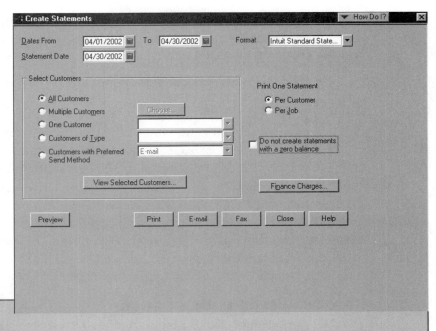

**Figure 5-4 • Creating statements starts with configuring the specifications for statements.**

## Selecting the Customers

It's normal procedure to send statements to all customers, but if that's not the plan, you can change the default selection.

If you want to send statements to a group of customers, click the Multiple Customers option to activate the Choose button that's next to it. Then click the Choose button to bring up a list of customers and select each customer you want to include. Click OK when all the appropriate customers are selected.

If you're sending a statement to one customer only, select One Customer, and then click the arrow next to the text box to scroll through the list of your customers and select the one you want.

To send statements to customers who are designated with a specific customer type, select the Customers of Type option, and then select the customer type you want to include from the drop-down list. This works, of course, only if you created customer types as part of your QuickBooks setup.

> **Tip** *If you want to send statements to certain customers only, that's a good reason in itself to create a customer type (name the type "stmnts"). Then link your statement customers to that type. See Chapter 2 to learn how to set up customer types.*

## Filtering for Send Methods

If your customers vary in the way you send them statements (mail, e-mail, or fax), you can opt to handle your statement delivery in batches, using one delivery method per batch. To do this, select the Customers With Preferred Send Method option, and then select the send method for this batch. Note that there isn't any send method named Mail; that's what the None option is for.

If you've used any method except Customers With Preferred Send Method to select customers, you can use the E-mail or Fax buttons to send e-mail or fax statements to all selected customers. QuickBooks will display a dialog box for every customer that's missing an e-mail address/fax number so you can fill in the data.

## Specifying the Printing Options

You can print one statement for each customer. That statement can list all transactions for all that customer's jobs, or you can print one statement for each job.

## Zero Balance Statements

The Do Not Create Statements With A Zero Balance check box means you can decide whether you want to send statements that have a zero balance. If you use statements only to collect money, you can select this option. If you use statements to make sure you and your customers have matching accounting records, don't select the option.

## Last Call for Finance Charges

If you haven't assessed finance charges, and you want them to appear on the statements, click the Finance Charges button. The Assess Finance Charges window opens, but this time no customers are selected and the charges are not yet assessed.

If you've already assessed finance charges for the selected time period, this window won't re-assess them (whew!). You'll be told that the finance charge for each customer is zero. Therefore, this window is useful only if you haven't already run the finance charge assessment for the period.

## Previewing the Statements

Before you commit the statements to paper, you can click the Preview button to get an advance look (see Figure 5-5). This is not just to see what the printed output will look like; it's also a way to look at the customer records, and to make sure that all the customers you selected are included.

Use the Zoom In button to see the statement and its contents close up. Click the Next Page button to move through all the statements. Click Close to return to the Create Statements window.

**Tip**    *If you see a statement that seems "funny," open a customer report to check the transactions.*

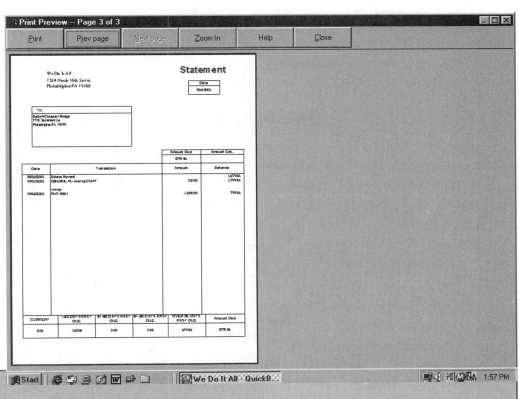

**Figure 5-5 • The Preview window provides a quick check before you send out the statements.**

## Printing the Statements

When everything is just the way it should be, print the statements by clicking the Print button in either the Print Preview window or the Create Statements window.

If you use the Print button in the Print Preview window, the statements print using the printer and printing options of your last print job, because no Print window is displayed.

If you click Close in the Preview window, return to the Create Statements window, and click Print, the Print Statement(s) window appears (as seen in Figure 5-6), and you can change the printing options.

## Customizing Statements

You don't have to use the standard statement form—you can design your own. To accomplish this, in the original Create Statements window, click the arrow to the right of the Format box and choose Customize. This opens the Customize Template window. Choose New in that window to open the Customize Statement window, shown in Figure 5-7.

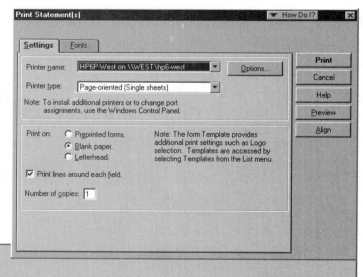

**Figure 5-6 • Change any options you wish and click Print.**

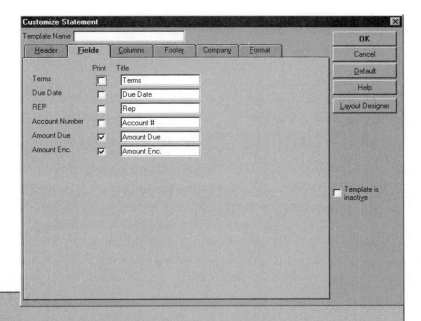

**Figure 5-7 • You may want to change the fields that appear on the statement columns.**

On the Fields tab, you might want to think about changing the following fields:

**Terms**    It's a good idea to select the Terms column title. It doesn't seem fair to tell a customer of amounts past due without reminding the customer of the terms.

**Amount Due**    This field isn't really necessary, because the same field and its data are positioned at the bottom of the statement page.

**Amount Enc**    If you use statements as bills, or expect payment for the amount of the statement, this field is supposed to contain an amount filled in by the customer. (The amount is supposed to match the amount of the check that's returned with the statement.) If you mail invoices and use statements as reminders (and your customers never send checks attached to the statements), deselect this field.

On the Footer tab, you can add text if you think there's anything to explain about the items on the statement. For example, if you create and list Debit Memos (see Chapter 4), you may want to explain what they are.

You must also supply a new name for this new template, because you cannot save the new design with the existing name. Click OK when you're finished.

> **Note**    *When you add fields to a template, QuickBooks may issue a warning that the fields overlap existing fields. If you choose Relayout, QuickBooks will attempt to fit all the fields onto the top of the statement columns. If you choose Skip, the fields will overlap; you should then choose the Layout Designer in the Customize Statement window to make everything neat and tidy. Information about using the Layout Designer is in Chapter 3.*

# Running Aging Reports

*Aging reports* are lists of the money owed you by your customers, and they're available in quite a few formats. They're for you, not for your customers. You run them whenever you need to know the extent of your receivables. Many companies run an aging report every morning, just to keep an eye on things.

A couple of aging reports are available in QuickBooks, and you can also customize any built-in reports so they report data exactly the way you want it. To see an aging report, choose Reports | Customers & Receivables, and then choose either A/R Aging Summary or A/R Aging Detail (these reports are explained next).

## Using Aging Summary Reports

The quickest way to see how much money is owed to you is to select A/R Aging Summary, which produces a listing of customer balances (see Figure 5-8).

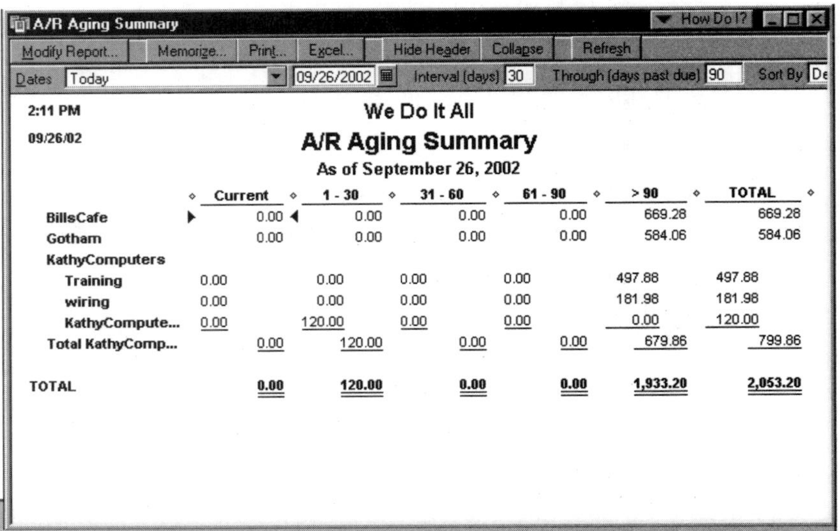

Figure 5-8 • A/R totals for each customer are displayed in an aging summary report.

Let's pause a moment and talk about the importance of the number for that A/R asset. In fact, banks give lines of credit and loans using the A/R balance as collateral.

When your accountant visits, you can bet one of the things he or she will ask to see is this report. When your accountant asks for an aging report, another safe bet is that you'll receive a request to see the amount posted to A/R in your general ledger. The general ledger A/R balance and the total on the aging report must be the same (for the same date)—not close, not almost, but *exactly* the same. If the figures are not identical, your general ledger isn't "proved" (jargon for, "I'm sorry, we can't trust your general ledger figures because they don't audit properly.").

## Using Aging Detail Reports

If you choose Aging Detail from the Accounts Receivable reports menu, you see a much more comprehensive report, such as the one seen in Figure 5-9. The report is sorted by aging interval, showing individual transactions, including finance charges, for each aging period.

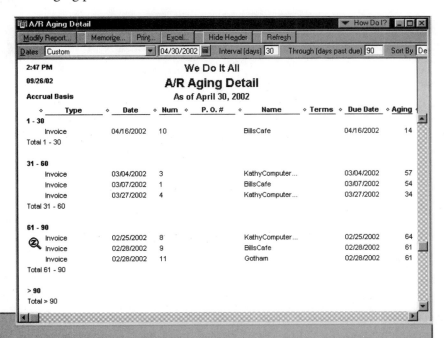

**Figure 5-9 • Scroll through the report to see all the information about your A/R aging.**

## Customizing Aging Reports

If you don't use (or care about) all of the columns in the aging detail report, or you'd prefer to see the information displayed in a different manner, you can customize the report before you print it. Start by clicking the Modify Report button on the report to see the Modify Report window.

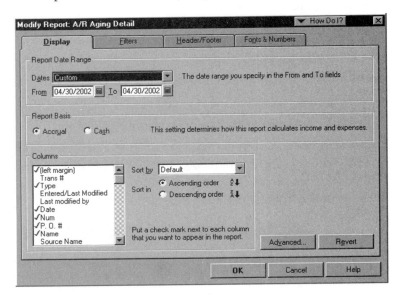

### Customizing the Columns

The most common customization is to get rid of any column you don't care about. For example, if you use the classes feature, but don't care about that information in your aging report, get rid of the column. Or you might want to get rid of the Terms column since it doesn't impact the totals.

To remove a column, scroll through the list of columns and click to remove the check mark. The column disappears from the report.

While you're looking at the list of column names, you may find a column heading that's not currently selected, but that contains information you'd like to include in your report. If so, click that column listing to place a check mark next to it. The column appears on the report and the data linked to it is displayed.

### Filtering Information

If you want to produce a report that isn't a straight aging report, you can easily filter the information that appears so that it meets criteria important to you. To filter your aging report, click the Filters tab.

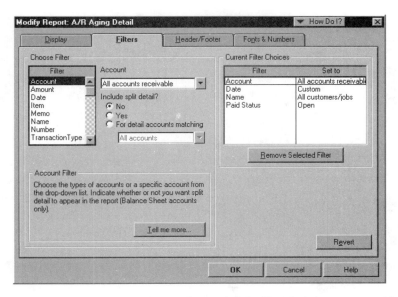

Select a filter and then set the limits for it. (Each filter has its own specific type of criteria.) For example, you can use this feature if you want to see only those customers with receivables higher than a certain figure, or older than a certain aging period: Select Amount from the Filter list, click the greater-than symbol (>), and then enter an amount in the text box.

## Customizing the Appearance

Click the Fonts & Numbers tab to change the format of the report.

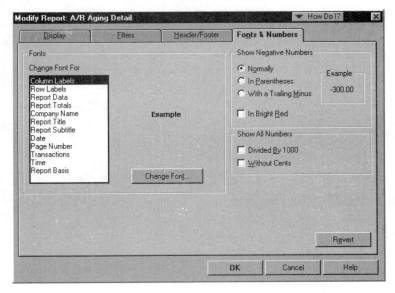

You can change the way negative numbers are displayed, and you can change the fonts for any or all the individual elements in the report.

When you close the report window, QuickBooks asks if you want to memorize the report. Choose Yes so you don't have to go through all the modifications again. See "Memorizing Aging Reports" later in this section.

## Printing Reports

Whether you're using the standard report or one you've customized, you'll probably want to print the report. When you're in a report window, click the Print button at the top of the window to bring up the Print Reports window (see Figure 5-10). If the report is wide, use the Margins tab to set new margins, and use the options on the Settings tab to customize other printing options.

## Memorizing Aging Reports

If you've customized a report and have the columns, data, and formatting you need, there's no reason to re-invent the wheel the next time you need the same information. Instead of going through the customization process again next month, memorize the report as you designed it. Then you can fetch it whenever you need it.

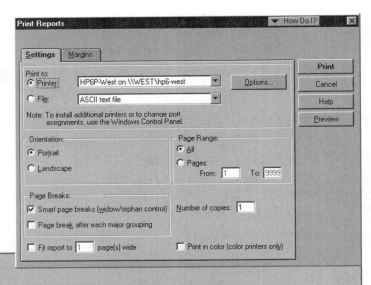

**Figure 5-10 • Set printing options before sending the report to the printer.**

Click the Memorize button in the report window. When the Memorize Report window appears, enter a new name for the report, optionally save it within a report group, and click OK.

From now on, this report name will be on the list of memorized reports you can select from when you choose Reports | Memorized Reports from the menu bar.

**Note**    *When you use a memorized report, only the formatting is memorized. The data is generated from the QuickBooks transaction records, so you get current, accurate information.*

# Running Customer and Job Reports

Customer and job reports are like aging reports, but they're designed to give you information about the customers instead of concentrating on financial totals. There are plenty of customer reports available from the menu that appears when you choose Reports | Customers & Receivables:

**Customer Balance Summary Report**    Lists current total balance owed for each customer.

**Customer Balance Detail Report**    Lists every transaction for each customer, with a net subtotal for each customer.

**Open Invoices Report**    Lists all unpaid invoices, sorted and subtotaled by customer and job.

**Collections Report**    A nifty report for nagging. Includes the contact name and telephone number, along with details about invoices with balances due. You're all set to call the customer and have a conversation, and you can answer any questions about invoice details.

**Accounts Receivable Graph**    Shows a graphic representation of the accounts receivable. For a quick impression, there's nothing like a graph (see Figure 5-11).

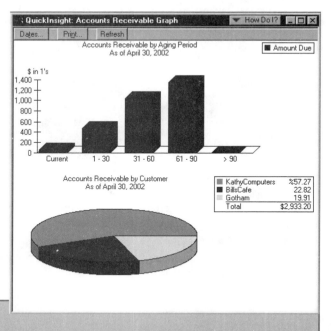

**Figure 5-11 •** Double-click a pie slice to see the details for that customer; double-click a bar to see a customer breakdown pie.

**Unbilled Costs By Job**   Tracks job expenses you haven't invoiced.

**Transaction List By Customer**   Displays individual transactions of all types for each customer.

**Customer Phone List**   Displays an alphabetical list of customers along with the telephone number for each (if you entered it in the customer card).

**Customer Contact List**   Displays an alphabetical list of customers along with the telephone number, billing address, and current open balance for each. Give this list to the person in charge of collections.

**Item Price List**   A list of all your items with their prices and preferred vendors.

## Using Reports to Make Collections

Martin Miser, the corporate controller at Buford Button Corp., is a fanatic about keeping the accounts receivables balances at the lowest possible number. The collection rate at Buford Buttons is quite good, thanks to the techniques Martin has instituted. No customer has terms longer than 30 days, and any customer more than 60 days overdue is put on a C.O.D. basis until checks are received to reduce the balance.

Buford does most of its sales by telephone, fax, or e-mail, and none of the company's sales reps work outside the office. To keep the receivables down, Martin has invented a number of protocols, some of which involve the sales reps.

He prints an aging summary report every morning at 9:00 A.M. (it sets his mood for the day). When the accounts receivable clerk completes the entry of payments that arrived in the mail (usually by noon), a collections report is printed. However, Martin did something clever with this report—he customized it to include a REP column. When the report is distributed, it's easy for each sales rep to find the right customers to call.

The reps are trained to ask for specific dates by which the customer promises to catch up. In addition, they ask the customers to send a series of post-dated checks. The company holds the checks and deposits them according to a schedule worked out between the rep and the customer.

Every Monday morning Martin prints another customized report, which is a collection report that he filters so that it shows only customers over a certain amount. That report is given to the A/R department head for Monday morning phone calls. By 2:00 P.M., Martin himself is on the telephone with those customers the department head feels weren't cooperating.

If a customer is constantly behind in payments, a customer type DUN is applied to the customer, and the dunning starts by sending statements weekly instead of monthly to all customers of that type.

The A/R total never gets out of hand at this company!

# Entering Accounts Payable Bills

## In this Chapter:

- *Enter vendor bills*

- *Enter inventory item purchases*

- *Enter vendor credit memos*

- *Use purchase orders*

- *Track reimbursable expenses*

- *Enter recurring bills*

Chapter 6

Entering your bills and then paying them through QuickBooks is *accrual accounting.* That means an expense is posted to your Profit & Loss statement when you enter the bill, not when you actually pay the bill. The total of unpaid bills is the amount posted to the Accounts Payable account. However, if your taxes are filed on a cash basis (an expense isn't posted until you pay the bill), be assured (and assure your accountant) that QuickBooks understands how to report your financial figures on a cash basis. (See Chapter 15 for information on financial reports.)

# Recording Vendor Bills

When the mail arrives, after you open all the envelopes that contain checks from customers (I always do that first), you should tell QuickBooks about the bills that arrived. Don't worry—QuickBooks doesn't automatically pay them. You decide when to do that.

To enter your bills, click the Bill icon on the icon bar (or select Vendors on the Navigators list and click the Enter Bills icon in the Vendors Navigator window.) You could also use the register for the Accounts Payable account and enter the bills directly into the register, but you get more tracking information if you use the Enter Bills window.

When the Enter Bills window opens (see Figure 6-1), you can fill out the information from the bill you received. The window has two sections: the heading section, which contains information about the vendor and the bill, and the details section, which records the data related to your general ledger accounts. The details section has two tabs: Expenses and Items. In this section, I'll cover bills that are posted to Expenses; the Items are covered later in this chapter when I cover purchasing inventory items.

Depending on the bill, you may be able to assign the entire bill to one expense account, or you may have to split the bill among multiple expense accounts. For example, your utility bills are usually posted to the appropriate utility account (electric, heat, and so on). However, credit card bills may be split among numerous expenses.

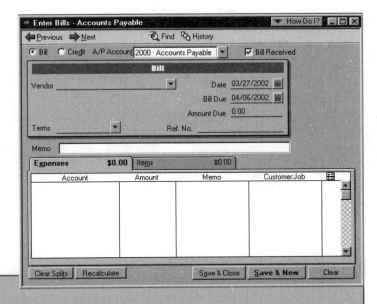

**Figure 6-1 • The Enter Bills window has a heading section and a details section.**

## Easy One-Account Posting

In the Vendor field, click the arrow to choose this vendor from the list that appears. If the vendor isn't on the list, choose <Add New> to add this vendor to your QuickBooks vendor list. Then fill out the rest of the bill as follows:

1. Enter the bill date. The bill due date fills in automatically, depending on the terms you have with this vendor. You can change this date if you wish. (If you have no terms entered for this vendor, the due date is automatically filled out using the default number of days for paying bills. QuickBooks sets this at 30 days, but you can change it in Edit | Preferences in the Purchases & Vendors section.)

2. You can enter the amount due, or you can let QuickBooks calculate it by adding up the items you enter in the Details section.

3. Enter the vendor's invoice number in the Ref. No. field.

4. In the Terms field, click the arrow to display a list of terms, and select the one you need. If the terms you have with this vendor aren't available, choose <Add New> to create a new Terms entry.

5. When you click in the Account column, an arrow appears. Click the arrow to display your chart of accounts. Select the account to which this bill is assigned. QuickBooks automatically assigns the Amount Due you entered in the Amount column.

6. If you wish, enter a note in the Memo column.

7. When you're finished, click Next to save this bill and bring up another blank Enter Bills window. I've skipped the Customer:Job column; see the discussions on charging customers for expenses that appear later in this section. When you've entered all your bills, click Save & Close.

## Splitting Expenses Among Multiple Accounts

Some bills aren't neatly assigned to one account in your general ledger; instead, they're split among multiple accounts. The most common example is a credit card bill.

To split a bill among multiple general ledger accounts:

1. Follow the first four steps in the instructions for entering bills in the previous section.

2. Click in the Account column to display the arrow you use to see your chart of accounts.

3. Select the first account to which you want to assign some portion of this bill.

4. If you've entered an amount in the Amount Due field on the bill heading, QuickBooks automatically applies the entire amount of the bill in the Amount column. Replace that data with the amount you want to assign to the account you selected.

5. Click in the Account column to select the next account and enter the appropriate amount in the Amount column.

As you add each additional account to the column, QuickBooks assumes that the unallocated amount is assigned to that account (see Figure 6-2). Repeat the process of changing the amount and adding another account until the split transaction is completely entered.

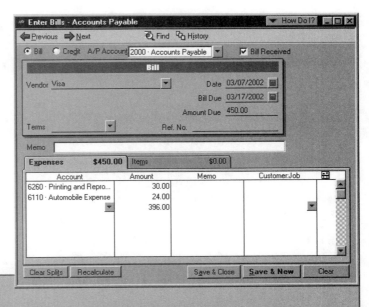

**Figure 6-2 • QuickBooks keeps recalculating, making it easy to enter split transactions.**

## Entering Reimbursable Expenses

A reimbursable expense is one that you incurred on behalf of a customer. Even though you pay the vendor bill, there's an agreement with your customer that you'll send an invoice to recover your costs.

There are two common ways to encounter the issue of reimbursable expenses:

- General expenses, such as long-distance telephone charges, parking and tolls, and other incidental expenses, are incurred on behalf of a client. Those portions of the vendor bill that apply to customer agreements for reimbursement are split out when you enter the bill.

- Specific goods or services are purchased on behalf of the customer. Amounts for these items that appear on the bill are charged to the customer.

## Recording the Reimbursable Expense

If you want to be reimbursed by customers for expenses you incurred on their behalf, you must enter the specific amounts you're charging to each customer:

1. Select the account, and then enter the portion of the bill that you're not charging back to a customer.
2. Select the account again, and then enter the portion of the bill you are charging back to the customer.
3. In the Customer:Job column, choose the appropriate customer or job (see Figure 6-3).
4. Repeat to include any additional reimbursable expenses or additional customers.

Of course, if the entire vendor bill is for a purchase you made on behalf of the customer, you don't have to go through all the steps of splitting the total amount; just select the customer and apply the entire amount of the bill.

The column with the strange-looking icon (to the right of the Customer:Job column) is a selection feature. The icon is supposed to represent an invoice, and it

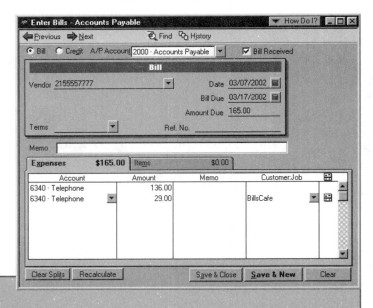

**Figure 6-3 • Charge portions of expenses to customers by splitting the vendor bill.**

appears automatically if you enter a customer in the Customer:Job column. You can click the column to put an X through the icon if you don't want to bill the customer for the expense, because you're merely tracking what you're spending on specific customers. If you disable the Invoice icon, the expense is associated with the customer in your records, but the amount isn't available for automatic billing to the customer.

## Invoicing the Customer for Reimbursable Expenses

When you save the vendor bill, the amounts you linked to a customer are saved in the customer file. If you placed an Invoice icon in the column next to the Customer:Job column on the vendor bill, you can collect the money from the customer.

When you next invoice the customer, you can add those amounts to the invoice. Here are the special steps to take during customer invoicing (see Chapter 3 for complete information about creating invoices for customers):

1. As you're creating the invoice, click the Time/Costs icon at the top of the Create Invoices window to open the Choose Billable Time And Costs window.

2. Move to the Expenses tab, which displays the reimbursable amounts you posted when you entered vendor bills.

3. Click in the Use column to select the expenses you want to include on the invoice you're currently creating (see Figure 6-4).

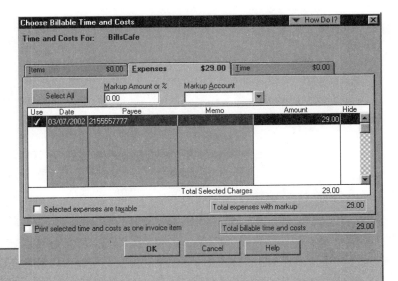

**Figure 6-4 •** Select the expense(s) you want to add to the customer invoice you're currently preparing.

4. Click OK to move the item to the invoice, where it appears in the line item section.

5. Add any other invoice items for this customer, and then save the invoice.

# Marking Up Reimbursable Expenses

You can mark up any expenses you're invoicing, which many companies do to cover any additional costs incurred such as handling, time, or general aggravation. The markup applies to each item in the Choose Billable Time And Costs window.

## Configuring Markups

You must set up your markup configuration ahead of time, which is accomplished with the following steps:

1. Choose Edit | Preferences to open the Preferences dialog box.
2. Click the Sales & Customers icon.
3. Click the Company Preferences tab.
4. Specify the percentage you want to use as your markup for reimbursed expenses (enter the number; QuickBooks automatically adds the percent sign).

**Caution** *QuickBooks uses the percentage you enter here to automate the pricing of inventory items. When you're entering the inventory items, as soon as you enter the cost, QuickBooks automatically adds this percentage and enters the price. This is frequently more annoying than helpful, and you'll constantly find yourself re-entering the item's price.*

5. To track the amount of money you receive as markups, select the option Track Reimbursed Expenses As Income.

When you select the option Track Reimbursed Expenses As Income, you can post the markup amount to an account you create for that purpose. You can create this markup account in either of the following ways:

- Use an Income account to add markup income to your Profit & Loss report.
- Use an Expense account to reduce your total expenses in your Profit & Loss report.

If you don't select this option, the amount you invoice is posted to the original expense account you selected when you entered the vendor's bill. Your Profit & Loss report could show a minus expense (income) for expenses you normally charge back to customers.

## Applying Markups to Customer Invoices

When you enable markups, the total on the Choose Billable Time And Costs window changes to reflect the markup (see Figure 6-5).

If you don't want your customer to see the markup, select the Print Selected Time And Costs As One Invoice Item option. You'll see the breakdown on the screen version of the invoice, but the printed invoice contains only the total.

**Caution**   *If you don't select the option to hide the markup, and later you return to edit the Invoice because you've changed your mind and want to hide the markup, the option is no longer available.*

If you change your mind and decide you never want to bill this customer for this expense, select the listing and click the Hide column. The expense will not show up when you open this window in the future.

If you want to mark up each item with a different amount, delete the formula in the Markup Amount or % box, and change the total in the amount column to reflect your markup. The difference between the original expense and the new total is not posted to the markup account; instead, the entire amount is posted to whatever income account you're posting this item to on the customer invoice.

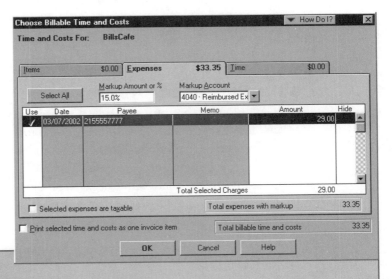

**Figure 6-5 • Notice the new total amount at the bottom of the window.**

If you reduce the amount, QuickBooks does not keep the remaining amount on the Billable Time And Costs window. You won't see it again, because QuickBooks makes the assumption you're not planning to pass the remaining amount to your customer in the future.

# Entering Inventory Item Bills

If the vendor bill you're recording is for inventory items, you need to take a different approach, because the accounting issues (the way you post amounts) are different. Two steps are involved when you buy items for your inventory:

1. You receive the inventory products.
2. You receive the bill for the inventory.

Once in a while, the bill comes before the products, and sometimes both events occur at the same time. (In fact, you may find the bill pasted to the carton or included inside the carton.)

Another twist to all of this is the change in procedures if you've used purchase orders. In this section, I'll go over all the available scenarios, including how to track purchase orders.

**Note** To use Inventory and Purchase Order features, you must enable them in the Purchases & Vendors category of Preferences (choose Edit | Preferences to open the Preferences dialog box).

## Using Purchase Orders

If you want, you can use purchase orders to order inventory items from your suppliers. However, it's not a great idea to use purchase orders for goods that aren't in your inventory—that's not what they're intended for.

Creating and saving a purchase order has no effect on your general ledger. No amounts are posted to an account, because purchase orders exist only to help you track what you've ordered against what you've received.

Here's how to create a purchase order:

1. Choose Vendors | Create Purchase Orders to open a blank Create Purchase Orders window.
2. Fill in the purchase order fields, which are easy and self-explanatory (see Figure 6-6).

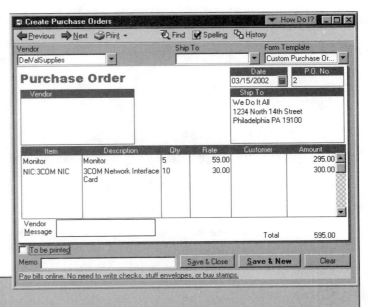

**Figure 6-6 • A purchase order looks like a vendor bill, but you don't incur any accounts-payable liability.**

**3.** Click Save & New to save the purchase order and move on to the next blank form, or click Save & Close if you have created all the purchase orders you need right now.

**Tip**   *If you're using job tracking, you can use the Customer column to keep track of your purchases for jobs or to treat the purchase as a reimbursable transaction.*

You can print the purchase orders as you create them by clicking the Print button as soon as each purchase order is completed. Be sure to select the option To Be Printed on each Create Purchase Orders window. If you'd prefer, you can print them all in a batch by clicking the arrow to the right of the Print button on the last purchase order window, and selecting Print Batch. If you want to print them later, just close the last purchase order; when you're ready to print, choose File | Print Forms | Purchase Orders from the QuickBooks menu bar.

Later, when the inventory items and the bill for them are received, you can use the purchase order to check those transactions and automate the receiving process.

**Tip** *Many companies don't print purchase orders; instead, they notify the vendor of the purchase order number when they place the order over the telephone, via e-mail, or by logging in to the vendor's Internet-based order system.*

## Receiving Inventory Items

Since this chapter is about accounts payable, we must cover the steps involved in paying for the inventory items. However, you don't pay for items you haven't received, and receiving the items merits some mention.

If the inventory items arrive before you receive a bill from the vendor, you must tell QuickBooks about the new inventory. Here's how:

1. Choose Vendors | Receive Items to open a blank Create Item Receipts window (see Figure 6-7).

2. Enter the vendor name, and if open purchase orders exist from this vendor, QuickBooks notifies you.

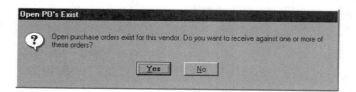

3. If you know there isn't a purchase order for this particular shipment, click No. Then fill out the Create Item Receipts window.

4. If you're not sure, or you know there is a purchase order, click Yes. QuickBooks displays all the open purchase orders for this vendor so you can choose the appropriate PO. (If the PO that matches this shipment isn't listed on the Open Purchase Orders List for this vendor, click Cancel on the Open Purchase Orders window to return to the receipts window.)

5. QuickBooks fills out the Create Item Receipts window using the information in the PO. Check the shipment against the PO and change any quantities that don't match. If no PO exists, fill out the Create Item Receipts window manually.

6. Click Save & New to receive the next shipment into inventory, or click Save & Close if this takes care of all the receipts of goods.

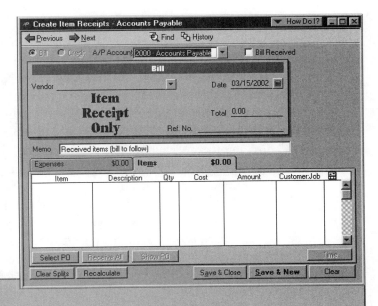

**Figure 6-7 • Receive items into inventory so they're available for sale.**

> **Tip**    *You can link this shipment to a purchase order as soon as you open the Create Item Receipts window by clicking the Select PO button at the bottom of the window. Find the right PO, and QuickBooks fills in the receipt information automatically.*

QuickBooks posts the amounts in the purchase order to your Accounts Payable account. This is not the standard, generally accepted accounting procedure (GAAP) method for handling receipt of goods, and if your accountant notices this QuickBooks action, you can stop the screaming by explaining that QuickBooks has a workaround for this (see the section "Understanding the Postings" later in this chapter).

I'll take a moment here to explain why your accountant might start screaming:

First, an accounts payable liability should only be connected to a bill. When a bill comes, you owe the money. While it's safe to assume that if the goods showed up, the bill will follow, and you'll owe the money in the end, technically you don't incur the A/P liability until you have a bill.

Second, costs on the PO may not be the current costs for the items, and the vendor bill that shows up may have different amounts. The PO amounts are taken from your inventory records, or by your own manual entry. It's not uncommon for purchasing agents to fill out a PO without calling the vendor and checking the latest cost. That works because the bill that arrives will have the correct costs, and those costs are the amounts that are supposed to be posted to the A/P account. If this situation occurs, QuickBooks changes the posting to A/P to match the bill.

Third, in order to avoid double-posting the A/P liability when the bill does arrive, you must use a special QuickBooks transaction window (discussed next). Because warehouse personnel frequently handle the receipt of goods, and receipt of bills is handled by a bookkeeper, a lack of communication may interfere with using the correct transaction methods. QuickBooks prevents this problem by alerting the data-entry person of a possible error. If the bookkeeper uses the standard Enter Bills transaction window, as soon as the vendor is entered in the window, QuickBooks displays a message stating that a receipt of goods record exists for this vendor and the bill should not be recorded with the standard Enter Bills window.

## Recording Bills for Received Items

After you receive the items, eventually the bill comes from the vendor.

To enter the bill, do *not* use the regular Enter Bills icon in the Vendors Navigator window, which would cause another posting to Accounts Payable. Instead, do the following:

1. Choose Vendors | Enter Bill For Received Items to open the Select Item Receipt window. Choose a vendor to see the current items receipt information for that vendor.

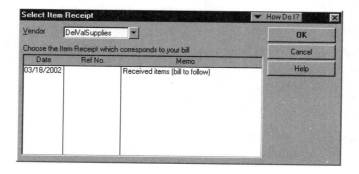

2. Select the appropriate listing and click OK to open an Enter Bills window. The information from the items receipt is used to fill in the bill information.
3. Change anything that needs to be changed: a different cost per unit, taxes and shipping costs that were added, etc.
4. Click Save & Close.
5. Whether you've made changes to the amounts or not, QuickBooks displays a message that you've changed the original transaction and asks if you want to save the changes. Say Yes. (Even if you didn't make changes, you've changed the transaction from a receipt of goods transaction to a vendor bill transaction, and QuickBooks replaces the original posting to Accounts Payable that was made when you received the items.)

## Receiving Items and Bills Simultaneously

If the items and the bill arrive at the same time (sometimes the bill is in the shipping carton), you must tell QuickBooks about those events simultaneously. To do this, choose Vendors | Receive Items And Enter Bill. This opens the standard Enter Bills window, but when you fill it out, QuickBooks receives the items into inventory in addition to posting the bill.

## Understanding the Postings

You need to explain to your accountant (or warn your accountant) about the way QuickBooks posts the receipt of goods and the bills for inventory items. It seems a bit different from standard practices if you're a purist about accounting procedures; but as long as you remember to use the correct commands (as described in the preceding sections), it works fine.

QuickBooks makes the same postings no matter how, or in what order, you receive the items and the bill. Let's look at what happens when you receive $400.00 worth of items and fill out the Receive Items window:

| Account | Debit | Credit |
| --- | --- | --- |
| Accounts Payable | | $400.00 |
| Inventory | $400.00 | |

Notice that the amount is posted to Accounts Payable, even if the bill hasn't been received. The entry in the Accounts Payable register is noted as a receipt of items with a transaction type ITEM RCF.

When the vendor bill arrives, as long as you remember to use Vendors | Enter Bill For Received Items, the amount isn't charged to Accounts Payable again; instead, the A/P register entry is changed to reflect the fact that it is now a bill (the item type changes to BILL). If you made changes to any amounts, the new amounts are posted, replacing the original amounts.

**Caution**    *If you use the standard Enter Bills listing, QuickBooks will warn you that this vendor has receipts pending bills and instructs you to use the correct command if this bill is for that receipt. If you ignore the listing, and the bill is indeed for items already received into QuickBooks, you'll have double entries for the same amount in your Accounts Payable account.*

Just for your information, and for your accountant's information, here's the posting you could expect from the receipt of $400.00 worth of items if you take the purist approach. In fact, most accounting software systems do use this two-step method, which separates the receipt of items from the receipt of the bill from the vendor. This approach requires an account in your chart of accounts that tracks received items. (It's usually placed in the Liabilities section of the Chart of Accounts list; you can call it whatever you wish.)

| Account | Debit | Credit |
| --- | --- | --- |
| Inventory | $400.00 | |
| Receipts holding account | | $400.00 |

Then, when the vendor bill arrives, a separate posting is made to the general ledger:

| Account | Debit | Credit |
| --- | --- | --- |
| Receipts holding account | $400.00 | |
| Accounts Payable | | $400.00 |

Because the postings to the receipts holding account are washed between the receipt of goods and the receipt of the bill, the bottom-line effect to your general ledger is the same when QuickBooks does it. The only thing missing in QuickBooks is the ability to look at the amount currently posted to the receipts holding account to see where you stand in terms of items in but bills not received (or vice versa). Some accountants and company bookkeepers want to track that figure.

As long as you use the correct commands to enter bills, you shouldn't have a problem. I'm covering this so you can reassure your accountant (who will probably want to know why QuickBooks didn't put a receipts holding account in your chart of accounts when you indicated you were using the inventory feature).

# Recording Vendor Credits

If you receive a credit from a vendor, you must record it in QuickBooks. Then you can apply it against an open vendor bill or let it float until your next order from the vendor. (See Chapter 7 for information about paying bills, which includes applying vendor credits to bills.)

QuickBooks doesn't provide a discrete credit form, nor does it provide a listing for vendor credits on the Vendors Navigator window. Instead, you can change a vendor bill form to a credit form with a click of the mouse:

1. Click the Bill icon on the QuickBooks toolbar to open the Enter Bills window.
2. Select Credit, which automatically deselects Bill and changes the available fields in the form (see Figure 6-8).
3. Choose the vendor from the drop-down list that appears when you click the arrow in the Vendor field.
4. Enter the date of the credit memo.
5. In the Ref. No. field, enter the vendor's credit memo number.
6. Enter the amount of the credit memo.
7. If the credit is not for inventory items, use the Expenses tab to assign an account and amount to this credit.
8. If the credit is for inventory items, use the Items tab to enter the items, along with the quantity and cost, for which you are receiving this credit.

> **Note**    *If you've agreed that the vendor pays the shipping costs to return items, don't forget to enter that amount on the Expenses tab.*

9. Click Save & Close to save the credit (unless you have more credits to enter—in which case, click Save & New).

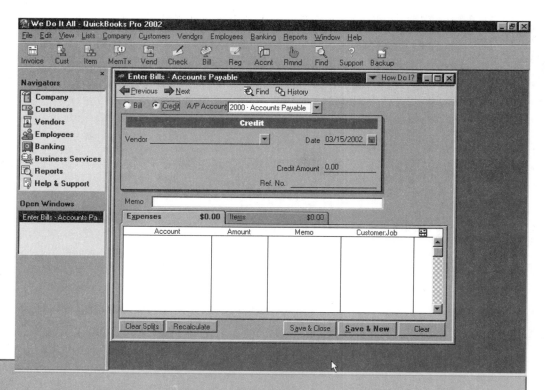

**Figure 6-8 •** Use the same QuickBooks form for vendor bills and credits—the Terms and Bill Due fields disappear when you are entering a credit.

Here are the postings to your general ledger when you save a vendor credit:

| Account | Debit | Credit |
|---|---|---|
| Inventory Asset | | Amount of returned items |
| Applicable expense accounts | | Amounts of expenses in the credit |
| Accounts Payable | Total credit amount | |

**Tip**    Don't use an RA (Return Authorization) number from your vendor as the basis for your credit. Wait for the credit memo to arrive so your records and the vendor's records match. This makes it much easier to settle disputed amounts.

# Entering Recurring Bills

You probably have quite a few bills that you must pay every month. Commonly, the list includes your rent or mortgage payment, payments for assets you purchased with a loan (such as vehicles or equipment), or a retainer fee (for an attorney, accountant, or subcontractor). You might even need to order inventory items on a regular basis.

You can make it easy to pay those bills every month without reentering the bill each time. QuickBooks provides a feature called *memorized transactions,* and you can put it to work to make sure your recurring bills are covered.

## Creating a Memorized Bill

To create a memorized transaction for a recurring bill, first click the Bill icon on the icon bar and fill out the bill, as shown in Figure 6-9.

**Tip**    *If the recurring bill isn't always exactly the same—perhaps the amount is different each month (your utility bills, for instance)—it's okay to leave the Amount Due field blank.*

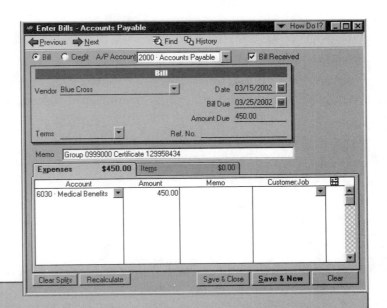

Figure 6-9 • Enter a bill in the normal fashion, then memorize it to use it again and again.

After you fill out the form, but before you save it, memorize it. To accomplish this, press CTRL-M (or choose Edit | Memorize Bill from the main QuickBooks menu bar). The Memorize Transaction window opens.

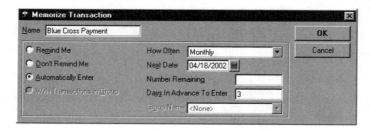

Use these guidelines to complete the Memorize Transaction window:

- Use the Name field to enter a name for the transaction. (It doesn't have to match the vendor or the expense.) Use a name that describes the transaction so you don't have to rely on your memory.
- Enter the interval for this bill in the How Often field.
- Enter the Next Date this bill is due.
- Select Remind Me to tell QuickBooks to issue a reminder that this bill must be put into the system to be paid.
- Select Don't Remind Me if you want to forego getting a reminder and enter the bill yourself.
- Select Automatically Enter to have QuickBooks enter this bill as a payable automatically, without reminders. Specify the number of Days In Advance To Enter this bill into the system.
- If this payment is finite, such as a loan that has a specific number of payments, use the Number Remaining field to specify how many times this bill must be paid.

Click OK in the Memorize Transaction window to save it, and then click OK again in the Enter Bills window to save the bill.

**Tip**    *If you created the bill only for the purpose of creating a memorized transaction, and you don't want to enter the bill into the system for payment at this time, close the Enter Bills window and respond No when QuickBooks asks if you want to save the transaction.*

**Caution**   *When you select the reminder options for the memorized bill, the reminders only appear if you're using reminders in QuickBooks. Choose Edit | Preferences and click the Reminders category icon to view or change reminders options.*

## Using a Memorized Bill

If you've opted to enter the memorized bill yourself (either by asking QuickBooks to remind you to do this, or by trusting your memory), you must bring it up to make it a current payable.

To use a memorized bill, press CTRL-T (or click the MemTx icon on the icon bar, or choose Lists | Memorized Transaction List). This opens the Memorized Transaction List window.

Select the transaction you want to use, right-click, and choose Enter Transaction from the shortcut men. This opens the bill in the usual Enter Bills window, with the next due date showing. Click Save & Close to save this bill, so it becomes a current payable and is listed when you pay your bills. (See Chapter 7 for information about paying bills.)

## Creating Memorized Bill Groups

If you have a whole bunch of memorized transactions to cover all the bills that are due the first of the month (rent, mortgage, utilities, car payments, whatever), you don't have to select and convert them to payables one at a time. You can create a group and then invoke actions on the group (automatically invoking the action on every bill in the group).

The steps to accomplish this are easy:

1. Press CTRL-T to display the Memorized Transaction List.
2. Right-click any blank spot in the Memorized Transaction window and choose New Group from the shortcut menu. In the New Memorized Transaction Group window, give this group a name.
3. Fill out the fields to specify the way you want the bills in this group to be handled.
4. Click OK to save this group.

Now that you've created the group, you can add memorized transactions to it:

1. In the Memorized Transaction List window, select the first memorized transaction you want to add to the group.
2. Right-click and choose Edit from the shortcut menu.
3. When the Schedule Memorized Transaction window opens with this transaction displayed, select the option named With Transactions In Group. Then select the group from the list that appears when you click the arrow next to the Group Name field.
4. Click OK and repeat this process for each bill in the list.

As you create future memorized bills, just select the same With Transactions In Group option.

If you have other recurring bills with different criteria (perhaps they're due on a different day of the month, or they're due annually), create groups for them and add the individual transactions to the group.

Now that all of your vendor bills are in the system, you have to pay them. Chapter 7 covers everything you need to know about accomplishing that.

## Memorizing Zero-Based Bills for Later Use

Fred is president of his own company, for which he has procured two company credit cards. He uses the AMEX card for travel and entertainment, which includes plane or train tickets, car rentals, and taking customers to dinner. He uses the Visa card for office supplies and charges for his Internet connection.

To make life easier and his work in QuickBooks faster, Fred clicked the Bill icon on the icon bar and created a bill for each credit card. He left the Amount field blank and then moved to the Expenses tab at the bottom of the form. For AMEX, he selected the Travel account, and then he immediately clicked in the Account column again and selected the Entertainment account. He didn't fill in any other information, which means that the amounts posted to those accounts were zero.

He pressed CTRL-M to memorize the bill and asked to be reminded monthly. He made the next due date a few days hence (which is when the current AMEX bill is actually due). He clicked OK and then canceled the original bill when he returned to that window. Then he repeated the process for the Visa card, entering the appropriate accounts for that card.

When the bills were due, he selected each bill from the Memorized Transaction List, and when the Enter Bills window opened, everything was already filled in except for the amounts—a nifty and easy way to make bookkeeping easier. Congratulations, Fred.

# Paying Bills

## In this Chapter:

- *Choose bills to pay*

- *Apply discounts and credits*

- *Write checks*

- *Make direct disbursements*

- *Set up sales tax payments*

## Chapter 7

The expression "writing checks" doesn't have to be taken literally. You can let QuickBooks do the "writing" part by buying computer checks and printing them. Except for signing the check, QuickBooks can do all the work.

# Choosing What to Pay

You don't have to pay every bill that's entered, nor do you have to pay the entire amount due for each bill. Your current bank balance and your relationships with your vendors have a large influence on the decisions you make.

There are all sorts of rules that business consultants recite about how to decide what to pay when money is short, and the term "essential vendors" is prominent. I've never figured out how to define "essential," since having electricity is just as important to me as buying inventory items.

Having worked with hundreds of clients, however, I can give you two rules to follow that are based on those clients' experiences:

- The government (taxes) comes first. Never, never, never use payroll withholding money to pay bills.
- It's better to send lots of vendors small checks than to send gobs of money to a couple of vendors who have been applying pressure. Vendors hate being ignored much more than they dislike small payments on account.

Incidentally, I'm not covering the payment of payroll tax obligations in this chapter, so be sure to read Chapter 9 to stay on top of those accounts payable items.

## Viewing Your Unpaid Bills

Start by examining the bills that are due. The best way to see that list is in detailed form, instead of a summary total for each vendor. To accomplish this, choose Reports | Vendors & Payables | Unpaid Bills Detail. All of your outstanding vendor bills are displayed, as shown in Figure 7-1.

You can see all your unpaid bills by selecting All in the Dates field (a good idea). Double-click any entry to see the original bill you entered, including all line items, and notes you made in the Memo column.

You can filter the report to display only certain bills. To accomplish this, click Modify Report and go to the Filters tab in the Modify Report window. Use the filters to change the display.

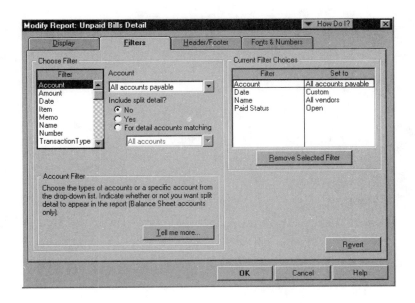

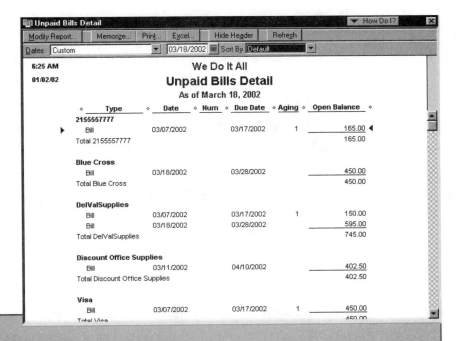

**Figure 7-1 • Check the details of current open bills.**

For example, you may want to see only one of the following types of bills:

- Filter for bills that are due today (or previously), eliminating bills due after today.
- Filter for bills that are more or less than a certain amount.
- Filter for bills that are more than a certain number of days overdue.

Print the report, and if you're short on cash, work on a formula that will maintain good relationships with your vendors.

## Selecting the Bills to Pay

When you're ready to tell QuickBooks which bills you want to pay, choose Vendors | Pay Bills. The Pay Bills window appears (see Figure 7-2), and you can begin to make your selections using the following guidelines.

**Due On Or Before**   Displays all the bills due within ten days, by default, but you can change the date to display more or fewer bills. If you have discounts for timely payments with any vendors, this selection is more important than it seems (see the section "Applying Discounts" later in this chapter).

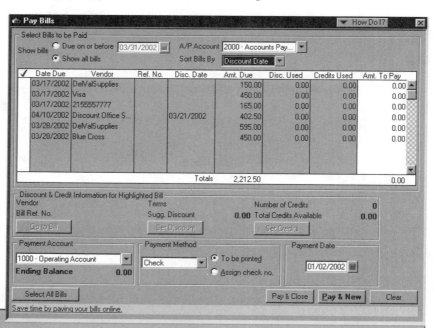

**Figure 7-2 • Paying bills starts in the Pay Bills window.**

**Show All Bills** Shows all the bills in your system, regardless of when they're due.

**A/P Account** If you have multiple A/P accounts, select the account to which the bills you want to pay were originally posted.

**Sort Bills By** Determines the manner in which your bills are displayed in QuickBooks. The choices are Due Date, Discount Date, Vendor, or Amount Due.

**Payment Account** The checking or credit card account you want to use for these payments.

**Payment Method** Offers two methods of payment: check or credit card. If you are paying by check and QuickBooks prints your checks, be sure the To Be Printed option is selected. If you're using manual checks, select Assign Check No. When you finish configuring bill payments, QuickBooks opens the Assign Check Numbers dialog box so you can specify the starting check number for this bill paying session.

**Note** *If you've configured your checking account for online banking, you'll see a third choice: Online Payment. (See Chapter 16 for more information about online bill paying.)*

**Payment Date** The date that you want to appear on your checks. By default, the current date appears in the field, but if you want to predate or postdate a check (or multiple checks), you can change that date. If you merely select the bills today and wait until tomorrow (or later) to print the checks, the payment date set here still appears on the checks.

**Tip** *You can tell QuickBooks to date checks by the day of printing by changing the Checking Preferences (see Chapter 21 to learn about preferences).*

After you've made changes to the data in the fields, your list of bills to be paid may change. If all the bills displayed are to be paid either in full or in part, you're ready to move to the next step. If there are still some bills on the list that you're not going to pay, you can just select the ones you do want to pay. Selecting a bill is simple—just click the leftmost column to place a check mark in it.

## Selecting the Payment Amounts

If you want to pay in full all the bills that are listed in the Pay Bills window, and there aren't any credits or discounts to worry about, the easiest thing to do is to click the Select All Bills button. This selects all the bills for payment (and the Select All Bills button changes its name to Clear Payments, so you have a way to reverse your action).

Here's what happens in your general ledger when you make straight payments of your bills:

| Account | Debit | Credit |
| --- | --- | --- |
| Accounts Payable | Total bill payments | |
| Bank | | Total bill payments |

I've had clients ask why they don't see the expense accounts when they look at the postings for bill paying. The answer is that the expenses were posted when they entered the bills. That's a major difference between entering bills and then paying them, or writing checks without entering the bills into your QuickBooks system. If you just write checks, you enter the accounts to which you're assigning those checks. For that system (the cash-based system) of paying bills, the postings debit the expense and credit the bank account.

## Making a Partial Payment

If you don't want to pay a bill in full, you can easily adjust the amount:

1. Click the check mark column on the bill's listing to select the bill for payment.
2. Click in the Amt. To Pay column and replace the amount that's displayed with the amount you want to pay. The total will change to match your payment when you save the window.

When the transaction is posted to the general ledger, the amount of the payment is posted as a debit to the Accounts Payable account (the unpaid balance remains in the Accounts Payable account) and as a credit to your bank account.

## Applying Discounts

When you want to take advantage of discounts for timely payment, the amount displayed in the Amt. Due column (or the Amt. To Pay column if you've selected the bill for payment) doesn't reflect the discount. You have to apply it:

1. Select the bill by clicking the check mark column. If a discount is available for this bill, information about the discount appears in the Discount & Credit Information For Highlighted Bill section when you select the bill's listing.
2. Click the Set Discount button to open the Discount And Credits window.

**3.** When the Discount And Credits window appears, it displays the amount of the discount based on the terms for this bill. You can accept the amount or change it, and then click Done to apply it.

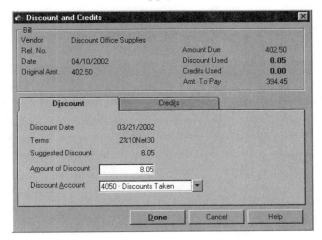

When you return to the Pay Bills window, the discount is applied and the Amt. To Pay column has the right amount.

**Tip** *Many businesses fill in the discount amount even if the discount period has expired. The resulting payment, with the discount applied, is frequently accepted by the vendor. Businesses that practice this protocol learn which vendors will accept a discounted payment and which won't (most will). Seeing that the discount you took has been added back in the next statement you receive is a pretty good hint that you're not going to get away with it.*

## Understanding the Discount Account

Notice that the Discount tab of the Discounts And Credits window has a field for the Discount Account. This account accepts the posting for the amount of the discount. If you don't have an account for discounts taken (not to be confused with the account for discounts given to your customers), you can create one now by clicking the arrow to the right of the field and choosing <Add New>.

The account for the discounts you take (sometimes called *earned discounts*) can be either an income or expense account. There's no right and wrong here, although I've seen accountants get into heated debates defending a point of view on this subject. If you think of the discount as income (money you've brought into your system by paying your bills promptly), make the account an income account. If you think of the discount as a reverse expense, make the account an expense account (it posts as a minus amount, which means it reduces total expenses).

For most companies, the only vendors who offer discounts are those from whom you buy inventory items (it's unusual for discounts to be offered by your landlord, electric company, office supply retailer, etc.). Your accountant may have told you to put the discount account in the section of your chart of accounts that holds the Cost of Goods Sold account, which makes a great deal of sense and is a very common scenario.

Sorry! QuickBooks won't let you select a COG account for posting discounts. This is an arbitrary decision on the part of QuickBooks programmers. I've contacted Intuit numerous times, during which I've protested, nagged, begged, and patiently explained things, but I've never received a response.

If you want to see your Profit & Loss reports reflect your discounts as part of COG, you have to use a "workaround" (a way to defeat the shortcomings of the software). Create a COG account named Discounts (which you can't use to post discounts). Also create an Expense account named Inventory Discounts and use that as your discount account. Then, periodically (monthly, quarterly, or end of year) do a journal entry to move the balance from the Expense account into the COG account.

Here's what posts to your general ledger when you take a discount. For example, suppose the original amount of the bill was $484.00 and the discount was $9.68; therefore, the check amount was $474.32. (Remember that the original postings when you entered the bill were for the total amount without the discount.)

| Account | Debit | Credit |
|---------|-------|--------|
| Accounts Payable | $484.00 | |
| Bank | | $474.32 |
| Discounts Taken | | $9.68 |

## Applying Credits

If the list of bills includes vendors for whom you have credits, you can apply the credits to the bill. Select the bill, and if credits exist for the vendor, information about the credits appears on the Pay Bills window. Click Set Credits to open the Discounts And Credits window. Select the credit, and click Done to change the Amt. To Pay column to reflect the credit.

# Saving the Pay Bills Information

There are two ways to save information about paying bills: save as you go or save at the end. You can select a bill, make adjustments (make a partial payment, apply a discount), and then click Pay & New to save that bill payment. That bill disappears from the list if it's paid in total, and reappears with the balance owing if it's partially paid. Or you can select each bill, making the appropriate adjustments. When you're finished applying all the credits, discounts, and partial payments, click Pay & Close.

Regardless of the approach, when you're finished selecting the bills to pay, QuickBooks transfers all the information to the general ledger and fills out your checkbook account register (or credit card account register) with the payments.

After you've paid the bills in QuickBooks, the bills aren't really paid; your vendors won't consider them paid until they receive the checks. You can write manual checks or print checks.

When you click Pay & Close in the Pay Bills window, all the bills you paid are turned into checks (albeit unwritten checks). You can see those checks in the bank account register, as shown in Figure 7-3 (click the Accnt icon on the icon bar and double-click the listing for your bank).

- If you indicated in the Pay Bills window that you would be printing checks (by selecting the To Be Printed option), your bank account register displays To Print as the check number. See the section "Printing Checks" later in this chapter.

- If you selected the Assign Check No. option because you manually write checks, your bank account register uses the check number you specified in the Assign Check Numbers dialog box. See the following section, "Writing Manual Checks."

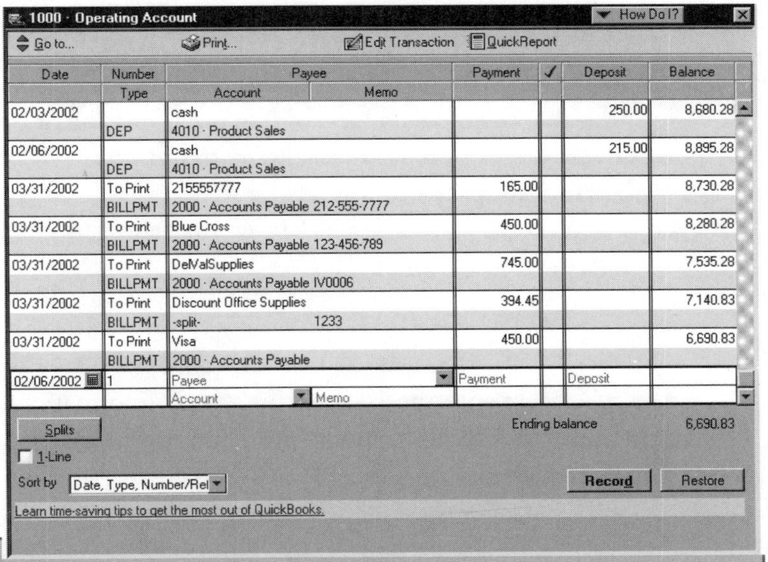

Figure 7-3 • The checks for paying bills are listed in your bank account.

# Writing Manual Checks

If you're not printing checks, you must make sure the check numbers in the register are correct. In fact, it's a good idea to print the register and have it with you as you write the checks. To accomplish that, with the register open in the QuickBooks window, click the Print icon at the top of the register window. When the Print Register window opens, select the date range that encompasses these checks (usually they're all dated the same day), and click OK to print.

Then, as you write the checks, note the correct check numbers on the printout. If they're different from the check numbers that were entered by QuickBooks, make the necessary corrections in the register.

# Printing Checks

Printing your checks is far easier and faster than using manual checks. Before you can print, however, you have some preliminary tasks to take care of. You have to purchase computer checks and set up your printer.

## Purchasing Computer Checks

You have several places to look for computer checks, and my own experience has been that there's not a lot of difference in pricing or the range of styles. Computer checks can be purchased for dot matrix printers (the check forms have sprocket holes) or for page printers (laser and inkjet).

Computer checks come in several varieties (and in a wide range of colors and designs):

- Plain checks
- Checks with stubs (QuickBooks prints information on the stub)
- Checks with special stubs for payroll information (current check, and year-to-date information about wages and withholding)
- Wallet-sized checks

## About Dot Matrix Printers

First of all, do not use a dot matrix printer that has a pull tractor for checks, because you'll have to throw away a couple of checks to get the print head positioned. Use a push-tractor printer.

I use dot matrix printers only for checks (I use my laser printer for QuickBooks reports). I gain a few advantages with this method, and you might like to think about them:

- I never have to change paper. I never accidentally print a report on a check. I never accidentally print a check on plain paper.
- They're cheap. Not just cheap—they're frequently free. Gazillions of companies have upgraded to networks and can now share laser printers. As a result, all of those dot matrix printers that were attached to individual computers are sitting in storage bins in the basement. Ask around.
- They're cheap to run (you replace a ribbon every once in a while) and they last forever. I have clients using old printers (such as an OKI 92) that have been running constantly for about 15 years. And I mean constantly—dot matrix printers are great for warehouse pick slips and packing slips, and some of my clients pick and pack 24 hours a day, seven days a week.

I have two dot matrix printers, both connected to a second printer port that I installed in my computer (the first printer port is connected to my laser printer). The second port is connected to a switch box, which switches between the printers. One switch position is marked "company checks" and the other is marked "personal checks." Printer ports cost less than $10 and are easy to install.

In fact, I really have three checking accounts and still never have to change paper. I have one of those dot matrix printers (an OKI 520) that holds two rolls of paper at the same time; one feeds from the back and the other from the bottom. You flip a lever to switch between paper (in my case, to switch between checking accounts). When I move the switch box to the "personal checks" position, I also flip the lever to feed the checks from the appropriate personal account (I have two personal checking accounts).

I have clients who want the additional security of making copies of printed checks. You can buy multipart checks, where the second page is marked "copy" so nobody tries to use it as a check. Law firms, insurance companies, and other businesses that file a copy of a check appreciate multipart checks, which require a dot matrix printer.

**Caution** *Lock the room that has the printer with the checks in it when you're not there.*

You have several choices for purchasing computer checks:

- Intuit, the company that makes QuickBooks, sells checks through its Internet marketplace, which you can reach at http://www.intuitmarket.com.
- Business form companies (there are several well-known national companies) sell them.
- Your bank may supply them (some banks have a computer-check purchasing arrangement with suppliers).

If you purchase checks from any supplier except Intuit, you just have to tell them you use QuickBooks. All check makers know about QuickBooks and offer a line of checks that are designed to work perfectly with the software.

## Setting Up the Printer

Before you print checks, you have to go through a setup routine. Take heart: You only have to do it once. After you select your configuration options, QuickBooks remembers them and prints your checks without asking you to reinvent the wheel each time.

Your printer needs to know about the type of check you're using, and you supply the information in the Printer Setup window. To get there, choose File | Printer Setup from the menu bar. Select Check/PayCheck as the form. Choose the Printer name and type that matches the printer you're using for checks. Your Printer Setup window should look similar to Figure 7-4.

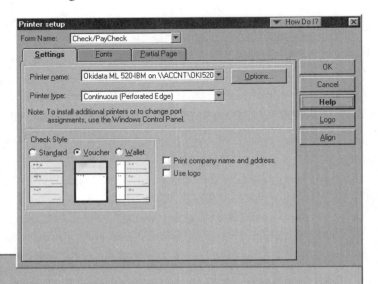

**Figure 7-4 • Use Printer Setup to configure check printing.**

## Choosing a Check Style

You have to select a check style, and it has to match the check style you purchased, of course. Three styles are available for QuickBooks checks, and a sample of each style appears in the window to show you what the style looks like.

- **Standard checks** are just checks. They're the width of a regular business envelope (usually called a *#10 envelope*). If you have a laser printer, there are three checks to a page. A dot matrix pin-feed printer just keeps rolling, since the checks are printed on a continuous sheet with perforations separating the checks.

- **Voucher checks** have additional paper attached to the check form. QuickBooks prints voucher information if you have voucher checks, including the name of the payee, the date, and the individual amounts of the bills being paid by this check. The voucher is attached to the bottom of the check. The check is the same width as the standard check (it's longer, of course, so you have to fold it to put it in the envelope).

- **Wallet checks** are narrower than the other two check styles (so they fit in your wallet). The paper size is the same as the other checks (otherwise, you'd have a problem with your printer), but there's a perforation on the left edge of the check, so you can tear off the check.

## Adding a Logo

If your checks have no preprinted logo and you have a bitmapped file of your company logo (the filename has a .bmp extension), you can select the Use Logo box and then tell QuickBooks where to find the file.

There's also a selection box for printing your company name and address, but when you buy checks, you should have that information preprinted.

 *Dot matrix printers can't handle graphics printing, so you can't choose a logo.*

## Changing Fonts

You can click the Fonts tab in the Printer Setup window and choose different fonts for the check information or for the payee's address block (or both).

Click the appropriate button and then choose a font, a font style, and a size from the dialog box that opens.

### Handling Partial Check Pages on Laser and Inkjet Printers

If you're printing to a laser or inkjet printer, you don't have the advantage that a pin-fed dot matrix printer provides—printing the check and stopping, leaving the next check waiting for the next time you print checks. QuickBooks has a nifty solution for this problem, found on the Partial Page tab (see Figure 7-5). Click the selection that matches your printer's capabilities.

## Printing the Checks

After your printer is configured for your checks, click OK in the Printer Setup window to save the configuration data. Now you can print your checks.

Choose File | Print Forms | Checks from the menu bar to bring up the Select Checks To Print window.

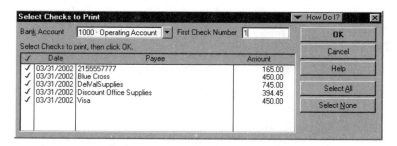

By default, all the unprinted checks are selected for printing. The first time you print checks, the first check number is 1; just replace that number with the first check number in the printer. Click OK when everything is correct.

The Print Checks window opens; everything should be correct, so just choose Print. If you're not using a dot matrix printer, QuickBooks asks how many checks are on the first page (in case you have a page with a check or two remaining). Fill in the number and place the page with leftover checks in the manual feed tray (QuickBooks prints those checks first). Then let the printer pull the remaining check pages from your standard letter tray. If you indicate there are three checks on the page, printing starts with the checks in the standard letter tray.

Click Print to begin printing your checks.

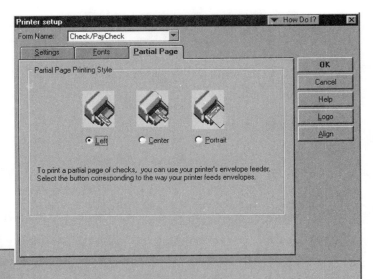

**Figure 7-5 • The QuickBooks partial page solution is based on the way your printer handles envelopes.**

## Reprinting in Case of Problems

Sometimes things go awry when you're printing. The paper jams, you run out of toner, the ribbon has no ink left, the dog chews the paper as it emerges, the paper falls off the back tray and lands in the shredder—all sorts of bad things can occur. QuickBooks knows this and checks the print run before it finalizes the printing process.

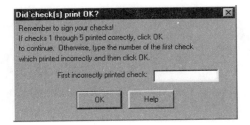

If everything is fine, click OK. If anything untoward happened, enter the number of the first check that is messed up. Put more checks into the printer (unless you're using a dot matrix printer, in which case you don't have to do anything). Then click OK to have QuickBooks reprint all the checks, from the first bad one on to the end of the check run.

After your checks have printed properly, put them in envelopes, stamp them, and mail them. *Now* you can say your bills are paid.

> **Tip**  *Just for the curious: Open the register for your bank account, and you'll see that the checks are numbered to match the print run.*

# Using Direct Disbursements

A *direct disbursement* is a disbursement of funds (usually by check) that is performed without matching the check to an existing bill. This is check writing without entering bills.

If you're not entering vendor bills, this is how you'll always pay your vendors. However, even if you are entering vendor bills, you sometimes need to write a quick check without going through the process of entering the invoice, selecting it, paying it, and printing the check. For example, when the UPS delivery person is standing in front of you waiting for a C.O.D. check and doesn't have time for you to go through all those steps.

## Writing Direct Disbursement Manual Checks

If you use manual checks, you can write your checks and then tell QuickBooks about it later. Or you can bring your checkbook to your computer and enter the checks in QuickBooks as you write them. You have two ways to enter your checks in QuickBooks: in the bank register or in the Write Checks window.

### Using the Register

To use the bank register, click the Reg icon on the QuickBooks toolbar, and then double-click the listing for the bank account. When the account register opens, you can enter the check on a transaction line, as follows:

1. Enter the date.
2. Press the TAB key to move to the Number field. QuickBooks automatically fills in the next available check number.

3. Press TAB to move through the rest of the fields, filling in the name of the payee, the amount of the payment, and the expense account you're assigning to the transaction.

4. Click the Record button to save the transaction.

5. Repeat the steps until all the manual checks you've written are entered into the register.

## Using the Write Checks Window

If you prefer a graphical approach, you can use the Write Checks window to tell QuickBooks about a check you manually prepared. To get there, click the Check icon on the icon bar or press CTRL-W. (Alternatively you can select Banking in the Navigators list and then click the Check icon in the Banking Navigator window, or choose Banking | Write Checks from the menu bar.)

When the Write Checks window opens (see Figure 7-6), select the bank account you're using to write the checks.

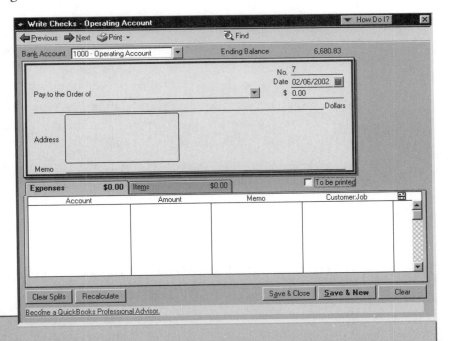

**Figure 7-6** • **Fill out the QuickBooks check the same way you fill out a paper check—they look the same.**

The next available check number is already filled in unless the To Be Printed option box is checked (if it is, click it to toggle the check mark off and put the check number in the window).

Fill out the check, posting amounts to the appropriate accounts. If the check is for inventory items, use the Items tab to make sure the items are placed into inventory. When you finish, click Save & New to open a new blank check. When you're through writing checks, click Save & Close to close the Write Checks window. All the checks you wrote are recorded in the bank account register.

## Printing Direct Disbursement Checks

You can print checks immediately, whether you normally enter bills and print the checks by selecting bills to pay, or you normally print checks as direct disbursements.

If you usually enter your vendor bills, but you need a check for which there is no bill in the system, you can use the Write Checks window to print an individual check quickly:

1. Click the Check button on the icon bar or press CTRL-W to open the Write Checks window. Make sure the To Be Printed option is selected.
2. Fill in the fields in the check and, when everything is ready, click Print.
3. The Print Check window opens and displays the next available check number. Make sure that number agrees with the next number of the check you're loading in the printer, and then click OK.
4. When the Print Checks window opens, follow the instructions for printing described earlier in this chapter.
5. When you return to the Write Checks window, click Save & New to write another check, or click Save & Close if you're finished printing checks.

## Printing Direct Disbursement Checks in Batches

If you don't enter vendor bills but instead pay your bills as direct disbursements, you can print checks in a batch instead of one at a time. To do so, open the Write Checks window and make sure the To Be Printed option is selected:

1. Fill out all the fields for the first check and click Save & New to move to the next blank Write Checks window.

2. Repeat step 1 for every check you need to print.
3. Click Save & Close when you are finished filling out all the checks.
4. Choose File | Print Forms | Checks from the menu bar.
5. Follow the instructions for printing checks described earlier in this chapter.

## Postings for Direct Disbursements

The postings for direct disbursements are quite simple:

| Account | Debit | Credit |
| --- | --- | --- |
| Bank account | | Total of all checks written |
| An expense account | Total of all checks assigned to this account | |
| Another expense account | Total of all checks assigned to this account | |
| Another expense account | Total of all checks assigned to this account (as many as needed) | |

# Remitting Sales Tax

If you collect sales tax from your customers, you have an inherent accounts payable bill, because you have to turn that money over to the state taxing authorities. The same thing is true for payroll withholdings; those payments are discussed in Chapter 9.

## Selecting the Sales Tax Payment Basis

There are two ways to remit sales tax to the taxing authorities; check with your accountant (and the state law) to determine the method you need to use:

**Accrual-basis method**   When the customer is charged (the invoice date)

**Cash-basis method**   When the customer pays

Choose Edit | Preferences from the menu bar. Click the Sales Tax icon in the left pane and select the Company Preferences tab to see the window, shown in Figure 7-7.

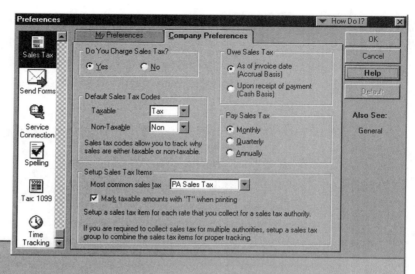

**Figure 7-7** • Be sure the specifications for remitting sales tax are correct, because QuickBooks goes on autopilot using these choices.

**Caution**    *If you collect taxes for more than one taxing authority and the rules are different for each, you're in for some additional work. QuickBooks does not permit separate configuration options for each state tax. You'll have to run detailed reports (see the next section, "Running Sales Tax Reports") and calculate your payments outside of QuickBooks.*

You also must indicate the frequency of your remittance to the state. Many states base the frequency on the amount of tax you collect, usually looking at your returns for a specific period of time (perhaps one specific quarter). If your sales tax liability changed dramatically during the examined period, you may receive notice from the state that your remittance interval has changed. (They'll probably send you new forms.) Don't forget to return to the Preferences window to change the interval.

**Note** | *The actual percentage of the tax, and any additional sales tax authorities you may have to collect and remit for (including their percentages), are configured in the sales tax items you establish. See Chapter 2 to learn about creating items.*

## Running Sales Tax Reports

If you collect sales tax for more than one state, or have to report separately on different rates (city and state), you must run sales tax reports to calculate your remittances. However, even if you only remit sales tax to one state, you should run a report to check your figures.

Choose Reports | Vendors & Payables | Sales Tax Liability. Use the Dates drop-down list to select an interval that matches the way you report to the taxing authorities. By default, QuickBooks chooses the last interval (as configured in Preferences). Figure 7-8 shows a Sales Tax Liability report for a monthly filer who reports to multiple states.

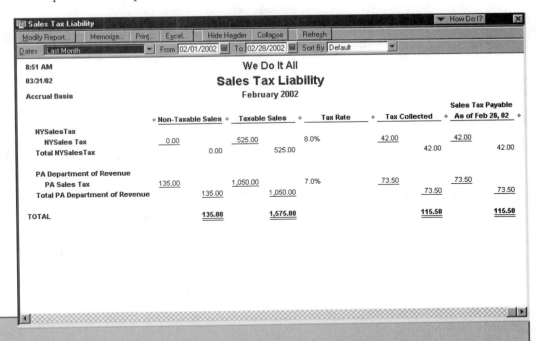

**Figure 7-8 •** The sales tax report always shows the nontaxable sales figures, because most states require that information on their sales tax forms.

## Paying the Sales Tax

After you check the figures (or calculate them, if you have multiple reports with different standards of calculation), it's time to pay the tax:

1. Chose Vendors | Sales Tax | Pay Sales Tax to open the Pay Sales Tax window.

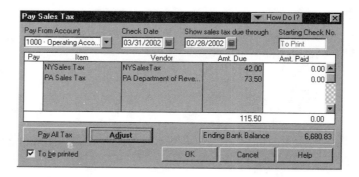

2. Select the bank account to use, if you have more than one.
3. Check the date that's displayed in the field named Show Sales Tax Due Through. It must match the end date of your current reporting period (for instance, monthly or quarterly).

**Note**   *QuickBooks doesn't ask for a start date, because it uses the current period as defined in your Preferences window.*

4. If you report to multiple taxing authorities, every one of them is listed in the window. Click in the Pay column to insert a check mark next to those you're paying now. If you're lucky enough to have the same reporting interval for all taxing authorities—it never seems to work that way, though—just click the Pay All Tax button.
5. If you're going to print the check, be sure to select the To Be Printed check box at the bottom of the dialog box.
6. Click OK when you've completed filling out the information.

The next time you print or write checks, the sales tax check is in the group waiting to be completed.

If, for some reason, you need to adjust the amount of sales tax due, select the sales tax (if you have more than one), then click the Adjust button to open the Sales Tax Adjustment dialog box. Specify the amount by which to increase or reduce the tax amount, and specify an Adjustment Account.

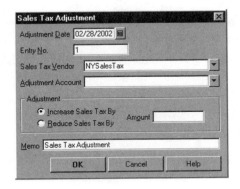

**Tip**    *If you have customers in a state other than the state in which you do business, you might be able to use another approach to sales tax. Technically, some states call this tax a Sales and Use tax, where the "use" part of the title means that the customer is responsible for remitting the tax. If the state permits it, you can skip the sales tax charge (and therefore skip the need to fill out forms and remit payments) and leave it up to the customer. The customer has to tell his or her state taxing authority that he or she purchased taxable goods from an out-of-state vendor (that's you) and remit the appropriate amount. Businesses that take advantage of this usually print a message on the invoice that says, "Sales taxes for this purchase are not collected by us and are your responsibility," or something to that effect. The truth is, you have no legal obligation to warn the customer if the out-of-state taxing authority is willing to let you skip sales tax collections, but it's nice to do.*

## Paying Sales Tax to Multiple Tax Authorities

Mary Mulligan has a garden supply business with customers in Pennsylvania and New Jersey. She has to collect and report sales tax for both states and they have different rules: Pennsylvania collects monthly on collected taxes, New Jersey collects quarterly on billed taxes. She has an item for each sales tax, and her QuickBooks preferences are set for Pennsylvania (she does more business there). Here's how she customized her QuickBooks system to make sales tax reporting easier.

She created three customer types and assigned a type to every customer:

- PA for taxable customers with Pennsylvania addresses
- NJ for taxable customers with New Jersey addresses
- NT for nontaxable customers

Then, she customized and memorized the Tax Liability Report:

1. She ran the report and clicked the Modify Report button on the report button bar.
2. When the Modify Report window opened, she clicked the Filters tab.
3. In the Report Filters window, she selected Customer Type as the filter and then selected PA as the customer type to filter for.
4. She memorized the report as PATax.
5. She repeated the procedure for New Jersey–taxable customers.

Now she uses these memorized reports (choosing Reports | Memorized Reports from the menu bar) before she runs her Pay Sales Tax routine. She can select the taxing authorities and correct the numbers when necessary, because she has the information she needs.

# Running Payroll

## In this Chapter:

- *Check tax status, deductions, and other employee information*

- *Sign up for QuickBooks payroll services*

- *Enter historical data*

- *Write payroll checks*

- *Use QuickBooks Deluxe Payroll Services*

Chapter 8

If you plan to do your own payroll rather than paying a payroll company, you'll find all the tools you need in QuickBooks. However, you can't use the payroll features unless you have an Internet connection, because you need to sign up for and implement payroll services from the QuickBooks Web site. All the information you need to set up and run payroll is covered in this chapter.

# Fine-Tuning Your Setup

Before you run the first payroll, all your setup tasks must be completed. You can't produce accurate payroll checks unless QuickBooks knows everything there is to know about the payroll taxes you have to withhold, the payroll taxes you have to pay as an employer, and the deductions you need to take for benefits, garnishes, union dues, or any other reason. And, of course, you need to configure each employee for dependents and deductions.

## Checking the Payroll Items

A QuickBooks *payroll item* is any element that is part of a payroll check. That means the elements that go into determining the gross amount of the payroll check (salary, wages, bonuses, and commissions), as well as the elements that determine the net amount of the payroll check (withheld taxes, deductions for benefits, and any other deductions).

You must create each payroll item (although QuickBooks creates many of them during your EasyStep Interview when you indicate you'll be using payroll). Each item you create has to be linked to an account in your chart of accounts. And because all the money you deduct is turned over to somebody else (the government, an insurance company, or a pension administrator), you must have vendors associated with each deduction.

Before you run your first payroll, it's a good idea to check your Payroll Item List to make sure everything you need has been entered, and also to double-check the links to accounts and vendors. Read Chapter 2 for step-by-step instructions about adding items to your Payroll Item List.

Open your list of payroll items by choosing Lists | Payroll Item List from the menu bar. Every item that's used to generate a paycheck must exist in the Payroll Item List.

Double-click each item to make sure it's linked properly. Double-clicking puts the item in edit mode, which brings up a wizard-like series of windows. The first window is for the name of the item; the way it appears on the payroll check stub. Click Next to move to the window that contains the links (see Figure 8-1).

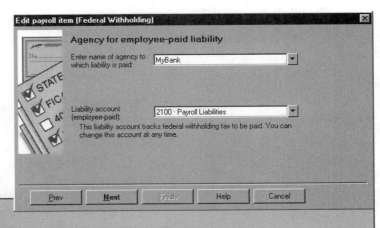

**Figure 8-1 • Be sure all the information is there, and be sure it's correct.**

If any item is missing or incorrect, you must make the necessary entries. You can create any additional vendor or general ledger accounts you need by selecting <Add New> from the drop-down list that appears when you click the arrow to the right of the field.

> **Tip** *Some payroll items have only two wizard windows; others have more because there's additional information needed about the item. If you come across anything you don't understand or don't know, it's best to call your accountant.*

## Checking Employee Information

The information about your employees must be perfectly, pristinely accurate, or you may hear about it in a very unfriendly manner.

> **Tip** *Make sure you pass around W-4 forms every year and insist that employees fill them out completely. Don't accept blank forms back with a notation that says "same as last year." This is your bible for entering employee data, and it's important to be able to prove that you entered information from the horse's mouth.*

To view your employee list, choose Lists | Employee List from the menu bar. When the list appears, double-click each employee's listing and move to the Payroll Info tab. Check the information against the W-4 form and also against any documents that employees sign to have specific deductions taken from their paychecks (medical benefits, pension plans, and so forth).

Click the Taxes button to check the tax status for this employee against the W-4 form.

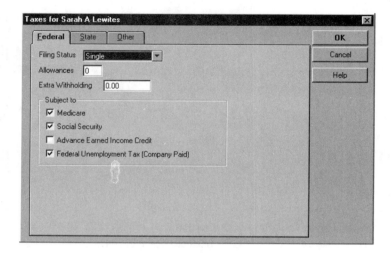

Click OK to return to the Payroll Info tab. The Sick/Vacation button, which is where you establish your sick- and vacation-day policies, is discussed in Chapter 2. The Direct Deposit button is used if you've signed up for direct deposit services with QuickBooks.

Most employees have all taxes withheld, but there are some exceptions to the rules. The employees who qualify for those exceptions usually know about it and their W-4 forms will reflect their special status. Here are some of the exceptions you might encounter:

- For federal income tax, there is a low-income exemption that is commonly used by students.
- FICA and Medicare exceptions can be taken by non-resident alien employees.
- A child under the age of 18 who is employed by a parent in an unincorporated business can claim exemption from FICA and Medicare withholding amounts. The parent must own more than half of the business for the child to qualify.

**Tip** *If your business is a corporation, you must separate compensation for corporate officers from the other employee compensation when you file your business taxes. To avoid having to perform all sorts of calculations outside of QuickBooks to determine these amounts, create a separate payroll item called "Officer Compensation." Assign it to its own account. Then open the Employee card for each officer and change the Earnings item to this new payroll item.*

# Signing Up for Payroll Services

You cannot do payroll within QuickBooks without signing up for payroll services. Actually, you can perform some payroll chores, such as generating gross payroll data, by entering employee hours. However, unless you've signed up for QuickBooks payroll services, no calculations occur against the gross amount of the paycheck. No withholding appears, no amounts are posted to employee and employer liability accounts, and there is no net amount.

You can, if you wish, use your own printed tax table and calculate the deductions manually, and then issue a paycheck for the net amount to each employee. If you don't want to face that chore, however, you must sign up for payroll services. QuickBooks offers two payroll service plans: Basic Payroll Services and Deluxe Payroll Services. In addition, you can sign up for direct deposit with either plan. I'll discuss the details for each plan in this section.

**Note** *QuickBooks also offers Premier Payroll Service. This is a standard payroll service company, and it is not integrated with your QuickBooks software. If you don't use a payroll service company, or you are unhappy with your current payroll service company, you might want to check out this new QuickBooks company. You can get more information by calling 800-542-1227 between 8 A.M. and 5 P.M. Pacific Time.*

## QuickBooks Basic Payroll Services

The QuickBooks Basic Payroll Service keeps your tax table up-to-date. You pay an annual fee, and each time you run your payroll you connect to the Internet to check the status of the tax tables and your service agreement. If everything is fine, the software engine that calculates paychecks is unlocked. The calculations are performed locally, on your computer, not on the Internet (you can disconnect your Internet connection before proceeding with payroll tasks). No employee information is exposed to the Internet during this process. If the tax table has changed, a new tax table is downloaded to your computer before the calculation engine is turned on.

Basic Payroll Services also provides direct deposit services (for an additional fee) and the ability to print federal tax forms from the software (940, 941, 1099, and W-2).

## QuickBooks Deluxe Payroll Services

The Deluxe Payroll Service includes all the functions in the Basic Payroll Service and then adds the following features:

- Automatic payment, by electronic transfer, of your federal and state withholdings
- Automatic electronic filing of all the federal and state forms required throughout the year
- Preparation of W-2 forms for each employee
- Preparation of W-3 forms for transmitting W-2 forms
- Direct deposit services

## QuickBooks Direct Deposit Services

With either the Basic or Deluxe Payroll Service, you can easily add direct deposit services for your employees. Employees must sign a form giving permission for direct deposit, and you can print those forms directly from your QuickBooks software (QuickBooks provides a link to display and print the forms during the sign-up process).

Employees can opt to deposit their entire paychecks into one bank account, or split the amount between two bank accounts.

## Applying for Payroll Services

To sign up for either service, choose Employees | Set Up Payroll to open the Payroll Setup wizard (see Figure 8-2).

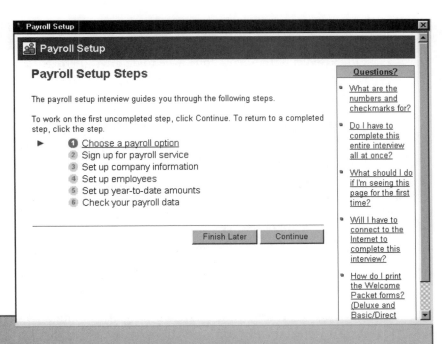

**Figure 8-2** • **The Payroll Setup feature starts with signing up for payroll services.**

Start by clicking Choose A Payroll Option, which opens a window where you can select either Basic or Deluxe payroll services. Make your choice, choose Sign Up, and click Continue. Make sure your company information (EIN number, company name, and company address) is correct, and then click Continue.

## Signing Up for Basic Payroll Services

For Basic Payroll Services you can complete your application online. Click Sign Up Now. QuickBooks opens your Web browser and travels to the QuickBooks payroll sign-up site. Click Continue to move through the windows (most of which contain information about the service). You can sign up for Basic Payroll with Direct Deposit, or for Basic Payroll only.

If QuickBooks has a problem with the company information you provide, a message appears asking you to contact Intuit to resolve the issue. You can call 800-499-3459 between 8 A.M. and 5 P.M. Pacific Time.

When the sign-up process is completed, QuickBooks periodically downloads the files you need to run payroll. The new files are automatically added to your QuickBooks system; you don't have to do anything to install them. Because this is the first time you've received payroll update files, the current tax table is added to your system.

### Signing Up for Deluxe Payroll Services

For Deluxe Payroll Services, you must first fill out some forms and receive a Personal Identification Number (PIN) from QuickBooks. Call QuickBooks at 800-332-4844 between 8 A.M. and 5 P.M. Pacific Time to get started. When you call, have the following information available:

- Number of employees
- Your EIN
- Your state ID numbers (income tax, unemployment tax, etc.)
- Bank account information (bank, account number, etc.)

When you receive your PIN, go through the online sign-up process, and enter the PIN when instructed. Then complete the rest of the sign-up process.

When the sign-up process is completed, QuickBooks downloads the files you need to run payroll. The new files are automatically added to your QuickBooks system; you don't have to do anything to install them. Because this is the first time you've received payroll update files, the current tax table is added to your system.

## Using Payroll on a QuickBooks Network

If you're using the network version of QuickBooks, always communicate with QuickBooks payroll services from the computer that's used to process payroll. If your payroll person is working from a QuickBooks installation on a computer that does not have Internet access, you can configure the QuickBooks network system to let that person have access to the files. To do so, from the computer that has Internet access, choose File | Update QuickBooks. Click the Options link and select On for the Share Download option so other network users can access the downloaded files. Then click Save and close the window. You must perform these steps before you begin using Payroll each week, because the tax tables are downloaded when you begin the Payroll run.

# Entering Historical Data

If you're not starting your use of QuickBooks at the very beginning of the year, you must enter all the historical information about paychecks. This is the only way to perform all those tasks required at the end of the year. You cannot give your employees two W-2 forms, one from your manual system and another from QuickBooks, nor can you file your annual tax reports on any piecemeal basis.

**Tip**    *No matter what your fiscal year is, your payroll year is the calendar year. Even though you can start using payroll for the current period before you enter the historical data, remember that the absence of historical data may affect some tax calculations. If there are withholding amounts that cease after a certain maximum (perhaps your state only requires SUI for the first $8,000.00 in gross payroll), you'll have to adjust those current paychecks manually to remove the withholding.*

## Entering the History Manually

The truth is, payroll is so easy to do if everything is set up properly that I usually advise clients to enter each historical payroll run individually. It's great training. For the first couple of pay periods, stop to look at the details and compare them to your manual records before saving the payroll. This gives you an opportunity to understand what QuickBooks is doing, in addition to checking accuracy.

If it's late in the year when you first begin using QuickBooks, I usually advise waiting until next year. If it's somewhere around the middle of the year, you may decide that my suggestion is crazy and refuse to go through the process of entering 26 or 30 weeks of payroll runs. I can understand your reluctance (although there's no such thing as being too careful when it comes to payroll), so read on to learn how to enter historical data in batches.

## Using the QuickBooks Payroll Data Wizard

QuickBooks provides assistance for entering prior payroll records in the form of a wizard. Choose Employees | Set Up Payroll from the QuickBooks menu bar. This opens the same Payroll Setup wizard you used to sign up for payroll. Unfortunately, you have to use this wizard one step at a time—there's no way to skip any steps.

Assuming you've completed all the steps to sign up for a payroll service, select Step 5: Set Up Year To Date Amounts. The YTD Introductory wizard window opens. Read the information and then click Next to proceed to your task. The wizard walks you through all the necessary steps. Remember that if you haven't gathered all the information you need, this won't go smoothly.

## Set the Dates for Payroll History

The initial wizard questions are about the dates you're using for historical data.

**Set a Starting Date for Historical Data**     If you've been entering payroll information to accounts because you've had a payroll service, or you've been doing manual payroll and posting the amounts in account registers, you don't want QuickBooks to enter those amounts again. Specify the starting date for posting amounts, which is after the last date you posted payroll data. If you've never posted any payroll data in QuickBooks, use the first day of the current year.

**Set a Starting Date for Using the QuickBooks Payroll Feature**     The next wizard window asks for the date on which you plan to go "live" with payroll. QuickBooks defines historical data as any data that precedes this date. On the "live" date, you'll be entering payroll checks and distributing them; those checks are not part of the historical data.

It's important to understand how the "live" date affects the task in front of you:

- Payroll records are summarized quarterly, because your 941 reports are due quarterly.
- You can't enter summarized data for the quarter that's current (the quarter that the "live" date falls in). Instead, for the current quarter, you must enter data for each individual pay period (weekly, biweekly, semi-monthly, or monthly). For previous quarters, you can enter quarterly totals.
- If you tell QuickBooks that your "live" date is any date in the first quarter, you will have to enter historical data for each pay period before the "live" date.
- If you tell QuickBooks that your "live" date is in the second quarter, QuickBooks will ask you to enter a quarterly total for the first quarter, and then ask you for individual pay period totals for the second quarter up to the "live" date.
- If you tell QuickBooks that your "live" date is in the third quarter, QuickBooks will ask you to enter quarterly totals for the first two quarters, and then ask you for pay period totals up to the "live" date.

To avoid a lot of data entry, it's a good idea to go "live" with payroll for the first pay period of a quarter.

### Enter Employee History

In the next window, a list of employees is displayed. Now it's time to enter the year-to-date information. You perform this task one employee at a time. Select the first employee and click Enter Summary (or double-click the employee listing). QuickBooks presents a screen with the pay period for this employee so you can fill out the amounts and click Next Period to move to the next pay period for this employee.

If you indicated a "live" date that's late in the year, QuickBooks offers quarterly pay periods to fill in the YTD amounts, except for the current quarter (as explained in the previous section).

Click OK when you have finished with this employee. You're returned to the list of employees, where you select the next employee and repeat the process.

When all the employee records are entered, you can use the wizard to enter all the payments you've made to remit withholding, pay taxes, and so on. QuickBooks assumes you've accounted for these in your opening trial balance, so whatever you enter does not affect your accounts (remember, you're entering historical payroll entries). You can change that assumption by instructing QuickBooks to post these amounts to the appropriate accounts.

## Running a Payroll Checkup

QuickBooks has a feature that checks your payroll configuration to make sure there aren't any discrepancies. This Payroll Checkup feature should be run whenever you add or modify payroll items or deductions. It's also a good idea to run the checkup after you've entered historical data so that QuickBooks can check your payroll system before you run your first payroll. If QuickBooks finds discrepancies or problems, you're told about them. No changes are made to your system unless you make those changes manually.

Choose Employees | Run Payroll Checkup to begin the process. It takes a few seconds to check your system (and display a disclaimer that QuickBooks is not responsible for errors), and then a window opens to display the results. Click the Edit buttons to open the appropriate windows so you can fix the problems. Then run the checkup again.

## Getting the Tax Tables

Before you can process payroll checks you must download the current tax tables from the QuickBooks Payroll Services Web site. That means you must be connected to the Internet. Choose Employees | Get Payroll Updates to open the QuickBooks

Payroll Information dialog box. Your current tax table version displays, along with other information about your payroll subscription status. Click Update. A progress bar displays to show you how things are going as you download the tax table to your computer.

# Running Payroll

It's payday. All the historical data is entered. It's time to run the payroll.

If you're using direct deposit services you need a two-day lead before the actual payday. If only some of your employees use direct deposit, you have two choices:

- Do all your payroll data entry two days before payday and hold the printed checks until payday (date the checks appropriately).
- Run the payroll procedure twice using the appropriate employees for each run.

## Selecting Employees to Pay

To begin, choose Employees | Pay Employees, to open the Select Employees To Pay dialog box shown in Figure 8-3.

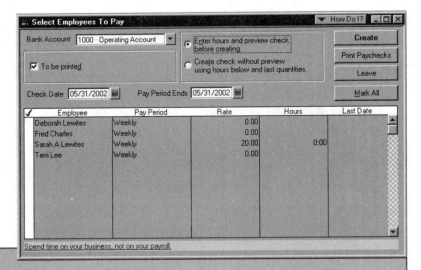

**Figure 8-3 • Select the employees who get a paycheck with this payroll run.**

The first time you run payroll, there's no information about the last payroll check for each employee. After you've completed this payroll run, that information will be available.

- For salaried employees, the information usually remains the same so you can create the checks without previewing information about hours.
- For hourly wage employees, if the number of hours are the same as the last check, you can repeat checks as if the employee were on salary.

For this first payroll, however, you must check the details before printing payroll checks:

1. Make sure the correct bank account is selected.

**Tip** *If you have a separate payroll account, be sure to go to Edit | Preferences and click the Checking icon. On the Company Preferences tab, select the default bank account for creating paychecks and the default bank account for paying payroll liabilities. This way, you won't accidentally use the wrong bank account when you're working in payroll.*

2. Select the option Enter Hours And Preview Check Before Creating.
3. Select the employees to be paid by clicking in the check mark column. If all employees are included in this payroll run (they're all direct deposit, or all printed checks) click the Mark All button.
4. Specify the check date and the end date for this payroll period.
5. Click Create to begin entering paycheck information.

**Note** *If you separate the payroll run between corporate officers and employees, you'll need to select each group separately.*

## Filling Out the Paycheck Information

The first employee's Preview Paycheck window opens (see Figure 8-4). If the employee is on an hourly wage, everything is blank until you fill in the Hours column. If the employee is salaried, the amounts are displayed.

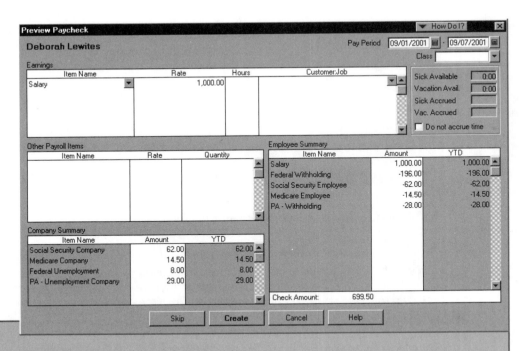

**Figure 8-4 • Fill in the hours for hourly employees; accept or change the rate for salaried employees.**

Complete the following steps:

1. Enter hours, if the employee is an hourly employee. Use the TAB key to move through the window.
2. Make any corrections necessary. Perhaps you need to add an additional pay item such as a bonus or enter a one-time deduction.
3. When everything is correct, click Create.
4. The next employee's record appears so you can repeat the process.
5. Continue to move through each employee.
6. When the last employee check is created, you're returned to the original Select Employees To Pay window.

Click Print Paychecks if you're ready to do that; otherwise, click Leave and print the paychecks later.

## Printing the Paychecks

When all the checks have been created, you must print the paychecks. Load the right checks in your printer (don't use your standard bank account checks if you have a separate payroll account).

1. Either choose Print from the Select Employees To Pay window, or choose File | Print Forms | Paychecks to open the Select Paychecks To Print window.
2. Select the bank account for this paycheck print run.
3. Make sure the First Check Number field contains the correct number for the first check loaded in the printer.
4. Deselect any paycheck you don't want to print at this time by clicking in the check mark column to remove the existing check mark.
5. Click OK when everything is configured properly.

The Print Checks window opens. Click Print to print the paychecks. QuickBooks displays a window in which you must confirm that everything printed properly or reprint any checks that had a problem. If everything is fine, click OK. If there's a problem, enter the number of the first check that had a problem and QuickBooks will reprint as necessary, starting with the next available check number.

**Note** *For direct deposits, QuickBooks prepares only a paycheck stub. To print those, choose File | Print Forms | Paystubs.*

## Sending Direct Deposit Information

If you use direct deposit services, you still go through the payroll process for the employees who opted for this service. You just don't print the checks. Instead, you notify QuickBooks to deposit the checks.

To make the direct deposit, open your Internet connection and then choose Employees | Send Payroll Data from the QuickBooks menu bar. A window opens to display the data you're about to upload, and you must confirm its accuracy. (If anything is amiss, cancel the procedure and return to the Pay Employees procedure to correct the information.) Click Go Online to begin the data transfer and follow the onscreen instructions.

## Sending Payroll Liability Information to Deluxe Payroll Services

If you've signed up for Deluxe Payroll Services, you must upload the information about the payroll run you just completed so that the service can remit your withholding to the appropriate government agencies.

Choose Employees | Send Payroll Data from the QuickBooks menu bar. A window opens to display the data you're about to upload, and you must confirm its accuracy. Click Go Online to begin the data transfer, and follow the onscreen instructions. When the information is received by QuickBooks, a confirmation window appears to show you the transactions that are being performed (for example, remittance of withholding taxes to the appropriate authorities) and the fees charged. The transactions are automatically entered in your checking account register.

## Handling Unusual Deductions

One of the employees at Bill's Diner has a garnishment for child support that has to be deducted and remitted to the local authorities. The garnishment order says that the employee must pay $30 if his paycheck is over $280 net, or 10% of his net pay if his net paycheck is under $280.

Since this is a choice, there's no way to create this deduction for automatic withholding. Here's what Bill has to do during the payroll process:

1. When the employee's Preview Paycheck window appears, enter the hours.
2. Note the Check Amount number that's displayed at the bottom of the window.
3. In the Other Payroll Items section of the window, click in the Name column.
4. Choose the garnishment deduction (which must exist in the Payroll Item List).
5. Enter the appropriate amount for this deduction.

This works because Bill created a separate garnishment payroll item for each type of garnishment order, without indicating an amount or percentage. Each remittance check is separate (even if Bill has multiple employees with the same type of garnishment order) in order to track everything more efficiently.

When Bill created the deduction for the employee, he had two choices:

- Enter the $30 amount and then correct it if the current amount is less.
- Leave the amount blank and enter it each week.

The issue of garnishment is becoming more significant to employers because government agencies are using it more frequently to collect child support payments and overdue student loans.

# Government Payroll Reporting

## In this Chapter:

- *Make tax deposits*

- *Remit withheld amounts and employer taxes*

- *Prepare quarterly and annual returns*

- *Print W-2 Forms*

Doing payroll in-house means having a lot of reports to print, forms to fill out, and checks to write. There's a logical order to these tasks, although the logic differs depending on the state and city (or town) you're in. In this chapter, we'll go over the procedures in the order in which most businesses have to perform the tasks.

If you've signed up for QuickBooks Deluxe Payroll services, you don't have to worry about the sections in this chapter that are concerned with remitting federal and state withholdings. You do, however, have to remit your local payroll tax withholding yourself.

# Making Federal Payroll Tax Deposits

The federal government requires you to deposit the withholding amounts, along with the matching employer contributions, at a specified time. That time period is dependent upon the size of the total withholding amount you've accumulated. You may be required to deposit monthly, semi-monthly, weekly, or within three days of the payroll. Check the current limits with the IRS or your accountant.

There's a formula for determining the size of the deposit check—it is the sum of the following amounts for the period:

- Federal withholding
- FICA withholding
- Medicare withholding
- FICA matching contribution from employer
- Medicare matching contribution from employer

You don't have to do the math—QuickBooks does it for you. But it's a good idea to know what the formula is so you can check the numbers yourself.

## Select the Liabilities for the Federal Deposit Check

To prepare the check, choose Employees | Pay Payroll Liabilities from the QuickBooks menu bar. Select the date range the check covers.

For a federal deposit, the date range must match your deposit frequency, which is determined by the amount of withholding. For most small businesses, monthly deposits are common. However, if your federal withholding amounts are very large, you may have to make a federal deposit within several days of each payroll. If your withholding amounts are relatively small, you may be able to file quarterly. Check Circular E, which is mailed to employers every year, or ask your accountant.

When you click OK, the Pay Liabilities window appears, listing all the payroll liabilities currently due. You could select everything and write all the checks (whether they're due at the moment or not) just to get them out of the way. I don't do that. I select only those liabilities that are due now. Besides, this section is about the federal deposit check.

To make it easier, click the arrow to the right of the Sort By field and choose Payable To, which arranges the list according to the agency that receives the payment. Then select the liabilities you want to pay.

Click in the check mark column to select the liabilities you want to pay. Notice that when you choose Medicare or Social Security, selecting the employee liability automatically selects the company liability (or vice versa). This is, of course, because you must pay the total of withholding and employer contributions at the same time.

Specify whether you want to create the check without reviewing it, or to review the check before finalizing it (I review everything before making payroll deposits!). Click Create when you've selected the liability payments you want to pay for your deposit payment. If you opted to review the check, it's displayed. If you need to make changes, do so (you shouldn't need to). Then click Save & Close to save the data.

## Print the Check

The check is created and needs only to be printed. (If you don't use printed checks, just go ahead and use the check register instead of following these steps for printing.) This is the easy part:

1. Choose File | Print Forms | Checks from the menu bar.
2. When the Select Checks To Print window opens, select the bank account you use for payroll.
3. Be sure all the payroll liability checks you created are selected.
4. Click OK to bring up the Print Checks window so you can print the checks.

The federal government sent you a book of coupons (Form 8109) you must use when you deposit the funds you owe. Fill out a coupon and take it, along with your check, to the bank in which you have your payroll account. Make the check payable to the bank, unless you've been given different instructions by the bank or your accountant.

**Note**   *Don't forget to fill in the little bullets on the coupon: one to indicate this is a 941 deposit, the other to indicate the quarter for which this payment is remitted.*

# Remitting State and Local Liabilities

Your state and local payroll liabilities vary depending upon where your business is located and where your employees live (and pay taxes). Besides income taxes, you are probably liable for unemployment insurance, as well. And many states have withholding for disability.

## State and Local Income Taxes

Most states have some form of an income tax, which might be calculated in any one of a variety of ways:

- A flat percentage of gross income
- A sliding percentage of gross income
- A percentage based on the federal tax for the employee

Local taxes are also widely varied in their approach:

- Some cities have different rates for employees of companies that operate in the city. There may be one rate for employees who live in the same city and a different rate for non-residents.
- Your business might operate in a city or town that has a *payroll head tax* (a once-a-year payment that is a flat amount per employee).
- You may have a head tax for the town in which your business operates and still be required to withhold local taxes for employees who live in another city.

State and local taxing authorities usually provide coupons to use for remitting income tax withholding. The frequency with which you must remit might depend on the size of your payroll, or it might be quarterly, semi-annual, or annual regardless of the amount.

To remit the withheld income tax for your state and local taxing authorities, choose Employees | Pay Payroll Liabilities from the QuickBooks menu bar. Select the date range this payment covers and click OK to open the Pay Liabilities window. Locate the state and local income tax liabilities. Mark them by clicking in the check mark column, and then click Create. Follow the steps to print the checks as described earlier. Mail them, along with your coupon, to the appropriate addresses.

**Tip** *Deselect the Show All Liabilities For This Period option to eliminate all the zero-based liabilities on this window.*

## Other State Liabilities

If your state has SUI or SDI or both, you have to pay those liabilities when they're due. Commonly, these are quarterly payments. Even if the payee name is the same as the payee that receives the income tax withholding, don't select these liabilities at the same time you select your income tax withholding liabilities. If you do, QuickBooks will cut one check for the grand total, and the SUI and SDI should be sent with a different form (and frequently to a different address).

**Tip** *It's a good idea to create a different payee name for SUI, SDI, and income tax withholding to make sure you don't accidentally send checks to the wrong place for the wrong thing.*

Not all states have SUI or SDI, and some have one but not the other. Some states collect SUI from the employee and the company; some collect only from the company. Check the rules for your state.

Use the same process described earlier of selecting the amounts due from the Pay Liabilities window when it's time to pay your state liabilities.

## Remitting Other Payroll Liabilities

The rules for remitting the paycheck deductions you take for other reasons—such as health benefits, pension, and so on—are specific to your arrangements with those vendors.

There are a great many ways to handle the way these payments are posted, and you have to decide what makes sense to you (or to your accountant). For example, if you pay a monthly amount to a medical insurer, you may want to post the employee deductions back to the same expense account you use to pay the bill. That way, only the net amount is reported as an expense on your taxes. Or you can track the deductions in a separate account and calculate the net amount at tax time.

Then you have to perform the steps to make sure the vendors get the right amount. For example, before you write the check to the medical insurance company, you must enter a regular vendor bill for the difference between the deducted amounts and the actual bill. That difference is your company contribution, of course. Then, when you write the check, both bills will be in the hopper, and the check will be in the correct amount.

# Preparing Your 941 Form

Every quarter you must file a 941 form that reports the total amount you owe the federal government for withheld taxes and employer expenses. If you have been paying the deposits regularly, no check is remitted with the 941. Instead, it's a report of amounts due and amounts paid, and they should match.

The 941 is concerned with:

- Gross wages paid
- Federal income tax withholding
- FICA (social security) withholding and matching employer contributions
- Medicare withholding and matching employer contributions

Many people fill out the 941 form they receive in the mail. You can gather the information you need from a QuickBooks report to do that, or you can have QuickBooks print the 941 form for you.

**Note** *The federal government is encouraging telephone filing, and instructions for that feature arrive with your 941 form every quarter. This is certainly an easy way to file. You can expect the government to begin encouraging online filing via the Internet very soon.*

# Creating the 941 Form

QuickBooks will prepare your 941 report, using the information in your QuickBooks registers. To prepare the report, follow these steps:

1. Choose Employees | Process Payroll Forms from the QuickBooks menu bar.
2. Select the option to Create Form 941.
3. Follow the onscreen instructions to complete the form and print it.

The printed form can be sent to the IRS if you use these printing criteria:

- The form must be printed with black ink on white or cream paper.
- The paper must be 8″ × 11″ or 8.5″ × 11″.
- The paper must be 18 lb. weight or heavier.

The printed report doesn't look exactly like the blank form you received, but it's close. More importantly, it's perfectly acceptable to the government.

You could also use the information in the printed report to fill in the blank 941 form you receive, or to transmit the information via telephone, saving your QuickBooks printout as your copy.

# Preparing Annual Returns

All the taxing authorities want annual returns. The feds, state, and local folks need reports and forms. Some of them need checks. You can get all the information you need from QuickBooks. In fact, all the usual QuickBooks reports work just fine, as long as you remember to set the Dates field to the entire year.

## Preparing State and Local Annual Returns

The state and local taxing authorities usually send you a form that asks for a reconciliation for the year. You may have to present quarterly totals as you fill out the form, which you can accomplish by changing the date range in the QuickBooks payroll reports.

Finish your State Unemployment annual report as soon as possible, because the payments you make to the state are relevant to the Federal Unemployment report (Form 940). Incidentally, for many states, the year-end State Unemployment report doesn't require a check because there's a limit to the wages that are eligible for applying the unemployment contribution rate.

## Preparing the 940 Report

For small businesses with only a couple of employees, the 940 report is frequently filed annually, along with a check. The 940 is the Federal Unemployment report (FUTA) and it's an employer expense.

To create your Form 940, choose Employees | Process Payroll Forms from the QuickBooks menu bar. Select the option to create the 940 form and follow the instructions that appear on the screen. Many small businesses qualify for Form 940EZ (which is shorter and easier).

# Printing W-2 Forms

You must print W-2 forms for your employees, the government agencies, and your own files. Everybody needs them.

Choose Employees | Process Payroll Forms from the QuickBooks menu bar and select Form W-2 to open the Process W-2s window. Click Mark All to select all the employees, and then choose Review W-2. Each employee's W-2 form is presented on the screen. If there is non-financial data missing (such as an address or ZIP code), you must fill it in.

Click Next to move through each employee's form. When everything is correct, load your W-2 forms in the printer and choose Print W-2s. The Print W-2s window opens so you can choose a printer and print the forms.

You must also print the W-3 form, which is a summary of your W-2 forms. It must be in the package you send to the IRS when you transmit the W-2 forms. Unfortunately, you can't preview the W-3 form.

All these payroll reports are a bit time-consuming, but you have no choice: These tasks are legally necessary. At least QuickBooks keeps the records and does the math.

# Configuring and Tracking Inventory

## In this Chapter:

- *Add items*

- *Deal with physical inventory counts*

- *Adjust the count*

- *Create pre-builds*

- *Use backorders*

## Chapter 10

For many businesses, the warehouse is a source of frustration, bewilderment, rage, and erroneous information. I'm using the term "warehouse" generically to indicate the place where you store inventory (which may not be a discrete building that looks like a warehouse).

# Creating Inventory Items

Inventory items are part of the Item List in your QuickBooks system. That list contains all the elements that might ever appear on a customer invoice, a purchase order, or a vendor bill. If you track inventory, many of the items in your Item List are the things you sell to customers from stock.

## Creating New Items

Instructions for adding items to the Item List are found in Chapter 2, but it's worth taking a moment here to go over the steps for inventory items.

Click the Item icon on the QuickBooks icon bar (or choose Lists | Item List from the menu bar) to open the Item List window, where all your inventory items are listed along with all the other types of items. The inventory items can be distinguished easily because they have their own type: Inventory Part. To see all the inventory items in a group, click the Type column heading to sort the list by type.

If you want to add a new item to your inventory items list, press CTRL-N while the Item List window is displayed. When the New Item window opens, fill in the information (Figure 10-1 is an example of an inventory item).

If you disabled automatic spell checks in the Preferences dialog box, click Spelling to make sure you have no spelling errors. This also lets the QuickBooks spelling checker add the words connected to this item to its dictionary (for example, the item code, the name of the vendor, and any technical jargon in the description). This obviates the need to check the spelling when you create an invoice or purchase order for the item. If you didn't disable automatic spell checks, the spelling tool will start when you click OK to save the item (See Chapter 21 to learn all about configuring and using the spelling checker.)

If you created any custom fields for items (discussed in Chapter 2), click Custom Fields and enter data in any custom field that's appropriate for this item.

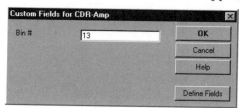

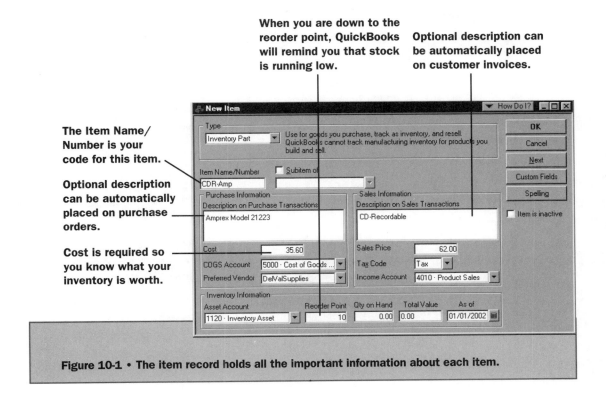

**When you are down to the reorder point, QuickBooks will remind you that stock is running low.**

**Optional description can be automatically placed on customer invoices.**

**The Item Name/ Number is your code for this item.**

**Optional description can be automatically placed on purchase orders.**

**Cost is required so you know what your inventory is worth.**

**Figure 10-1 • The item record holds all the important information about each item.**

If you want to add additional custom fields, click Define Fields.

You can also enter the current Qty On Hand in this window. If you're entering inventory as part of your original configuration of QuickBooks, that might be a suitable way to do it. If you've already started QuickBooks with an opening balance sheet from your accountant, you may want to enter the quantity on hand through the inventory adjustment tool, discussed in the section "Making Inventory Adjustments" later in this chapter. In fact, you should ask your accountant for his or her advice on making the inventory adjustment before you start performing the tasks noted here.

The reason for the accountant query is the way inventory value is posted in QuickBooks. If you enter the quantity on hand through the New Item window, the value of that quantity is entered into your inventory asset account, and the balancing entry is made to your current equity account.

If you use the inventory adjustment window, the balancing entry is made to an account of your choice. When you're performing standard adjustments (after a physical count of the inventory), the account you use is the inventory adjustment account. However, you can invent and use any account for offsetting the inventory adjustment, and your accountant may want to use an equity account you've invented for prior years or some other balance sheet account instead of touching the preconfigured equity balance. See the detailed explanations for using the inventory adjustment window later in this chapter and discuss this issue with your accountant.

**Tip** *To edit an item, open the Item List and double-click the item you want to change. Make the necessary changes and click OK.*

## Creating Subitems

Subitems are used when there are choices for items and you want all the choices to be part of a larger hierarchy so you can track them efficiently. For instance, if you sell widgets in a variety of colors, you may want to create a subitem for each color: red widget, green widget, and so on. Or perhaps you sell widgets from different widget manufacturers: Jones widgets, Smith widgets, and so on.

In order to have a subitem, you must have a parent item. Figure 10-2 shows a new item that has been specifically created as a parent item.

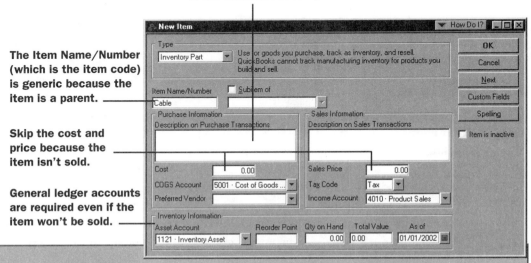

Figure 10-2 • This item won't be sold to customers; it exists only as a parent item.

Having created the parent item, subitems are easy to create by opening a blank New Item window:

1. In the Item Name/Number field, enter the code for this item. It can be an item, a color, a manufacturer name, or any other code that specifies this subitem as compared to other subitems under the same parent item. For instance, the first subitem I created under the parent item shown in Figure 10-2 was named Cat5-6 (indicating Category5 cable that is 6 feet long).

2. Check the box named Subitem Of, and then select the parent item from the drop-down list that appears when you click the arrow to the right of the field.

3. Enter the descriptions you want to appear on purchase orders and invoices.

4. Enter the cost and price.

5. Enter the general ledger account information.

6. Enter the reorder point if you're using that feature.

7. Continue to add subitems to each parent item in your system.

## Making Items Inactive

Sometimes you have inventory items that you aren't buying or selling at the moment. Perhaps they're seasonal, or the cost is too high and you want to delay purchasing and reselling the item until you can get a better price.

As long as you're not using the item, you can make it inactive. It doesn't appear on the items list, which means that the list is shorter and easier to scroll through when you're creating an invoice. And QuickBooks won't nag you with reorder reminders.

To declare an item inactive, open the Item List window and right-click the item. Then choose Make Inactive from the shortcut menu.

When an item is inactive, it's not just invisible on the list of items for sale that appears during invoice data entry; it doesn't even appear on the Item List window. However, you can change the appearance of the Item List window to display inactive items.

When you make any item inactive, the Show All check box becomes activated in the Item List window. If no items are marked inactive, the Show All option is grayed out and inaccessible. Click the Show All check box to display the inactive items along with the active items. Any inactive item is displayed with an X to the left of the item listing (see Figure 10-3). To make an inactive item active again, choose the Show All option so you can see the inactive items, and then click X to deselect it.

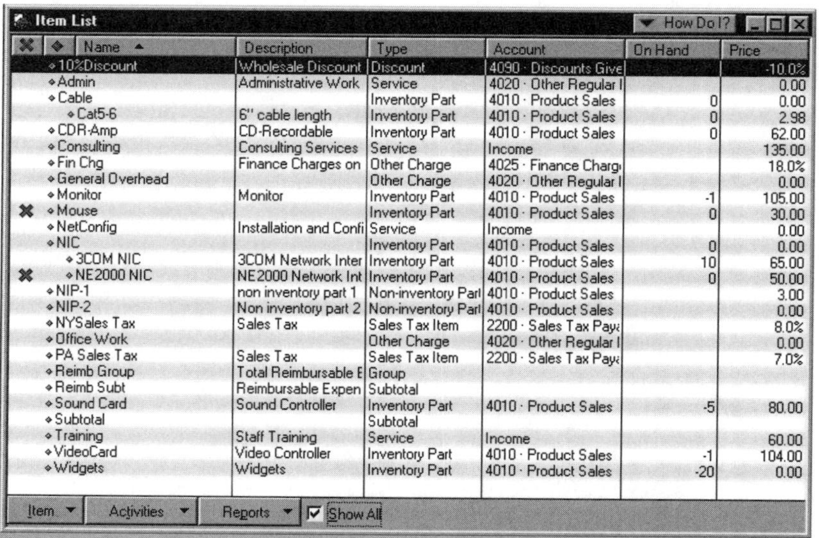

**Figure 10-3 • Inactive items remain in your system, and you can display them when you need to see a complete items list.**

---

**Caution** *You can make any individual subitem inactive, but if you make a parent item inactive, all of its subitems are also made inactive.*

## Activate All Items Before Running Reports

If you make an item inactive, QuickBooks pretends it doesn't exist. An inactive item doesn't show up in any inventory report. Worse, all calculations about the worth of your inventory, including reports that aren't directly connected to inventory (such as your balance sheet reports), fail to include any amounts connected to inactive items.

You must activate all inventory items, except those that have never been received into stock and never sold, before running any reports on inventory. You should also activate all inventory items before running financial statements.

# Running Inventory Reports

You'll probably find that you run reports on your inventory status quite often. For most businesses, tracking the state of the inventory is the second most important and frequently run set of reports (right behind reports about the current accounts receivable balances).

QuickBooks provides several useful, significant inventory reports, which you can access by choosing Reports | Inventory as the report type to see the available reports, which are discussed in this section.

## Inventory Valuation Summary Report

This report gives you a quick assessment of the value of your inventory. By default, the date range is the current month to date. Each item is listed with the following information displayed in columns:

**Item Description**   The description of the item, if you entered a description for purchase transactions.

**On Hand**   The current quantity on hand, which is the net number of received items and sold items. Because QuickBooks permits you to sell items you don't have in stock (perhaps you didn't use a QuickBooks transaction to bring them into stock), it's possible to have a negative number in this column.

**Avg Cost**   Each receipt of inventory transaction is used to calculate this figure.

**Asset Value**   The value posted to your Inventory account in the general ledger. The value is calculated by multiplying the number on hand by the average cost.

**% of Tot Asset**   The percentage of your total inventory assets that this item represents.

**Sales Price**   The price you've set for this item. This figure is obtained by looking at the item's configuration window. If you entered a price when you set up the item, that price is displayed. If you didn't enter a price (because you chose to determine the price at the time of sale), $0.00 displays. QuickBooks does not check the sales records for this item to determine this number, so if you routinely change the price when you're filling out a customer invoice, those changes aren't reflected in this report.

**Retail Value**   The current retail value of the item, which is calculated by multiplying the number on hand by the retail price.

**% of Retail Value**   The percentage of the total retail value of your inventory that this item represents.

## Inventory Valuation Detail Report

This report lists each transaction that involved each inventory item. For a while, it bothered me that the report showed no financial information about the price charged to customers, but then I realized that the report is about the value of inventory. That's a cost-based amount, and is irrelevant to the retail price. You can double-click any sales transaction line to see the details (and the amount you charged for the item).

## Inventory Stock Status

There are two Stock Status reports: By Item and By Vendor. The information is the same in both reports, but the order in which information is arranged and subtotaled is different. You can use these Stock Status reports to get quick numbers about inventory items, including the following information:

- The preferred vendor
- The reorder point
- The number currently on hand
- A reminder (a check mark) for ordering items that are below the reorder point
- The number currently on order (purchase order exists but stock has not yet been received)
- The next delivery date
- The average number of units sold per week

**Note** *Very few customization options are available for inventory reports—you can change the date range and filter some of the items, but you cannot add or remove columns.*

## Getting Quick Inventory Reports

QuickBooks provides a reporting feature called QuickReports that provides valuable information about an individual inventory item or all inventory items. QuickReports are available from the Item List window.

In the Item List window, select an item and press CTRL-Q (or click the Reports button and choose QuickReport) to open the QuickReport shown in Figure 10-4. You can change the date range for the report, and you can double-click any transaction line to drill down to the transaction details.

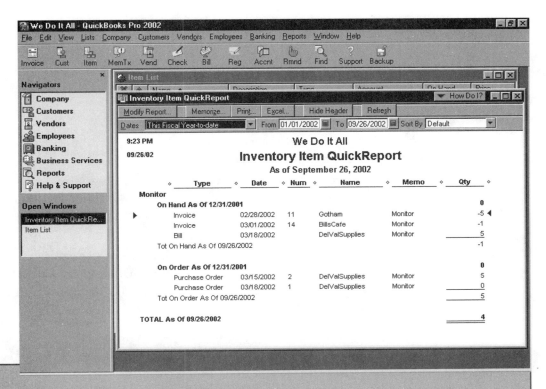

**Figure 10-4 • A quick report is an activity report for an item.**

# Counting Inventory

I can hear the groans. I know—there's nothing worse than doing a physical inventory. However, no matter how careful you are with QuickBooks transactions, no matter how pristine your protocols are for making sure everything that comes and goes is accounted for, you probably aren't going to match your physical inventory to your QuickBooks figures. Sorry about that.

## Printing the Physical Inventory Worksheet

The first thing you must do is print a Physical Inventory Worksheet (see Figure 10-5), which is one of the choices on the Inventory Reports menu in the Report Finder.

This report lists your inventory items in alphabetical order, along with the current quantity on hand, which is calculated from your QuickBooks transactions. In addition, there's a column that's set up to record the actual count as you walk around your warehouse with this printout in hand.

If you have a large number of inventory items, you may have some problems with this worksheet:

- You cannot change the way the worksheet is sorted, so you cannot arrange the items to match the way you've laid out your warehouse.

- If you use bins, rows, or some other physical entity in your warehouse, QuickBooks has no feature to support it, so you cannot enter the location on this worksheet (nor can you sort by location, which is an extremely useful method).

- I have no idea why the Pref Vendor column exists, because I've never experienced a physical inventory in which that information was used. If you stock by manufacturer, the manufacturer's name is usually referred to in the code or description. However, you cannot get rid of it.

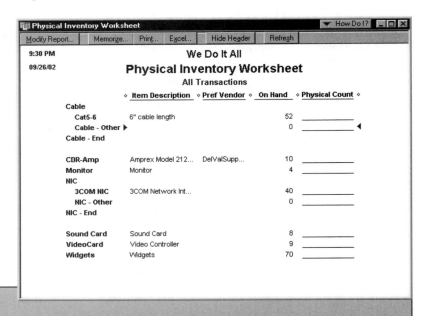

**Figure 10-5 • The worksheet's most important column is the one with the blank lines that you use to enter the physical count.**

Click the Print button in the worksheet window to bring up the Print Reports window. In the Number Of Copies box, enter as many copies as you need (one for each person helping with the count).

**Tip**    *Don't hand every person a full report—cut the report to give each person the pages he or she needs, and keep one full copy to use as a master.*

## Exporting the Report to a File

You can also export the worksheet, which is useful if you want to print additional columns or rearrange the way the report is sorted. Exporting is accomplished by printing to a file instead of the printer:

1. Click the Print button on the Physical Inventory Worksheet window.
2. In the Print To field of the Print Reports window, select File.
3. Click the arrow to the right of the File text box and select a format for the file. Then click Print.
4. In the Create Disk File dialog box, select a folder to hold this file and give the file a name. Then click Save to save the file.
5. Open the appropriate software and manipulate the file to make a worksheet that fits your exact needs.

**Tip**    *If you want to send the file to a word processor and use the Table feature, select Tab Delimited as the file type. Then, in the word processor, select the text and convert it to a table, using tabs to determine the columns (most word processors have this option).*

## Sending the Report to Microsoft Excel

You can automatically export your file to Microsoft Excel without printing the report to a file. This gives you a way to rearrange the report before you print it. More important, it provides a way to enter the physical count and then re-sort the report using those numbers, creating any type of inventory reports you need. Click the Excel button on the report button bar, and then select an option for saving this exported file. Your choices are:

- Send report to a new Excel spreadsheet
- Send report to an existing Excel spreadsheet

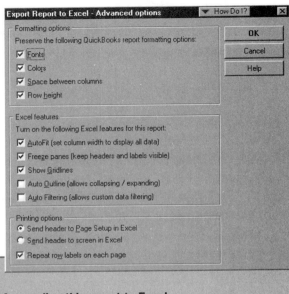

**Figure 10-6 • Select the options you need for sending this report to Excel.**

For even more control, click the Advanced button and select the options you want to take advantage of (see Figure 10-6).

**Note** *For information on using QuickBooks with Microsoft Office applications, see Appendix C.*

## Planning the Physical Count

QuickBooks lacks a "freeze" feature like the one found in most inventory-enabled accounting software. Freezing the inventory means that after you've printed the worksheet and begun counting, any transactions involving inventory are saved to a holding file in order to avoid changing the totals. When you've finished your physical count, you unfreeze the inventory count and print a report on the holding file. Make your adjustments to the count using the information in that file, and then make the final adjustments to the count.

You can perform these actions manually. After you print the worksheet (which you don't do until you're ready to start counting), be sure that all sales invoices will be handled differently until after the inventory count is adjusted. There are a number of ways to do this:

- Print an extra copy of each invoice and save the copies in a folder. Don't pick and pack the inventory for the invoices until after the count.
- Prepare a form for sales people to fill out the name and quantity of inventory items sold during the freeze, and delay picking and packing the inventory until after the count.
- Delay entering invoices until after the count is over. (This is not a good idea if counting takes a couple of days.)
- Don't receive inventory in QuickBooks (don't fill out a Receive Items or Receive Bill form) until after the count.
- If inventory arrives in the warehouse, don't unpack the boxes until after the count.

When you start counting the inventory, be sure there's a good system in place. The most important element of the system is *having somebody in charge*. One person, with a master inventory worksheet in hand, must know who is counting what. When each counter is finished, his or her sheet should be handed to the person in charge and the numbers should be duplicated onto the master inventory worksheet. (This is why you print multiple copies of the worksheet.) Note the date and time the count was reported.

After the count, bring in any inventory that's arrived during the count. Then start picking and packing your orders so you can generate income again.

## Making the Inventory Adjustments

After you've finished counting the inventory, you may find that the numbers on the worksheet don't match the physical count. Most of the time the physical count is lower than the QuickBooks figures. This is called *shrinkage*. Shrinkage is jargon for "stuff went missing for an unexplained reason," but most of the time the reason is employee theft. Sorry, but that's a well-documented fact. Another reason for shrinkage is breakage, but most of the time that's reported by employees, and you can adjust your inventory because you know about it. When you don't know about it, suspect the worst, because statistics prove that suspicion to be the most accurate.

## Adjusting the Count

You have to tell QuickBooks about the results of the physical count, and you accomplish that by choosing Vendors | Inventory Activities | Adjust Quantity/ Value On Hand. The Adjust Quantity/Value On Hand window opens, which is shown in Figure 10-7.

Here are the guidelines for filling out this window:

- Enter the date (usually inventory adjustments are made at the end of the month, quarter, or year, but there's no rule about that).

- Use an optional Ref. number to track the adjustment. The next time you enter an adjustment, QuickBooks will increment the Ref. number by one.

- Enter the inventory adjustment account in your chart of accounts. Click the arrow to see a display of all your accounts. If you don't have an inventory adjustment account, choose Add New and create one.

**Tip** *An inventory adjustment account must exist in order to adjust your inventory. Usually it's an expense account.*

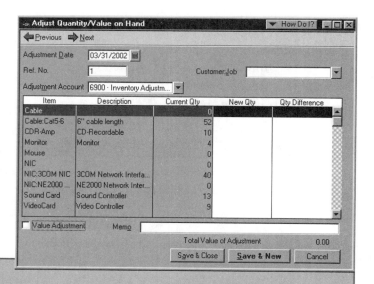

**Figure 10-7 • Correct the value of your inventory by adjusting the quantities to match the physical count.**

- The Customer:Job field is there in case you're sending stuff to a customer (or for a job) but not including the items on any invoices for that customer or job. QuickBooks provides this feature to help you when you do that (which is usually as a result of a job-costing scheme you're using). The inventory is changed and the cost is posted to the job.
- If you've enable the Class feature, a Class field appears.
- Use either the New Qty column or the Qty Difference column to enter the count (depending on how you filled out the worksheet and calculated it). Whichever column you use, QuickBooks fills in the other column automatically.
- Anything you enter in the Memo field appears on your Profit & Loss Detail report, which eliminates the question "what's this figure?" from your accountant.

When you have completed entering all the information, click Save & Close.

## Adjusting the Value

When you complete the entries, the total value of the adjustment you made is displayed in the window. That value is calculated by using the average cost of your inventory. For example, if you received ten widgets into inventory at a cost of $10.00 each, and later received ten more at a cost of $12.00 each, your average cost for widgets is $11.00 each. If your adjustment is for minus one widget, your inventory asset value is decreased by $11.00.

You can be more precise about your inventory valuation by eliminating the average valuation and entering a true value:

1. Click the Value Adjustment check box.
2. A column named New Value opens in the window (see Figure 10-8).
3. The value of the total adjusted count is displayed for each item, and you can change the value to eliminate the effects of averaging costs.

Of course, to do this, you must have the information you need, and then make the appropriate calculations in order to enter the correct total value. To obtain the information, follow these steps:

4. Click the Item icon on the icon bar to open the Item List window.
5. Click the Reports button at the bottom of the window.
6. Choose Reports On All Items | Purchases | Purchases By Vendor Detail.

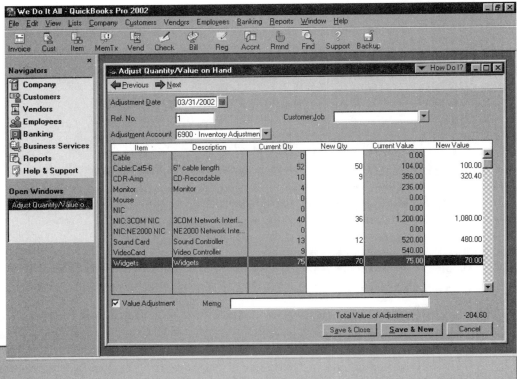

Figure 10-8 • You can manually change the current total value of any inventory item.

This report presents a history of your purchases so you can make the necessary calculations.

> **Tip** | *In case your accountant asks, QuickBooks does not support FIFO or LIFO costing for inventory. Essentially, you create your own FIFO/LIFO calculations by using the information in the vendor reports.*

Return to the Adjust Quantity window and enter the data. When you've finished making your changes, click Save & Close to save your new inventory numbers.

## Understanding the Postings

When you adjust the inventory count, you're also changing the value of your inventory asset. When you save the adjustment, the inventory asset account register changes to reflect the differences for each item (see Figure 10-9).

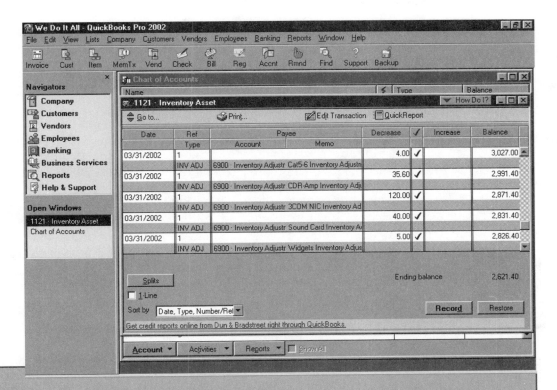

**Figure 10-9 •** Inventory adjustments are posted with the transaction type INV ADJ, instead of a sale or receipt of goods.

But this is double-entry bookkeeping, which means there has to be an equal and opposite entry somewhere else. For example, when you sell items via customer invoices, the balancing entry to the decrement of your inventory account is made to cost of sales. When you're adjusting inventory, however, there is no sale involved (nor is there a purchase involved). In this case, the balancing entry is made to the inventory adjustment account, which must exist in order to adjust your inventory.

If your inventory adjustment lowers the value of your inventory, the inventory asset account is credited and the adjustment account receives a debit in the same amount. If your adjustment raises the value of your inventory, the postings are opposite.

## Making Other Adjustments to Inventory

You can use the Adjust Quantity/Value On Hand window to make adjustments to inventory at any time and for a variety of reasons:

- Breakage or other damage.
- Customer demo units.
- Gifts or bonuses for customers or employees.
- Removal of inventory parts in order to create pre-built or pre-assembled inventory items. (See the upcoming section on pre-builds.)

The important thing to remember is that tracking inventory isn't just to make sure that you have sufficient items on hand to sell to customers (although that's certainly an important point). Equally important is the fact that inventory is a significant asset, just like your cash, equipment, and other assets. It affects your company's worth in a substantial way.

# Creating Pre-Builds

*Pre-builds* are products that are assembled or partially assembled using existing inventory parts. QuickBooks does not have any capacity for tracking pre-builds automatically, but you can create a system that works if you have a couple of pre-built items you want to place into inventory and sell to your customers. If you build assembled products as a matter of course, and it's a large part of your business, QuickBooks is not the software for you.

Software that supports pre-builds automates all the processes, using the following steps:

- Permits the creation of a pre-built inventory item, asking which inventory parts (and how many of each) are used.
- Receives the pre-built item into inventory (after you physically build it), automatically removing the individual parts from inventory.
- Automatically creates a cost for the new pre-built item based on the cost of the individual parts.

**Tip**    *Most software that supports pre-builds also permits a labor charge to be added as part of the cost.*

Each of these steps can be performed manually in QuickBooks and, although it's more time-consuming, you can create pre-builds yourself.

## Creating the Pre-Built Item

Start by putting the item into your items list, as shown in Figure 10-10.

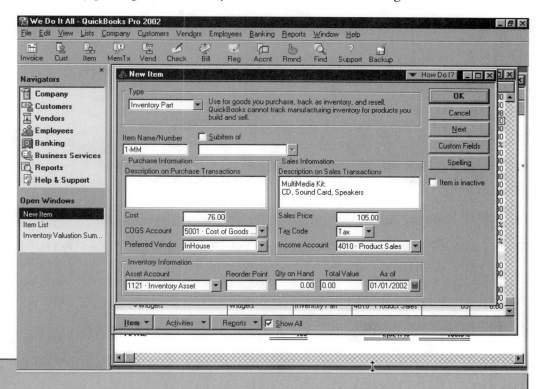

**Figure 10-10 • You create pre-builds in the same manner as a purchased item.**

The protocols I've used for entering the item shown in Figure 10-10 are specially designed for pre-builds, and you can consider this a guideline for your own entries if you find it helpful:

- The Item Name is unique in its starting character to force the pre-built items into a contiguous list at the beginning or end of any reports. If you normally use numbers for items, use a letter for the first character of your pre-builds (X or Z usually works well).
- The cost is the aggregate cost of the original inventory parts (which means you have to look them up before you perform this action).
- A vendor named "InHouse" was invented for this item.

Notice that there is no quantity on hand (it's brought into inventory when built). You may want to enter a reorder point for this item.

## Putting Pre-Builds into Inventory

When you bring your pre-built items into inventory, you don't receive them the way you receive the inventory items you purchase (there's no vendor). Instead, you must take the items you used to build them out of inventory and put the pre-build into inventory:

1. Choose Vendors | Inventory Activities | Adjust Quantity/Value On Hand.
2. In the Adjust Quantity/Value On Hand window, use the Qty Difference column to add the number of pre-builds and remove the number of original items that were used to create these pre-builds. As you enter each amount in the Qty Difference column, QuickBooks automatically makes entries in the New Qty column (see Figure 10-11).
3. Click OK to save the new quantities.

Notice that the total value of adjustment is zero, because we're replacing components with a pre-build.

**Tip** *If you use other paraphernalia for pre-builds (nails, screws, labels, whatever), add those items to the inventory items list so you can make the cost more exact.*

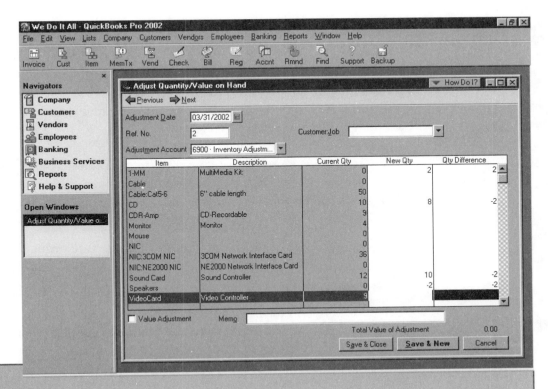

**Figure 10-11** • Use the Adjust Quantity feature to move items in and out of inventory for pre-builds.

# Handling Backorders

Backorders are nerve-wracking on both ends, whether you're waiting for items that your supplier didn't have, or you need to ship items to customers and you're out of them. However, you don't have to lose customer business because you're out of an item—you can backorder. QuickBooks doesn't have a backorder feature, but it does have features you can use to create your own backorder protocol for your business.

## Handling Pre-Builds Accurately

The Potter County Bicycle Shop sells and repairs bikes. Many of the bikes have special additional gadgets attached, and since some of these gadgets are very popular, the owners pre-attach them. This creates assembled, pre-built products, which are entered into inventory as the assembly is completed.

The owners are savvy business people who want to account for every penny of cost. Here's how they set up their pre-assembled products. First, they entered the items they need into their items list, and then they performed the following steps:

1. They entered all of the bikes they carry as inventory items.
2. They entered all of the gadgets they carry as inventory items.
3. They entered all of the combinations of bikes and gadgets that they pre-assemble as inventory items.

Before they performed step 3, they printed an Inventory Valuation Summary report, which provided the cost figures for all their inventory items. Then they figured out how much time it would take to assemble each pre-built item and used that time to add other costs to the pre-built items.

- For each pre-built inventory item they totaled the cost of the bike and the gadget they were attaching. This is a *direct materials* cost.
- They used the average employee hourly rate and applied that figure to the amount of time each pre-built unit required. This is a *direct labor* cost.
- They added the burden (employer costs, including benefits) using the same proportional hourly figure. This is also a *direct labor* cost.
- They added a proportional cost for the use of tools and equipment that aren't tracked as items in inventory, such as screws, paint, oil, polishing equipment, and so on. This is an *overhead* cost.

The grand total became the cost of the pre-built items.

Some accountants assign different categories to the various costs that can be applied to the assembly or manufacture of goods—this is how The Potter County Bicycle Shop's accountant set up the costs. Your accountant may do it a bit differently.

# Determining Customer Preferences

Part of the trick of keeping your customers' business is keeping your customers' preferences straight. The issue of backorders is important, because not all customers have the same attitude. Generally, there are three different approaches your customers take:

- "Okay, ship me whatever you have and send the backorders when you get them."

- "Just ship me what you have and take the other items off the order, and I'll order the other stuff when you get it." (This may really mean, "I'm going to look elsewhere, but if everyone else is out of it, I'll call you back.")

- "Hold the order until the backordered items are in, and then ship everything at once."

Nobody expects you to remember each customer's preference, but Quick-Books has some features that help you handle backorders to each customer's satisfaction.

## Using the Notepad for Backorder Instructions

QuickBooks has this nifty item called "customer notes," which you can use for keeping backorder instructions:

1. Open the Customer:Job List and double-click the customer listing to which you want to add a note.

2. When the Edit Customer window opens, click the Notes button.

3. In the Notepad window, enter a notation about the customer's attitude regarding backorders (see Figure 10-12).

4. Click OK twice to save the note and close the customer record.

When you're filling out an invoice for this customer, you can view the customer notepad. With the customer's invoice on the screen, choose Edit | Notepad from the QuickBooks menu bar, and the notepad for that customer appears.

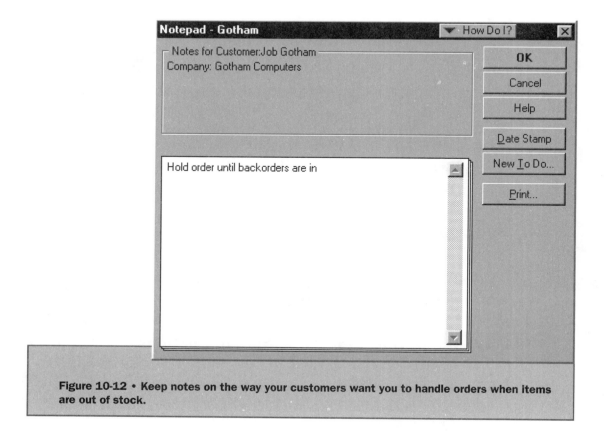

**Figure 10-12 •** Keep notes on the way your customers want you to handle orders when items are out of stock.

## Using a Backorder Handling Field

You can formalize your backorder handling by creating a Backorders field on the customer cards. Then you can put the field on the invoice form so it's right in front of you when you're filling out an order. Actually, there are three tasks involved if you want to use this protocol:

- Create the field for backorder preferences in the customer form.
- Add data to the field for each customer.
- Add the field to your invoice form.

## Adding a Field to the Customer Form

You can add a custom field to all the customer cards in your system by creating the new field in any existing customer record:

1. Click the Cust icon on the icon bar or press CTRL-J to open the Customer: Job List.
2. Double-click the listing for any existing customer.
3. Click the Additional Info tab, and then click Define Fields.
4. When the Define Fields window opens (see Figure 10-13), enter a label for the backorder field.
5. Select Customers:Jobs to use this field on your customer cards, and then click OK. QuickBooks displays a message telling you that you can use this custom field in templates (which is exactly what we're going to do). Click OK to make the message go away. Notice that you can tell it never to come back.
6. When you return to the customer window, click OK.

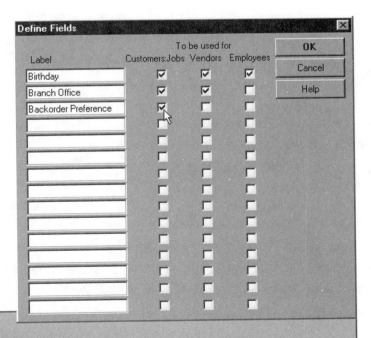

**Figure 10-13** • **Create a label for the new field and indicate where you want to use it.**

## Enter Data in the Customer Records

The customer list is still on your QuickBooks screen, which is handy because now you must enter information in the new field for each customer that orders inventory items from you:

1. Double-click a customer listing to open an Edit Customer window.
2. Move to the Additional Info tab (see Figure 10-14).
3. Enter this customer's backorder preference in the Backorders field you created.
4. Click OK to save the information.
5. Repeat the process for each customer.

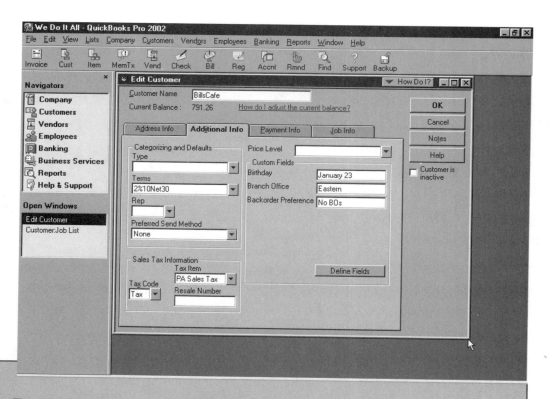

**Figure 10-14 • The field you invented is available for entering data.**

Unlike most of the fields that are built into the customer record, custom fields don't have their own list files; therefore, you don't have a drop-down list available when you want to enter data—data entry is manual. You should create some rules about the way you use this field so everyone in the office uses the same phrases. Don't let people create abbreviations or "cute" entries; make sure the data makes the customer's backorder status absolutely clear. For example, for a backorder preference, consider creating easy-to-understand data entries such as: Ship Separate, Hold Order, and No BOs.

## Put the Field on Your Invoice Forms

The information about a customer's backorder preferences is important when you're filling an order and you're out of something the customer wants. So you might as well have the information in front of you, which means putting it right on the invoice form. Complete information about customizing invoices is in Chapter 3. Here we'll just customize the invoice by adding this new field:

1. Click the Invoice icon on the icon bar.
2. Click the arrow to the right of the Form Template box at the upper right of the blank invoice form, and choose Customize.
3. When the Customize Template window opens, select the Intuit Product Invoice from the Template list and click the New icon to open the Customize Invoice window.
4. Move to the Fields tab, where you'll find that the field you added to the customer form is listed.
5. Enter the text you want to use for this field on the invoice (see Figure 10-15).
6. Select Screen to make sure this field and its data are on the screen when you're filling out an invoice. If you want to print the field and its data (so the customer is reminded of the preference), select Print also.
7. At the top of the window, enter a name for this new invoice template.
8. Click OK to save the new template.

You may get a message from QuickBooks about the position of fields, and usually it's best to opt to lay out the fields again. Check Chapter 3 for more information about field positions on templates, including moving your new field to a different position on the invoice.

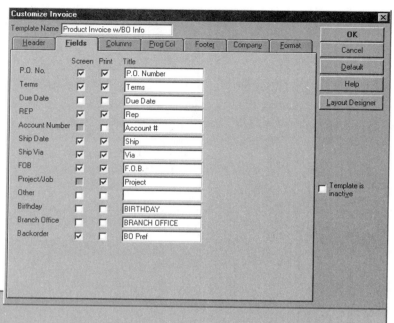

**Figure 10-15 • Add customer backorder preferences to your invoice form.**

Now when you need to enter a product invoice, use this new template. As soon as you enter the customer name in the Create Invoices window, the backorder preferences for that customer are displayed (see Figure 10-16).

## Recording a Backorder Invoice

Now that you're all set and can fill backorders the way your customers want them filled, here's how to create a backorder invoice in QuickBooks:

1. Fill out the invoice form, putting backordered items on the line items (see Chapter 3 for information about creating invoices).

2. When the invoice form is completely filled out, right-click anywhere on the form and choose Mark Invoice As Pending from the shortcut menu. The word "Pending" appears on the invoice form.

3. Save the invoice by clicking Save & Close (or click Save & New if you have more invoices to complete).

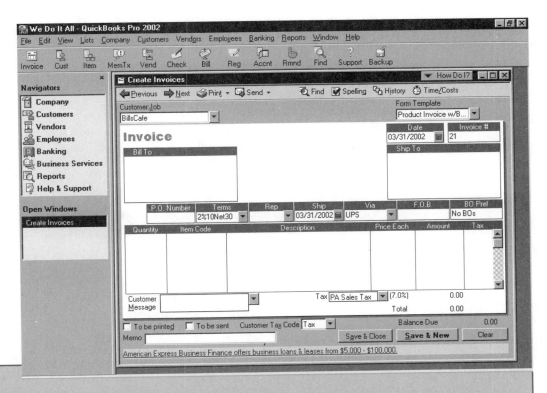

**Figure 10-16 • It's hard to make a mistake when the backorder preference is in your face.**

**Note** *A pending invoice does not post any amounts to the general ledger.*

Later, when the backordered products arrive and have been entered into inventory, you can release the pending status:

1. Choose Reports | Sales | Pending Sales.
2. When the list of pending sales appears, double-click the listing for the sale you want to finalize. The original invoice (still marked "Pending") is displayed on your screen.
3. Choose Edit | Mark Invoice As Final from the QuickBooks menu bar.

4. Click Save & Close to save the invoice.
5. Pick it, pack it, and ship it.

The point of going through this work is to reinforce the notion that the better you satisfy your customers, the more money you'll make.

Another important lesson in this chapter is that even though QuickBooks doesn't inherently support a feature you want to use, once you understand the software you can frequently manipulate it to do what you need.

# Making Checkbook Adjustments

## In this Chapter:

- *Make deposits*

- *Transfer funds between accounts*

- *Deal with bounced checks*

- *Void disbursements*

- *Track ATM transactions*

- *Understand petty cash*

- *Balance credit card statements*

Before you started using accounting software, did your checkbook register have entries crossed out? Pencil notes next to inked-in entries? Inked notes next to penciled-in entries? Transactions that were made in April entered in the middle of a string of June transactions ("The statement came—I forgot about that transaction")? Lots of corrections for math errors?

If so, don't relax; the only thing QuickBooks can take care of for you is the last problem—the math errors. Computers don't make math mistakes. Even with QuickBooks, you still have to enter your transactions. The advantage is that most of your transactions (your customer payments and the checks you write) are entered for you automatically.

# Making a Deposit

Even though QuickBooks automatically enters deposits into your bank account when you record customer payments, there are times when you receive money that's unconnected to a customer payment.

Entering a deposit (one that's not a customer payment) into your QuickBooks check register isn't much different than entering a deposit into a manual checkbook register. Actually, it's easier because you don't have to make any calculations— QuickBooks takes care of that.

Click the Reg (it stands for check register) button on the icon bar and choose the bank account you want to work with. Fill in the date, and then click in the deposit column to enter the amount (see Figure 11-1). Assign the deposit to an account. You should use the memo field for an explanation, because your accountant will probably ask you about the deposit later (and sometimes create a journal entry to re-assign the amount). Click the Record button. That's it!

You can, if you wish, enter a payee name in the Payee column, but QuickBooks doesn't require that. If the payee doesn't exist in any of your name lists, after you enter the name QuickBooks displays a Name Not Found message offering you the following selections:

- Quick Add, which lets you enter a name without any additional information
- Set Up, which lets you create a new name using the regular Create Name window
- Cancel, which returns you to the account register so you can either choose another name or delete the Payee entry

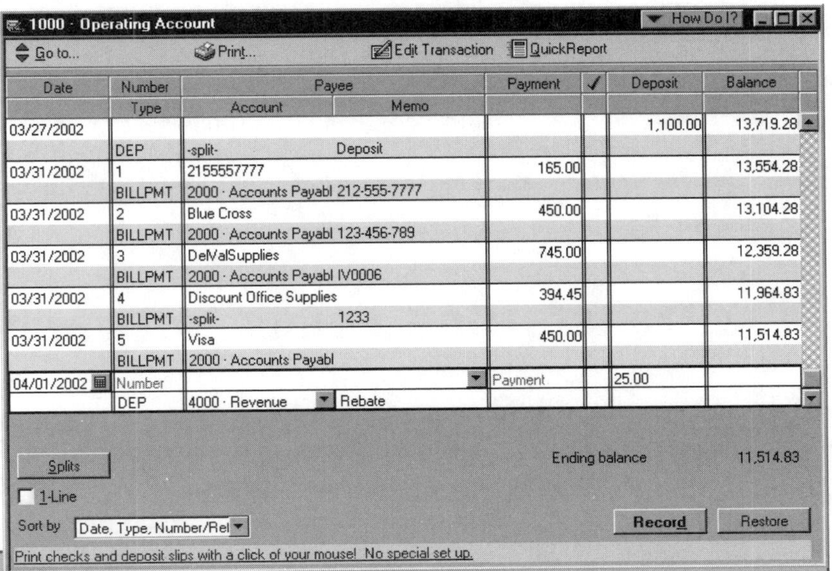

**Figure 11-1 • The simplest way to record a deposit is to use only the required fields: date, amount, and posting account.**

If you select Quick Add or Set Up, you'll be asked which type of Name you're adding: Vendor Customer, Employee, or Other. Unless this payee will become a Vendor or Customer (I think we can eliminate Employee from this procedure), choose Other.

Usually the account you assign is an income account, because you're receiving revenue even though it may not be from an actual sale to a customer. You can use a miscellaneous revenue account or create a revenue account specifically for this type of income. However, if you're making a deposit that's a refund from a vendor, you can post the amount to the expense account that was used for the original expense.

If you're depositing your own money into the business, that's capital; in this case, you should use the capital account (it's an equity account) or establish a liability account if you're making a loan to your company.

When in doubt, post the amount to the most logical place and call your accountant. You can always edit the transaction later or make a journal entry to post the amount to the right account.

> **Tip** *It's a good idea to set up accounts for transactions that you're unsure how to post. I have two such accounts. For income about which I want to ask my accountant, I use account #9998, titled MysteryIncome. Account #9999 is titled MysteryExpense. If the account has a balance, it means I should call my accountant and find out where to post the income or expense I temporarily "parked" in that account. I can use a journal entry, or edit the transaction, to put the money into the right account.*

# Transferring Funds Between Accounts

Moving money between bank accounts is a common procedure in business. If you have a bank account for payroll, you have to move money out of your operating account into your payroll account every payday. Some people deposit all the customer payments into a money market account and then transfer the necessary funds to an operating account when it's time to pay bills. Law firms deposit some funds into an escrow account and then transfer the portion that belongs to them into the operating account. The rest of the escrow deposit goes to the client.

The difference between a regular deposit and a transfer isn't clear if you think about the end result as being nothing more than "money was disbursed from one account and deposited into another account." However, that's not the way to think about it. When you work with accounting issues, every action has an effect on your general ledger, which means there's an effect on your financial reporting (and your taxes). A transfer isn't a disbursement (which is an expense that's assigned to a specific account), and it isn't a regular deposit (income received). A transfer has no effect on your profit and loss.

> **Tip** *If you don't use the transfer protocol, you run the risk of posting a deductible expense or taxable income to your profit and loss reports.*

To make a transfer, follow these steps:

1. Choose Banking | Transfer Funds from the menu bar.
2. Fill out the fields (see Figure 11-2).
3. Click Save & Close (or Save & New if you have another transfer to make).

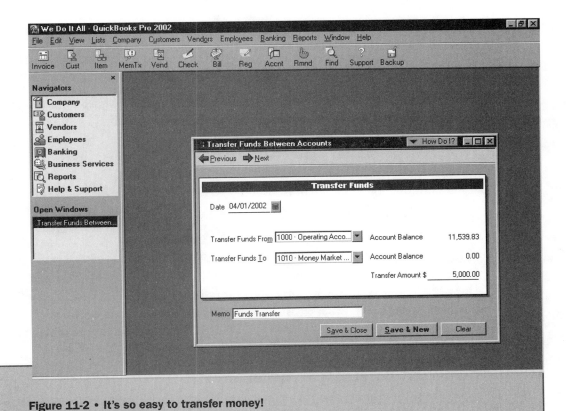

**Figure 11-2 • It's so easy to transfer money!**

QuickBooks posts the transaction (you'll see it marked as TRANSFR in both bank accounts if you open their registers) without affecting any totals in your financial reports. All the work is done on the balance sheet, but the bottom line of your balance sheet doesn't change.

| Account | Debit | Credit |
|---|---|---|
| Sending Bank Account | | Amount of Transfer |
| Receiving Bank Account | Amount of Transfer | |

**Tip**    *In order to facilitate a transfer of funds, you really should have both of the accounts set up in your QuickBooks system. Although you can create accounts during the transfer procedure, it's always quicker and easier to have everything set up in advance.*

# Handling Bounced Checks

Customer checks sometimes bounce. When that happens, you have several tasks in front of you:

- Deduct the amount of the bounced check from your checking account
- Record any bank charges you incurred as a result of the bounced check
- Remove the payment applied to the customer invoice (if it wasn't a cash sale)
- Recover the money from the customer

In addition, you might want to collect a service charge from the customer (at least for the amount of any charges your own bank assessed).

## Adjusting the Account Balances

You must remove the amount of the bounced check from your bank account, and also adjust the Accounts Receivable account if the bounced check was an invoice payment. If the check was a payment for a cash sale, nothing was posted to Accounts Receivable; however, you must adjust the income account to which you posted the cash sale.

### Using the Bank Account Register

If you deposited the check directly into the bank instead of using the Undeposited Funds account, and the deposit was an invoice payment, its listing has a type of PMT. You must delete the payment (there's no Void option for payments), by pressing CTRL-D or by choosing Edit | Delete Payment from the QuickBooks menu bar. QuickBooks displays a message telling you that the payment was used to pay an invoice and that deleting it will result in unpaid balances (which is exactly what should happen). Click OK, and the invoice that was paid returns to its balance due before the payment. The Accounts Receivable account is also adjusted. The invoice will show up as unpaid the next time you send a statement to the customer, and you should also invoice the customer for any bounced check charges you incurred, and for any service charge you want to charge the customer (see "Invoicing Customers for Bounced Checks" later in this section).

If you used the Undeposited Funds account, you can create a journal entry to remove the amount paid from the customer's balance. Then you must re-invoice the customer (see "Invoicing Customers for Bounced Checks" later in this section).

### Using a Journal Entry

You can create a journal entry to adjust the amounts. Choose Banking | Make Journal Entry to open the General Journal Entry window. Then take these steps:

1. Click the Account column, then click the arrow and select the bank into which you deposited the payment.
2. Press TAB twice to move to the Credit column, and enter the amount of the bounced check.
3. Press TAB to move to the Memo column to write yourself a note (e.g., Smith Ck #2345 bounced).
4. Click in the Account column and choose the Accounts Receivable account. QuickBooks automatically fills in the amount in the Debit column.
5. Click in the Name column and select the customer whose check bounced.
6. Click Save & Close.

## Recording Bank Charges for Bounced Checks

If your bank charged you for a returned check, you have to enter the bank charge. To do so, start by opening the register for your bank account. Then fill out the fields, pressing the TAB key to move from one field to the next:

1. Click the Date field in the blank line at the bottom of the register and enter the date that the bank charge was assessed.
2. In the Number field, QuickBooks automatically fills in the next available check number. Delete that number and press TAB. QuickBooks fills in the word "Number."
3. Leave the Payee field blank.
4. In the Payment field, enter the amount of the service charge for the returned check.
5. In the Account field, assign this transaction to the account you use for bank charges.
6. Click the Record button in the register window to save the transaction.

Your bank account balance is reduced by the amount of the service charge. You should charge the customer for this, and in the following sections I'll cover the steps needed to accomplish that.

## Invoicing Customers for Bounced Checks

In order to re-invoice your customers after a check bounces, you must create items for bounced checks and for any service charges. Then you can use those items in the invoice.

### Creating an Item for a Bounced Check Replacement

You have to re-invoice the customer for the bounced check. To do that, you need an item for bounced checks:

1. Click the Item icon on the icon bar to open the Item List window.
2. Press CTRL-N to enter a new item.
3. Select Other Charge as the item type.
4. Name the item appropriately (for instance, "Returned Check").
5. Enter an optional description.
6. Leave the amount blank (you will fill it in when you create the invoice).
7. Clear the Taxable check box.
8. Link the item to your sales income account.

The reason you link the item to the sales income account is to replace the income that was removed when you voided the deposited check. After all, the customer still has the product or service you sold. If you have multiple income accounts, create a new, general income account for this item (call it "Bounced Checks" if you wish). Later, you can do a journal entry to move the income from the general account to the specific account that was used at the time of the cash sale.

### Creating an Item for Customer Service Charges

To create an item for invoicing customers for service charges, follow these steps:

1. Click the Item icon on the icon bar to open the Item List window.
2. Press CTRL-N to enter a new item.
3. Select Other Charge as the item type.
4. Name the item appropriately (for instance, "RetChkChg").
5. Enter a description (for example, Service charge for returned check).
6. Leave the amount blank (you will fill it in when you create the invoice).

7.  Clear the Taxable check box.

8.  Link the item to an income account, such as to Other Income or to an account you create for situations like this (perhaps "Customer Service Charges").

## Creating the Invoice

Now you need to send an invoice to the customer for the bounced check.

> **Tip**    *You might want to select the Service Invoice—which I find is easier and "cleaner" for this type of invoice—from the Custom Template box.*

1.  Click the Invoice icon on the icon bar.

2.  When the Create Invoices window opens, enter the name of the customer who gave you the bad check.

3.  Enter the date on which the check bounced.

4.  Click in the Item column and select the item you created for returned checks.

5.  Enter the amount of the returned check.

6.  Add another line item for the service charge you incurred for the bounced check, using the item you created for service charges.

7.  Click Print so you can send the invoice to the customer, and then click Save & Close to save the invoice.

# Voiding Disbursements

Sometimes you have to void a check that you've written. Perhaps you decided not to send it for some reason, or perhaps it was lost in the mail. Whatever the reason, if a check isn't going to clear your bank, you should void it.

The process of voiding a check is quite easy, and the only trouble you can cause yourself is *deleting* the check instead of *voiding* it. Deleting a check removes all history of the transaction, and the check number disappears into la-la land. This is not a good way to keep financial records. Voiding a check keeps the check number, but sets the amount to zero.

To void a check, open the bank account register and click anywhere on the check's transaction line. Right-click to see the shortcut menu and choose Void Check. The corresponding entry in the expense account (or multiple expense accounts) to which the check was written is also adjusted.

# Tracking Petty Cash Transactions

Aren't those ATM gadgets wonderful? They're everywhere, even at the supermarket checkout! It's so easy to take cash out of your bank account.

And it's so easy to forget to enter the transaction in your account register. You must create a system for yourself that ensures your ATM withdrawals are accounted for. Having said that, I'll move on to the accounting procedures involved with ATM transactions, because QuickBooks cannot help you remember to enter transactions.

**Tip** *I have one of those consoles with a flip-up lid between the front seats of my car, and the only use I ever make of it is as a receipts container. I keep ATM, gas station, credit card, and bank deposit receipts in it. Every so often I bring everything in the console into the office and enter the ATM amounts. (I get a monthly bill for the gas I put into my car and the credit card bills, and I only save the receipts because my accountant insists on it.) Then I put all the receipts into a large manila envelope. If I need to check anything when a bill comes in, I look in the envelope. At the end of the year, the envelope is filed away with my copy of my tax returns. I'm ready if they audit me!*

When you withdraw cash from an ATM machine, there's an assumption that you need the cash for a business expense. (Don't withdraw cash from a business bank account for personal spending.) In effect, you're taking a petty cash advance, and you have to account for it. That means you have to account for the portion of it you spend, and the portion that's still in your pocket. The way to track expenses for which you've taken money in advance is to use a petty cash account. You can also use these procedures for "real" petty cash, which means you actually carry cash around. That cash belongs to the business, and you must account for it.

## Creating a Petty Cash Account

If you spend cash for business expenses, your chart of accounts should have a petty cash account. This account functions like a cash till: You put money in it, then you account for the money that's spent, leaving the rest in the till until it, too, is spent. Then you put more money into the till. The petty cash account doesn't represent a real bank account; it just represents that portion of the money in the real bank account that you've put into the till.

If you don't have a petty cash account in your chart of accounts, create one:

1. Click the Accnt icon on the icon bar to open the Chart of Accounts window.
2. When the Chart of Accounts window appears, press CTRL-N to open a blank New Account window.
3. Fill in the account information using the following guidelines:
   - The Account Type is Bank.
   - If you number your accounts, use a number that places your new petty cash account near the other (real) bank accounts in your chart of accounts.
   - Leave the opening balance at zero.

Now that you have the petty cash account, you can use it to track your ATM withdrawals. You can use the same technique for money you take from the petty cash drawer (the till).

## Putting Money into Petty Cash

When you withdraw money from your bank account with your ATM card, it's not an expense; it's just cash. You've put cash into a till (literally, the till is your pocket, but to your accounting system it's a petty cash container). It becomes an expense when you spend it (remember to get a receipt so you can enter the expense into your system).

Bring the ATM receipt and receipts for the stuff you purchased with the ATM cash back to the office. In QuickBooks, perform the procedures necessary to track the cash you spent and the cash you didn't spend.

The first thing you have to do is take the cash out of your QuickBooks bank account, because you stood in front of an ATM dispenser and took cash out of your actual bank account. However, this is double-entry bookkeeping, and there has to be an equal and opposite posting to another account. That's what the petty cash account is for.

1. Choose Banking | Transfer Funds from the menu bar.
2. In the Transfer Funds Between Accounts window, fill out the information needed, which is just the two accounts and the amount. Then click Save & Close.

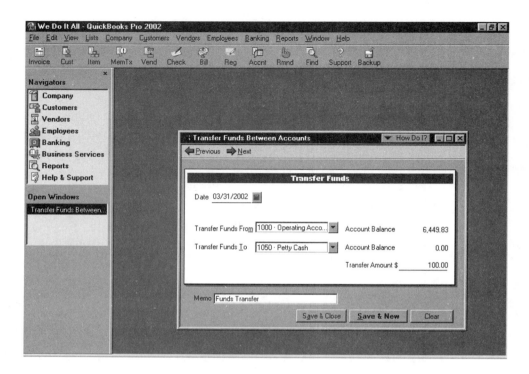

The money in your petty cash account is the same as the money in your pocket, and you're responsible for it. As you spend it, you must account for it, which is covered next.

# Entering the Cash Disbursements

As you spend the money you withdraw via an ATM transaction or by taking cash out of the petty cash box in the office, you must record those expenditures in the petty cash account. There are a couple of valid methods for accomplishing this, all of which start with opening the petty cash account register.

When you open the petty cash account register, the next available transaction line is highlighted automatically. Now you can enter the amount of cash you actually spent, using either of the methods described here:

- Enter each individual cash transaction you make.
- Enter one large transaction, splitting the transaction among all the appropriate expense accounts.

To enter each transaction separately, you can invent a payee named "PettyCash" (use the Other Name type) for each transaction, or enter a real payee for each transaction ("Joe's Hardware Store," "Mary's Office Supplies," and so on). Quick-Books uses automatic numbering, thinking each entry is a check. It's OK to let those numbers stand (you never reconcile this account with a bank statement). Enter the appropriate expense account for each transaction.

If you want to enter one transaction and split it among multiple expense accounts, use the payee named PettyCash. After you enter the amount and move to the Account field, click the Splits button in the register window. This opens a Splits window in the account register (see Figure 11-3).

Enter the accounts to which your expenditures should be posted. When you finish entering accounts for the split transaction, click Record.

If you spent less than the amount of cash you withdrew from the till, the balance stays in the petty cash account. You'll probably spend it later, and so you will repeat this task to account for that spending.

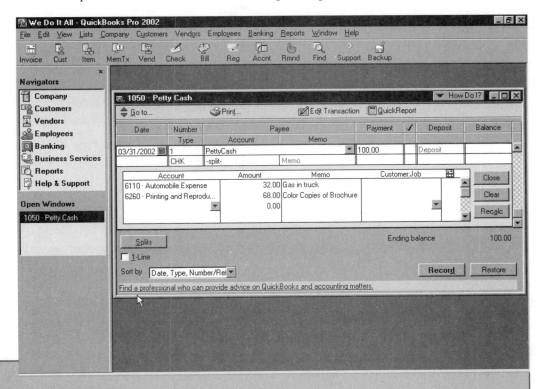

**Figure 11-3 • It's faster to account for all the petty cash you spent in one split transaction.**

## Tracking Petty Cash

Sally and Sarah are partners in a consulting firm. They have one employee, a salesperson named Susan. There's a constant need for petty cash as all three of them pursue their work: parking fees, tolls, cab fare, and so on.

They established a petty cash system that makes each person accountable for the money she receives and also automatically replenishes the cash as it's spent. Here's what they did to start this system:

- They established a separate petty cash account in the chart of accounts for each person.
- They wrote three checks to cash ($100.00 each), posting each check to an individual petty cash account.

Each woman cashed her check. During the course of each day, that money is spent and receipts are saved. (This means everyone has to remember to ask for a receipt, because the policy is "no receipt, no cash.")

Every week, usually on Friday, each woman fills out an expense account form. (Sarah created it in a word processor and printed a whole bunch of copies.) Each type of expense is listed and subtotaled. Receipts are attached to the form. Then the following tasks are completed:

- A check is written (the payee is Cash) to each person for the total amount on the expense account form. This means each woman is now back at $100.00 because the check amount is the difference between the original $100.00 and the expenditures.
- Sally opens the petty cash account registers and records the information from the expense account forms, assigning the correct expense accounts to each subtotal.
- The forms, with the attached receipts, are filed in case they're ever needed (such as for an IRS audit).

This is a terrific, efficient system, and Sally and Sarah have made their accountant very happy.

# Managing Your Credit Cards

When you use a business credit card, you have a number of choices for tracking and paying the credit card bill. First, you can either pay the entire bill every month, or pay part of the bill and keep a running credit card balance. Second, you can choose between two methods of handling credit card purchases in QuickBooks: Treat the credit card bill as an ordinary vendor and deal with the bill when it arrives, or treat the credit card bill as a liability and track each transaction as it's made instead of waiting for the bill.

## Treating Credit Cards as Vendors

You can set up the credit card as an ordinary vendor and enter the bill into QuickBooks when it arrives. Most of the time, the expenses are posted to multiple accounts, so the credit card bill transaction is a split transaction (see Figure 11-4).

If you don't pay off the card balance, be sure to enter the current interest charges so your current balance is accurate. (The running balance is already included in your Accounts Payable balance.)

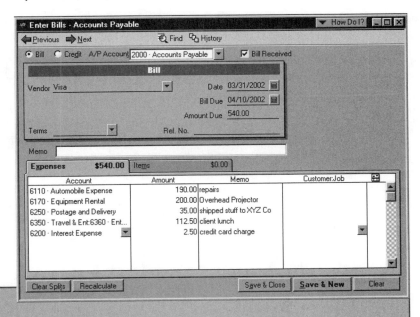

**Figure 11-4 • Credit cards bills are usually split transactions.**

When you pay the credit card bill, you can enter the amount you want to pay against each bill in the system. Always start with the oldest bill, making a partial payment or paying it in full. Then move to the next oldest bill, making a partial payment or paying it in full.

> **Tip** *If you always pay your credit card bill in full, you can use a direct disbursement (write a check) instead of entering the bill and then paying it.*

## Treating Credit Cards as Liability Accounts

You can also treat credit cards as liability accounts, tracking each transaction against the account as it occurs. Then when the bill arrives, you match the transactions against the bill and decide how much to pay. Your running balance is tracked specifically against the credit card, instead of being part of your Accounts Payable balance.

### Creating a Credit Card Account

To use credit cards in this manner, you must have an account for each credit card in your chart of accounts. If you don't have such an account as a result of the EasyStep Interview, you can create one now, using an account type of Credit Card. Check out Chapter 2 for information about adding items to your chart of accounts.

> **Caution** *QuickBooks arranges the chart of accounts by account types. If you're using numbers for your accounts, the numbering is ignored in favor of account types. To make sure your credit card account is displayed in the right order, use a number that fits in with current liabilities (credit card accounts come right after accounts payable accounts).*

### Entering Charges on the Credit Card Account

If you want to track your credit card charges as they're assumed, instead of waiting for the bill, you have to treat your credit card transactions like ATM transactions—enter them as you go. QuickBooks has a built-in feature to help you accomplish this.

Choose Banking | Enter Credit Card Charges from the QuickBooks menu bar to open the Enter Credit Card Charges window seen in Figure 11-5.

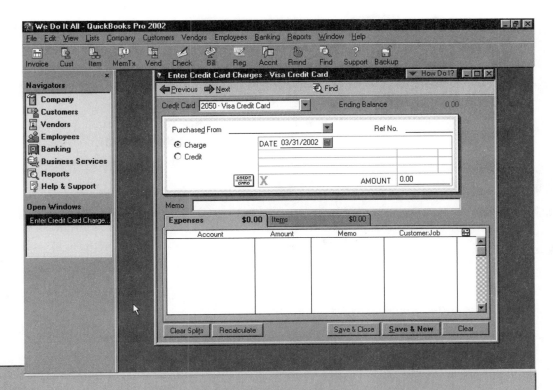

**Figure 11-5** • You can enter individual credit card transactions as you make them.

Select the appropriate credit card account and then use the store receipt as a reference document to fill in the transaction. Here are some guidelines for making this transaction easy and quick to complete:

- In the Purchased From field, enter a generic vendor. Create a vendor called "CredCard" or something similar. Then use the Memo field for each transaction to note the name of the real vendor, if that information is important to you. If you use a real, individual vendor name in the Purchased from field, each time you use your credit card at a new vendor, QuickBooks will force you to add the vendor to your vendor list. You'll end up with a gazillion vendors with whom you don't have a real vendor relationship (they don't send you bills), and you won't be able to delete them from your QuickBooks file because they have transactions.

- If the transaction is a return, be sure to select the Credit option at the top of the window.
- Enter the receipt number in the Ref No. field.
- Enter the date of the purchase (frequently earlier than the date you're entering the transaction).
- Use the Expenses tab for general expenses; use the Items tab if you used the credit card to buy inventory items (items you sell to customers).
- If you use the credit card for an expense or an item for a customer, enter the customer information so you can bill the customer for reimbursement (see Chapter 6 for details about entering reimbursable expenses).

Click Save & Next to save the record and move to another blank credit card entry window to enter the next receipt, or click Save & Close if you're finished entering credit card charges.

**Tip** *You can also enter these charges directly in the register of your credit card account. (Some people find it faster to work in the register.)*

## Reconciling the Credit Card Bill

Eventually, the credit card bill arrives, and you have to perform the following chores:

- Reconcile the bill against the entries you recorded.
- Decide whether to pay the entire bill or just a portion of it.
- Write a check.

Choose Banking | Reconcile from the QuickBooks menu bar to open the Reconcile window. In the Account to Reconcile field, select the credit card from the drop-down list. In the Begin Reconciliation dialog box (see Figure 11-6), enter the appropriate data.

- Enter the ending balance from the credit card bill.
- Enter any finance charges on the bill in the Finance Charges box, along with the date on which the charges were assessed. Enter the account you use to post finance charges (or create one if you don't have one—it's an expense).

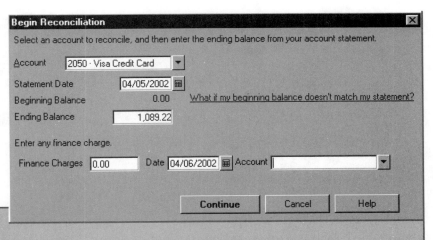

**Figure 11-6 • Specify the dates and charges, using the information in the bill.**

**Note**   *The first time you do this, there won't be an opening balance for this credit card. If you don't pay the entire bill, you'll see an opening balance the next time you use this window.*

Click Continue to open the Reconcile Credit Card window, which displays the purchases you entered, as shown in Figure 11-7.

Click the check mark column for each transaction on your window that has a matching transaction on the credit card bill (make sure the amounts match, too). That includes payments, credits, and charges.

**Note**   *The first time you use the Reconcile Credit Card window, your payments to the credit card won't appear.*

Add any transactions you forgot to enter by opening the credit card register (click the Accnt icon on the QuickBooks toolbar) and entering the transactions. (To find the receipts, search your pockets, desk, pocketbook, the floor of your car, and the kitchen junk drawer.) When you return to the Reconcile Credit Card window, the new transactions are added and you can check them off.

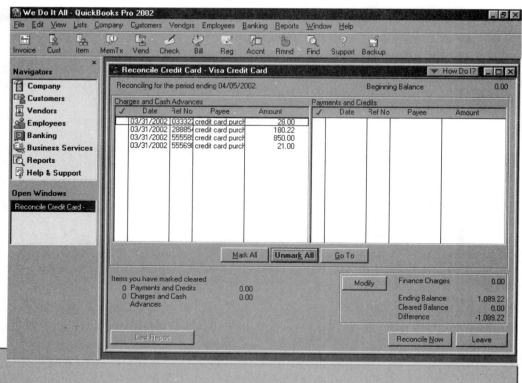

**Figure 11-7 •** Check the bill against the transactions you entered.

**Tip** *Finance charges for businesses are tax deductible; the finance charges you incur in your personal financial dealings aren't.*

Now look at the box at the bottom of the window where the totals are displayed. If the difference is $0.00, congratulations! Everything's fine. Click Reconcile Now (QuickBooks offers a congratulatory message). If the difference is not $0.00, you have to figure out the problem and make corrections.

## Finding the Problem

If your account doesn't balance, try these procedures to find a solution:

- Count the number of transactions on the bill and make sure the same number of transactions appear in your window. Don't forget that the finance charge entry at the bottom of the window is a transaction on the bill.

- Check the numbers again, making sure that the amount you originally entered for each transaction matches the amount on the bill. If the difference is divisible by 9, it's quite possible you transposed a number when you entered the transaction in the register.

Usually one of these problems is the culprit. If this is the case, make the appropriate corrections:

- Click the Modify button at the bottom of the window to return to the Modify Reconciliation window if you entered the ending balance or finance charge incorrectly.
- Right-click a transaction with an incorrect amount and choose Edit Transaction from the shortcut menu. Correct the data in the Amount field and click Save & Close. Answer Yes when QuickBooks asks if you want to record the changes.

## Deferring the Problem

If you can't figure it out, and you just don't have time to work on it now, click Leave. QuickBooks will keep the transaction information you've entered thus far (but not the ending balance or finance charge you entered), and it will be waiting for you when you return to finish reconciling the account.

## Adjusting the Difference

If there's a difference you just cannot resolve, and you want to finalize the reconciliation, you can make an adjusting entry. Then later, if you find the transaction that caused the problem, you can delete the adjusting entry and record the correct transaction. To accomplish this, click Reconcile Now even though the difference isn't $0.00. QuickBooks displays this Reconcile Adjustment window.

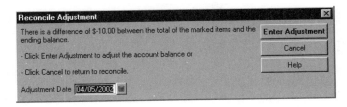

Click OK to let QuickBooks create an adjustment entry. Later, if you figure out what the problem was, open the credit card account register and remove the adjusting entry. Replace it with a real entry that solves the problem.

## Paying the Credit Card Bill

When you click Reconcile Now in the Reconcile Credit Card window (or accept an adjusting entry), QuickBooks moves on to pay the bill by asking you whether you want to write a check now or create a vendor bill that you'll pay the next time you pay your bills.

Select the appropriate response and complete the transaction window. If you don't want to pay the entire bill, change the amount. The unpaid amount will appear as an opening balance the next time you reconcile the account.

**Tip**    *All the detailed information you need to create vendor bills is covered in Chapter 6, and everything about writing checks is in Chapter 7.*

# Reconciling Bank Accounts

## In this Chapter:

- *Enter data from your bank statement*

- *Clear transactions*

- *Reconcile the differences*

- *Make adjustments*

Reconciling bank accounts is fancy terminology for "I have to balance my checkbook," which is one of the most annoying tasks connected with financial record keeping.

> **Note** *The first time you reconcile your bank accounts in QuickBooks, you'll find there's a bit more work involved than in subsequent reconciliations.*

# Entering Data from the Statement

After your bank statement arrives, you must find some uninterrupted moments to compare it to the information in the QuickBooks account register.

If your bank sends your canceled checks in the envelope along with the statement (some banks don't include the physical checks), you can arrange the checks in numerical order before you start this task. However, instead of sorting and collating the physical checks, it's much easier to use the list of check numbers on your statement. They appear in numerical order. An asterisk or some other mark usually appears to indicate a missing number (usually a check that hasn't cleared yet, a check that cleared previously, or perhaps a voided check).

## Beginning the Reconciliation

To start, choose Banking | Reconcile to open the Begin Reconciliation dialog box. This is the place to enter the ending balance, and also enter any bank charges or interest earnings.

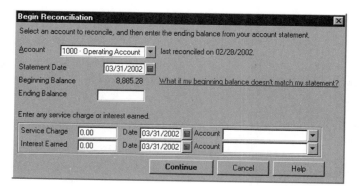

Check the Beginning Balance field in your window against the opening balance on the bank statement. (Your bank may call it the *starting balance*.) If this is the first time you've reconciled this account in QuickBooks, a difference probably exists. You cannot change this figure in the Begin Reconciliation dialog box. See the suggestions that follow if this is the first reconciliation you're performing.

Enter the ending balance from your statement in the Ending Balance field. Also enter the statement date.

## Resolving First-Time Balance Problems

The reason the beginning balance doesn't match the first time is that your QuickBooks beginning balance includes the initial entry you made for this bank account during setup (if you made one). The number may have been derived from an opening trial balance, the account balance on the day you started your QuickBooks setup, or any other scheme you used to get started in QuickBooks. The bank is using a running total that began way back when, starting when you first opened that bank account. The only QuickBooks users who have it easy are those who opened their bank accounts the same day they started to use QuickBooks. (A minuscule number of people, if any, fit that description.)

If you entered a beginning balance for your checking account during the QuickBooks setup procedure (which put an offsetting entry into your equity account), the opening bank balance probably doesn't match the statement's opening balance. In fact, one big difference is probably the date—your opening balance date is not the same as the opening balance date on the statement (which is a date within the past month).

You cannot change the opening balance directly in the Reconcile window. However, you can change the opening balance in your account register, or you can let QuickBooks create an adjustment to reconcile the difference during the reconciliation process.

Personally, I prefer the latter choice—it's much less confusing to your accountant. But since it is possible to change the opening balance, I'll explain how.

To change the opening balance to match the bank statement, move to the account register and find that first transaction entry. Change the amount to match the opening balance and change the date to match the statement date. Write yourself a note so you can give your accountant a coherent explanation, because your equity account will have to be recalculated at the end of the year.

Information on how to tell QuickBooks to make an automatic adjusting entry to account for the difference is found later in this chapter, in the section "Reconciling the Difference."

# Entering Interest and Service Charges

Your statement shows any interest and bank service charges if either or both are applicable to your account. Enter those numbers in the appropriate fields in the Begin Reconciliation window and make sure the appropriate account is linked.

By "bank charges," I mean the standard charges banks assess, such as monthly charges (sometimes assessed for failure to maintain a minimum balance). Bank charges do not include special charges for bounced checks (yours or your customers'), nor any purchases you made that are charged to your account (e.g., purchase of checks or deposit slips). Those should be entered as discrete transactions, making them easier to find in case you have to talk to the bank about your account.

# Clearing Transactions

After you've filled out the information in the Begin Reconciliation dialog box, click Continue to open the Reconcile window, shown in Figure 12-1.

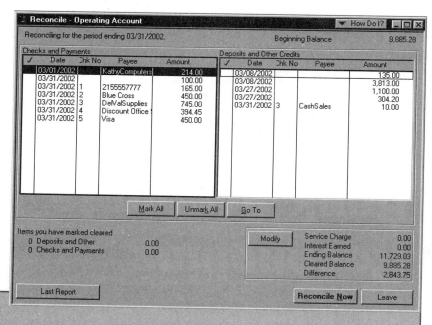

**Figure 12-1 •** All the transactions in your bank register that haven't yet been cleared by reconciling the account are displayed.

Now you must tell QuickBooks which transactions have cleared. All the transactions that are on your bank statement are cleared transactions. If the transactions are not listed on the statement, they have not cleared.

**Note**   *The only transactions displayed in the Reconcile window are those that have not yet cleared. Any transactions you've cleared in previous months are permanently cleared—they won't appear in the window. This makes it easier to work with this window.*

Click each transaction that cleared. A check mark appears in the left-most column to indicate that the transaction has cleared the bank. If you clear a transaction in error, click again to remove the check mark—it's a toggle.

**Tip**   *If all, or almost all, of the transactions have cleared, click Mark All. Then deselect the transactions that didn't clear. This is easier that marking a great many transactions one at a time.*

As you check each cleared transaction, the Difference amount in the lower-right corner of the Reconcile window changes. The goal is to get that figure to 0.00.

## Adding Transactions During Reconciliation

While you're working in the Reconcile window, if you find a transaction on the statement that you haven't entered into your QuickBooks software (probably one of those ATM transactions you forgot to enter), you don't have to shut down the reconciliation process to remedy the situation. You can just enter the transaction into your register.

To open the bank account register, right-click anywhere in the Reconcile window and choose Use Register from the shortcut menu. When the bank register opens, record the transaction. Return to the Reconcile window, where that transaction is now listed. Pretty nifty! Check it off as cleared, of course, because it was on the statement.

You can switch between the Reconcile window and the register for the account you're reconciling by clicking on the windows. (Ah, the wonders of multitasking.) Use the Open Windows list on the Navigators list to move between them.

**Tip**   *I automatically open the register of the account I'm reconciling as soon as I start the reconciliation process. In addition to making it easier to enter those transactions I missed, it's a quick way to look at details when I see a transaction that puzzles me ("Why did I write a check to Joe Fool?").*

## Deleting Transactions During Reconciliation

Sometimes you find that a transaction that was transferred from your account register to this Reconcile window shouldn't be there. The most common occurrence of this is an ATM withdrawal that you entered twice. Or perhaps you forgot that you'd entered a deposit, and a couple of days later you entered it again. Whatever the reason, there are occasionally transactions that should be deleted.

To delete a transaction, move to the account register and select that transaction. Press CTRL-D to delete it. When you return to the Reconcile window, the transaction is gone.

## Editing Transactions During Reconciliation

Sometimes you'll want to change some of the information in a transaction. For example, when you see the real check, you realize you'd made it out to Sam Smith, but your account register says Stan Smith. Or perhaps the amount on the check is wrong. You might even have the wrong date on a check. (These things only happen, of course, if you write checks manually.)

Whatever the problem, you can correct it by editing the transaction. Double-click the transaction's listing in the Reconcile window to open the original transaction window. Record the necessary changes, which are reflected when you return to the Reconcile window.

# Reconciling the Difference

If this isn't the first reconciliation you're performing, there's a good chance that that Difference figure at the bottom of the Reconcile window is at 0.00. If this is the first reconciliation, and you changed the opening balance in the account register (as explained earlier in this chapter), you probably have no difference showing.

If that's true, you've finished this part of the reconciliation. Click Reconcile Now and read the section "Printing the Reconciliation Report" later in this chapter. If Difference shows an amount other than 0.00, read the next section.

## Pausing the Reconciliation Process

If there are differences and you don't have the time, energy, or emotional fortitude to track them down at the moment, you can stop the reconciliation process without losing all the transactions you checked against the bank statement and cleared.

Click the Leave button in the Reconcile window and do something else for a while. Go home and have dinner, play with the cat, help the kids with homework, whatever. When you return and bring up the Reconcile window again, you'll have to re-enter the amounts in the Ending Balance field, as well as the Service Charge And Interest Earned fields. Everything else will be exactly the way you left it.

# Finding and Correcting Problems

When you're ready to investigate the cause of a difference between the ending balance and the cleared balance, here are some guidelines for finding the problems:

- Count the number of transactions on the statement and make sure the same number of transactions are cleared in your Reconcile window. (Look in the lower-left corner of the window—the number of items you have marked cleared is displayed.) If the numbers differ, the problem is in your QuickBooks records; there's a transaction you should have cleared but didn't, or a transaction you cleared that you shouldn't have.
- Check the amount of each transaction against the amount in the bank statement.
- Check your transactions and make sure a deposit wasn't inadvertently entered as a payment (or vice versa). A clue for this is a transaction that's half the difference. If the difference is $220.00, find a transaction that has an amount of $110.00 and make sure it's a deduction if it's supposed to be a deduction.
- Check for transposed figures. Perhaps you entered a figure incorrectly in the register, such as $549.00 when the bank clears the transaction as $594.00. A clue that a transposed number is the problem is that the reconciliation difference can be divided by nine.

If you find the problem, correct it. When the Difference figure is 0.00, click Reconcile Now.

**Tip** *You might want to let somebody else check over the statement and the register, because sometimes you don't see your own mistakes.*

## Permitting an Adjusting Entry

If you cannot find the problem, you can tell QuickBooks to make an adjusting entry to force the reconciliation to balance. The adjusting entry is placed in the register, and if you ever do figure out what the problem is, you can make the proper adjustment transaction and delete the adjusting entry.

To have QuickBooks create an adjusting entry, click Reconcile Now even though there's a difference. A message appears similar to the one shown in the following illustration. Click Enter Adjustment to permit the adjusting entry.

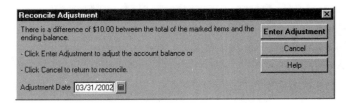

**Note** *Back in your account register, all the cleared transactions are distinguished by a check mark in the column that has a check mark in the column heading.*

# Printing the Reconciliation Report

When you have a balanced Reconcile window, QuickBooks offers congratulations and offers to print a reconciliation report. Click Cancel if you don't want a report.

## Deciding on the Type of Report

QuickBooks offers two reconciliation report types: Detail and Summary. Here are the differences between them:

- The Detail Report shows all the transactions that are cleared (cleared transactions), and all the transactions that haven't cleared ("in transit" transactions) as of the statement closing date. Any transactions dated after the statement closing date are listed as being "new transactions."
- The Summary Report breaks down your transactions in the same way, but it doesn't list the individual transactions; it shows only the totals for each category (Cleared, In Transit, and New).

Selecting the Detail Report makes it easier to resolve problems in the future. You have a list of every check and deposit, and when it cleared.

## Print vs. Display

You also have to decide whether to Print or to Display the report. Your decision should be made according to how you think you might use the report in the future. Also, you must be aware that if you're using QuickBooks Basic or QuickBooks Pro, you will never again be able to generate this report. QuickBooks does not keep a copy of the information, and it does not track when transactions clear, so you can never ask for a report that shows in which month a transaction cleared the bank.

**Note** *QuickBooks Premier versions keep copies of reconciliation reports, and you can retrieve them whenever you need them.*

## Printing a Reconciliation Report

If you opt to print the report, you have a choice between printing to a printer and printing to a file. The Print Reports dialog box offers both options, as shown in Figure 12-2.

If you send the file to the printer, you can file it for future reference. If you send the file to a disk file you can open it in the appropriate software (and also print it if you wish) any time in the future. The following file types are available in the File drop-down list:

- *ASCII text* is straight, unformatted text. The space between columns is filled in with spaces, not tab markers, so when you open the file you won't see the columns unless you use a monospaced font (such as Courier).

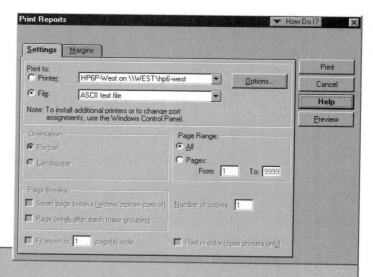

**Figure 12-2 •** Unlike the normal Print dialog box, the QuickBooks Print Reports dialog box offers a choice of disk files in addition to the physical printer.

- *Comma delimited* automatically puts a comma between each field (column entry). Select this option if you want to use the file in a spreadsheet or database program capable of importing comma-delimited files. Most spreadsheet software can handle comma-delimited files.
- *Tab delimited* is the same as comma delimited, but the field delimiter is a tab marker instead of a comma. All spreadsheet and database software can handle tab-delimited files.

## Displaying a Reconciliation Report

If you choose to display the report, you see the usual QuickBooks report format. You can modify the report to change the font, the columns, etc. In addition, if you're using QuickBooks Pro or QuickBooks Premier you can click the Excel icon at the top of the report window and automatically create a spreadsheet file. You can sort the columns (by date, by check number, by amount, etc.).

# Using Budgets

## In this Chapter:

- *Configure a budget*

- *Create different kinds of budgets*

- *Report on budgets versus actual figures*

- *Export budgets*

**Chapter 13**

A budget is a tool for tracking your progress against your plans. A well-prepared budget can also help you draw money out of your business wisely, because knowing what you plan to spend on inventory, staff, or equipment prevents you from carelessly withdrawing profits and living high on the hog whenever you have a good month.

You can prepare your budget from a variety of budget types in QuickBooks, ranging from a standard P&L (Profit & Loss) budget to a budget based on a combination of accounts, customers, and classes. The Budget window is always the same; your budget is created around the components you include in your budget design.

In this chapter, I'll discuss basic P&L budgets and Job budgets. Once you understand how to create and use either of these budgets, you can create any other kind of budget you need.

## Budgeting Income and Expenses

The most common (and useful) budget is based on your income and expenses. After you've set up a good chart of accounts, creating a budget is quite easy.

To create a P & L budget, choose Company | Set Up Budgets from the QuickBooks menu bar. A blank Set Up Budgets window appears, ready to receive your configuration options (see Figure 13-1).

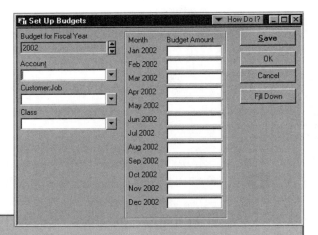

**Figure 13-1 • Budgets start in the Set Up Budgets window.**

## Entering the Budget Figures

Click the arrow to the right of the Account text box and choose the first account you want to budget. (For a P&L budget, select only income and expense accounts.) Then enter the budget amount for that account for the first month.

> **Note**   *If the first month in the Set Up Budgets window isn't the first month of your fiscal year, you didn't enter your company information properly during company setup. Choose Company | Company Information from the menu bar and change the information in the First Month In Your Fiscal Year field.*

You don't have to type the amounts for the other 11 months—you can use QuickBooks' Fill Down feature. Click the Fill Down button to see the Fill Down window.

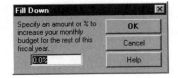

- Enter the per-month growth or reduction that you want to plan on for your chosen account. You can use an amount, such as $1,000, or a percentage.
- Type the % symbol if you want to budget by percentage.
- Use the minus sign (–) if you're working with an account in which you plan to reduce the amount.
- Leave the amount at 0 if you just want to fill in each month with the same number.

Figure 13-2 shows a company with a budgeted income from consulting services of $25,000 in the first month, and then a 4% growth per month.

> **Caution**   *It's almost impossible to predict balance sheet accounts (assets, liabilities, and equity accounts), so don't include them in your budget. In fact, predicting and planning balance sheet account figures is so complicated that it's generally only performed as part of a thesis for an MBA degree—or for a complicated study from a Wall Street mergers-and-acquisitions firm.*

The Fill Down feature works from the current month (the one you're using to enter a figure) down, so you can enter static numbers for a couple of months, and then budget in automatic changes.

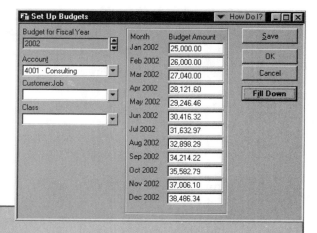

**Figure 13-2 • This company is looking for monthly measured growth of 4% over the preceding month.**

Click Save to record the budget for that account, and repeat the procedure for the next account. Click OK when you have finished entering figures for all the accounts you want to budget.

> **Tip** It's common to budget using only certain P&L accounts instead of budgeting for every income and expense account. Many people skip the accounts over which they have little or no control (for instance, rent or mortgage).

## Viewing the Budget

After you select the accounts and figures you want to use for your budget, take a look at it. Choose Reports | Budget | Profit & Loss Budget Overview. Your budget appears as a report (see Figure 13-3) in the Profit & Loss Budget Overview window.

If you use subaccounts in your budget, you can click the Collapse button in the budget window to see only the parent account totals. The button name changes to Expand after you click it.

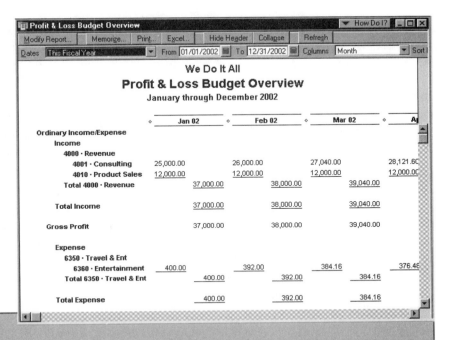

**Figure 13-3 •** Scroll through the report to see all the budget figures you created and their totals over the course of the year.

To condense the numbers, change the interval in the Columns drop-down list box. The default is Month, but you can choose another interval, and QuickBooks will calculate the figures to fit. For example, you might want to select Quarter to see four columns of three-month subtotals.

You can make changes to the budget by repeating the steps for creating it—the same budget appears, and you can change amounts or add/remove accounts.

# Comparing Your Budget with Reality

When you create a P&L budget, you can run Budget vs. Actual reports, which means you can see how your real numbers stack up compared to your budget figures. The report also displays the difference between the two.

## View the Budget vs. Actual Report

To see how close you are to meeting your budget figures, choose Reports | Budget | Profit & Loss Budget vs. Actual. When the report appears, you can scroll through it to look at the month-by-month details (see Figure 13-4).

## Customize and Memorize the Budget vs. Actual Report

The first thing you'll notice in the report is that all the accounts in your general ledger are listed, regardless of whether or not you included them in your budget. However, only the accounts you used in your budget show budget figures. You can change that by customizing the report to include only your budgeted accounts.

Click the Modify Report button at the top of the Budget report window. In the Modify Report window that opens, click the Advanced button to open the Advanced Options window. Click the option labeled Show Only Rows And Columns With Budgets.

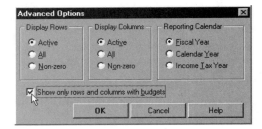

Click OK to return to the Modify Report window, and then click OK again to return to the Profit & Loss Budget vs. Actual report window. The data that's displayed is only that data connected to your budgeted accounts.

You can also use the options in the Modify Report window to make other changes:

- Change the report dates.
- Change the calculations from Accrual to Cash (which means that unpaid invoices and bills are removed from the calculations, and only actual income and expenses are reported).

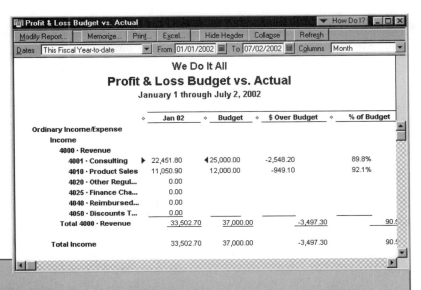

**Figure 13-4 •** Generate the Budget vs. Actual report to see how closely your real numbers match the expectations you had when you created your budget.

You should memorize the report so you don't have to make these modifications the next time you want to view a comparison report. Click the Memorize button at the top of the report window, and then give the report a meaningful name. Only the formatting changes you make are memorized, not the data. Every time you open the report, it displays current data.

Select the option to save the report to a Memorized Report Group if you want to categorize your memorized reports to make locating them easier. You can create a group for budgets by choosing Reports | Memorized Reports | Memorized Report List. Click the Memorized Report button and select New Group.

## View the Memorized Budget vs. Actual Report

To view the report after you memorized it, choose Reports | Memorized Reports from the QuickBooks menu bar. Your report name appears on the Memorized Reports submenu (or on a Group submenu if you opted to put the report in a group).

# Budgeting by Customer or Job

If you have a customer or project you want to track, create a budget for it. While it's useful to create budgets if you think there might be a problem with costs, it's equally valid to create a budget just for the information you gain. For example, if you're beginning to accept projects on which you'll have to submit a bid or an estimate, tracking the first few jobs with a budget may produce an important pattern. Perhaps you always under-budget one item or over-budget another. Use the information you gather to bid and estimate in a smarter fashion.

## Creating Specific Budgets for Customers and Jobs

You start customer and job budgets the same way you start P&L budgets: by choosing Company | Set Up Budgets from the QuickBooks menu bar. This brings up the Set Up Budgets window. Click the arrow to the right of the Customer:Job field and select either a customer or a job. Configure the budget with the following guidelines:

- To track everything (income and expenses) for this customer or job, you can skip the accounts and just enter a budget amount in each month. Part of the Budget vs. Actual report will show the net income against the net budget amount.

- To track an entire project when you don't care about the month-by-month details, enter the entire budget amount in the first month.

- To track only certain accounts for a customer or job, select the accounts and enter a monthly budget amount for each account.

When you're finished filling out the fields, click OK to save the budget.

## Creating Budgets for Multiple Customers or Jobs

QuickBooks only recognizes one Customer:Job budget. You can, however, track multiple customers and/or jobs within the same budget. The quick way to create multiple budgets for different customers is to finish the first customer's configuration and click Save instead of OK. Then, choose another customer or job and configure that one. Continue until your single budget contains budgets for all the customers and jobs you need to track. Then click OK.

## Viewing Customer and Job Budget Reports

Both the Overview and Budget vs. Actual reports that are discussed earlier for P&L budgets are available for budgets that are configured for customers and jobs. To see your budget, choose Reports | Budget | Profit & Loss Budget By Job Overview.

To see a Budget vs. Actual report, choose the Profit & Loss Budget vs. Actual by Job report. Unfortunately, this report shows you all customers, not just the customers you included in your budget. To confine the report to budgeted customers, click the Modify Report button on the report window. Then click the Advanced button on the Display tab and select Show Only Rows And Columns With Budgets.

# Deleting Budgets

You can't delete a budget. That sounds strange, but the fact is that budgets aren't files in QuickBooks—they're not discrete components of your data. Therefore, there's nothing to point to in order to choose a Delete command.

What you *can* do is remove the figures from an existing budget, which effectively destroys the budget information. In order to do that, you must know which accounts were included in your budget, so the first step is to print a budget report (use the steps described earlier in this chapter). Then follow these steps:

1. Choose Company | Set Up Budgets to open a blank Set Up Budgets window.
2. Select the first account, customer, job, or class you used in the budget you want to get rid of.
3. Select the amount in the first month and replace its contents with a zero.
4. Click the Fill Down button and copy the zero to all of the other months.
5. Repeat for each account, customer, job or class you originally used for the budget.
6. Click Save to save the changed (empty) budget.
7. Click OK.

# Copying Budgets to the Next Year

If you want to use the same budget for the next year, you can copy the budget to the next year, but this isn't a one-step procedure. In fact, you're not making a copy at all; you're exporting the budget to another software program, changing the year field, and then importing the budget back into QuickBooks. However, there are some serious limitations to this procedure. You cannot select specific budget accounts to export—it's all or nothing. And when you import the new budget into QuickBooks, it replaces the current budget.

## Exporting to a File

You can export the budget to any software program that lets you manipulate documents that contain delimited fields (your best bet is a spreadsheet program). Here are all the steps for copying budgets to another year:

1. Choose File | Utilities | Export from the QuickBooks menu bar.
2. When the Export dialog box opens, it displays all the QuickBooks lists. Select the item named Budgets and click OK.
3. Another Export dialog box opens (it looks like the Save dialog box you're used to seeing in Windows software). Select a folder in which to save this exported file, or leave it in your QuickBooks folder. I usually change the folder to the location where I keep files for the program I'm going to use for the exported file.
4. You must also give this exported list a filename (QuickBooks will automatically add the extension .iif to the filename). "Budgets.iif" is the most logical name.
5. Click Save. QuickBooks displays a message telling you that your data has been exported successfully. Click OK.

**Caution**    *When you enter the filename, don't forget to delete the asterisk (\*) that QuickBooks placed in the field.*

## Importing the Budget into the Software Program

Now, you must open the software in which you want to manipulate the budget date, and import the .iif file into the software:

1. Click the Open icon (or use the Open command) in the software you're using. When the Open dialog box appears, move to the folder where you stored your .iif file.
2. In the Files Of Type field of the Open dialog box, change the specification to All Files (otherwise, you won't see your .iif file in the listings).
3. Double-click your exported .iif file to open it.

4. Your software application should recognize that this file doesn't match its own file type and therefore begin the procedures for importing a file. In case your software doesn't figure it out, your .iif file is a tab-delimited file.

5. When the import procedures are completed, your budget is displayed in the window of your software program.

6. Move to the column labeled STARTDATE, and update the dates so they apply to the following year.

7. Save the file (it must have an .iif extension).

8. Close the software.

## Importing the Budget Back into QuickBooks

Okay, you changed the year in the other software, and now you have to import the budget, with its new year, back into QuickBooks:

1. Open QuickBooks and choose File | Utilities | Import from the menu bar.

2. When the Import dialog box opens, double-click the file you saved.

3. QuickBooks flashes a message to tell you the import was successful. Click OK.

Now open a budget report and change the Date fields to reflect the new year. Instead of blank lines, you have figures displayed, duplicating last year's budget.

# Using Microsoft Excel for Budgeting

You can transfer your budget data into Microsoft Excel and perform all your budget manipulations, reporting, and "what if" scenarios there, instead of using QuickBooks.

After you create a budget, display its Overview report as described earlier in this chapter. Then click the Excel button on the button bar of the report window. QuickBooks asks whether you want to use a new Excel spreadsheet for this budget or send the budget to an existing spreadsheet. In this case, choose a new spreadsheet.

Microsoft Excel launches, and your budget appears on the screen, where you can make whatever changes you need to. Following are the common changes to consider:

- Change the year so you can use the budget next year and match it against next year's real figures.

- Change the amounts.
- Change the formula for changing the amounts each month.

**Note** *See Appendix C for more information about using QuickBooks with Microsoft Excel.*

You can, of course, export your budgets at any time and for any reason—you don't have to wait until you need a copy of the budget for next year. You can use spreadsheet software to play "what if" games with the figures, or add fields and calculations that don't exist in QuickBooks. The more comfortable you are with spreadsheet software, the more power you'll gain from your budgets.

# Using Journal Entries

## In this Chapter:

- *Work in the General Journal Entry window*

- *Enter the opening trial balance*

- *Make adjustments to the general ledger*

- *Depreciate fixed assets*

- *Journalize outside payroll services*

Chapter 14

**A**s you work in QuickBooks, the amounts involved in the financial transactions you complete are transferred to your general ledger. In addition to transaction totals, numbers can be placed into the general ledger directly. This is called making a *journal entry.*

Journal entries shouldn't be made without a specific purpose, and usually that purpose is to enter figures that cannot be added to an account via a standard transaction (e.g., an invoice or a check).

## Using the General Journal Entry Window

The General Journal Entry window represents the standard approach to viewing the general ledger: columns for account numbers, debit amounts, and credit amounts. In addition, QuickBooks provides some additional columns that hold data related to the journal entry. To make a journal entry, follow these steps:

1. Choose Banking | Make Journal Entry. QuickBooks displays a message telling you that automatic numbers are now assigned to journal entries (a new feature in QuickBooks). Unless you want to see this message every time you make a journal entry, select Do Not Display This Message In The Future, and then click OK to see the General Journal Entry window.

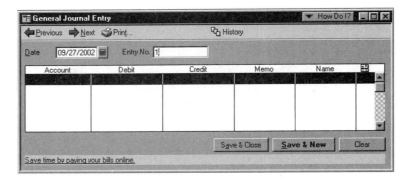

2. Click in the Account column, and then click the arrow to see your chart of accounts. Choose the account you need.
3. Move to the Debit or Credit column (depending on the data you're entering), and enter the amount for that account.
4. Repeat for all the accounts in the journal entry.

As you enter each amount, QuickBooks presents the offsetting total in the next line. For example, if the line items you've entered so far have a higher total for the credit side than the debit side, the next entry presents the balancing offset (see Figure 14-1).

Here are the guidelines for using the columns QuickBooks adds to a traditional journal entry window:

- Use the Memo column to write a comment about the amount on this line of the entry.

> **Note**    *If you're using QuickBooks Premier version, you can select the Autofill Memo option to have the memo you enter on the first line appear automatically on all lines.*

- Use the Name column to assign a customer, vendor, employee, or other name to the amount on this line of the entry.
- The column with the icon is a "billable" flag. It means that the amount is billable to the name in the Name column. Click the column to put a line through the icon to prevent making this a billable entry. This column is only available if you are using an expense account and you enter a customer name in the Name column.
- If you are using the Classes feature, you can link this line of the entry to a class. (See Chapter 21 for information about classes.)

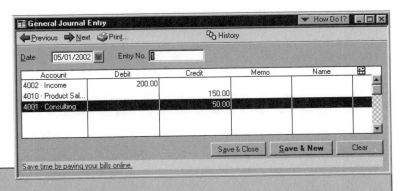

**Figure 14-1 • QuickBooks keeps the running offset figure available—you don't have to enter a figure for the last entry.**

The truth is, except for the memo, there is rarely a reason to use any of those columns, because journal entries shouldn't be used in place of transactions, and these columns are connected to transaction issues.

# Opening Trial Balance

If you opted to skip entering opening balances during your EasyStep Interview when you first started using QuickBooks, eventually you'll need to enter the opening balances for your company. All that's necessary is the opening balances for the balance sheet accounts. Then you can add all the transactions that took place since the beginning of the year to create a thorough history of transactions while you're posting the current year's activity to the general ledger.

## Entering the Opening Balances

QuickBooks does not have an item or feature called the "opening balance," per se. However, every account register is sorted by date, so using the first day of your fiscal year creates an opening balance automatically.

> **Tip**    *Create a separate equity account for your previous equity; it makes it easier to maneuver numbers at the end of the year when you're closing books. QuickBooks will post profit (or loss) to the retained earnings equity account, but you'll have historical numbers in the other account. At the end of each year, you can make a journal entry to move the current year's equity into the previous equity account.*

Confer with your accountant to develop the opening balance, and then enter it as a journal entry by using the steps described in the previous section.

## Workarounds for QuickBooks Limitations

There are a couple of QuickBooks idiosyncrasies you may run into when working with journal entries.

In QuickBooks, a journal entry can contain only the A/P account or the A/R account; you cannot use both of those accounts in the same journal entry (and the odds are good that both accounts have balances in your opening balance). You'll get an error message that says, "You cannot use more than one A/R or A/P account in the same transaction" (which is not a clear explanation). Unfortunately, QuickBooks doesn't issue the error message until you've entered all the data and try to save the journal entry. This restriction does not have its roots in accounting standards. It's an arbitrary rule built into the QuickBooks software.

Another problem is that QuickBooks insists you attach a single customer or vendor name to the entry if you're making a journal entry that involves either the A/R or the A/P account. You can't just enter an A/P balance against your equity. If you're keeping customer info outside of QuickBooks (perhaps you have a retail business and keep customer charges elsewhere), you're out of luck.

If you decide that's OK, and you're willing to enter customer opening balances, you have another problem: You can't enter A/R for more than one customer. QuickBooks won't permit more than one A/R line in the journal entry (the same restrictions apply to A/P).

QuickBooks' approach is to enter the opening balance when you create a customer or vendor. The Additional Info tabs in both the New Customer and New Vendor windows have a field for this purpose. Those totals are posted to A/R and A/P as of the date you enter, which should be the first day of the fiscal year if you're trying to create an opening trial balance.

Neither of these data entry methods—A/R lines or opening balances during customer setup—are a good idea anyway. The entry is only a total, and you cannot enter discrete invoices or bills, saddling you with several annoying drawbacks:

- You can't easily deal with disputes over specific invoices or bills (you'll have to find the original paperwork).
- Customer payments have to be applied as partial payments against the total you entered. This makes it more difficult to have conversations with customers about their accounts.
- You don't have the opportunity to enter memos on invoices or bills.
- It makes it difficult to track those amounts that are for reimbursed expenses.

Here's the best solution to both problems:

Enter your opening trial balance without the A/R and A/P entries. Adjust the equity account if your accountant preconfigured the opening trial balance for you. (Also avoid using an opening balance when you set up customers and vendors). Then enter the open invoices for customers and the open bills from vendors, using your opening balance date for the transactions, and let QuickBooks post the totals to the general ledger.

You can create one comprehensive invoice per customer/vendor and pay it off if you don't want to bother with the individual invoices that created the opening balance. The equity account will automatically adjust itself back to your accountant's original totals as you enter the transactions.

# Making Adjusting Entries

There are some circumstances, such as changing accounts and tracking depreciation, that require adjusting entries to your general ledger. Read on to find out how to handle these situations.

## Making Journal Entries for Changed Accounts

I've had many clients who decided, after they'd been using QuickBooks for a while, that they wanted to track income differently. Instead of one income account (income received), they opted for separate income accounts that are more specific. For example, an income account for fees and another income account for products sold. This made business analysis easier.

This transaction is quite simple. Create the new account and then take the appropriate amount of funds out of the original account and put them into the new account. Revenue is a credit-side item, so:

- Debit the original account for the amount that belongs in the new account.
- Credit the new account for that same amount.

Then, of course, you'll have to go to the items list and change the necessary items to reflect the new income account so you don't have to keep making journal entries.

The same decision is frequently made about expenses, as business owners decide to split heretofore comprehensive accounts. Perhaps you feel Insurance accounts should be Car Insurance, Equipment Insurance, Building Insurance, Malpractice Insurance, and so on.

For expense accounts, the journal entry goes to the opposite side of the ledger, because expenses are a debit-side item:

- Credit the original expense account for the amount you're taking out of it and putting into the new account(s).
- Debit the new account(s) for the appropriate amount(s).

The same logic applies to an asset account named Automobiles that you want to divide into more specific accounts (track the truck separately from the car, for instance, especially if they were purchased in different years). This means you can also separate out any accumulated depreciation so it's assigned to the correct asset. (You can get that information from your tax returns, or ask your accountant.)

# Making Depreciation Entries

*Depreciation* is a way to track the current value of a fixed asset that loses value as it ages. The loss of value can be viewed as just part of aging or because the asset probably won't last more than a given number of years (it either becomes obsolete or just doesn't work anymore). The basis of an asset's depreciation from an accounting point of view, however, is really determined by a complicated set of rules. The IRS makes these rules, and the rules change frequently (and many of them seem to defy logic).

**Note**    *Your accountant should determine the amount and schedule of any asset's depreciation; your depreciation deductions are part of your business tax return.*

Depreciation is a journal entry activity. Most small businesses enter the depreciation of their assets at the end of the year, but some companies perform depreciation tasks monthly or quarterly.

Depreciation is a special journal entry because the accounts involved are very restricted—this is not a free choice where you can use whichever account strikes your fancy. The account that is being depreciated must be a fixed asset. The offset entry is to an account named Depreciation Expense (or Depreciation), and it is in the expense section of your chart of accounts.

## Creating Accounts for Tracking Depreciation

I'm assuming that you've created your fixed asset account and that the assets you've purchased have been posted there. You might have multiple fixed asset accounts if you want to track different types of fixed assets separately. (For instance, my chart of accounts has three fixed asset account sections: Equipment, Furn & Fixture, and Automobile.)

When it comes to accounting procedures that have a direct bearing on my taxes and for which I might need information at a glance (especially if I'm called upon to explain it), I like to be very explicit in the way I work. Therefore, for every fixed asset account in my chart of accounts I have families of accounts for depreciation. I create a parent (account) and children (subaccounts) for each type of fixed asset. For example, the fixed asset section of a chart of accounts I create would look like this:

```
Equipment Assets (Parent)
Equipment (Subaccount)
Equipment-Accum Depr (Subaccount)
Furn & Fixture Assets (Parent)
```

```
Furn & Fixture (Subaccount)
Furn/Fixture-Accum Depr (Subaccount)
Automobile Assets (Parent)
Automobiles (Subaccount)
Automobile-Accum Depr (Subaccount)
```

Each account has an account type of Fixed Asset.

If you use numbers for your chart of accounts (actually, I do), create a numbering system that makes sense for this setup. For example, if Equipment is 1600, the subaccounts start with 1601; Furn & Fixture starts with 1620, and the subaccounts start with 1621; Automobile starts with 1640, and so on.

I post asset purchases to a subaccount I create for the specific purchase, and I make my journal entry for depreciation in the Accum Depr subaccount. I never use the parent account. There are several reasons for this:

- Both the asset subaccount and the depreciation asset subaccount are "pure." I can look at either one to see a running total instead of a calculated net total.

- Tracing the year-to-year depreciation is easy. I just open the depreciation asset subaccount register—each line represents a year.

- It's just plain easier and quicker to open the depreciation asset subaccount if I'm asked about the depreciation total (handy if you sell the asset and have to add back the depreciation).

The net value of my fixed assets on the balance sheet is correct. A Balance Sheet report shows me the details (see Figure 14-2).

You can further refine this paradigm by creating subaccounts for specific fixed assets. For instance, you may want to create a subaccount for each automobile asset (or one for cars and one for trucks) and its accompanying accumulated depreciation. If your equipment falls under a variety of depreciation rules (e.g., manufacturing equipment vs. computer equipment), you may want to have a set of subaccounts for each type.

If you're really obsessive, you can create a different subaccount for each year of depreciation, for instance, under your Automobile-Accum Depr subaccount, you could have Automobile-Depr 1999, Automobile-Depr 2000, Automobile-Depr 2001, and so on. Then your balance sheet shows a complete year-by-year depreciation schedule instead of accumulated depreciation—and the math still works properly. Of course, after a number of years, you'll have destroyed an entire forest with all the paper it takes to print your balance sheet.

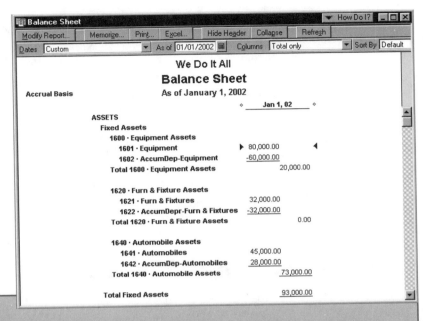

**Figure 14-2 • Use subaccounts for fixed assets and their depreciation to get a detailed display of depreciation activity.**

## Creating a Depreciation Entry

In order to depreciate fixed assets, you must have a depreciation offset account in the Expense section of your chart of accounts. Here's how to make your depreciation entry:

1. Choose Banking | Make Journal Entry from the menu bar.
2. Choose the first asset depreciation subaccount.
3. Enter the depreciation amount in the Credit column.
4. Choose the next asset depreciation subaccount and enter its depreciation amount in the Credit column. (QuickBooks automatically puts the offsetting amount in the Debit column, but you can ignore that as you work).
5. Continue until all your depreciation figures are entered in the Credit column.
6. Choose the Depreciation Expense account. The total amount of the credits is automatically placed in the Debit column.
7. Click Save & Close.

## Reversing Entries

Your accountant may enter, or tell you to enter, *reversing entries*. These are general journal entries that are applied on one date and then reversed on another date. For example, on 12/31/02, you may have a journal entry that adjusts your A/R and A/P accounts in order to prepare for tax filing on a cash basis (some accountants prefer this method to asking QuickBooks to print cash-basis reports). On 1/1/03, the entry will be reversed. After you enter both general journal entries, the totals you see are dictated by the way you fill out the Date field in the report window.

**Note**   *If you have QuickBooks Premier version, an automated reversing journal entry is available.*

# Journalizing Outside Payroll Services

If you have an outside payroll service, you have to tell QuickBooks about the payroll transactions that took place. You get a report from the service, so all the numbers are available. It's just a matter of entering them.

It's common for businesses to perform this task via a journal entry (even businesses that don't use computers and have to haul out the big ledger books). Like all other journal entries, this one is just a matter of entering debits and credits.

There are three parts to recording payroll:

- Transferring money to the payroll account
- Entering the payroll figures
- Entering the employer expense figures

## Transferring Money to the Payroll Account

You must have a separate bank account for payroll if you have an outside payroll service—in fact, a separate payroll account is a good idea even if you do your own payroll with QuickBooks.

Outside payroll services reach into your checking account; in fact, they have checks, and you certainly don't want to be giving away checks for your regular operating account. Another reason for a separate payroll account, even if you do your own payroll, is the discipline involved in holding on to your employee withholdings until you pass them along to insurance companies, other vendors, and the government—*especially* the government. The money you withhold and leave in your bank account until you're ready to transmit it to the government is not your money. You cannot spend it. It doesn't matter if you need the money to save your business from total bankruptcy—you cannot spend the money. People have done that and gotten into serious trouble, including jail. Keeping all the money associated with payroll in a separate bank account removes it from the amounts you have available to run your business.

To transfer the money you need for this payroll, choose Banking | Transfer Funds. Then transfer the money from your regular operating account to your payroll account (see Figure 14-3).

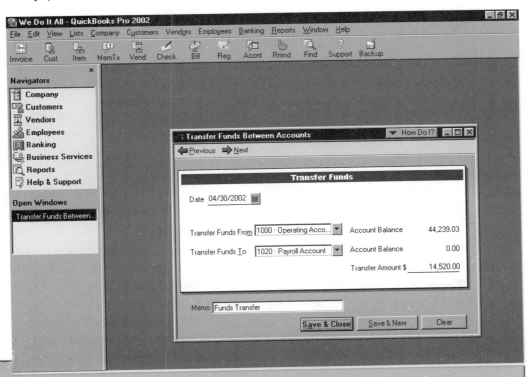

**Figure 14-3 • A transfer is really a journal entry, crediting the sending account and debiting the receiving account.**

Be sure to transfer enough money for the gross payroll plus the employer payroll expenses, which include:

- Employer-matching contributions to FICA and Medicare
- Employer-matching contributions to pension plans
- Employer-matching contributions to benefits
- Employer state unemployment assessments
- Employer FUTA
- Any other government or benefit payments due

Even though some of these aren't transmitted every payday, you should transfer the amounts at that time anyway. Then, when it's time to pay them, the correct amount of money will have been amassed in the payroll account.

## Recording the Payroll

The *payroll run* (jargon for "printing the paychecks") produces a fairly complicated set of debits and credits. Many businesses record a journal entry for the run, then a separate journal entry for the employer expenses when they're transmitted.

If your payroll service takes care of remitting employer expenses, you can journalize the payments. If you do the employer reports yourself and send the checks directly, your check-writing activity will record the payments.

Here's a typical template for recording the payroll run as a journal entry:

| Account | Debit | Credit |
| --- | --- | --- |
| Salaries and Wages (Expense) | Total Gross Payroll | |
| FWT (liability) | | Total Federal Withheld |
| FICA (liability) | | Total FICA Withheld |
| Medicare (liability) | | Total Medicare Withheld |
| State Income Tax (liability) | | Total State Tax Withheld |
| Local Income Tax (liability) | | Total Local Tax Withheld |
| State SDI (liability) | | Total State SDI Withheld |
| State SUI (liability) | | Total State SUI Withheld |
| Benefits Contrib (liability) | | Total Benefits Withheld |
| 401(k) Contrib (liability) | | Total 401(k) Withheld |
| Other Deductions (liability) | | Total Other Ded Withheld |
| Payroll Bank Account (asset) | | Total of Net Payroll |

It's possible that you don't have all the expenses shown in this list (for instance, not all states have employee unemployment assessments). And you may have additional withholding such as union dues, garnishments against wages, and so on. Be sure you've created a liability account in your chart of accounts for each withholding category you need, as well as a vendor for each transmittal check.

## Recording Employer Payments

You need to record the employer payments if your payroll service is taking care of them for you (if you do it yourself, just write the checks from the payroll account). Typically, the journal entry looks something like this:

| Account | Debit | Credit |
| --- | --- | --- |
| Federal Payroll Expenses (expense) | FICA and Medicare Employer Total | |
| Federal Withholdings (liability) | All Individual Withholding Totals (FIT, FICA, etc.) | |
| State and Local Withholdings (liability) | All Withholding Totals (taxes, SDI, SUI, etc.) | |
| SUTA (expense) | Employer SUTA | |
| FUTA (expense) | Employer FUTA | |
| Employer Contributions (expense) | All Benefit, Pension, Other Contributions | |
| Payroll Bank Account (asset) | | Total of Checks Written |

The entry involving the transmittal of withholdings is posted to the same account you used when you withheld the amounts. In effect, you "wash" the liability accounts; you're not really spending money, you're remitting money you've withheld.

You can have as many individual employer expense accounts as you think you need, or you can post all the employer expenses to one account named "Payroll Expenses."

**Tip** *Don't have your payroll service take their fee from the payroll account. Instead, write them a check from your operating account. The service is not a payroll expense; it's an operating expense.*

# Reconciling the Payroll Account

The problem with journal entries for payroll is that, when the bank statement comes for the payroll account, reconciling it is a bit different. When you open the payroll account in the Reconcile window, you see the journal entry totals instead of the individual checks.

## Reconciling Outside QuickBooks

You have the report from the payroll service, and it lists each check number. You can therefore reconcile the account outside of the Reconcile window (using a manual system or creating a spreadsheet in your spreadsheet software).

**Tip** *See if your payroll service can send you a file containing check#/payee/ amount information that can be opened in spreadsheet or database software.*

**Note** *Most people find that the payroll checks themselves are cashed quickly and clear rapidly, which always makes reconciliation easier. Payments to government agencies may not clear quite as fast.*

## Entering Fake Payroll Checks

If you feel you really need to perform the reconciliation in QuickBooks, you could enter the checks without posting them to an account, instead posting them back to the payroll account. (The journal entry took care of all the real postings.) You have a little bit of setup to do, then you can perform this task every payday.

Create a name, "Payroll," with a type Other Name. (Choose Lists | Other Names List from the menu bar.) You can use this name for every check.

Alternatively, you could create a name for each employee in the Other Name list, using initials, last name only, or some other name that isn't the same as the original employee name. The reason you have to create these fake names is that QuickBooks will not let you write a direct check to a real employee. Employee checks can only be written via the real Payroll feature. The only reason to go through this work is if you feel you must have all the details in your QuickBooks register instead of looking up the check number and employee name in the payroll service report you received.

Now you have a payee name for the payroll checks. Grab the report from the payroll service and enter the individual checks:

1. Click the Reg icon on the QuickBooks toolbar and select the payroll account register.

2. On the next available transaction line, enter the payroll check date.
3. TAB to the Number field and enter the first check number on the payroll service report.
4. Enter the payee Payroll (unless you've entered all your employee names as Other Name types, in which case enter the appropriate name).
5. Enter the amount of the net paycheck.
6. In the Account field, choose the Payroll account. QuickBooks will flash a message warning you that you're posting the payment to the source account.

7. Click OK. (In fact, you might want to click the check box that tells QuickBooks to omit this warning in the future.)
8. Click the Record button to save this check, and then enter the next check.

Continue the process until all the checks are entered. As shown in Figure 14-4, each entry is automatically duplicated (although the amounts are in different columns).

The amounts are in different columns because QuickBooks is automatically writing the balancing entry (which is what double-entry accounting software does); in this case, the balancing entry is to the payroll account instead of an expense account.

You can also enter the checks the payroll service wrote to transmit your withholdings or pay your taxes. As long as each entry you make was entered into the journal entry, you can post everything back to the payroll account. You're "washing" every transaction, not changing the balance of the account. Then when you want to reconcile the payroll account, the individual checks are in the Reconcile window. The fact is, this procedure is quite easy and fast, and you only have to do it on payday (or once a month if you want to wait until the statement comes in).

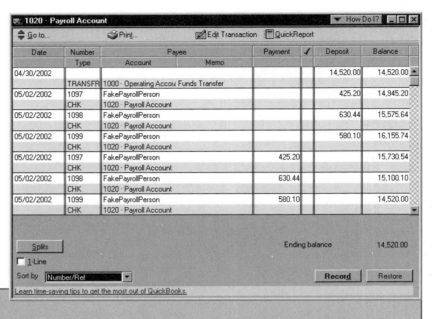

**Figure 14-4 •** The ending balance is the same as the starting balance after you enter all the checks.

## Using Journal Entries to Produce Business Reports

Telma and Louisa have a bookkeeping business. Their clients are local small businesses, none of which own computers. This means that producing reports about income and expenses is time-consuming for the clients. None of their clients has employees, so there aren't any payroll issues.

Both women installed QuickBooks on their laptop computers and travel to the clients' offices where they produce reports for the clients' accountants. This is much cheaper for their clients than having their accountants visit and do the same work the women can do easily with QuickBooks. (Luckily, QuickBooks permits multiple company files.)

All the work is done via one journal entry per month. Here are the details:

- All the deposit slips are added up, and the total is posted as a debit to the bank account. The deposit slips are marked with a "Q" for QuickBooks, so none will be accidentally entered again next month.

- All the checks that were written are totaled, and the total is entered as a credit against the bank account. Each check stub is marked with a "Q" for QuickBooks as it's added to the total, so next month it's clear which checks have not yet been accounted for.

- Each check stub is also marked with an account code, and the amount of the check is debited against that account in the journal entry window. Most of the checks are for expense accounts, but some are for the purchase of equipment or other assets, and some are posted to Owners Draw, which is an equity account.

- If there's a question about how to post a check, it's posted as a debit to an expense account named To Be Resolved, and a note is left for the client to call the accountant for instructions. Then next month, a separate journal entry is used to credit the To Be Resolved account and debit the correct account.

When the journal entry is completed and saved, everything necessary for a Balance Sheet report, a Profit and Loss statement, and a Trial Balance is in the QuickBooks files.

# Running General Ledger Reports

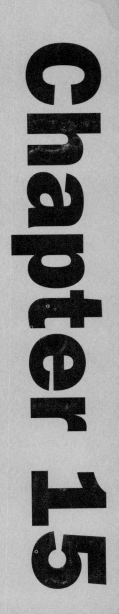

## In this Chapter:

- *Report the trial balance*

- *Create a Balance Sheet*

- *Create a Profit & Loss statement*

- *Create an accountant's review copy*

If QuickBooks is your first accounting software program, and you've been using manual bookkeeping procedures, you've already discovered how much easier it is to accomplish bookkeeping tasks. However, even with the ease and power you've gained with QuickBooks, bookkeeping probably isn't fun. I can't give you any QuickBooks tips to make it fun (it isn't—it's precise, repetitive work), but I can tell you how to feel better about all the work you do in QuickBooks.

It's the reports you get out of the software that make the work worthwhile. These are reports you'd have to spend hours on using a manual bookkeeping system. And you can change, customize, and manipulate these reports to get all sorts of information about your business. Most of the results you obtain from QuickBooks reports couldn't be gained from a manual system. (Well, maybe they could, if you made a lifetime career out of it and spent weeks on each report.)

# Reporting the Trial Balance

A *trial balance* is a list of all your general ledger accounts and their current balances. It's a quick way to see what's what on an account-by-account basis. In fact, you can use the individual totals and subtotal them to create a Balance Sheet and a Profit & Loss (P&L) statement. However, you don't have to do that because both of those important reports are also available in QuickBooks.

To see a trial balance, choose Reports | Accountant and Taxes | Trial Balance.

Your company's trial balance is displayed on your screen and looks similar (in form, not content) to Figure 15-1. You can scroll through it to see all the account balances. The bottom of the report has a total for debits and a total for credits, and they're equal. Click the Print button on the report's button bar to print the report.

## Configuring the Trial Balance Report

You can change the way the trial balance report displays information, using the configuration options available for this report. Click the Modify Report button on the report's button bar to bring up the Modify Report window shown in Figure 15-2.

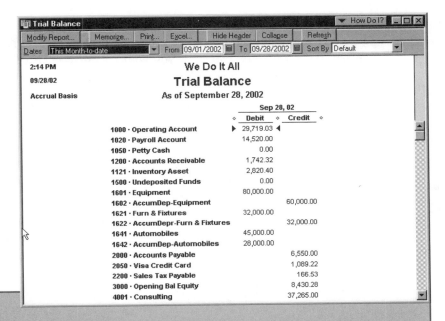

Figure 15-1 • The trial balance shows the current balance for each account.

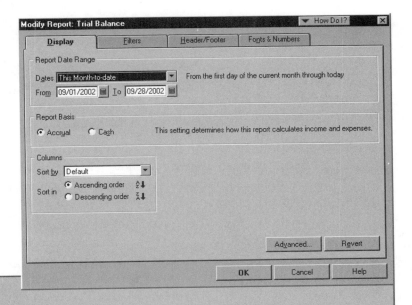

Figure 15-2 • Modify the Trial Balance report output by changing configuration options.

### Accrual vs. Cash Trial Balance

One important control in the Customize Report window is the Report Basis selection. QuickBooks can show you your balances on an accrual basis or on a cash basis:

- Accrual numbers are based on your transaction activity. When you invoice a customer, that amount is considered to be revenue. When you enter a vendor bill, you've entered an expense.

- Cash numbers are based on the flow of cash. Revenue isn't real until the customer pays the bill, and your vendor bills aren't expenses until you write the check.

By default, QuickBooks, like most accounting software, displays accrual reports. It's generally more useful as you analyze your business.

### Setting Advanced Options

Click the Advanced button on the Display tab to see the Advanced Options window, where you have two choices for changing the criteria for displaying information, and a choice for determining the calendar basis of the report.

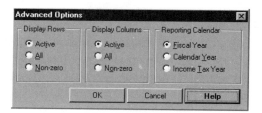

The two display choices (Rows and Columns) change the criteria for displaying information.

- Select Active to display only those accounts in which financial activity occurred. This includes accounts that have amounts of $0.00 as a result of financial activity.

- Select All to see all accounts, irrespective of whether they had activity or have a balance of $0.00.

- Select Non-zero to see only those accounts that had activity and have a balance other than $0.00.

The Reporting Calendar option determines the calendar basis of the report. You can change the option if your company preferences are not set for a fiscal year and a tax year that coincide with the calendar year:

- Fiscal Year sets the reporting calendar to start at the first month of your company's fiscal year.
- Calendar Year sets the reporting calendar to start at January 1.
- Income Tax Year sets the reporting calendar to start on the first day of the first month of your company's tax year.

Click OK to return to the Modify Report window.

## Filtering the Data

Click the Filters tab in the Modify Report window to filter the contents of the report (see Figure 15-3).

Select a category (Filter) from the list in the Choose Filter box and decide how each category should be displayed. You can also exclude category data with filters. Different categories have different filtering criteria. For instance, you can filter amounts that are less or greater than a certain amount.

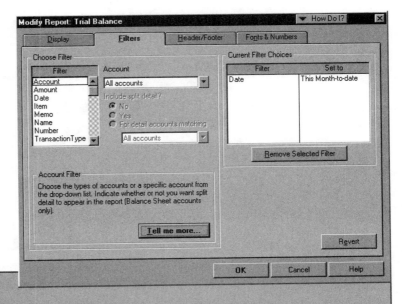

**Figure 15-3 • Change what's reported by filtering the data in the report.**

**Caution**    *Once you start filtering accounts and amounts, you probably will have a trial balance that no longer balances. At that point, you can't call it a trial balance; you're creating a list of account balances.*

## Changing the Header and Footer

You can customize what appears on the header and footer of your report by changing the options on the Header/Footer tab, shown in Figure 15-4.

The options you configure here have no bearing on the figures in the report; this is just the informational stuff. Most of the fields are self-explanatory, but the Date Prepared field may confuse you. That's not a date that has anything to do with you, your QuickBooks files, or your system; it's a sample format. Click the arrow to the right of the field to see other formats for displaying the date.

## Changing the Fonts and Number Display

The Fonts & Numbers tab, shown in Figure 15-5, lets you change the font you use for the various elements in the report. Select any part of the report from the list on the left side of the dialog box and click Change Font. Then select a font, a style (bold, italic, etc.), a size, and special effects such as underline.

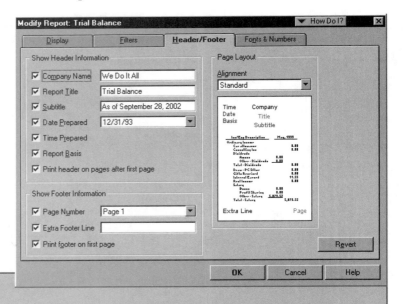

**Figure 15-4 • Change the information at the top and bottom of the report.**

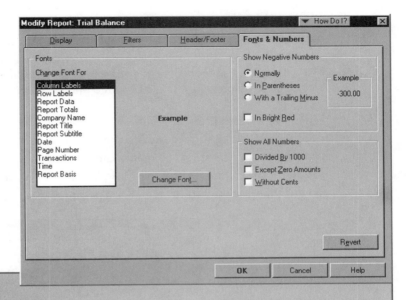

**Figure 15-5 • Change the appearance of the text and numbers in your report.**

On the right side of the dialog box, you can configure the way numbers display and print on your report. Select a method for showing negative numbers. If you wish, you can also select a method for displaying all the numbers on the report:

- Divided By 1000 reduces the size of the numbers by showing them as multiples of 1000. This is useful for companies who report 7-digit and 8-digit numbers.
- Except Zero Amounts removes all instances of $0.00.
- Without Cents eliminates the decimal point and the two digits to the right of the decimal point from every amount. Only the dollars show, not the cents. QuickBooks rounds the cents to the nearest dollar.

## Memorizing a Customized Trial Balance

I find that I like to glance at the trial balance report occasionally, just to see what certain totals are. Calling up the trial balance to view five or six account balances is faster than opening five or six account registers to examine the current balance. I only need to see the accounts that have a balance; I have no interest in zero-balance accounts. My accountant, on the other hand, likes to see all the accounts. He finds significance in some accounts being at zero.

> **Tip** *Balance sheet accounts display their current balances in the Chart of Accounts list window, so you don't have to print a report to see those numbers.*

The solution to providing both of us with what we want is in memorizing each modified version of the report. After you've configured the report to display the information you want, in the manner in which you want it, click the Memorize button on the report's button bar. The Memorize Report window appears so you can give this customized format a name.

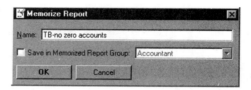

> **Tip** *Be sure to use a reference to the report type in the memorized name. If you use a name such as My Report, you'll have no idea what the report is about.*

You can recall a memorized report by choosing Reports | Memorized Reports from the QuickBooks menu bar and selecting the report name.

# Generating a Balance Sheet

QuickBooks offers several Balance Sheet reports, and each of them is explained in this section. Select the one you want to see by choosing Reports | Company & Financial and then choosing the report.

A Balance Sheet report is specifically designed to show only the totals of the balance sheet accounts (assets, liabilities, and equity) from your chart of accounts. It's really a report on your financial health. The reason a balance sheet balances is that it's based on a formula:

Assets = Liabilities + Equity

Before you glance at the trial balance you just printed and prepare to write me a note saying, "Excuse me, you don't know what you're talking about; I just added those accounts up, and it doesn't balance," let me redefine one of the terms: equity.

When you generate a Balance Sheet report, the equity number is a calculated number and is arrived at with these steps:

1. All the income accounts are added up.
2. All the expense accounts are added up.
3. The expense total is subtracted from the income total.
4. The result of the calculation in step 3 is added to the totals in existing equity accounts (which could be Opening Balance Equity, Prior Retained Earnings, Retained Earnings, and so on).
5. The total that's calculated in step 4 becomes the figure for equity in a Balance Sheet report.

If you have more expenses than you have income, you're operating at a loss; consequently, it's a negative number that is combined with the existing equity accounts. This means that the equity number that appears on your balance sheet could be lower than the equity number that shows on your trial balance.

## Balance Sheet Standard

The standard Balance Sheet reports the balance in every balance sheet account (unless the account has a zero balance), and subtotals each account type: asset, liability, and equity. The report is automatically configured for year-to-date figures, using your fiscal year and the current date. The fiscal year is the same as the calendar year for most small businesses.

## Balance Sheet Detail

This report is similar to a detailed general ledger transaction report, showing every transaction in every balance sheet account. By default, the report covers a date range of the current month to date. Even if it's early in the month, this report is lengthy. If you change the date range to encompass a longer period (the quarter or year), the report goes on forever.

If you want to see a balance sheet only to get an idea of your company's financial health, this is probably more than you wanted to know.

## Balance Sheet Summary

This report is a quick way to see totals, and it's also the easiest way to answer the question, "How am I doing?" All the account types are listed and subtotaled, as shown in Figure 15-6.

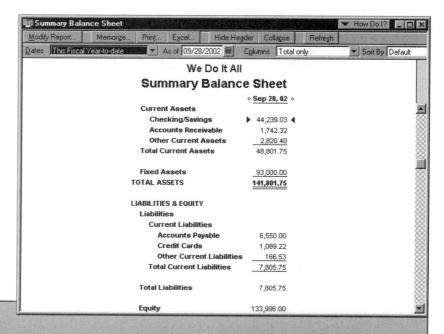

**Figure 15-6 • Get a quick check-up on your financial health with a Summary Balance Sheet.**

If you miss seeing the details, hold your mouse pointer over any total (your pointer turns into a magnifying glass) and double-click. An itemized list of the transactions for each account represented by that total appears. For example, Figure 15-7 shows the display that appears when I double-click the total for Fixed Assets. Close the detail report to return to the Summary Balance Sheet.

## Balance Sheet Previous Year Comparison

The comparison balance sheet is designed to show you what your financial situation is compared to a year ago. There are four columns in this report:

- The year-to-date balance for each balance sheet account
- The year-to-date balance for each balance sheet account for last year
- The amount of change between last year and this year
- The percentage of change between last year and this year

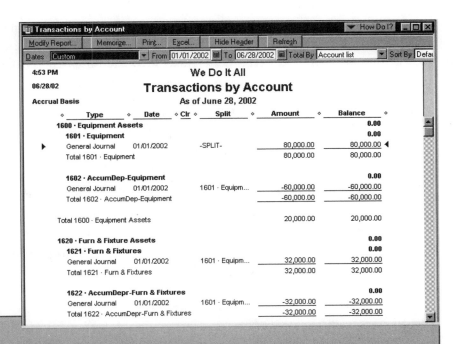

**Figure 15-7 • Details are available for any total in the balance sheet summary report.**

If you've just started using QuickBooks this year, there's little reason to run this report. Next year, however, it'll be interesting to see how you're doing compared to this year.

## Customizing and Memorizing a Balance Sheet

When your balance sheet is on the screen, you can use all of the customization features mentioned for the Trial Balance report. Then when you have the configuration you need, memorize the report.

# Generating a Profit & Loss Statement

Your P&L report is probably the one you'll run most often. It's natural to want to know if you're making any money. A P&L report is also called an *income report*. It shows all your income accounts (and displays the total), all your expense accounts (displaying the total), and then puts the difference between the two totals on the last line. If you have more income than expenses, the last line is a profit.

All of the P&L reports are available by choosing Reports | Company & Financial. The report types are explained in this section.

## Profit & Loss Standard Report

The standard P&L report is a straightforward document, following the normal format for an income statement:

- The income is listed and totaled.
- The Cost of Goods Sold accounts are listed, and the total is deducted from the income total in order to show the gross profit.
- The expenses are listed and totaled.
- The difference between the gross profit and the total expenses is displayed as your Net Income (or Net Loss).

**Note** *If you don't sell inventory items, you probably don't have a Cost of Goods Sold section in your P&L.*

While the format is that of a normal income statement, the end result isn't. The default date range for the QuickBooks standard P&L is the current month-to-date. This is not a year-to-date figure; it uses only the transactions from the current month. Click the arrow to the right of the Dates field and change the date range to This Fiscal Year-To-Date. The resulting display is what you want to see—a normal income statement for your business for this year (see Figure 15-8).

## Profit & Loss Detail Report

The Profit & Loss Detail report is for terminally curious people. It lists every transaction for every account in the P&L format. It goes on forever.

This report is almost like an audit trail, and it's good to have if you notice some numbers that seem "not quite right" in the standard P&L. I don't recommend it as the report to run when you just need to know if you're making money.

## Profit & Loss YTD Comparison Report

The YTD (year-to-date) comparison report compares the current month's income and expense totals with the year-to-date totals. Each income and expense account is listed.

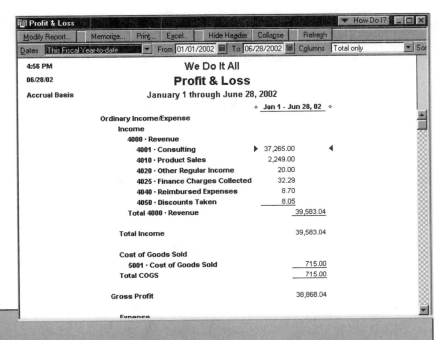

**Figure 15-8 • Scroll to the bottom to see your profit.**

## Profit & Loss Previous Year Comparison Report

If you've been using QuickBooks for more than a year, this is a great report! If you recently started with QuickBooks, this will be a great report next year!

This is an income statement for the current year-to-date, with a column that shows last year's figure for the same period. This gives you an instant appraisal of your business growth (or ebb). So that you don't have to tax your brain doing the math, there are two additional columns: the difference between the years in dollars and the difference in percentage.

## Profit & Loss by Job Report

This report presents a year-to-date summary of income and expenses posted to customers and jobs. In effect, it's a customer P&L. Each customer gets its own column and the bottom row of each column is the net income.

### Profit & Loss by Class Report

If you've enabled Class tracking, this report appears on the Reports menu. Each class is subtotaled for its own P&L.

## Customizing and Memorizing P&L Reports

Use the QuickBooks Customize features discussed earlier in this chapter to tailor P&L reports so they print exactly the way you want to see the information. You might want to customize several formats: for you, for your accountant, and perhaps for your bank (your bank also wants to see a Balance Sheet). Then memorize the perfect custom reports you design.

# Creating an Accountant's Review

Many accountants support QuickBooks directly, which means they understand the software and know how to use it. In fact, they have a copy of QuickBooks on their own computer system.

At various times during the year, your accountant might want to look at your books. There might be quarterly reports and adjustments, a physical inventory that resulted in serious changes in your balance sheet, expenses that should be reappropriated, or any of a hundred other reasons. Almost definitely this will occur at the end-of-year process you have to go through in order to close your books for the year.

This could result in your accountant showing up and sitting in front of your computer, making the necessary changes (almost always journal entries), moving this, reversing that, and generally making sense out of your daily transaction postings. By "making sense," I mean putting transaction postings into categories that fit your tax reporting needs.

While your accountant is using the software, you can't get much accomplished. You could say, "Excuse me, could you move? I have to enter an invoice." But remember, you're paying for the accountant's time.

Or if your accountant doesn't want to visit, he or she may request printouts of various reports, then write notes on those printouts: "Move this, split that, credit this number here, debit that number there." Or you receive a spreadsheet-like printout with an enormously long and complicated journal entry, which means you have to stop entering your day-to-day transactions to make all those changes.

QuickBooks has a better idea. Give your accountant a disk with a copy of your QuickBooks records. Let your accountant do the work back at his or her office. When the disk comes back to you, the necessary changes have been placed on the disk. QuickBooks merges the changes into your copy of the software. It's magic!

**Note** To work with your QuickBooks 2002 files, your accountant must have QuickBooks 2002 installed.

## Creating an Accountant's Review Copy

You can create the accountant's review copy on a floppy disk, or save it to a file and send it to your accountant via e-mail:

1. Choose File | Accountant's Review | Create Accountant's Copy from the QuickBooks menu bar. The Save Accountant's Copy To dialog box appears so you can save the information for your accountant.

2. Change the location to your floppy drive if you plan to send a floppy disk to your accountant. If you're going to transmit the file via e-mail, you'll save some time searching for the file if you save it in the folder that your e-mail software uses as the default location.

3. The filename must have an extension of .qbx. You can change the name of the file if you want to, but generally it's a good idea to keep the filename QuickBooks suggests (which is based on your company name).

4. Click Save to create the accountant's copy.

QuickBooks notifies you when the process is complete. If the file won't fit on a floppy disk, you'll be asked to insert a second floppy disk to complete the process. If you've password-protected your QuickBooks data file, you must tell your accountant what the admin password is. Otherwise, your accountant won't be able to open the file.

## Working During the Accountant's Review

Because parts of your QuickBooks data have been locked, it's important to know what you can and cannot accomplish until you receive data back from your accountant. Your accountant also has restrictions. Table 15-1 describes what you (the client) can and can't do while your files are locked, and Table 15-2 describes what an accountant can and cannot do with the accountant's copy file.

| Clients Can | Clients Cannot |
|---|---|
| Create transactions | Delete an entry in a list |
| Edit transactions | Rename an item in a list |
| Delete transactions | Change an account to a subaccount in the Chart of Accounts list |
| Add new items to lists | Change a subaccount to an account in the Chart of Accounts list |
| Edit items in lists | |

**Table 15-1 • What You Can Do with Your QuickBooks Files While Your Accountant Has an Accountant's Copy**

| Accountants Can | Accountants Cannot |
|---|---|
| Create journal entries | Delete list entries |
| Edit account names | Make list entries inactive |
| Change account numbers (if you use numbers for your chart of accounts) | Create transactions (except journal entries) |
| Edit tax information for accounts | |
| Adjust inventory quantities and values | |
| Print 1099 forms | |
| Print 941 forms | |
| Print 940 forms | |
| Print W-2 forms | |

**Table 15-2 • What Accountants Can Do While Working in the Accountant's Copy**

# Unlocking Your Files Without a Review

If you make an accountant's review copy in error, or if your accountant tells you there are no changes to be made, you can unlock your files. This puts everything back as if you'd never created an accountant's review copy.

Choose File | Accountant's Review | Cancel Accountant's Changes. QuickBooks asks you to confirm your decision.

## Merging the Accountant's Changes

When your accountant returns your files to you, the changes have to be imported into your QuickBooks files, as follows:

1. Place the floppy disk you received from your accountant into the floppy drive. If you received the file via e-mail, note the folder and filename you used to store it on your hard drive.
2. Choose File | Accountant's Review | Import Accountant's Changes.
3. QuickBooks insists on a backup of your current file before importing. Click OK and proceed with the backup as usual.
4. When the backup is complete, QuickBooks automatically opens the Import Changes from Accountant's Copy window. Make sure the Look In field at the top of the window matches the location of the accountant's review file.
5. Choose the import file, which has an extension of .aif, and click Open (or double-click on the .aif file).

Your QuickBooks data now contains the changes your accountant made, and you can work with your files normally.

**Tip**    *Make sure your accountant sends you a note or calls to tell you about the changes. QuickBooks does not indicate what has changed after the import.*

# Using Online Banking Services

## In this Chapter:

- *Set up a connection to QuickBooks on the Web*

- *Set up online bank accounts*

- *Perform online transactions*

- *Receive online payments from your customers*

## Chapter 16

If you have an Internet connection, you can use the wide range of online services offered by QuickBooks. In fact, you can register your software, get updates, find information about using QuickBooks more efficiently, and perform banking chores.

Banking chores are the subject of this chapter. You'll discover that QuickBooks and its parent company, Intuit, have used the Internet to make banking a snap. You can sign up for online banking, which means you can view the status of your account, see which transactions have cleared, and generally maintain your account via your modem. You can also sign up for online payments, which means you send money to vendors via the Internet as well. The money is deposited directly into your vendor's bank account, or a check is automatically generated (depending upon the way your vendor works). And you can also make arrangements for online payments from your customers.

# Setting Up a Connection

Before you can use the QuickBooks online services, you have to let the software know how you get online. After this simple, initial step, QuickBooks does its online work on autopilot.

The first step is to let QuickBooks know how you reach the Internet. Choose Help | Internet Connection Setup from the menu bar. This launches the Internet Connection Setup wizard, which presents a question in the first window (see Figure 16-1).

The choices on the first wizard window cover all the possibilities. One of them fits your situation, and in this section I'll explain how QuickBooks handles the setup for each type of connection.

## Dial-up Connections

The option Use The Following Connection refers to a dial-up connection, using your modem. This connection could be through an ISP (Internet Service Provider), which you reach using the dial-up capabilities built into your operating system (Dial-Up Networking). Or you may have a connection through a proprietary software program that connects you to a particular host such as CompuServe or America Online. These proprietary programs first connect you to their host server, where there are preconfigured sections of information. Then the systems permit you to wander off on your own on the Internet.

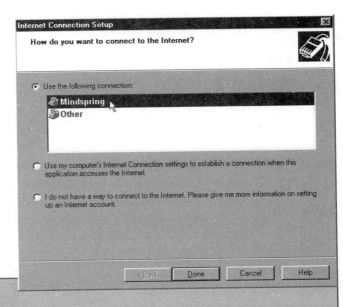

**Figure 16-1 • The first step is to tell QuickBooks how you reach the Internet.**

Any dial-up connections you've configured appear in the Internet Connection Setup window. If no connection appears, and you know you've configured a dial-up connection to your ISP, QuickBooks had a problem finding it or identifying it. Close the window (but don't shut down QuickBooks), open your dial-up connection, and connect to the Internet. Then open this window again, and QuickBooks should identify it.

Select the connection so it's highlighted. Then click Done on the Internet Connection Setup window. You're all set. Any time you need to travel to the Internet while you're working in QuickBooks, QuickBooks will open the connection (unless you're already connected to the Internet) and take you to the right site.

**Caution**    *If QuickBooks didn't detect your connection during setup, and you had to connect to the Internet before configuring your connection, you'll have to connect manually every time you want to use Internet services in QuickBooks.*

## Network or Always-On Connections

If you connect to the Internet via a cable modem, DSL, or a network Internet connection server, select the option Use My Computer's Internet Connection

Settings. Then click Next to see an explanation of the connection QuickBooks found, which is referred to as a direct connection. Click the Connection Settings button if you need to check the settings (but that shouldn't be necessary). Then click Done.

## No Internet Connection

If you don't have Internet access, you can run QuickBooks without taking advantage of the online services, or you can sign up for an Internet service. If you select the option I Do Not Have A Way To Connect To The Internet, and click Next, you'll see an explanation that you must sign up for Internet service before using the Internet Connection Setup wizard.

After you're signed up, use the Internet Connection wizard built into Windows (the way to get to that wizard varies among the different versions of Windows, so check your Help files). Then return to this window and set up your QuickBooks online connection.

# Setting Up Online Accounts

You have to establish online access for your bank accounts, both with your bank and with QuickBooks. Your bank must support QuickBooks online access procedures. There are three online banking services available:

- Online account access
- Online bill paying
- Online credit card services

You can sign up for any or all of these services. If your bank doesn't support online bill paying or online credit card services, QuickBooks does and you can work directly with QuickBooks online banking sites. See "Using the QuickBooks Online Payment Service" and "Using the QuickBooks Credit Card Service" later in this chapter.

The process of enabling online banking has three steps:

1. Enable a QuickBooks bank account (or multiple accounts) for online services.
2. Apply for online services with your bank.
3. Receive a personal identification number (PIN) from your bank to make sure your online account is secure.

# Understanding Online Account Access

If you sign up for online account access, you have the ability to connect to your bank's computer system and look at your account. Once you're plugged in to your account records online, there are a number of tasks you can accomplish:

- Check your balance as of this moment.
- Transfer money between accounts. (Both accounts must be at this bank and enabled within QuickBooks for online services.)
- Download information about all the cleared transactions to your computer. The information is automatically placed into your QuickBooks bank register.

One of the advantages of this system is that you can do all these things at your own convenience; if you want to do your banking in the middle of the night, you can. Check with your bank, however, to see if there's a time period when online access isn't permitted (usually in the wee hours of the morning). Some banks reserve a few hours each night to perform maintenance tasks on their computers.

# Understanding Online Bill Paying

You can pay your bills online, transferring money directly from your account to your vendors. This point-and-click method of paying bills is certainly a lot easier than writing out checks. If you don't have printed checks, I can't imagine not using online payment, because writing out a check manually is a whole lot of work! Even if you do have printed checks, you might want to consider online payments because it's usually easier and quicker than mailing checks.

When you make an online payment, the following information is transmitted to your vendor in addition to money:

- The date and number of the invoice(s)
- Information about any discounts or credits you've applied to the invoice(s)
- Anything you inserted as a memo or note when you prepared the payment

If the vendor is set up to receive electronic payments, the money is transferred directly from your bank account to the vendor's bank account. Incidentally, being set up to receive electronic payments does not mean your vendor must be using QuickBooks; there are many and varied methods for receiving electronic payments, and many companies have these arrangements with their banks.

If the vendor's account is not accessible for online payments, your bank writes a check and mails it, along with all the necessary payment information.

## Understanding Online Credit Card Services

You can also pay your credit card bills online either by using QuickBooks online payment features (if the bank that holds your credit card supports it) or by signing up for a QuickBooks credit card (that definitely supports online payments).

## Finding Your Bank Online

You may already have learned about your bank's online services—many banks enclose information about this feature in the monthly statements, or have brochures available when you visit the bank.

**Note** *If you've already applied for online services, you can skip this part and move to the section "Enabling Your Online Bank Accounts."*

Before you run to the neighborhood bank branch to sign up, you can find out what your bank expects from you by going online. In fact, you may be able to sign up online.

Choose Banking | Set Up Online Financial Services from the menu bar. The submenu has two commands:

- Apply For Online Banking, which opens a wizard that lets you find your bank on the Internet and fill out an application (if your bank offers that service).
- Online Financial Institutions List, which opens an Internet window in your browser so you can see the list of participating financial institutions. If your bank is on the list, it may offer sign-up from this window

### Check the Online Financial Institutions List

If you haven't discussed online services with your bank, you can choose Online Financial Institutions List to see if your bank participates. QuickBooks opens the Financial Institutions Directory Web site (see Figure 16-2).

**Tip** *The best way to find out what your own bank offers is to select Any Services as the service type. If you find your bank on the list, it's likely the opening Web page, which contains a list of the service types offered.*

Scroll through the list to find your bank and click its listing. The right pane of your browser window displays information about the bank's online services, along with a link to its online Web site. Many banks also display an Apply Now button (or one similarly named), and clicking it opens an application.

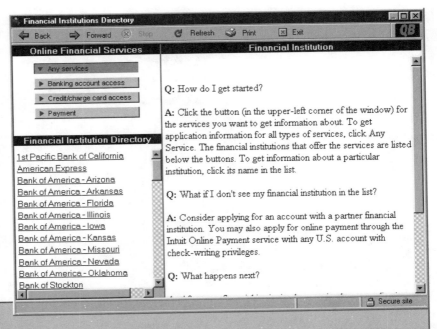

**Figure 16-2 •** Select the type of online banking service you want to look for, then scroll through the list to see if your bank participates.

## Apply for Online Services

If you already know that your bank has online services, but you haven't filled out an application, you can apply online by selecting the command Apply For Online Banking from the Set Up Online Financial Services submenu. The Online Banking Setup Interview wizard seen in Figure 16-3 opens to guide you through the process.

Click Next to begin. In the next wizard window, select I Would Like To Get Application Information Over the Internet. Click Next to move to the next window, and click the Apply Now button. QuickBooks takes you to the Financial Institutions Directory Web site, which is the same location described in the previous section.

Scroll through the list to find your bank, and click on its listing. In the right pane, click the Apply Now button (if there isn't one, follow the instructions your bank has placed in the right pane).

**Figure 16-3 • Use the Online Banking wizard to apply for services at your bank.**

**Caution** *You may see a warning that you are about to send information to an Internet zone in which it might be possible for other people to see the data you send. Select Yes to continue (you might want to select the option not to be warned in the future). If this makes you nervous, forget online banking, because there's no guaranteed security on the Internet—even though Intuit and your bank both make every possible effort to keep data secure.*

When your bank's application form appears in the browser window, fill it out and submit it. Your bank will send you information about using its online service, along with a PIN that's been assigned. All banks provide a method of changing the PIN to one of your own choosing. In fact, many banks insist that you change the PIN the first time you access online services.

**Note** *If your bank doesn't accept applications online, you should see a telephone number for online services on the Web site.*

## Using the QuickBooks Online Payment Service

If your bank doesn't participate in online services, and if your prime motivation for banking online is paying your bills via the Internet, you can sign up for that service directly with QuickBooks.

When the Financial Institutions list is displayed in your browser window, scroll through the list to find and choose QuickBooks Bill Pay Service in the left pane. QuickBooks travels to the Intuit Online Payment Service site on the Internet. Read the information (see Figure 16-4) and, if you're interested, click Apply Now.

An application form appears on your screen. Fill out the information and click the Print icon on your browser toolbar to print it (or print the blank form and fill it in manually). Then take these steps:

1. Sign the application (two signatures if this is a joint application).
2. Mark one of your bank account checks VOID (just write the word "VOID" in the payee section of the check). Be careful not to obliterate the important information that's encoded along the bottom of the check (your account number and the bank routing number).
3. If you are signing up for online payment for multiple bank accounts, send a voided check for each account. QuickBooks collects its fees directly from your checking account, so indicate which bank account is the billing account by writing "Billing Account" on the back of the appropriate check.
4. Mail your completed, signed application, along with the voided check(s) to the address indicated on the application.

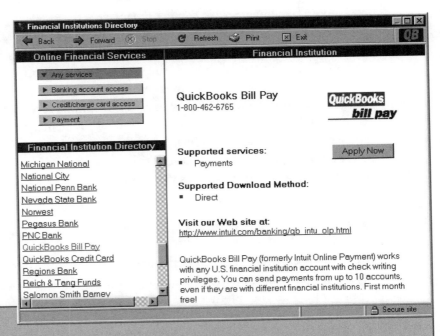

**Figure 16-4 • If your bank won't work directly with your QuickBooks software, QuickBooks will work with your bank to let you pay bills online.**

In a couple of weeks, you'll receive all the information you need to begin paying your bills online.

## Using the QuickBooks Credit Card Service

If your bank doesn't provide online credit card processing services, you can use the QuickBooks services. Follow the instructions to access the QuickBooks online payment service, except choose QuickBooks Credit Card instead of QuickBooks Bill Pay Service in the left pane.

Click Apply Now in the right pane or click the link for more information about this service before you apply. This is actually an application for a QuickBooks credit card that you can use to pay business expenses.

## Enabling Your Online Bank Accounts

After you've signed up with your bank and have your secret PIN, you must configure your QuickBooks bank account(s) for online services.

**Note** *Some banks use passwords instead of PINs.*

Choose Banking | Set Up Online Financial Services | Apply For Online Banking. The Online Banking Setup Interview wizard appears, and this time you should click the Enable Accounts tab. Follow the instructions and answer the questions as you proceed through the wizard. (Click Next to keep moving along.)

As you go through the steps in the wizard, you're configuring a bank account as an online account. You'll be asked to select the online services you'll use with this account. Choose online account access, online payments, or both (depending on the services you've signed up for).

You can create online bank accounts in QuickBooks for as many accounts and different financial institutions as you need.

# Performing Online Transactions

After you've set up your online banking permissions with your financial institutions and established your online bank account(s) in QuickBooks, you're ready to do your banking on the Internet.

# Accessing Your Bank Account Online

You can connect to your online bank records and check the balance and activity of your account. When you're viewing your account online, the list of transactions can be downloaded to your computer in order to update your QuickBooks register. (You'll have to enter your PIN or password, of course, to view your account.) Follow the directions on the screen to place the information into your QuickBooks system.

# Transferring Money Between Accounts Online

If you have multiple accounts at your financial institution, you can transfer money between those accounts. For example, you may have a money market account for your business in addition to your checking account.

To transfer money online, you must have applied at your financial institution for online banking for both accounts. You'll probably have a unique PIN for each account. To make your life less complicated, you should make changes while you're online to ensure both accounts have the same PIN. In addition, you must have enabled both accounts for online access within QuickBooks.

There are two methods you can use to transfer funds between online accounts: Use the transfer funds function, or use the register for either account.

## Using the Transfer Funds Function

The simplest way to move money between your online accounts is to use the QuickBooks Transfer Funds Between Accounts window, which you reach by choosing Banking | Transfer Funds from the menu bar.

Specify the sending and receiving accounts (remember, both must be enabled for online access) and enter the amount you want to transfer. Be sure to select the option for Online Funds Transfer. Click Save & Close. Then choose Banking | Online Banking Center, make sure the transaction has a check mark, and click Send.

## Using the Bank Register to Transfer Funds

You can enter a transfer directly into the account register of the bank account from which you are sending the money. The significant data entry is the one in the check number column; instead of a check number, type the word **send**. Don't enter a payee, enter the amount, and enter the receiving account in the account field. Then choose Banking | Online Banking Center, make sure the transaction has a check mark, and click Send.

## Paying Bills Online

You can pay your bills in QuickBooks, then go online to send the payments to the payees. You may either use your own bank (if it's capable of working with QuickBooks to pay bills online) or use the QuickBooks bill paying service. In this section, when I say "bank," you can mentally substitute the QuickBooks service if that's what you're using.

If your vendor can accept electronic funds, this is a breeze. What happens is that your bank's software transmits the payment electronically, and the vendor's bank uses its software to accept it—no paper, no mail, no delays. If your vendor cannot accept electronic funds, your bank actually prints a check and mails it.

There are three methods for creating the transaction in QuickBooks:

- Use the Write Checks window.
- Use the Pay Bills window.
- Use the register for the account you use for online payments.

I think the easiest way is using the Write Checks window. Here's how it works:

1. Click the Check icon on the icon bar, press CTRL-W, or choose Banking | Write Checks from the menu bar to open the Write Checks window.
2. Select the bank account.
3. Select the Online Banking option.
4. Select the vendor. If your information on the vendor doesn't include an address, telephone number, and bank account number, QuickBooks will ask you to provide whatever information is missing.
5. Enter the delivery date, which is the date on which you want the funds to be delivered.

**Note** *The first time you use online bill paying, the default delivery date is two days after the current date. Thereafter, the default delivery date will be one day after the current date.*

6. Enter the amount of the online payment.
7. Enter an optional memo if you want to include a message to the vendor.

**Caution**     *A memo can only be delivered as a voucher or stub, which means that your payment will not be made electronically even if the vendor is able to accept electronic payments. Instead, a check is sent, which delays the payment.*

8. Assign the expense account (or item sale) in the line item section of the window.

9. Repeat this process for each payment you're making.

Finally, go online to transmit the information to the Online Banking Center. Choose Banking | Online Banking Center. In the Online Banking Center window, click Send. Your payments are sent to the big bill-paying machine on the Net.

## Creating Online Transaction Reports

You can track your online activities using the available QuickBooks reports. The quickest way to see your online transactions is to choose Reports | Accountant & Taxes | Transaction Detail By Account.

In the report window, click the Modify Report button, and click the Filters tab. In the Filter list box, select Online Status. Click the arrow to the right of the Online Status box and select the online status option you need:

**All**     Reports all transactions whether they were online transactions or not (don't choose this option if you're trying to get a report on your online transactions).

**Online To Send**     Reports the online transactions you've created but not yet sent online.

**Online Sent**     Reports only the online transactions you've sent.

**Any Online**     Reports on all the online transactions you've created, both sent and waiting.

**Not Online**     Excludes the online transactions from the report. (Don't choose this option either.)

After you've set the filter options, click OK to return to the report window.

## Doing Business with Big Business

Jerry's Computer Upgrades is a thriving small business, specializing in adding memory, peripherals, gizmos, and doodads to PCs. Jerry buys lots of memory chips, and his supplier has offered a 10 percent price reduction if Jerry will deposit his payments electronically (and on time, for which Jerry already gets a 2-percent deduction in the bill amount).

The supplier explained that online payments are much less work because they eliminate the labor and time involved in opening mail, crediting Jerry's account, writing a deposit slip, and taking the check to the bank. Jerry called around and asked other vendors if they had the ability to accept online payments. Many of them did (but nobody else offered Jerry a discount for using online bill paying).

Jerry went to his bank and opened a separate account for his online bill paying. He also enabled online transactions for his regular operating account so he could transfer money into the online bill-paying account as he needed it.

Now Jerry can hold onto his money until a day before payment is due to his vendors (why should they get the interest?) instead of sending checks several days ahead in order to ensure that his 2-percent discount for timely payment is valid.

His normal procedure is to go online, upload the checks he's written for online bill paying, and then transfer the appropriate amount of money from his operating account to his bill-paying account.

Because the accounts are separate, generating reports about his online transaction activity is easy. Because he doesn't have to sign checks, put them in envelopes, place stamps on the envelopes, and take the envelopes to the mailbox, Jerry is saving time. And Jerry, like all good business people, believes that time is money.

# Receiving Customer Payments Online

Besides the online activities that permit you to track your own bank account activity, transfer money, and pay your own bills, QuickBooks offers a way for your customers to pay you online. This service is provided by the QuickBooks online billing service.

The QuickBooks online billing service offers your customers a way to pay your bills on the QuickBooks online payment site. The customer can enter a credit card number to pay the bills, or use an online payment service.

You can notify the customer about this online service by e-mailing the invoice with the online service URL in the cover note, or by snail-mailing the invoice and sending an e-mail message with the online service URL. The customer clicks the link to the URL to travel to the QuickBooks Web site and arrange for payment.

QuickBooks notifies you that the payment is made, and you can download the payment information into your bank register using the standard online banking procedures.

To learn more about this service, or to sign up, choose Customers | Customer Services | Get Paid Faster. In the Online Billing window (see Figure 16-5), use the links to learn more about the service or to sign up.

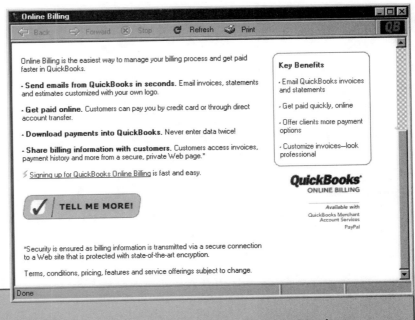

**Figure 16-5 •** Learn about online customer payments and decide if you want to sign up.

# Year-End Procedures

## In this Chapter:

- *Run reports on your financial condition*

- *Print 1099 forms*

- *Make year-end journal entries*

- *Get ready for tax time*

- *Close the books*

## Chapter 17

The end of the year is a mad house for bookkeepers, and that's true for major corporations as well as small businesses. There is so much to do, so many reports to examine, corrections to make, entries to create—whew!

You can relax a bit. You don't have to show up at the office on January 1st (or the first day of your new fiscal year if you're not on a calendar year). Everything doesn't have to be accomplished immediately. QuickBooks is date-sensitive so you can continue to work in the new year. As long as the dates of new transactions are after the last day of your fiscal year, the transactions won't work their way into your year-end calculations.

Meanwhile, even after the first day of the next fiscal year, you can continue to work on transactions for the current fiscal year, making sure you change the transaction dates any time a transaction window opens with the current (next year) date.

# Running Year-End Financial Reports

The standard financial reports you run for the year provide a couple of services for you:

- You can see the economic health of your business.
- You can examine the report to make sure everything is posted correctly.

To run financial reports, click the Reports menu listing. For year-end reports, you'll need to access several types of reports (see Chapter 15 for lots of information about creating and modifying reports).

## Running a Year-End P&L Report

Start with a Profit & Loss Standard report (also called an *income statement*), which is one of the reports in the Company & Financial listing. Set the date range as This Fiscal Year. Voilà! The report displays the year-end balances for all the income and expense accounts in your general ledger that had any activity this year.

Examine the report, and if anything seems out of line, double-click the total to see the postings for that account. You can double-click any of the posting lines to see the original transaction.

If there's a transaction that now looks as if it's in error, you can take corrective action. You cannot delete or void a bill you paid, nor a customer invoice for which you received payment, of course. However, you might be able to talk to a customer or vendor for whom you've found a problem and work out a satisfactory arrangement for credits. Or you may find that you posted an expense or income transaction to the wrong general ledger account. If so, make a journal entry to correct it (see the section on making journal entries later in this chapter). Then run the year-end P&L report again and print it.

## Running a Year-End Balance Sheet

Your real financial health is demonstrated in your balance sheet. To run a year-end balance sheet, select Balance Sheet Standard from the Report Finder and set the date range for This Fiscal Year. Your year-end balance sheet figures appear in the report.

The balance sheet figures are more than a list of numbers; they're a list of chores. Check with your accountant first, but most of the time you'll find that the following advice is offered:

- Pay any payroll withholding liabilities with a check dated in the current year in order to clear them from the balance sheet and gain the expense deduction for the employer taxes.

- If you have an A/P balance, pay some bills ahead of time. For example, pay your rent or mortgage payment that's due the first day of the next fiscal year during the last month of this fiscal year. Enter and pay vendor bills earlier than their due dates in order to pay them this year and gain the expense deduction for this year.

# Issuing 1099 Forms

If any vendors are eligible for 1099 forms, you need to print the forms and mail them. First, make sure your 1099 setup is correct by choosing Edit | Preferences and selecting the Tax: 1099 icon. Click Company Preferences to see your settings (see Figure 17-1).

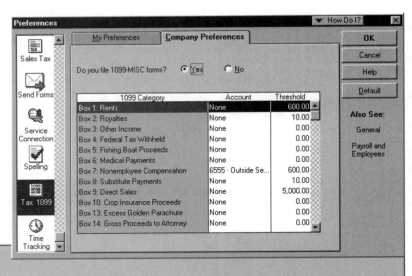

**Figure 17-1 • Check the threshold and posting account information in your 1099 preferences.**

Check the latest IRS rules and make any changes to the threshold amounts for the categories you need. Also assign an account to each category for which you'll be issuing Form 1099 to vendors.

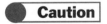 **Caution** *You cannot assign the same account to more than one category.*

## Run a 1099 Report

Before you print the forms, you should print a report on your 1099 vendors. To accomplish this, choose Reports | Vendors & Payables and select one of the 1099 reports:

- 1099 Summary lists each vendor eligible for a 1099 with the total amount paid to the vendor.
- 1099 Detail lists each transaction for each vendor eligible for a 1099.

You can make adjustments to transactions, if necessary, in order to make sure your 1099 vendors have the right totals.

It's also a good idea to go through your entire Vendor list to find any vendors who did not appear on the 1099 report but who should be receiving 1099s. If you find any, edit the Vendor record to make sure the 1099 option is selected on the

Additional Info tab. You must also have an identification number for the vendor, in the form of either a Social Security number or a federal EIN number if the vendor is a business (proprietorship or partnership—corporations do not receive 1099s).

## Print 1099 Forms

To print the 1099 forms, choose File | Print Forms | 1099s. The specific type of 1099 form that's offered depends on the preferences you set for 1099s and vendors. Most businesses use the 1099-MISC form.

- Be sure the dates are correct in the Printing 1099 Forms window and click OK.
- When the list of 1099 recipients appears, any vendor who is over the appropriate threshold should have a check mark.
- Click Preview to see what the form will look like when it prints. Zoom in to make sure your company name, address, and EIN number are correct. Click Close on the Preview window to return to the 1099 window. Then load the 1099 forms into your printer and click Print.
- If you're using a laser or inkjet printer, set the number of copies so you have enough for your own records—you'll need three. Dot matrix printers use multipart forms.

When the forms are printed, send one to the vendor, one to the government, and put the third copy in your files. You must deliver the forms to vendors by January 31.

Repeat these procedures for each type of 1099 form you are required to print (most businesses only need to worry about the 1099-MISC form).

# Making Year-End Journal Entries

There are probably a couple of journal entries your accountant wants you to make before you close your books for the year:

- Depreciation entries
- Prior retained earnings moved to a different account
- Any adjustments needed for cash versus accrual reporting (these are usually reversed on the first day of the next fiscal year)

**Note**    *See Chapter 14 for detailed information about making journal entries.*

You can send the P&L and balance sheet reports to your accountant, and you'll receive journal entry instructions. Or you can send your accountant an accountant's review copy of your company data, and let your accountant make the journal entries and import the changes when the review copy is returned. See Chapter 15 to learn how to use the accountant's review copy feature.

# Running Tax Reports

Some small business owners prepare their own taxes manually or by using a tax software program like TurboTax. Many small businesses turn the tax preparation chores over to their accountants. No matter which method you choose for tax preparation, you should run the reports that tell you whether your QuickBooks data files are ready for tax preparation. Is all the necessary data entered? Do the bottom line numbers call for some special tax planning or some special tax considerations?

# Check Tax Line Information

If you're going to do your own taxes, every account in your chart of accounts that is tax-related must have the right tax form in the account's tax line assignment. To see if any tax line assignments are missing, choose Reports | Accountant & Taxes | Income Tax Preparation. When the report appears, all your accounts are listed, along with the tax form assigned to each account. If you created your own chart of accounts, the number of accounts that you neglected to assign to a tax form is likely to be quite large, as shown in Figure 17-2.

Before you can prepare your own taxes, you must edit each account to add the tax information. To do so, open the chart of accounts and select an account. Press CTRL-E to edit the account and select a tax form from the Tax Line entry drop-down list. Your selections vary depending upon the organizational type of your company (proprietorship, partnership, S corp, C corp, etc.). Your organizational type is part of the Company Information data, which you can see by choosing Company | Company Information from the QuickBooks menu bar.

> **Note** *Be sure the Income Tax Form Used field is filled out properly on your Company Information dialog box. If it's blank, you won't see the tax information fields on your accounts.*

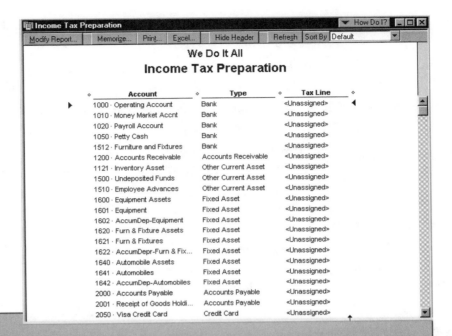

**Figure 17-2 •** Look what happens at the end of the year if you don't take the time to assign tax forms when you create your chart of accounts.

If the account is an expense account, and you invoice customers for reimbursement, select the check box Track Reimbursed Expenses and specify the account to which you post the reimbursed monies (usually an income account). This field only appears in expense accounts if you've enabled the feature to track reimbursed expenses as income. Configure this function by choosing Edit | Preferences, clicking the Sales & Customers icon, and selecting the Company Preferences tab. Then click the Track Reimbursed Expenses As Income check box.

This feature provides a method for netting out the expense on your tax return. However, you can see a total for your expenses, and a separate total for the amount of money you received by way of reimbursement from customers. If you don't track the reimbursements to a separate account, but instead you write the postings for reimbursement back to the original account, that account is automatically netted out.

**Note**    *One of the selections in the drop-down list is Not Tax-Related, which may be appropriate for some accounts.*

If you don't know which form and category to assign, here's an easy trick for getting that information:

1. Choose File | New Company to create a new company in QuickBooks.
2. Begin answering the wizard questions, using a fake company name.
3. Choose a company type that's the same as (or close to) your own type of business.
4. When prompted, save the new company file.
5. Tell the EasyStep Interview wizard to create a chart of accounts.
6. After the chart of accounts is created, click Leave to stop the interview.
7. Choose File | Open Company and open the new company.
8. Open the chart of accounts list and press CTRL-P to print the list.
9. The printed list has the tax form information.
10. Open your real company, open the chart of accounts, and use the information on the printed document to enter tax form information.

## Calculate Other Important Tax Information

There are some taxable numbers that aren't available through the normal QuickBooks reports. One of the most common is the report on company officer compensation if your business is incorporated.

If your business is a C corporation, you file tax form 1120, while a Subchapter S corporation files tax form 1120S. Both of these forms require you to separate compensation for corporate officers from the other employee compensation. You will have to add those totals from payroll reports (either QuickBooks payroll or an outside payroll service).

You can avoid the need to calculate this by creating a separate Payroll item called Officer Compensation and assigning it to its own account (which you'll also have to create). Then open the Employee card for each officer and change the Earnings item to the new item. Do this for next year; it's probably too late for this year's end-of-year process.

## Using TurboTax

If you purchase TurboTax to do your taxes, you don't have to do anything special in QuickBooks to transfer the information. Open TurboTax, and tell it to import your QuickBooks company file.

Almost everything you need is transferred to TurboTax. There are some details you'll have to enter directly into TurboTax (for example, home office expenses for a Schedule C form).

# Closing Your Books

After all the year-end reports have been run, any necessary journal entries have been entered, and your taxes have been filed (and paid), it's traditional to go through the exercise of closing the books.

Typically, closing the books occurs some time after the end of the fiscal year, usually within the first couple of months of the next fiscal year (right after the tax forms have been sent to the government).

The exercise of closing the books is performed in order to lock the books. No user can change anything. After taxes have been filed based on the information in the system, nothing can be changed. It's too late. This is it. The information is etched in cement.

## Understanding Closing in QuickBooks

QuickBooks doesn't use the traditional accounting software closing procedures. In most other business accounting software, closing the year means you cannot post transactions to any date in that year, nor can you manipulate any transactions in the closed year. Closing the books in QuickBooks does not etch the information in cement; it can be changed and/or deleted by users with the appropriate permissions.

QuickBooks does not require you to close the books in order to keep working in the software. You can work forever, year after year, without performing a closing process. However, many QuickBooks users prefer to lock the transactions for a year as a way to prevent any changes to the data.

The QuickBooks closing (locking) procedure is tied in with the users and passwords features that are part of the software. This is so closing can lock some users out of changing anything in last year's books and still permit an administrator (and selected users) to make changes. If a restricted user attempts to change (or delete) a transaction in the closed period, an error message appears telling the user he or she is denied access.

 **Tip**  *If you haven't set up users, read Chapter 21.*

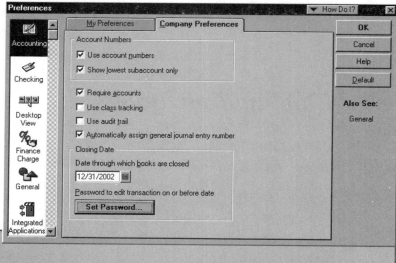

**Figure 17-3 • Entering a closing date is the first step to locking down data.**

## Closing the Year

In QuickBooks, you close the year by entering a closing date. This inherently does nothing more than lock users out of the previous year's transactions. At the same time, you can reconfigure user rights to enable or prevent entry into closed transactions with the following steps:

1. Choose Edit | Preferences to open the Preferences dialog box.
2. Click the Accounting icon.
3. Select the Company Preferences tab.
4. Enter the closing date, which is the last date of your fiscal year (see Figure 17-3).

If your fiscal year is different from a calendar year, don't worry about payroll. The payroll files and features (including 1099s) are locked into a calendar year configuration and closing your books doesn't have any effect on them.

## Preventing Access to Closed Books

To prevent users from changing transactions in the closed year (or to permit them to), assign a password for manipulating closed data. Click Set Password. In the Set

Closing Date Password dialog box, enter the password, then press TAB and enter it again in the Confirm Password field.

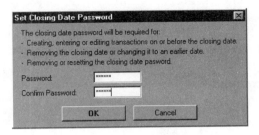

**Caution**    *If you've set up users and passwords for access to your QuickBooks data file, only the QuickBooks Administrator can set the closing date and password.*

The characters you type are displayed on the screen as asterisks (in case somebody is peeking over your shoulder). If you don't enter exactly the same characters in both fields, QuickBooks asks you to start over. If that happens, you may have chosen a password so complicated that it invites typos, which could mean you'll have a problem using the password when you need it. Here are some guidelines for creating effective passwords:

- Don't use a password that is easy to figure out. Your birthday, your spouse's name, your nickname, your dog's name, and other similar phrases are easy to guess.

- If you distribute the password to other users to whom you want to grant the right to manipulate closed data, don't post a note on their desk lamps, or office doors, and don't yell down the hall. Use e-mail if nobody else has access to their Inbox (users who habitually leave their Inbox windows loaded on the screen can't say that).

- Write yourself a note with the password and put it in a secure place (your wallet, a locked desk drawer, etc.). Even if you're sure you'll remember the password when you need it, don't fail to take this step. History has already proven you wrong (and you can confirm this by querying any QuickBooks consultant or any Intuit support technician, who had to pass along the bad news that the file had to be sent to Intuit for unlocking—for a fee).

**Note** | If you're upgrading to QuickBooks 2002 from a previous version, the closing date password is a new implementation of the password feature. Password protection for closed books is available, even if you don't use the User/Password features for your QuickBooks files.

If you need to change or remove the closing date (although I can't imagine the circumstances under which this would occur), QuickBooks requires the password to perform this action.

**Note** | If you're using the Premier Version of QuickBooks, you can also enable auditing, which means users who have password rights to manipulate transactions within the closed year period leave behind a file that tracks everything they did.

## Creating a Year-End Backup

After all the numbers are checked, all the journal entries are made, and the books have been closed by entering a closing date as described in the previous section, do a separate backup. Don't put this backup on one of the floppy disks you're using for your normal backups. If you use other removable media for backups (such as Zip or Jaz drives), use a fresh disk or create a folder on the removable drive for this backup. Label the disk (or folder) "Year-End Backup 2002." Make several copies.

# Using Time and Billing

*Lots of service businesses sell time; it's the most important commodity they have. Actually, most service businesses are really selling knowledge and expertise, but nobody's ever figured out how to put a value on those assets. The solution, therefore, is to charge for the time it takes to pass along and use all that expertise (that explanation was originally voiced by Abraham Lincoln as he explained why and how attorneys charge for time).*

*If you've installed the Time and Billing features of QuickBooks, Part Three of this book covers all the steps you need to take to set your system up for maximum efficiency and accuracy. Then we'll discuss all the ways you can use the functions and tools that are available within the system.*

**Part Three**

# Using Time Tracking

## In this Chapter:

- *Configure time tracking*

- *Fill out timesheets*

- *Edit timesheets*

- *Bill for time*

## Chapter 18

You can track time just to see how much time is spent completing a project or working for a customer, or you can track time for the purpose of billing the customer for the time. Time tracking does not have to be connected to time billing. In and of itself, time tracking is a way to see what everyone in your company is doing, and how much time they spend doing each thing. Some of those activities may be administrative and unconnected to customers.

You can use this information in a variety of ways, depending on what it is you want to know about the way your business runs. If you charge retainer fees for your services, time tracking is a terrific way to figure out which customers may need to have the retainer amount raised.

# Configuring Time Tracking

When you first install QuickBooks Pro, and whenever you create a new company, you're asked if you want to track time. If you respond affirmatively, QuickBooks Pro turns on the time-tracking features. If you opted to skip time tracking, you can turn it on if you change your mind later. In fact, if you did turn it on, you can turn it off if you find you're not using it.

If you're not sure whether you turned on time tracking when you installed your company, choose Edit | Preferences from the QuickBooks menu bar. Select the Time Tracking icon and click the Company Preferences tab. Make sure the Yes option button is selected.

## Configuring Your Work Week

By default, QuickBooks Pro assumes your work week starts on a Monday. However, if your business is open every day of the week, you might want to use a standard Sunday-to-Saturday pattern for tracking time.

You can turn on, turn off, or configure time tracking quite quickly. Use the Time Tracking Preferences dialog box and specify the first day of your work week. Then click OK.

**Tip**    *If you've been tracking time and decide you don't want to bill customers for time any longer, you can turn off time tracking. Any time records you've accumulated are saved—nothing is deleted. If you change your mind again later and turn time tracking back on, the records are available to you.*

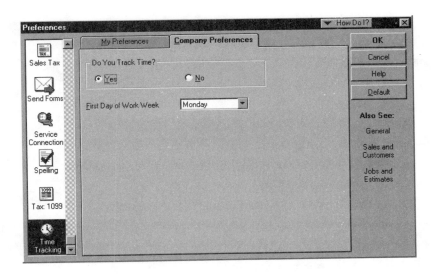

## Configuring Workers

If you're tracking time for your employees, outside contractors, or yourself, everybody who must keep track of his or her time must exist in the system. Each person must also fill out a timesheet.

### Tracking Employee Time

If you are running the QuickBooks payroll feature, you already have employees in your QuickBooks system. You can track the time of any employee who fills out a timesheet (timesheets are covered later in this chapter).

You can also use the timesheet data to pay the employee, using the number of hours reported in the time-tracking system to determine the number of hours for which the employee is paid. For this to work, however, the employee must be linked to his or her timesheet. As a result, you must modify the employee record:

1. Choose Lists | Employee List from the menu bar to open the Employee List.
2. Double-click the listing of the employee you want to link to time tracking.
3. Move to the Payroll Info tab of the employee record (see Figure 18-1).
4. Select the Use Time Data To Create Paychecks check box.
5. Click OK.

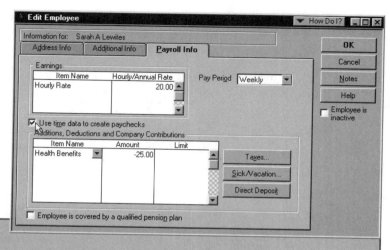

**Figure 18-1** • Link an employee to the time-tracking system if you want to use timesheets to calculate the paycheck.

## Tracking Vendor Time

Any vendor in your system who is paid for his or her time can have that time tracked for the purpose of billing customers. Most of the time these vendors are referred to as outside contractors, or subcontractors. You don't have to do anything to the vendor record to effect time tracking; you merely need to record the time used as the vendor sends bills.

## Tracking Other Worker Time

You may need to track the time of people who are neither employees nor vendors. The word "employees" means you have established QuickBooks payroll services. If you have employees, but you don't use QuickBooks payroll, they're not employees to your QuickBooks software.

QuickBooks provides a system list called Other Names. You use this list to amass names or descriptions that don't fit in the other QuickBooks lists. You can track time for people by entering their names into the Other Names List. Here are some situations in which you'll need to use the Other Names feature:

- You have employees and use QuickBooks payroll, but you are not an employee because you take a draw instead of a paycheck. In this case, you must add your own name to the Other Names List if you want to track your own time.

- You have employees and are not using QuickBooks payroll, so there is no Employees list in your system. You must add each employee name to the Other Names List in order to track employee time.

- You have no employees and your business is a proprietorship or a partnership. Owner or partner names must be entered into the Other Names List in order to track time.

## Configuring the Tasks

Most of the tasks you track already exist in your system as service items. These are the items you use when you bill customers for services. However, because you can use time tracking to analyze the way people in your organization spend their time, you may want to add service items that are relevant to non-customer tasks.

For example, if you want to track the time people spend performing administrative tasks for the business, you can add a service item called Administrative to your items list. If you want to be more specific, you can name the particular administrative tasks you want to track (for example, Bookkeeping, Equipment Repair, New Sales Calls, Public Relations, and so on).

To enter new items, click the Item button on the icon bar. When the Item List window opens, press CTRL-N to open a new item form. Select Service as the item type and name the new item. Here are some guidelines for administrative items:

- If you're specifying administrative tasks, create a service named Administration, and then make each specific administrative task a subitem of Administration.

- Don't put an amount in the Rate box. You're not charging a customer for this service, and you can calculate the amount you're paying the recipient when you make the payment (via payroll or vendor checks).

- Because you must assign an account, choose or create an innocuous revenue account (such as Other Revenue). No money is posted to the account.

Because time tracking is connected to customers, in order to track administrative work, you must also create a customer for the occasions when no real customer is being tracked. The easiest way to do that is to create a new customer to represent your company. For example, you may want to create a customer named House, or InHouse.

## Configuring User Permissions

If you're using multiple user and password features in QuickBooks, you must edit each user to make sure people can use the time-tracking forms. See Chapter 21 for detailed information about setting up users and permissions.

# Using Timesheets

QuickBooks offers two methods for recording the time you spent on tasks: Single Activity and Weekly Timesheet.

- Single Activity is a form you use to enter what you did when you perform a single task at a specific time on a specific date. For example, a Single Activity form may record the fact that you made a telephone call on behalf of a customer, or you repaired some piece of equipment for a customer, or you performed some administrative task for the company which is unrelated to a customer.

- Weekly Timesheet is a form in which you indicate how much time and on which date you performed work. Each Weekly Timesheet entry can also include the name of the customer for whom the work was performed.

Your decision about which method to use depends on the type of work you do and on the efficiency of your workers' memories. People tend to put off filling in Weekly Timesheets and then attempt to reconstruct their activities in order to complete the timesheets. This frequently ends up being less than accurate as an approach. The method only works properly if everyone remembers to open the timesheets and fill them in as soon as they complete each task. Uh huh, sure.

**Tip**   *If you fill out a Single Activity form, every time you open a Weekly Timesheet form any single activity within that week is automatically inserted into the Weekly Timesheet.*

## Using the Single Activity Form

Use the Single Activity form when you need to record one event you want to track. Use these steps to open and fill out the form:

1. Choose Employees | Time Tracking | Time/Enter Single Activity from the menu bar to open the Time/Enter Single Activity window (see Figure 18-2).

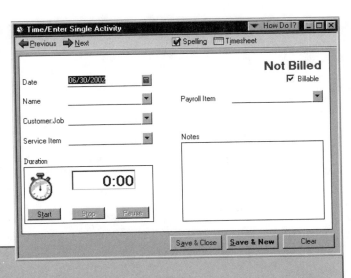

**Figure 18-2 • Fill out the details to indicate how you spent your time.**

2. The Date field is automatically filled in with the current date. If this activity took place previously, change the date.

3. Click the arrow to the right of the Name field and select the name of the person who performed the work from the list that appears. The list contains vendors, employees, and names from the Other Names List. (You can use <Add New> to add a new name.)

**Note**   *If you select an employee name from the list, and that employee is not configured for using time data to create paychecks, QuickBooks asks if you'd like to change that configuration. If the employee is just tracking time for job costing purposes, and is not paid from these timesheets, click No.*

4. If your time was spent working on a task for a customer rather than performing an administrative task, select the customer or job in the Customer:Job field. Do this whether or not the customer is going to be billed for the time.

5. In the Service Item field, select the task.

6. In the Duration box, enter the amount of time you're reporting in the format hh:mm.

7. If this time is billable to the customer, the Billable check box should be marked (it is by default). If the time is not going to be billed to the customer, click the box to remove the check mark.

8. If the Payroll Item field appears, select the payroll item that applies to this time (for example, salary or hourly wages). This field only appears if an employee has been linked to the time-tracking system, as explained earlier in this chapter.

9. Click in the Notes box to enter any comments or additional information you want to record about this activity.

10. Click Save & New to fill out another Single Activity form, or click Save & Close to finish.

## Using the Stopwatch

You can let QuickBooks track the time you're spending on a specific task. Click the Start button in the Duration box of the Activity window when you begin the task. QuickBooks tracks hours and minutes as they elapse.

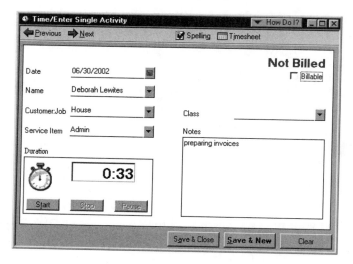

- To pause the counting when you're interrupted, click Pause. Then click Start to pick up where you left off.
- To stop timing, click Stop. The time is recorded in the Weekly Timesheet.

Click Save & New to fill out the next activity; click Save & Close if you're finished recording your time.

You can set the format for reporting time, both on the activity sheet and in the stopwatch window. Some companies prefer the hh:mm format; other companies prefer a decimal format (e.g., 1.6 hours). To establish your preference, choose Edit | Preferences and click the General icon. Then select the Company Preferences tab, and use the options in the Time Format section of the dialog box to select the appropriate format.

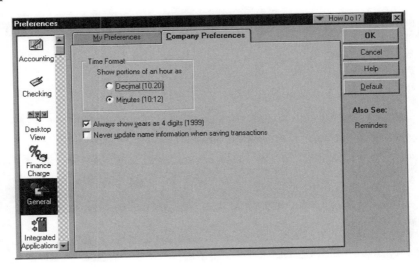

## Using Weekly Timesheets

A Weekly Timesheet records the same information as the Single Activity form, except that the information is recorded in week-at-a-time blocks. To use this form, choose Employees | Time Tracking | Use Weekly Timesheet to open the Weekly Timesheet window (see Figure 18-3).

1. Select your name from the list that appears when you click the arrow to the right of the Name field.

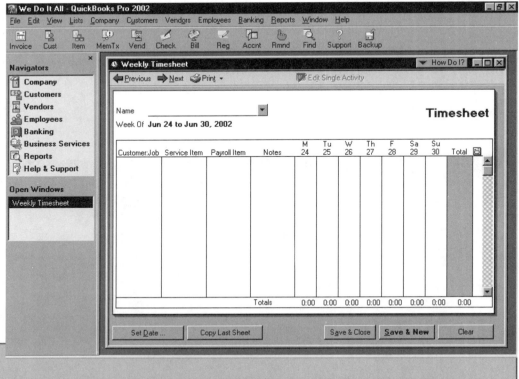

**Figure 18-3 •** You may find it easier and quicker to enter information on a weekly basis.

2. If you want to enter time for a different week, click the Set Date button and enter the first day of any week for which you want to enter activities. (The first day of your company work week is set in Edit | Preferences | Time Tracking.)

3. Click in the Customer:Job column to display an arrow which you click to see the Customer List. Select the customer connected to the activity (or select the in-house listing if you're performing administrative work unconnected to a customer).

4. Enter the service item that describes your activity.

5. If you're an employee whose paycheck is linked to your timesheets, select the Payroll Item that fits the activity. If your name is attached to the Other Name or Vendor list, or you're an employee who is not paid from the timesheets, you won't see a Payroll Item column.

6. In the Notes column, enter any comments you feel are necessary.

7. Click the column that represents the day for which you are entering a timesheet activity and enter the number of hours worked on this task.

8. Move to the beginning of the next row to enter the next timesheet entry, repeating until you've accounted for your time for the week.

9. For each row, indicate whether the time is billable in the right-most column. By default, all time entries linked to a customer (in the first column) are billable. (The icon in the right-most column is supposed to look like an invoice.) Click the icon to put an X atop it if the time on this row is not billable.

10. Click Save & New to use a timesheet for a different week. Click Save & Close when you are finished entering time.

**Tip** If this week's timesheet has the same entries as the last timesheet this person filled out, click the Copy Last Sheet button to move the entries into this timesheet.

# Reporting Timesheet Information

Before you use the information on the timesheets, you can check the data and the other important elements (for example, whether billable and non-billable items are accurate). You can edit information, view and customize reports, and print the original timesheets.

## Running Timesheet Reports

To run reports on timesheets, choose Reports in the Navigator List, and select Jobs & Time as the type of report. Use one of these four reports:

- **Time By Job Summary** reports the amount of time spent for each service on your customers and their jobs.
- **Time By Job Detail** reports the details of the time spent for each customer and job, including dates and whether or not the time was marked as billable (see Figure 18-4). A billing status of Unbilled indicates the time is billable but hasn't yet been transferred to a customer invoice.

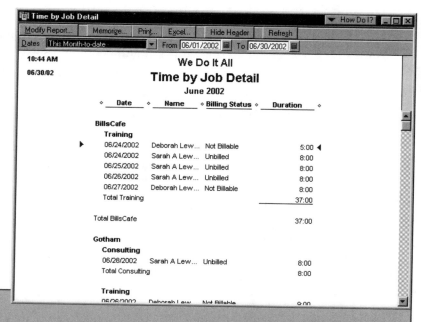

**Figure 18-4 •** Details from timesheets are sorted by customer and job in this report.

- **Time By Name** reports the amount of time each user tracked.
- **Time By Item** provides a quick analysis of the amount of time spent performing services your company is providing and to whom.

If you've made it a practice to encourage people to enter comments in the Notes section of the timesheet, you should change the report format so it includes those comments. You can do this only in the Time By Job Detail report:

1. Open the Time By Job Detail report and click the Modify Report button on the button bar.
2. In the Modify Report window, select Notes from the Columns list.
3. Click OK.

To make sure you always see the notes, you should memorize this report. Click the Memorize button on the report button bar and name the report. Hereafter, it will be available in the Memorized Reports list.

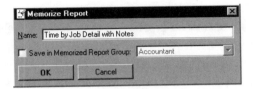

## Editing Entries in the Report

While you're browsing the report, double-click an activity listing to see the original entry, an example of which is seen in Figure 18-5. You can make changes on the original entry, which is necessary for the activity shown in Figure 18-5 because in-house administration tasks aren't billed to the in-house customer.

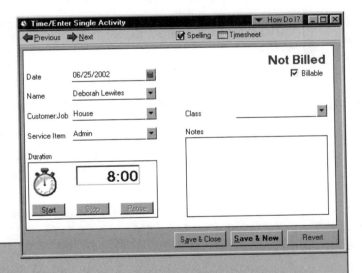

**Figure 18-5 • Check the original timesheet to see that the data is correct.**

If you make changes, when you click Save & Close to return to the report window, QuickBooks displays a message to ask whether you want to refresh the report to accommodate the changes. Click Yes.

## Editing Entries in the Timesheets

Before you use the timesheets for customer billing or payroll, make sure you examine them and make any needed corrections. In fact, you may want to take this step before you view any of the Jobs & Time reports.

The common revision is the billable status. If you have outside contractors or employees filling out timesheets, it's not unusual to have some confusion about which customers receive direct time billings. In fact, you may have customers to whom you send direct time bills only for certain activities and provide the remaining activities as part of your basic services.

To check timesheets, just open a new timesheet (choose Employees | Time Tracking | Use Weekly Timesheet). Select the person connected to the timesheet you want to inspect. Use the Previous or Next arrows at the time of the timesheet window, or click the Set Date button at the bottom of the window, to move to the timesheet you want to inspect. Then edit the information as necessary:

- You can change the number of hours for any activity item.
- Click the icon in the Billable column (the last column) to reverse the current status (it's a toggle). Line entries that are not billable have an X over the icon.
- To view (and edit if necessary) any notes, first click in any of the weekday columns to activate the Edit Single Activity icon at the top of the timesheet window. Click that icon to see the entry as a single activity, with the entire note available for viewing or editing.

**Caution** *If you've already used the timesheet data to bill the customer or pay the employee, the changes you make are useless. It's too late. Customer invoices and payroll records are not updated with your edits.*

## Printing the Weekly Timesheets

It's a common practice to have employees print their Weekly Timesheets and distribute them to the appropriate people. Usually that means your payroll person (or the person who phones in the payroll if you use an outside payroll service) or a personnel manager. However, you may want to designate one person to print all the timesheets.

To print timesheets, choose File | Print Forms | Timesheets from the QuickBooks menu bar to open the Select Time Sheets To Print window shown in Figure 18-6.

- By default, all timesheets are selected. To remove a timesheet, click the column with the check mark to de-select that listing. You can click Select None to de-select all listings, then click in the column to select one or more specific users.
- Change the date range to match the timesheets you want to print.
- To see any notes in their entirety, select the Print Full Activity Notes option. Otherwise, the default selection to print only the first line of any notes is empowered.

Click OK to print the selected timesheets. (Click Preview to see an onscreen display of the printed timesheets. From the Preview window you can click Close to return to the Select Timesheets To Print window or click Print to open the Print window.)

When the Print window opens, you can change the printer or options. Change the number of copies to print to match the number of people to whom you're distributing the timesheets.

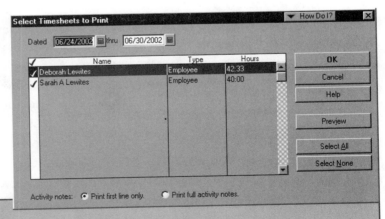

**Figure 18-6 • Print timesheets and distribute them to the appropriate people.**

One thing you should notice about printed (or previewed) timesheets is that there's a single column to indicate the billing status. The entries are codes:

- B = billable but not yet billed to the customer
- N = not billable
- D = billable and already billed to the customer

# Creating Invoices with Timesheets Data

After you've configured QuickBooks to track time, you can use the data you amass to help you create customer invoices quickly. For a full and detailed discussion about invoicing customers, please turn to Chapter 3.

## Plugging in Time Charges

When you're ready to bill customers for time, click the Invoice button on the icon bar and follow these steps:

1. In the Create Invoices window, select the customer or job.
2. Enter the date of this invoice (if it isn't today, which is the date that appears by default). Unbilled activities up to and including the invoice date are available for this invoice.
3. Click the Time/Costs button on the top of the invoice form to open the Choose Billable Time And Costs window. Click the Time tab to see the entries from timesheets, as shown in Figure 18-7.
4. Select the entries you want to include on this invoice (click Select All to use all the entries, otherwise click in the Use column to put a check mark on the entries you want to include).
5. If you don't want to change any options (see the following section), click OK to transfer the items to the invoice.
6. Click Save & New to continue to the next invoice, or Save & Close if you are finished creating invoices.

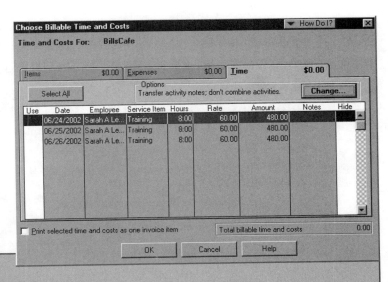

**Figure 18-7 • Timesheet entries for this customer/job are displayed so you can choose the ones you want to include on the invoice.**

# Changing Options for Time Charges

You can change the way you transfer data from the timesheets to the invoice. All the necessary tools for accomplishing this are on the Time tab of the Billable Time And Costs window that opens when you click the Time/Costs button on the Create Invoices window.

## Printing One Invoice Item

If you just want to invoice a total amount for time charges instead of showing each activity, click the check box next to the selection Print Selected Time And Costs as One Invoice Item. Then click OK to return to the invoice. Now you're going to go crazy unless you realize you have to take the word "print" literally. After you make the selection and return to the invoice form, you see every individual item listed on the invoice, with individual totals for each item. However, two things have changed on the invoice: The first line item is now an item named Reimb Group, and it has no amount. A new description appears below the individual time items, and it has an amount that is the total of the individual time charges. This entry is the description attached to the Reimb Group item.

Don't worry, the only thing that prints is this new Reimb Group, that last item. It prints as one item; the onscreen invoice is not the same as the printed invoice any more. If you're a skeptic, click the Preview button to see what the printed invoice will look like (told ya so!).

## Combining Service Items

If you don't want to combine all the time charges into one line, you can still be selective about the way information is transferred to the invoice. Click the Change button at the top of the Choose Billable Time And Costs dialog box to see your options.

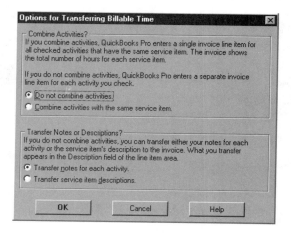

You can select the option Combine Activities With The Same Service Item to enter a single line item for each activity type. For example, if you have Consulting and Training as separate services, and there are several activities for each of those services, the invoice will have a line item for Consulting and another line item for Training. Each line will have the total for that service.

In the Transfer Notes Or Descriptions section of the Options window, you can choose to print the notes on each timesheet (the notes are printed in the Description column of the invoice). Select the option to transfer notes if you want the Description field to contain the notes from the timesheet entry instead of the description of the service. Select the option to transfer the service item description if you want the Description field filled in with the description attached to the service item.

**Caution** *Don't transfer notes unless you check every timesheet to make sure an employee hasn't entered a note you'd prefer the customer didn't see. Delete any such notes from the activity window when you edit the timesheets.*

## Using Timesheets for Internal Controls

In addition to billing his clients from timesheets, attorney Ernie Esquire uses the information to track the activities of his employees, all of whom are salaried (which means he doesn't use timesheet hours for payroll). Ernie has two office rules, and they both influence the way timesheets are configured and filled out:

- Billing time is entered in 10-minute blocks. This policy isn't uncommon in professional offices; it means that no matter how much time is spent on a client's work, the employee must round it up to the next 10-minute figure on the timesheet.
- An employee's day belongs to the company. Every moment of the eight-hour day for which the employee's salary is designated must be reported.

The billing time minimum means that when Ernie examines timesheets, he frequently finds many more minutes (or even hours) listed than the actual time the employee spent at work. Within a real 10-minute period, an employee who completes a quick activity for each of three clients can enter 30 minutes on the timesheets.

To permit employees to track their non–client-related time, Ernie has created a number of additional activity/service items: Lunch, Personal, Thinking. When he set up these items, he configured them for zero value and posted them to a miscellaneous expense account (it doesn't matter because there will never be an invoice for the services, so nothing will ever post). He uses the information he garners from the timesheets to analyze the way employees work and to decide whether or not his employees need assistants.

Because Ernie congratulates employees for effective use of time, including personal and thinking time, there's no particular threat in being honest when they fill in the timesheets. In fact, one of the interesting byproducts of his system is that there are notes frequently appended to the Lunch activity ("Sat near Judge Johnson's clerk at the corner deli and heard that the Judge is planning a long vacation in June, and since we're trying to avoid him for the Jackson case, let's press for a June date."). Similarly, employees sometimes enter notes about the time they spend just thinking ("We need more chocolate choices in the vending machine.").

# Using Timesheets for Payroll and Job Costing

## In this Chapter:

- *Configure payroll from timesheets*

- *Configure services and reports for job costing*

## Chapter 19

When you turn on time tracking, you can connect it to your QuickBooks payroll functions. This ability to track the information on the timesheets and transfer it to payroll does more than create paychecks—you can use it for job costing by tracking your payroll expenses against jobs.

# Setting Up Timesheet Data

If you want to link employee time to payroll or job costing, you must configure your QuickBooks system for those features.

## Configuring the Employee Record

To link an employee to time tracking, you must select the time-tracking option on the Payroll Info tab of the employee record. To accomplish this for an existing employee, open the Employee List and double-click the employee's listing. Move to the Payroll Info tab and select the option Use Time Data To Create Paychecks. Select this option when you enter a new employee.

Opting to link paychecks to time data doesn't mean that the employee's paycheck is absolutely and irrevocably linked to the employee's timesheets. It means only that when you prepare paychecks, QuickBooks checks timesheets before presenting the employee's paycheck form. You have total control over the number of hours and pay rate for the paycheck.

While the link to time tracking is advantageous for creating paychecks for hourly workers, you can link salaried employees to time tracking in order to track job costing.

## Configuring Payroll Preferences for Job Costing

If your time tracking is just as important for job-costing analysis as it is for making payroll easier, you can configure your payroll reporting for that purpose:

1. Choose Edit | Preferences from the menu bar.
2. Click the Payroll & Employees icon, and then click the Company Preferences tab.
3. At the bottom of the window (see Figure 19-1), select the option Report All Payroll Taxes By Customer:Job, Service Item, And Class (if you're using classes).

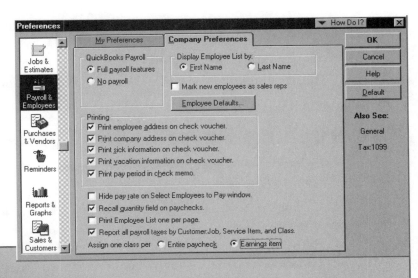

**Figure 19-1 • Use payroll costs in your job-costing reports.**

4.  If you're using classes, specify the way to assign a class:
    *   Entire Paycheck means you assign a class to all payroll expenses on a check (including company-paid taxes), instead of assigning a class to individual payroll items. If you're using time tracking, this means you can't assign classes to Employee activities that are transferred from timesheets to the paycheck.
    *   Earnings Item means you can assign a class to each payroll item in the Earnings section of the paycheck.
5.  Click OK to save your preferences.

## Training Employees to Use Timesheets

If your employees only keep timesheets to indicate the billable work they do, that's not going to do much to automate the payroll process. Few employees will have a full 40-hour week, and you'll have to fill in the remaining information manually when you create the paycheck.

*   Create at least one payroll item to cover non-billable work. You can call it Administration, In-Office, or any other designation. No customers are attached to these entries.

- Make sure employees account for every hour of the day and every day of the week.
- Have employees fill in days for sick pay or vacation pay on their timesheets. Those items are probably already part of your payroll items.

# Running Payroll with Timesheets Data

When it's time to run the payroll, you can use the data from the timesheets to create the paychecks:

1. Choose Employees | Pay Employees from the menu bar.
2. When the Select Employees To Pay window opens, the Hours column displays the number of hours that employees accounted for in their timesheets (well, at least those employees who filled out timesheets).
3. Select the option to enter hours and preview the check.
4. Select the employees to pay.
5. Click Create.

Each employee's paycheck is previewed (see Figure 19-2). For employees who are configured to have their paychecks generated from timesheets, the data from the employee's timesheet is transferred to the Earnings section. Some hourly employees will have billable hours that filled their week, and other employees may have administrative tasks that filled their week. Still others will have entered only the billable hours, and you'll have to fill in the rest yourself.

If the timesheet data that is transferred to the paycheck doesn't account for all the time the employee is entitled to, you'll have to add the administrative items yourself:

1. Click the Item Name column in the Earnings section, and enter a non-billable (administrative) payroll item.
2. In the Rate column, enter this employee's pay rate.
3. In the Hours column, enter the number of hours needed to complete this employee's work week.
4. Click Create.

 **Caution**   *Changes you make to the payroll window are not updated on the timesheet.*

See Chapter 8 for detailed information about creating payroll checks.

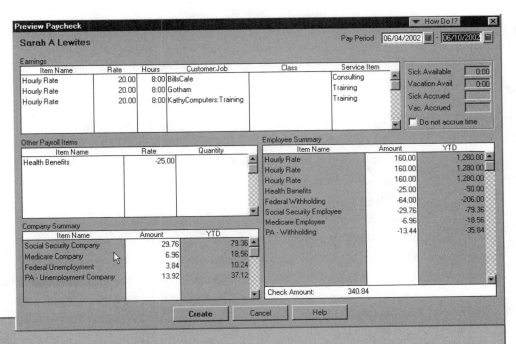

**Figure 19-2 • If the timesheet didn't account for all the hours in the pay period, the paycheck comes up short.**

# Running Payroll Reports for Cost Information

When you use time tracking, you can see reports on your payroll expenses as they relate to customers and jobs. The one I find most useful is the Payroll Transaction Detail report. To get to it, choose Reports | Employees & Payroll | Payroll Transaction Detail. When the Payroll Transaction Detail report appears, enter the date range you want to examine.

This report probably has more information than you really need, but the customer and job data is there. However, I've found that this report needs a bit of customization to make it useful. Click the Modify Report button to start customizing the report:

1. Click the Display tab and deselect the Wage Base column and the Trans # column, because they're not important.

2. You can change the way the data is sorted by clicking the arrow next to the Sort By text box and selecting a different category (I find it useful to sort by Name).

3. Click the Filter tab; in the Filter list, select Payroll Item.

4. Click the arrow to the right of the Payroll Item field and choose Selected Payroll Items.

5. Select the payroll items you want to track for customers and jobs (Salary, Hourly Rate, and Overtime Hourly Rate are the ones I find useful).

6. Click OK twice to return to the report window with its new configuration.

7. Click the Memorize button to make this configuration permanent, giving it a name that reminds you of why you need the report (for example, payroll-costing).

Now you're all set! You can get the information you need whenever you need it.

# Using the Onscreen Timer

## In this Chapter:

- *Install Timer*

- *Make copies for others*

- *Use Timer*

- *Export activities*

- *Export information to Timer users*

- *Import files from Timer*

## Chapter 20

If you have QuickBooks Pro or QuickBooks Premier, you can install a Timer program that permits you and other people connected to your company to track time automatically. It works by providing an onscreen clock that ticks away as you perform tasks. Each time you start a task, you tell Timer what you're doing, and the program keeps track of the amount of time it takes to complete each task.

# Installing Timer

The Timer software must be installed separately; it's not part of the standard QuickBooks Pro or Premier installation procedure. After you install it, you can give copies of the program to employees, subcontractors, or anyone else whose time you must track in order to send invoices to customers or perform cost analysis. Those folks do not have to have QuickBooks installed on their computers.

The Timer program works separately; you cannot launch it from within QuickBooks. It has its own menu choice on your computer's Program menu. However, you can interact with Timer from QuickBooks, importing and exporting files between QuickBooks and the Timer software.

## Installing the Program Files

To use Timer, you must install it on your computer from the original QuickBooks install disc. Before you begin the installation, close any programs that are open (including QuickBooks).

Put the QuickBooks 2000 CD in the CD-ROM drive. If AutoRun launches the CD and asks if you want to install QuickBooks, click No. Choose Start | Programs | QuickBooks Pro | Install QuickBooks Pro Timer (or, if you have QuickBooks Premier, substitute "Premier" for "Pro"). The installation program launches, and you need only follow the prompts. The Installation wizard displays the directory into which Timer will be installed (by default, C:\QBTIMER). If you have some reason to move the software to a different directory, choose Browse and select another location. You also have to approve the location of the Timer program listing on your Programs menu (by default, in the QuickBooks program submenu). The files are transferred to your hard drive, which takes only a short time. Then the installation program notifies you that the files have been installed, and you must restart your computer to use the software. Choose Yes, and after you've restarted the computer, QuickBooks Pro Timer appears on the submenu under QuickBooks Pro.

## Creating Disks for Others

Everybody who performs work for you should have a copy of the Timer program. (This is perfectly legal, and your QuickBooks Pro Timer software license permits it.) As they track their activities, the data is saved in files that you can import into QuickBooks in order to fill out timesheets. The information in the files includes the customer for whom the work is being performed, the amount of time, and all the other information a timesheet should track. Using Timer is far more efficient and accurate than relying on everyone's memory.

1. Label three blank formatted floppy disks with a disk number (1, 2, and 3).

**Tip** *Be sure you indicate the word "Timer" on the floppy disk labels; it's confusing to your recipients to have a disk labeled #1 without a software name indicated.*

2. Put the QuickBooks CD in the CD-ROM drive. If it starts the installation program automatically, answer No to the query about installing QuickBooks.

**Tip** *Press and hold the SHIFT key when you insert the CD to stop the AutoRun feature temporarily.*

3. Put the disk labeled Timer Disk #1 into your floppy disk drive.
4. Click the Start button on your taskbar and move to Programs. Then move to the QuickBooks Pro program item to display the submenu. Click the submenu program item named Create Timer Install Disks.

A wizard opens, presenting a series of instructions, all of which are easy to handle. Just keep going until the three disks are created. It takes a while, by the way, and part of the reason is that CD-ROMs aren't as fast as hard drives, and floppy disk drives are slower than snails.

After the first set of floppy disks is created, you can either repeat the process or use the disks themselves to make copies.

## Installing Timer Disks

On the receiving end, the installation of Timer disks is straightforward and easy. You can give these directions to your recipient. Or perhaps you are your own recipient— you might have multiple computers in your office and want to install the Timer program on a computer that is used by an employee to track his or her time.

1. Put floppy disk #1 into the floppy disk drive and click the Start button on the task bar.

2. Choose Run from the Start menu.
3. In the Open text box enter **a:\install**.
4. Click OK.

The installation program asks for each floppy disk as required, and when the Timer software is installed, a Programs menu listing for QuickBooks Pro/Premier appears on the recipient's computer, and the Timer program is in the submenu. The recipient has to restart the computer after the installation is complete in order to use the Timer program.

## Exporting Data Lists to Timer Users

You must export information from your company files to the Timer program so the program has data to use. The information is the data in your lists: employees, customers (and jobs), vendors, and service items. If you're using classes in QuickBooks, that data is also exported.

1. Choose File | Timer | Export Lists For Timer from the QuickBooks menu bar.
2. The Export Lists For Timer window opens, as shown in Figure 20-1.
3. Click OK to begin the export process. You can also select the option to skip this opening screen in the future.

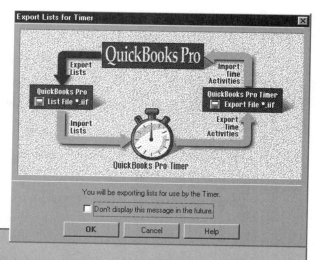

**Figure 20-1** • The people who are tracking time need information from the QuickBooks company file.

When the Export window opens (see Figure 20-2), choose a location for the file and give the file a name, using the following guidelines:

- If you are creating the export file for your own use, save it in a folder on your hard drive. The default folder is your QuickBooks folder, which is as good a choice as any.

- If you are creating an export file on a floppy disk for another user, click the arrow to the right of the Save In field and choose your floppy drive. Make sure you have a blank, formatted floppy disk in the drive.

- If you are creating the export file for another user, and you're going to send it via e-mail, you can save it to any folder on your hard drive. However, it's faster if you save it to the default folder selected by your e-mail software when you choose to upload a file.

- Give the file a name that will remind you of the company to which the data is attached. For instance, if the company name is A.J. Backstroke, Inc., you might want to name the export file "AJB."

- Don't forget to delete the asterisk (*) that QuickBooks places in the filename box.

QuickBooks adds an .iif file extension automatically. Click Save to save the export file. QuickBooks displays a message announcing that the data has been exported successfully. Now you can use the file and give it to any Timer user.

Incidentally, you only have to save this file once, even if you're shipping it to multiple Timer users. You can make your own copy, saving it on your hard drive. Then copy that file to a floppy disk as many times as you need to, or send it via e-mail. However, if you add items, names, or other important data to your system files, you must export it again to include those items.

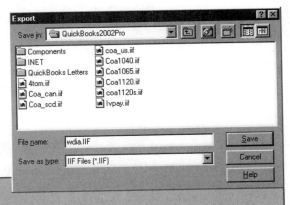

**Figure 20-2 • Name the export file and save it to a folder or a floppy disk.**

# Using Timer

You use Timer to track your work and report the time you spend on each task. In order to report your time, the Timer software keeps a data file. That file can be brought into QuickBooks and imported into a timesheet. Then you get paid for the time.

You don't have to have QuickBooks installed on your computer to use Timer. You do, however, have to have information about the company for which you're doing the work. That information is contained in files you import to your Timer software (the same files I discussed in the previous section). Then, when you use Timer, you can configure your tasks to tell the software who you are, what services you're performing, and which customer is being serviced.

## Using Timer for the First Time

The first time you use Timer you have a little setup work to do, after which you can go onto autopilot.

Start Timer by choosing Start | Programs | QuickBooks | QuickBooks Pro Timer. When the software opens for the first time, there's no file established for saving the data. Timer offers three choices for remedying this problem. Select Create New Timer File. Then click OK.

> **Tip** *QuickBooks provides a sample data file you can use to explore and play with, but this software is easy enough to use that you can jump right in and create your own file.*

When the New Timer File window opens (see Figure 20-3), enter a location and a filename for your personal Timer data. By default, Timer offers to save the file in the same folder in which the software exists. If you're working on a network and saving your files to a network location, click the Network button. Timer creates a mapped drive for you, so the network folder to which you're saving your data must already be shared.

For the filename, it's a good idea to use your name or initials, because Timer files are connected to a specific user. If you expect to keep files for multiple companies, make the filename a reflection of both the company name and your own name. For example, if your name is Debby Doright, and you perform tasks for companies named Creative Consultants and WeAreWidgets, you might create one file named "DDCC" and another file named "DDWAW."

Click OK to save the filename. Timer displays a message telling you that you must import company information before you can use your new file, and it also offers to open a Help file that explains how to perform this task. You can click No, because the instructions are available right here.

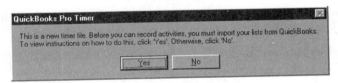

The Timer window is on your screen and the name of your file is on the title bar. However, because no data file is attached to it (yet), the important menu items aren't accessible.

Luckily, since you read the explanation earlier in this chapter about how to create the data file, a file with the needed data has already been created and exported, so you can import it (when you control all sides of this process, it's terribly efficient).

1. Choose File | Import QuickBooks Lists from the menu bar of the Timer window to open the Import QuickBooks Lists window.

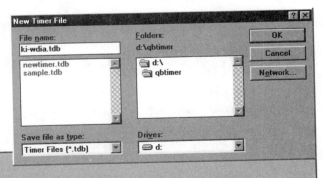

**Figure 20-3 •** The filename should reflect your name and the company name.

2. Click Continue to display the Open File For Import window.

3. If the folder displayed in the right pane of the window is not the location of the exported file, move through your computer's drives and folders to choose the right folder. If the file is on a floppy disk, click the arrow to the right of the Drives field and select the floppy disk drive.

4. Select the file that has been prepared for you and click OK.

Timer imports the file and then displays a message telling you that the file was imported successfully. Click OK to clear the message from the screen. Now it's time to go to work—and track your time as you work.

## Using the Timer Window

The Timer software window opens, and now all the menu items are accessible.

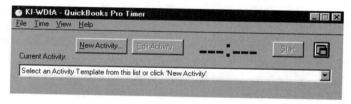

However, you have to set up an activity before the software can do its job. An activity is the work performed by a Timer user for one customer, during one day. Work performed for multiple customers requires multiple activities. An activity links three elements:

- The person using Timer
- The type of work that person is performing
- The customer for which that work is performed

## Setting Up an Activity

Click the New Activity button to open the New Activity window and complete the form to establish this activity (see Figure 20-4).

The date is automatically filled in with the current date, and all the other fields are very easy to fill in. You just have to click the arrow to the right of each field to see the list that's been imported from the company you're working with. (Of course, there's no preconfigured list for the Notes field, which you can use to make comments.) If the activity is billable to the customer, be sure that option is selected.

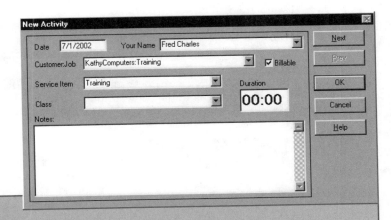

**Figure 20-4 • Designing an activity means specifying who, for whom, and what.**

**Tip** *Your name must be in the list that appears in the Your Name field, which means you've either been established as an employee, a vendor, or an "other name" in the original company's files.*

**Caution** *There is no option to add a new item to any list; you can only work with the items provided by the company's imported file.*

After you've configured this activity, click Next to set up another activity or click OK to return to the Timer window. Now the Timer window is ready to let you work (see Figure 20-5).

**Tip** *Whether you leave the Timer window at its opening size or reduce it to a little square digital readout of time (like a digital clock), you can move it to a corner of your screen by dragging the title bar.*

The activity you design is a template, containing the customer, the service, and your name (the user). All that's missing is the amount of time you spent working. It's available all the time, and when you use it to time your activities, a copy of the template is loaded, and that copy is used for today's work (Timer works by the day).

The title bar displays the name of the file you're working in.

Click this button to reduce the software window to the size of the Timer clock readout (the same icon is on the small window so you can restore the original size).

Click New Activity to set up an activity.

Click Edit Activity to make changes to the configuration of the current activity.

Click Start to start and stop Timer (the button changes its name).

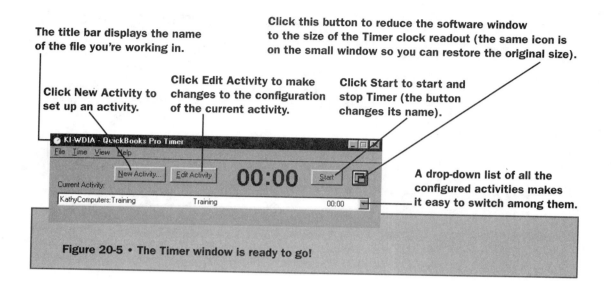

A drop-down list of all the configured activities makes it easy to switch among them.

**Figure 20-5 • The Timer window is ready to go!**

## Editing the Activity

Click the Edit Activity button to open a window with the original fields for the current activity. Then make the changes you need to make. Commonly, the changes involve a different service item for the same customer, or a change as to whether or not this is billable work.

## Timing Your Work

Go to work. That might mean you're doing research, making telephone calls, building an ark, writing a white paper, or anything else for which the company pays you (and probably bills its customers).

1. Choose the activity from the Current Activity drop-down list

2. Click the Start button. The Activity bar displays "-Timing-" to indicate that timing is activated, and the elapsed minutes appear on the Timer window.

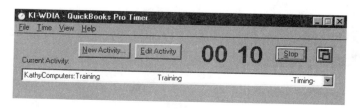

3. If you need to stop working for a while, click the Stop button. The button changes its name to Resume.

4. If you stop working because you've finished the task, you can create another activity, choose a different activity from the Activity bar or close the software.

> **Tip**    *You can keep multiple activities running and switch between them. Each activity is automatically paused when you switch to another.*

Each day, as you work with Timer, you can choose an activity from the Activity bar. As you switch from activity to activity in the same day, you're resuming the activity, not starting a new one. In fact, when you return to an activity any time in the same day, the Resume button is active.

## Setting Timer Preferences

After you've used Timer for a while, you may want to set preferences so the software works the way you prefer. To accomplish this, choose File | Preferences from the Timer menu bar to display the submenu, and use the following submenu items to configure Timer.

**Default Name**    You can select a name that is automatically entered in the Your Name field when you launch an activity.

**Number Of Days To Remember Activities**    You can specify the number of days that the Timer keeps an activity template (the default is 30).

**Turn On All One Time Messages**    You can bring back the message dialog boxes for which you selected the option "Don't Show This Message Again."

**Show Time When Minimized**    Specify whether you want to see the elapsed time counter when you minimize the Timer window. Minimize means minimized to a task bar button, which is not the same as reducing the Timer window to a smaller size.

The most useful preference is the one that enters a default name every time you create a new activity. That name, of course, should be your own name. When you select this option, the Choose A Default Name window opens so you can select your name from the list. You can also set a default option for whether or not your work is billable to customers.

> **Tip**    *If more than one person uses Timer on your computer, it's probably better not to enter a default name. However, if you do enter a default name, the other user just has to choose the activity and click the Edit Activity button to change the name.*

# Exporting Your Time Files

When you've completed your tasks or stopped for the day, you can send the company the information about your working hours. Some companies may want daily reports; others may want you to wait until you've completed a project.

## Viewing the Log

Before you send your files back to QuickBooks, you should take a look at the information. Choose View | Time Activity Log from the Timer menu bar. When the Time Activity Log window opens, it shows today's activities (see Figure 20-6).

If you wish, you can view a larger range of activities by changing the dates covered by this log. Click the arrow to the right of the Dates field and choose a different interval, or enter dates directly in the From and To fields.

## Editing an Entry

You can change the information in any entry by double-clicking it (see Figure 20-7). The most common reasons to do this are to change the time (especially if you worked on this activity away from your computer, so no timer was running) or to add a note. If you want to change the time, enter the new time in the Duration field.

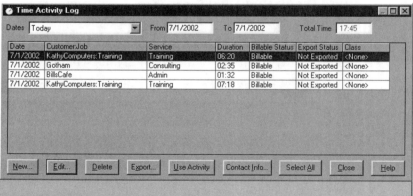

**Figure 20-6 • What did you do today?**

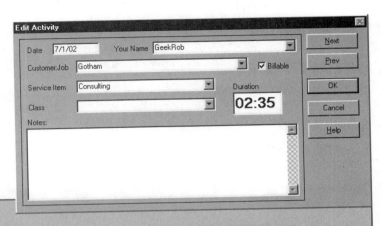

**Figure 20-7 • You can make adjustments or add notes before you export an activity.**

## Creating an Export File

If you want to get paid, you must export your information to QuickBooks so your timesheet can be used to calculate payment. You can either choose specific entries for export, or export all the information in your Timer system.

1. Open the Time Activity Log.
2. To export specific entries, click the first entry you want to export and hold down the CTRL key as you click any additional entries. To export all entries, click the Select All button.
3. Click the Export button to launch the Export Time Activities process.
4. Click Continue if the opening explanation window is displayed. (Remember, you can select the option to stop showing this window.)
5. In the Export Time Activities window, select All Unexported Time Activities, and then enter the date you want to use as the cut-off date for selecting activities. Timer has already selected the option to send all or some of the activities, depending on your selections in the Time Activity Log.

6. Click OK.

**Tip** *If you know you're ready to export all your files, you don't have to open the Time Activity Log. Instead, from the QuickBooks Pro Timer window, choose File | Export Time Activities. Timer exports all your unexported time activities.*

When the Create Export File window opens, select a location for the file and give it an appropriate name.

**Caution** *Timer won't accept filenames longer than eight characters.*

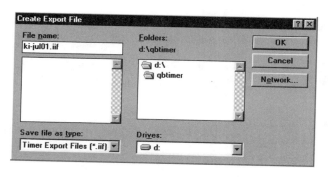

It's a good idea to use your initials in the name so there won't be any problems back at the QuickBooks computer if multiple Timer users are sending files. (I also put the date in the filename.) Click OK when you've entered the information.

Timer displays a message telling you that the file was exported successfully. When you view your activity log, the Export Status column reflects the export process (see Figure 20-8).

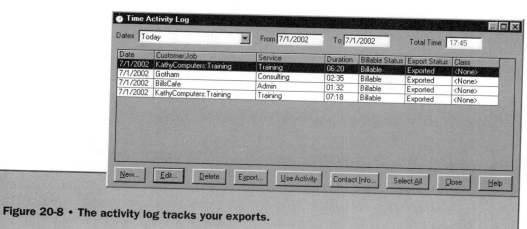

**Figure 20-8 • The activity log tracks your exports.**

After you've exported an activity, it's still available in the Activity bar for the rest of the day (it disappears tomorrow). Don't use it. Even though QuickBooks will permit you to export it again with the new number for time spent on the activity (although you do get a warning), it's not a clean way to work. Instead, open the template and start a new Timer activity.

# Importing Timer Files Back into QuickBooks

When you receive Timer files from employees and subcontractors, you must import them into QuickBooks. This is a simple process, and QuickBooks takes care of putting the information you've received into the appropriate files.

## Importing the File

On the QuickBooks menu bar, choose File | Timer | Import Activities From Timer. This opens the Import window, and you must specify the location of the file in the Look In drop-down list in order to see the exported files that are available. Double-click the file you want to use.

**Note**    *The first time you perform this task, you see an explanatory window welcoming you to the file importing process. Select the option to skip this window in the future so you can get right to work.*

Before importing the file, QuickBooks does a quick check of the contents. If any Timer user is an employee, QuickBooks checks to see if that employee's information specifies that timesheets are used to create the paycheck. If the employee is not set up for this method of computing the paycheck, QuickBooks asks you if you want to change the employee's setting.

It's common to track employee time without making the paycheck dependent on data from Timer (especially if the employee is salaried instead of paid by the hour), so you don't have to change the employee's settings to use the data from Timer. In this case, click No.

On the other hand, if this is an hourly employee, and you forgot to change the settings and would like to specify that the payroll program should use timesheets to create the paycheck, click Yes.

QuickBooks notifies you when the file has been imported and displays a summary of the contents.

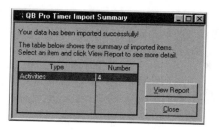

If you want to see details, click View Report to see a Timer Import Detail report, as shown in Figure 20-9.

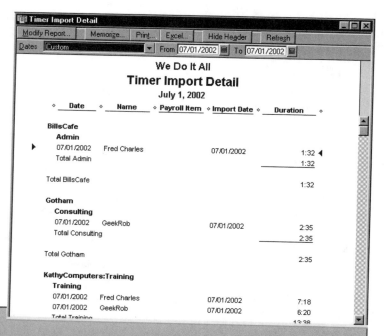

**Figure 20-9 • You can view the information that's in the imported Timer file.**

Double-click a line item in the report to see even more details in the form of the Timesheet that's created. You can edit the Timesheet if you wish; it's common to make the final decision at this point about whether the activity is going to be billed to the client.

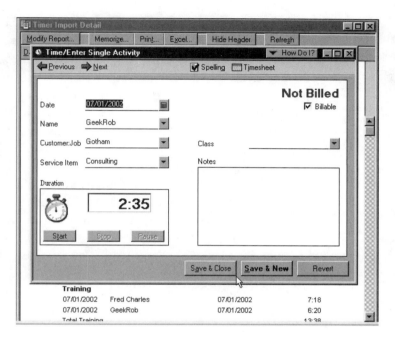

## Using Timer Data with Timesheets

What makes all of this seem almost miraculous is the way you can use this data without doing anything. It's just there, waiting for you. Timer data is sent to the user's timesheet and from there on, everything is on autopilot.

Open the Weekly Timesheets (choose Employees | Time Tracking | Use Weekly Timesheet) and select the name of the person who sent you the Timer file. Voilà! Everything's there.

For employees who are paid using their timesheets, wait until pay day and head right for the Create Paychecks window (choose Employees | Pay Employees). Once again, everything's there (having been transferred from the timesheets).

See Chapter 18 for more information about using timesheets; see Chapter 19 for information about integrating timesheets with payroll.

# Handling Multiuser Activities in Timer

ABC Engineers is a consulting firm, and most of their work is as a subcontractor to another company. One of their clients uses QuickBooks Pro, and ABC has received the Timer software along with instructions to use it for tracking the time they spend working for this client company.

Three of the ABC employees are assigned to this client, and each employee installed the Timer software on his own computer. The Names list on the file that was imported from the client contained a listing called ABC Engineers, and all three employees made this name the default for all activities.

As work is completed on the computer, on paper, and via telephone calls (they track the time used in conversations with the client), Timer runs.

Every Friday afternoon each employee exports a file that covers all unexported activities up to the current date and sends it back to the client company via e-mail. The filename contains the employee initials, so the client receives three separate files.

Back at their client company, the files are imported into QuickBooks Pro. This automatically places the information into timesheets. Since ABC Engineers is a vendor/subcontractor, there are no payroll issues to worry about.

The QuickBooks user chooses Reports | Jobs & Time | Time By Name to view a report that displays the information sorted by the name of the person who performed tasks with Timer. The ABC timesheet entries are displayed, along with a total.

A customer invoice is created. Clicking the Time/Costs button on the Invoice window produces a list of all the timesheet entries connected to the customer on the Time tab. Some of the entries are from in-house employees and were accumulated through the use of a timesheet. Other entries have been imported from the Timer program. The appropriate charges are marked for billing, and the invoice is completed automatically.

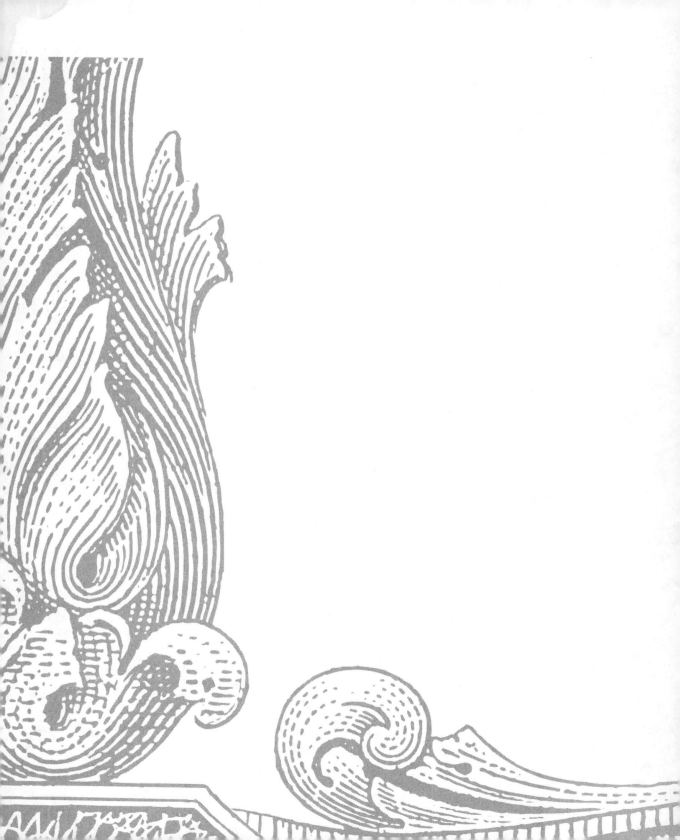

# Managing QuickBooks

*All software needs TLC, and accounting software needs regular maintenance to ensure its accuracy and usefulness.*

*In Part Four of this book, you'll learn how to customize QuickBooks so it works more efficiently, matching the way you like to work. The chapters in Part Four cover the features and tools you can use to make QuickBooks even more powerful. In addition, you'll learn how to maintain the file system, create additional company files, and use QuickBooks in network mode (so more than one person can be working in QuickBooks at the same time).*

*Of course, I'm going to cover backing up your data, which is the most important maintenance task in the world. Once you put your accounting data into QuickBooks, your business life depends on it. Hard drives die, motherboards freak out, power supplies go to la-la land, and all sorts of other calamities are just waiting to happen. We'll discuss the preventive measures you can take to make sure your business continues to live after your computer dies.*

# Customizing QuickBooks

## In this Chapter:

- *Change general preferences*

- *Customize the QuickBooks window*

- *Create users and passwords*

- *Use QuickBooks on a network*

- *Create classes*

## Chapter 21

Q uickBooks, "out of the box," is set to run efficiently, providing powerful
bookkeeping tools that are easy to use. However, you may have specific
requirements because of the way you run your company, the way your accountant
likes things done, or the way you use your computer. No matter what your special
requirements are, it's likely that QuickBooks can accommodate you.

# Changing Preferences

The preferences you establish in QuickBooks have a great impact on the way data is
kept and reported. It's not uncommon for QuickBooks users to change or tweak
these preferences periodically. In fact, the more you use QuickBooks and understand
the way it works, the more comfortable you'll be about changing preferences.

You can reach the Preferences window by choosing Edit | Preferences from the
QuickBooks menu bar. When the Preferences window opens for the first time, the
General section of the window is selected (see Figure 21-1).

The My Preferences tab is where you configure your preferences as a QuickBooks
user, and each user you create in QuickBooks can set his or her own preferences.
QuickBooks will apply the correct preferences as each user logs in to the software.

The Company Preferences tab is the place to configure the way QuickBooks
accounting features work for the current company.

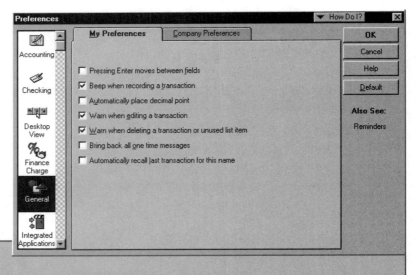

**Figure 21-1 • Configure QuickBooks to behave the way you prefer.**

As you select options and move from one section of the Preferences window to another, you'll be asked to save the changes in the section you just completed.

## Setting General Preferences

Since the Preferences window starts us in the General section, let's begin there.

### Setting My Preferences for the General Section

The My Preferences tab of the General section offers a number of options you can select. They're all designed to let you control the way QuickBooks behaves while you're working in transaction windows.

**Pressing Enter Moves Between Fields**   This option exists for people who constantly forget that the normal key for moving from field to field in Windows software is the TAB key. Of course, when they press ENTER, the record they're working on is saved even though they haven't finished filling out all the fields. Rather than force users to learn Windows procedures, QuickBooks lets you change the procedures to match your instincts.

**Beep When Recording A Transaction**   This is inaccurate; it's not a beep you hear, it's the *ka-ching!* noise of a cash register. Deselect the option to turn it off.

**Automatically Place Decimal Point**   This is a handy feature once you get used to it. It means that when you enter monetary characters in a field, a decimal point is placed to the left of the last two digits. Therefore, if you type 5421, when you move to the next field the number automatically becomes 54.21. Of course, if you want to type in even dollar amounts, you have to enter the zeros, as in 6500, which becomes 65.00. You can also type a period after you enter 65, and QuickBooks will automatically add two zeroes to the right of the period.

**Warn When Editing A Transaction**   This option, which is selected by default, tells QuickBooks to flash a warning when you change any transaction and try to close the window without explicitly saving the changed transaction. This means you have a chance to abandon the edits. If you deselect the option, the edited transaction is saved, unless it is linked to other transactions (in which case, the warning message appears).

**Warn When Deleting A Transaction Or Unused List Item**   When selected, this option produces a warning when you delete a transaction or an item that has not been used in a transaction. (Actually it's a message asking you to confirm your action.) If you try to delete an item that has been used in a transaction, QuickBooks won't permit you to complete the deletion.

**Bring Back All One-Time Messages**    One-time messages are those introductory windows that include a Don't Show This Message Again option. If you've selected the Don't Show Me option, select this check box to see those messages again (and you can once again select the Don't Show Me Again option).

**Automatically Recall Last Transaction For This Name**    This option means that QuickBooks will present the last transaction for any name (for instance, a vendor) in full whenever you use that name. This feature is useful for repeating transactions, but you can turn it off if you find it annoying.

### Setting Company Preferences for the General Section

The Company Preferences tab in the General section has three choices:

**Time Format**    Select a format for entering time, choosing between decimal (for example, 11.5 hours) or minutes (11:30).

**Always Show Years As 4 Digits**    If you prefer to display the year with four digits (1/1/2002 instead of 1/1/02), select this option.

**Never Update Name Information When Saving Transactions**    By default, QuickBooks asks if you want to update the original information for a list item when you change it during a transaction entry. For example, if you're entering a vendor bill and you change the address, QuickBooks offers to make that change back on the vendor record. If you don't want to be offered this opportunity, select this option.

## Setting Accounting Preferences

Click the Accounting icon on the left pane of the Preferences window to move to the Accounting preferences. There are only Company Preferences available for this section; the My Preferences tab has no options available (see Figure 21-2).

**Use Account Numbers**    Choose this option if you want to use numbers for your chart of accounts in addition to names.

**Show Lowest Subaccount Only**    This option, which is available only if you use account numbers, is useful because it means that when you see an account number in a field (in a transaction window), you only see the subaccount. If the option is not selected, you see the parent account followed by the subaccount, and since the field display doesn't show the entire text unless you scroll through it, it's hard to determine which account has been selected.

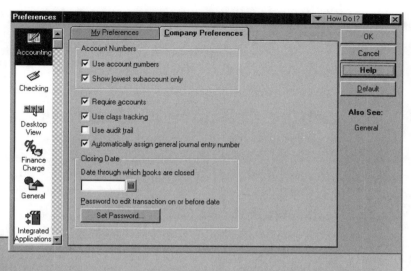

**Figure 21-2 • Choose the accounting options you require in order to run your company efficiently.**

**Require Accounts**   Select this option to require that every item and transaction you create in QuickBooks has to be assigned to an account. If you don't select this option, transaction amounts are posted to Uncategorized Income or Uncategorized Expense.

**Use Class Tracking**   This option turns on the Class feature for your QuickBooks system (which is discussed later in this chapter).

**Use Audit Trail**   Select this option to keep a log of changed transactions (not a log of all transactions, just those that are changed after they're first entered). What's important about this option is that deleted transactions are listed in the audit trail. To see the audit log, click the Reports listing on the Navigation bar. Choose the Accountant & Taxes report type, then choose Audit Trail.

**Automatically Assign General Journal Entry Number**   This option is new to QuickBooks 2002. It means that every time you create a general journal entry, QuickBooks automatically assigns the next available number to it. In previous versions of QuickBooks, you had to track JE entry numbers yourself (or skip numbering altogether).

**Closing Date** This option is also new to QuickBooks 2002. It sets a password-protected closing date for your QuickBooks data file. Once you set the date and create a password, nobody can manipulate any transactions that are dated on or before the closing date unless they know the password.

## Setting Checking Preferences

This section has options in both the My Preferences and Company Preferences tabs. On the My Preferences tab, you can select default bank accounts for different types of transactions. The Company Preferences tab offers several options concerned with check printing, described in this section.

**Print Account Names On Voucher** This option is useful only if you print your checks and the check forms you purchase have vouchers (stubs). If so, selecting this option means that the stub will show the Payee, the posting account, and the first 16 lines of any memo you entered on the bill you're paying. If the check is for inventory items, the item name appears instead of the posting account. If the check is a payroll check, the payroll items and amounts are printed on the voucher.

**Change Check Date When Check Is Printed** Selecting this option means that at the time you print checks, the current date becomes the check date. If you don't select this option, the check date you specified when you filled out the check window is used (even if that date has already passed).

**Start With Payee Field On Check** This option forces your cursor to the Payee field when you first bring up the Write Checks window. If the option is off, the bank account field is the first active field (needed if you write checks from different bank accounts).

**Warn About Duplicate Check Numbers** When this option is selected (which it is, by default), QuickBooks will warn you if a check number you're filling in already exists.

**Autofill Vendor Account Number In Check Memo** Most vendors maintain an account number for their customers, and your account number can be automatically printed when you print checks. In order for this to occur, you must fill in your account number in the Vendor card (on the Additional Information tab).

**Select Default Accounts To Use** You can set the default bank accounts for payroll checks and payroll liability payments.

# Setting Desktop View Preferences

This section of the preferences configuration lets you design the way the QuickBooks window looks and acts. Only the My Preferences tab contains configuration options.

In the View section, you can specify whether you always want to see one QuickBooks window at a time, or view multiple windows.

- Choose One Window to limit the QuickBooks screen to showing one window at a time, even if you have multiple windows open. The windows are stacked atop each other, and only the top window is visible. To switch between multiple windows, use the Open Window List. If you don't display the Open Window List (covered later in this chapter), you must use the Window menu on the QuickBooks menu bar to select the window you want to work in.

- Choose Multiple Windows to make it possible to view multiple windows on your screen. Selecting this option activates the arrangement commands on the Windows menu item, which let you stack or arrange windows so that more than one window is visible at a time.

In the Navigators section, you can select Show Company Navigator When Opening A Company File if you want to display the Company Navigator window whenever you open a company. The Company Navigator window contains icons and links to tasks and features (see Figure 21-3). You can open a different company by choosing File | Open, or by choosing File | Open Previous Company (the submenu lists the last company files you've worked in).

In the Desktop section, you can specify what QuickBooks should do when you exit the software, choosing among the following options:

- **Save When Closing Company** means that the state of the desktop is remembered when you close the company (or exit QuickBooks). Whatever QuickBooks windows were open when you left will reappear when you return. You can pick up where you left off.

- **Save Current Desktop** displays the desktop as it is at this moment every time you open QuickBooks. Select this option after you've opened or closed the QuickBooks windows you want to see when you start the software. If you choose this option, an additional choice named Keep Previously Saved Desktop appears on the window.

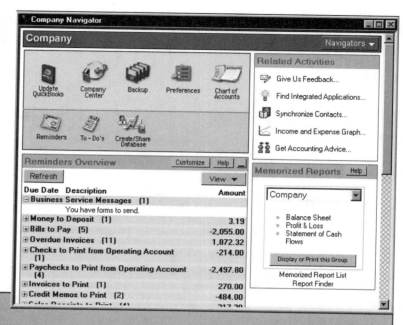

**Figure 21-3 • The Company Navigator provides quick access to tasks and features.**

- **Don't Save The Desktop** tells QuickBooks to display an empty QuickBooks desktop when you open this company, or when you start QuickBooks again after using this company. The desktop isn't really empty—the menu bar, icon bar, and any other navigation bars are on the desktop, but no transaction or list windows are open.

- **Keep Previously Saved Desktop** (available only if you select Save Current Desktop) tells QuickBooks to display the desktop as it was previous to the current desktop.

In the Color Scheme section, you can select a scheme from the drop-down list. In addition to a group of color schemes, you have the option of selecting the standards you set for Windows.

In addition to the options on this preferences tab, two buttons are available to configure general settings for Display and Sounds. Clicking either button opens the associated applet in your Windows Control Panel. The configuration options you change in these dialog boxes affect your computer and all your software, not just QuickBooks.

**Tip**    *QuickBooks takes quite a bit of time to open after you select it from your Programs menu or a desktop icon. In addition, when you exit QuickBooks, it takes a long time for the program window to close. If you hate to wait, you can speed QuickBooks up by making the following choices for Desktop View preferences:*

- *Select the Don't Save The Desktop option*
- *Deselect the Show Company Navigator option*

## Setting Finance Charge Preferences

Click the Finance Charge icon (which has only Company Preferences available) to turn on, turn off, and configure finance charges (see Figure 21-4).

Finance charges can get a bit complicated, so read the complete discussion about this topic in Chapter 5.

## Setting Integrated Applications Preferences

For QuickBooks Pro and Premier versions, you can let third-party software have access to the data in your QuickBooks files. Click the Integrated Applications icon and move to the Company Preferences tab to specify the way QuickBooks works with other software programs. You can give permission to access all data, no data, or some data. (See Appendix C for a discussion about finding and using applications that are designed to work with QuickBooks data.)

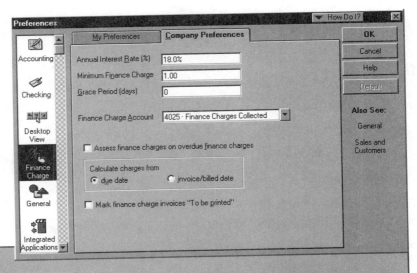

**Figure 21-4 •** **Configure the method you want to use for imposing finance charges on customers who don't pay on time.**

## Setting Jobs & Estimates Preferences

For QuickBooks Pro and QuickBooks Premier, you can configure the way your estimates and invoices work, as shown in Figure 21-5. The options are self-explanatory.

## Setting Payroll & Employees Preferences

Use the Company Preferences tab of this section of the Preferences window to set all the configuration options for payroll. Read Chapter 8 to understand the selections in this window.

## Setting Purchases & Vendors Preferences

The Company Preferences tab has several configuration options for using purchase orders and paying vendor bills:

**Inventory And Purchase Orders Are Active** Select this option to tell QuickBooks that you want to enable the inventory features; the purchase orders are automatically enabled with that action.

**Warn If Not Enough Inventory To Sell** This option turns on the warning feature that is useful during customer invoicing. If you sell ten widgets, but your stock of widgets is fewer than ten, QuickBooks displays a message telling you there's insufficient stock to fill the order. (You can still complete the invoice; it's just a message, not a functional limitation.)

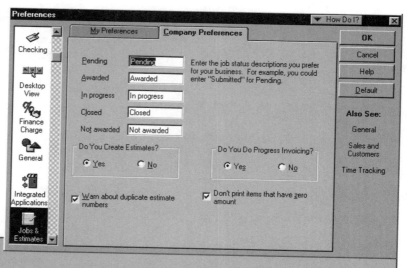

**Figure 21-5 • Turn estimating on or off and configure the lingo you want to use.**

**Warn About Duplicate Purchase Order Numbers**    When this option is enabled, any attempt to issue a purchase order with a P.O. number that already exists will generate a warning.

**Entering Bills**    Use the options in this section to set default payment terms for vendors (you can change the terms for individual vendors) and to issue a warning if you enter a vendor bill with the same invoice number twice.

**Paying Bills**    If you select the automatic discounts option, QuickBooks will apply any credits from the vendor to the open bills automatically, and take any discount that the vendor's terms permit. (The vendor terms are specified in the vendor's file.) If you select this option, enter the account to which you want to post discounts taken.

# Setting Reminders Preferences

The Reminders section of the Preferences window has options on both tabs. The My Preferences tab has one option, which turns on the Reminders feature and displays a Reminders list when you open a company file.

The Company Preferences tab enumerates the available reminders, and you can select the ones you want to use (see Figure 21-6).

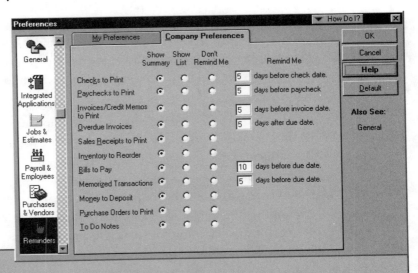

**Figure 21-6 • Decide which tasks you want to be reminded about.**

For each item, decide whether you want to see a summary (just a listing and the total amount of money involved), a complete detailed list, or nothing at all. You can also determine the amount of lead time you want for your reminders.

> **Tip** If you choose Show Summary, the Reminder List window has a button you can click to see the details.

# Setting Reports & Graphs Preferences

This is another section of the Preferences window that has choices on both tabs, so you can set your own user preferences, and then set those options that affect the current company. Let's start with the My Preferences tab (see Figure 21-7), which configures performance issues for graphs.

## Updating Reports and Graphs

While you're viewing a report or a graph, you can make changes to the format or to the data behind it. Most of the time, QuickBooks automatically changes the report/graph to match the changes. However, if there is anything else going on (perhaps you're also online, or you're in a network environment and other users are manipulating data that's in your report or graph), QuickBooks stops making changes automatically. The reason for the shutdown of automatic refreshing is to keep your computer running as quickly and efficiently as possible. At that point, QuickBooks has to make a decision about when and how to refresh the report or graph. You must give QuickBooks the parameters for making the decision to refresh.

- Choose Prompt Me To Refresh to see a message asking you whether you want to be reminded to refresh the report or the graph after you've made changes to the data behind it. When the reminder appears, you can click Yes to refresh the data in the report.

- Choose Refresh Automatically if you're positively compulsive about having up-to-the-second data and don't want to remember to click the Refresh button. If you work with QuickBooks on a network, this could slow down your work a bit because whenever any user makes a change to data that's used in the report/graph, it will refresh itself.

- Choose Don't Refresh if you want to decide for yourself, without any reminder from QuickBooks, when to click the Refresh button. (Incidentally, when I selected this option, reports continued to refresh automatically.)

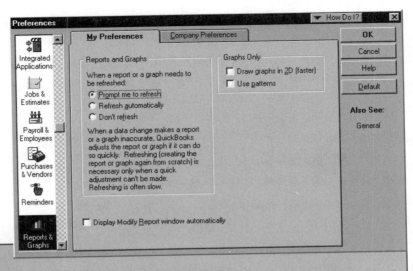

**Figure 21-7 •** Set the parameters you want to use when you create reports and graphs.

## Display Modify Report Window Automatically

If you find that almost every time you ask for a report, you have to customize it, you can tell QuickBooks to open the Modify Report window whenever a report is brought to the screen. Click the check box next to Display Modify Report Window Automatically.

## Graphs Only

You can also provide instructions to QuickBooks about how you want your graphs created:

- Choose Draw Graphs In 2D (faster) to have graphs displayed in two dimensions instead of three. This doesn't impair your ability to see trends at a glance; it's just not as "high-tech." The main reason to consider this option is that the 2-D graph takes much less time to draw on your screen.
- Choose Use Patterns to draw the various elements in your graphs with black-and-white patterns instead of colors. For example, one pie wedge may be striped, another speckled. This is handy if you print your graphs to a black-and-white printer.

## Setting Company Preferences for Reports

Move to the Company Preferences tab of the Reports & Graphs window to set company preferences (see Figure 21-8).

**Summary Reports Basis**   Specify whether you want to see summary reports as accrual-based or cash-based.

**Aging Reports**   Specify whether you want to generate A/R and A/P aging reports using the due date or the transaction date.

**Reports—Show Accounts By**   Specify whether you want accounts listed by their account names, their descriptions, or both.

## Setting Report Format Defaults

You can set the default formatting for reports by clicking the Format button and making changes to the default configuration options. Use this feature if you find yourself making the same modifications over and over.

## Configuring the Cash Flow Report

A cash flow report is really a complicated document, and before the days of accounting software, accountants spent many hours creating such a report. QuickBooks has configured a cash flow report format that is used to produce the cash flow reports available in the list of Company & Financial reports.

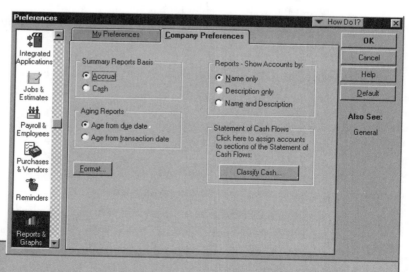

**Figure 21-8 •  Configure the options for reports.**

You can view the format by clicking the Classify Cash button, but you shouldn't mess around with the selections in the window that appears unless you check with your accountant.

## Setting Sales & Customers Preferences

You can set a few options as defaults in the Sales & Customer section of the Company Preferences window:

**Usual Shipping Method**   Use this to set the default shipping method.

**Default Markup Percentage**   Specify a markup for items that have both a cost and price.

**Usual FOB**   Set the FOB language for invoices. FOB (Free On Board) is the location from which shipping is determined to be the customer's responsibility. This means more than just paying for freight; it's a statement that says, "At this point you have become the owner of this product." The side effects include assigning responsibility if goods are lost, damaged, or stolen.

**Track Reimbursed Expenses As Income**   This option changes the way your general ledger handles payments for reimbursements. When this option is enabled, the reimbursement can be assigned to an income account (which you should name "reimbursed expenses"). When the option is not enabled, the reimbursement is posted to the original expense account, washing away the expense.

**Automatically Apply Payments**   This option tells QuickBooks to apply payments automatically to open invoices. If the payment amount is an exact match for an open invoice, it is applied to that invoice. If the payment amount is smaller than any open invoice, QuickBooks applies the payment to the oldest invoice. Without this option, you must manually apply each payment to an invoice (which is the way I work, because frequently the customer's check stub indicates the invoice the customer wants to pay even if it's not the entire amount).

**Warn About Duplicate Invoice Numbers**   This option tells QuickBooks to warn you if you're creating an invoice using an invoice number that's already in use.

**Use Price Levels**   This option turns on the Price Level feature, which is explained in Chapter 2.

**Round All Sales Prices Up To The Next Whole Dollar**   If, after you apply a price level, the amount contains any cents over a penny, the price is rounded up to the next whole dollar.

## Setting Sales Tax Preferences

This is one section of the Preferences window that is easy to configure, because most of the options are pre-decided by laws and rules. Figure 21-9 shows my configuration; yours may differ.

## Setting Send Form Preferences

This preference category controls the cover sheets for faxing or e-mailing invoices and estimates. You can create text and determine how the recipient's name is displayed. See Chapter 3 to learn how to send forms.

## Setting Service Connection Preferences

If you purchase services from QuickBooks, use this window to specify the way you want to connect to the Web site for those services. (These settings do not apply to Payroll and Online Banking services.)

- Choose Automatically Connect Without Asking For A Password to let all users log in to the QuickBooks Business Services network automatically.
- Choose Always Ask For A Password Before Connecting to force users to enter a login name and password in order to access QuickBooks Business Services.

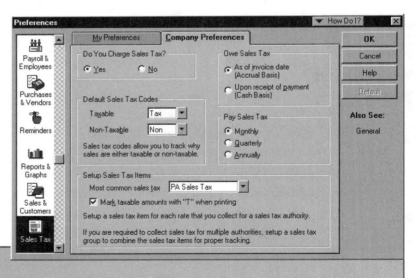

**Figure 21-9 • Most sales tax preferences are a matter of following the rules.**

- Choose Allow Background Downloading Of Service Messages to let QuickBooks check the Intuit Web site for updates and information periodically, when you're connected to the Internet (even if you aren't using QuickBooks).

More information about buying services from QuickBooks is in Appendix D.

## Setting Spelling Preferences

This is where you control the way the spelling checker works. You can instruct QuickBooks to check spelling automatically before saving or printing any form. In addition, you can specify those words you want the spelling checker to skip, such as Internet address, numbers, and solid capital letters that probably indicate an abbreviation.

## Setting 1099 Form Preferences

Use this section of the Preferences window to establish the 1099 form options you need. For each type of 1099 payment, you must assign an account from your chart of accounts.

## Setting Time-Tracking Preferences

Use this section to turn on Time Tracking and to tell QuickBooks the first day of your work week (which really means the first day listed on your timesheets). Read all about tracking time in Chapter 18.

# Working with Multiple Users

If you have the QuickBooks Pro or Premier multi-user version, the first time you used QuickBooks, the EasyStep Interview program asked if other people use your computer to perform work in QuickBooks. If you answered Yes, you were asked to provide names and passwords for each person. After the additional users are configured, you, as the administrator, can determine who can use the various features in QuickBooks. You can add users, delete users, and change access permissions at any time. Only the administrator can perform these tasks. If you said No during the interview, you can change your mind and set up multiple users now.

# Creating, Removing, and Changing User Information

When you want to create or modify users, choose Company | Set Up Users from the QuickBooks menu bar. If you are setting up multiple users for the first time, QuickBooks displays the Set Up QuickBooks Administrator window. You must have an administrator (I'm assuming it's you) to manage all the other user tasks.

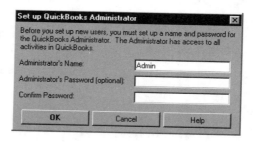

It's a good idea to leave the Administrator's name as Admin. If you want to password-protect the Administrator's login, move to the Administrator's Password box and enter a password. Enter the same password in the Confirm Password to confirm it. You won't see the text you're typing; instead, the system shows asterisks as a security measure (in case someone is watching over your shoulder).

**Tip**   While the use of a password is optional, omitting passwords altogether can put your system's security at risk.

## Creating a New User

When you click OK in the Set Up QuickBooks Administrator dialog box (or if you already set up the configuration option to have multiple users) you see the User List window.

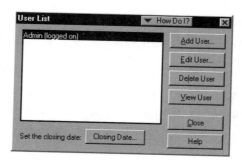

To add a new user to the list, click Add User. This launches a wizard that assists you in setting up the new user. In the first wizard window, fill in the necessary information:

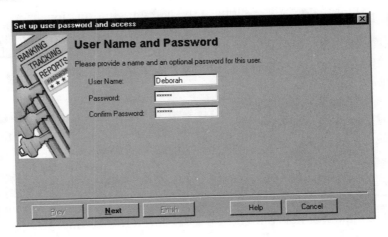

1. Enter the user name, which is the name this user must type to log in to QuickBooks.
2. If you want to establish a password for this user (it's optional), enter and confirm the user's password.
3. Click Next to set up the user's access to QuickBooks features. See the section "Setting User Permissions" later in this section.

**Tip**   *Make a note of all user passwords and keep that list in a safe place. Inevitably, a user will come to you because he or she cannot remember a password.*

## Deleting a User

If you want to remove a user from the User List, select the name and then click the Delete User button. QuickBooks asks you to confirm your decision.

## Editing User Information

You can change the configuration options for any user. Select the user name in the User List window and click Edit User. This launches a wizard similar to the Add User wizard, and you can change the user password, access permissions, or both.

# Setting User Permissions

When you're adding a new user or editing an existing user, the wizard walks you through the steps for configuring the user's permissions. Click Next on each wizard window after you've supplied the necessary information.

The first permissions window asks if you want this user to have access to selected areas of QuickBooks or all areas. If you want to give the user full permission to do everything, you're asked to confirm your decision, and there's no further work to do in the wizard.

## Configuring Rights to Individual Areas of QuickBooks

If you want to limit the user's access to selected areas of QuickBooks, select that option and click Next. The ensuing wizard windows take you through all the QuickBooks features (Accounts Receivable, Check Writing, Payroll, and so on) so you can establish permissions on a feature-by-feature basis for this user. You should configure permissions for every component of QuickBooks that you installed. Any component not configured is set as No Access for this user.

For each QuickBooks component, you can select from these permission options:

**No Access**   The user will be denied permission to open any windows in that section of QuickBooks.

**Full Access**   The user can open all windows and perform all tasks in that section of QuickBooks.

**Selective Access**   The user will be permitted to perform tasks as you see fit.

If you choose to give selective access permissions, you'll be asked to specify the rights this user should have. Those rights vary slightly from component to component, but generally you're asked to choose one of these permission levels:

- Create transactions
- Create and print transactions
- Create transactions and create reports

**Tip**   You can select only one of the three levels, so if you need to give the user rights to more than one of these choices, you must select Full Access instead of configuring Selective Access.

## Configuring Special Areas of QuickBooks

There are two wizard windows for setting permissions that are not directly related to any specific area of the software: sensitive accounting activities and sensitive accounting reports.

Sensitive accounting activities are those tasks that aren't directly related to specific QuickBooks features:

- Making changes to the Chart of Accounts list
- Manipulating the register for any balance sheet account
- Using online banking
- Transferring funds between banks
- Reconciling bank accounts
- Creating journal entries
- Preparing an accountant's review
- Working with budgets

Sensitive financial reports are those reports that reveal important financial information about your company, such as:

- Profit & Loss reports
- Balance sheet reports
- Budget reports
- Cash flow reports
- Income tax reports
- Trial balance reports
- Audit trail reports

### Configuring Rights for Existing Transactions

If a user has permissions for certain areas of QuickBooks, you can limit his or her access to manipulate existing transactions within those areas. This means the user can't change or delete a transaction, even if he or she created it in the first place.

When you have finished configuring user permissions, the last wizard page presents a list of the permissions you've granted and refused. If everything is correct, click Finish. If there's something you want to change, use the Prev button to back up to the appropriate page.

## Configuring Classes

QuickBooks provides a feature called Classes that permits you to group items and transactions in a way that matches the kind of reporting you want to perform. Think of this feature as a way to "classify" your business activities. To use classes, you must enable the feature, which is listed in the Accounting section of the Preferences window.

Some of the common reasons to configure classes include

- Reporting by location if you have more than one office.
- Reporting by division or department.
- Reporting by business type (perhaps you have both retail and wholesale businesses under your company umbrella).

You should use classes for a single purpose; otherwise, the feature won't work properly. For example, you can use classes to separate your business into locations or by type of business, but don't try to do both.

When you enable classes, QuickBooks adds a Class field to your transaction windows. To fill it in, you must create the classes you want to use.

## Adding a Class

To create a class, choose Lists | Class List from the QuickBooks menu bar to display the Class List window. (Remember that you must enable Classes in the Accounting Preferences to have access to the Class Lists menu item.) Press CTRL-N to add a new class. Fill in the name of the class in the New Class window.

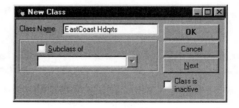

Click Next to add another class, or click OK if you are finished. It's a good idea to create a class called "Other." This gives you a way to sort transactions in a logical fashion when there's no link to one of your real classes.

## Using a Class in Transactions

When you're entering transactions, each transaction window provides a field for entering the class. For example, the invoice form adds a Class field at the top (next to the Customer:Job field) so you can assign the invoice to a class. However, you can also link a class to each line item of the invoice (if you expect the line items to require separate links to classes). You must customize your invoice forms to add classes as a column. When you do, you should add the column to the screen form, but not the printed form, because your customers don't care. See Chapter 3 to learn how to customize invoice forms.

# Reporting by Class

There are two types of reports you can run for classes:

- Individual class reports
- Reports on all classes

## Reporting on a Single Class

To report on a single class, open the Class list and select the class you want to report on. Then press CTRL-Q to open a QuickReport on the class. When the Class QuickReport appears, you can change the date range or customize the report as needed.

## Reporting on All Classes

If you want to see one report in which all classes are used, open the Class list and click the Reports button at the bottom of the list window. Choose Reports On All Classes and then select either Profit & Loss By Class, or Graphs. The Graphs menu item offers a choice of an Income & Expenses Graph, or a Budget vs. Actual Graph.

### Profit & Loss by Class Report

The Profit & Loss By Class report is the same as a standard Profit & Loss report, except that each class uses a separate column. The Totals column provides the usual P&L information for your company.

Totals for items not assigned to a class appear in a column called Unclassified. This is likely to be a rather crowded column if you chose to enable class tracking after you'd already begun using QuickBooks.

You can find detailed information about running and customizing Profit & Loss reports in Chapter 15.

### Graphs That Use Class Data

You can also display a graph for Income & Expenses sorted by class, or one that compares budget versus actual figures sorted by class.

## Customizing Other Reports for Class Reporting

Many of the reports you run regularly can also be customized to report class information (for example, aging reports). Use the Filters tab to add all, some, or one class to the report.

# Using Classes to Track Partners

Carl, Pete, and Lucy are veterinarians with a busy practice. Before they formed their partnership, each of them had practiced independently. They each brought a certain amount of equity into the partnership (including cash, equipment, and patients), and they want to track the individual equity amounts by using the profits each provides. In effect, each of their examining rooms is run as an individual profit center.

Each partner name is established as a class, and there are two additional classes:

- Other, which is used to mean "this particular item is practice-wide."
- Split, which is used to mean "add this up at the end of the year and assign a percentage to each partner."

All revenue transactions are assigned to a partner class. Each line item on every vendor bill is assigned to a class, as follows:

- Certain overhead items such as rent, utilities, and so on are assigned to Other.
- Consumable overhead items, such as towels, syringes, and medical supplies, are assigned to Split.

At the end of the year, when the reports are run, the totals for the Split class are reapportioned with a journal entry. The percentage of income is used as a guideline for the percentage of the split, because the assumption is that a partner with a certain amount of revenue must have used a certain amount of consumable items in order to produce that revenue. While this system isn't terribly exact, it is as ingenious and fair as a system could be.

When the year is closed, a percentage of the retained earnings figure is posted to each partner's equity account. The profit for each partner is the revenue, less the expenses incurred by each partner (including the Split class percentage).

This system also provides a nifty way to figure end-of-year bonuses, since the partners can base the amount of the bonus (a draw) on the amount of the current year retained earnings for each partner.

# Using QuickBooks on a Network

If you're using QuickBooks Pro or Premier, you and other users can use the software on a network. Multiple users can be working in QuickBooks at the same time.

You must purchase a separate copy of QuickBooks Pro for each user who will access the network files and install that copy on the user's computer. Look for special network packages of QuickBooks with special pricing (for example, the five-user pack).

## Setting Up the Network Installation

The first thing you must do is install QuickBooks Pro on every computer that will be involved in this network setup. One of those installed copies becomes the main network copy. That copy can reside on a network server or on a user's computer. To set up shared access of the QuickBooks company files, perform the following steps:

1. On the computer that will act as the QuickBooks server, open Windows Explorer and right-click the folder into which you installed QuickBooks Pro.
2. Choose Sharing from the shortcut menu to open the Folder Properties dialog box.
3. Select Shared As. The folder name is automatically entered as the Share Name, and that is probably a good choice. However, you can change the name of the share if you wish.
4. Set permissions for Full Control.
5. Click OK.

If you're using Windows 98 or Windows ME, the permissions are configured on the Sharing tab of the Properties dialog box. If you're using Windows NT, Windows 2000, or Windows XP, click the Permissions button on the Sharing tab to use the Permissions dialog box.

It's a good idea to map the shared folder as a drive on the other users' computers. It's not necessary, but it speeds up access to the company files:

1. On each user's computer, open the Network icon (Network Neighborhood or My Network Places) and select the remote computer that's acting as the server for QuickBooks Pro.
2. Right-click the shared folder for QuickBooks.
3. Choose Map Network Drive from the shortcut menu.

4. In the Map Network Drive dialog box, select a drive letter for this resource.
5. Select the Reconnect At Logon option.
6. Click OK.

## Switching Between Multi-user Mode and Single-user Mode

On the computer that's acting as the host/server, you must enable multi-user mode before other users can access the data files. To accomplish this, make sure the company you want users to work in is the current company. Then choose File | Switch To Multi-user Mode from the QuickBooks menu bar.

All the QuickBooks windows are closed while the switch is made. Then a message appears to tell you that the company file is working in multi-user mode. The title bar of the QuickBooks window also announces that the software is in multi-user mode, and displays the name of the user. If you haven't set up any users, QuickBooks offers to begin that process now.

If you need to return to Single-user Mode, use the File menu, where the command has changed to Switch To Single-user Mode. A number of administrative tasks must be performed in single-user mode:

- Backing up
- Restoring
- Compressing files
- Deleting items from lists
- Exporting or importing accountant's review copies
- Certain other setup and preferences tasks (QuickBooks displays a message telling you to switch to single-user mode when you access those setup tasks)

## Accessing QuickBooks Pro from Other Computers

Users at computers other than the QuickBooks host/server computer can reach the network data easily:

1. Launch QuickBooks Pro (from the Program menu or a desktop shortcut).

2. Choose File | Open Company/Login from the QuickBooks menu bar to see the Open A Company dialog box.

3. Click the arrow to the right of the Look In field to display a hierarchy of drives and shared resources.

4. Select the drive letter if the resource is mapped.

5. If the resource is not mapped, select Network Neighborhood. Then select the host computer and continue to make selections until you find the shared QuickBooks folder.

6. In the Open A Company window, choose the company you want to use and click Open, or double-click the company name.

**Note**   *If you attempt to open a company that someone else on the network is currently using, you see a message that QuickBooks has opened in multi-user mode because someone else is using the file. Click OK.*

7. When the QuickBooks Login window appears, enter your login name and password. Then click OK.

**Caution**   *Your login name exists in the User list, and if anyone is already accessing the files with that name, you are told to use a different name or try later.*

The first time each user logs on, it's a good idea to choose Edit | Preferences and establish personal preferences in all the My Preferences tabs that contain configuration options. (Only the administrator can make configuration changes to the Company Preferences tabs.)

# Customizing the Icon Bar

QuickBooks put icons on the icon bar, but the icons QuickBooks chose may not match the features you use most frequently. Putting your own icons on the icon bar makes using QuickBooks easier and faster. You can also change the way the icon bar and the icons it holds look. To customize the icon bar, choose View | Customize Icon Bar to open the Customize Icon Bar dialog box.

**Caution**   *The icon bar must be visible in order to customize it. If it's not on your QuickBooks screen, choose View | Icon Bar from the QuickBooks menu bar.*

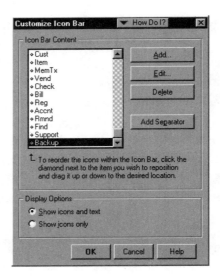

If you log in to QuickBooks, either because a single computer is set up for multiple users, or because you're using QuickBooks on a network, the settings you establish are linked to your user name. You are not changing the icon bar for other users.

## Changing the Order of Icons

You can change the order in which icons appear on the icon bar. The list of icons in the Customize Icon Bar dialog box reads top-to-bottom representing the left-to-right display on the icon bar. Therefore, moving an icon's listing up moves it to the left on the icon bar (and vice versa).

To move an icon, click the small diamond to the left of the icon's listing, hold down the left mouse button, and drag the listing to a new position.

## Changing the Icon Bar Display

You can change the way the icons display in several ways, which I'll explain in this section.

### Display Icons Without Title Text

By default, icons and text display on the icon bar. You can select Show Icons Only to remove the title text under the icons. As a result, the icons are much smaller (and you can fit more icons on the icon bar). Positioning your mouse pointer over a new, small icon still works—the description of the icon's feature appears as a Tool Tip.

## Change the Icon's Graphic, Text, or Description

To change an individual icon's appearance, select the icon's listing and click Edit. Then choose a different graphic (the currently selected graphic is enclosed in a box), change the Label (the title), or change the Description (the Tool Tip text).

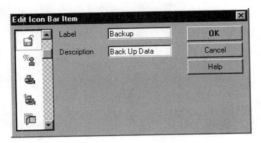

### Separate Icons

You can insert a separator between two icons, which is an effective way to create groups of icons. The separator is a gray vertical line. Select the icon that should appear to the left of the separator bar and click Add Separator. QuickBooks inserts "(space)" to the listing to indicate the location of the separator.

## Removing an Icon

If there are any icons you never use, or use so infrequently that you'd rather use the space they take up for icons representing features you use a lot, remove them. Select the icon in the Customize Icon Bar dialog box and click Delete. QuickBooks does not ask you to confirm the deletion; the icon is just zapped from the list (although it remains on the icon bar until you close the Customize Icon Bar dialog box).

## Adding an Icon

You can add an icon to the icon bar in either of two ways:

- Choose Add in the Customize Icon Bar dialog box.
- Automatically add an icon for a window (transaction or report) you're currently using.

### Using the Customize Icon Bar Dialog Box to Add an Icon

To add an icon from the Customize Icon Bar dialog box, click Add. If you want to position your new icon at a specific place within the existing row of icons (instead of at the right end of the icon bar), first select the existing icon that you want to sit to the left of your new icon. Then click Add. The Add Icon Bar Item dialog box opens.

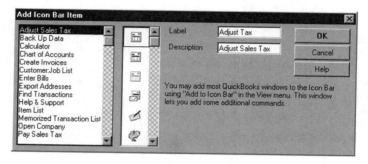

Scroll through the list to select the task you want to add to the icon bar. Then choose a graphic to represent the new icon (QuickBooks selects a default graphic, which appears within a box). If you wish, you can change the name (the title that appears below the icon) or the description (the text that appears in the Tool Tip when you hold your pointer over the icon).

### Adding an Icon for the Current Window

If you're currently working in a QuickBooks window, and it strikes you that it would be handy to have an icon for fast access to this window, you can accomplish the deed quickly. While the window is active, choose View | Add "*Name of Window*" To Icon Bar. A dialog box appears where you can choose a graphic, name, and description for the new icon.

# Using the Navigators List

The Navigators list is a vertical toolbar that has two functions:

- It provides a list of Navigators. Click an item to open its Navigator window.
- It provides a list of the currently open windows (in the Open Windows List box). Click an item to switch to that window.

The real name of this vertical toolbar is Open Window List, but because it has the title "Navigators" at the top, it's common to refer to it as the Navigators list.

Navigator windows are an assortment of related functions and features. For example, the Customers Navigator has links to QuickBooks customer functions and reports, as well as to Web-based information and features (see Figure 21-10).

**Tip**     *When any navigator is open, you can also quickly switch to any other navigator window by clicking the arrow next to the word "Navigators" in the upper-right corner of the window to see a drop-down list of navigators.*

The Open Windows list is like your Windows task bar, providing quick access to any currently opened window.

To display or hide the Navigators/Open Window list, choose View | Open Window List. The command is a toggle, and if the list is on the screen, a check mark appears on the command. When the list is displayed, you can quickly close it by clicking the X in its upper-right corner.

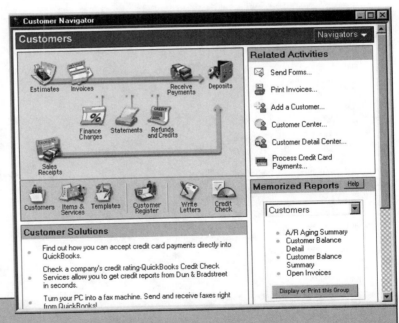

**Figure 21-10 •** All the functions and features related to customers are grouped together on the Customers Navigator window.

If you log in to QuickBooks, either because a single computer is set up for multiple users, or because you're using QuickBooks on a network, the settings you establish are linked to your user name. You are not changing the off/on setting for the Navigators/Open Window list for other users.

## Using and Customizing the Shortcut List

The Shortcut list is a vertical toolbar that combines the features of the icon bar and the Navigators list (see Figure 21-11). You can add it to your QuickBooks screen by choosing View | Shortcut List.

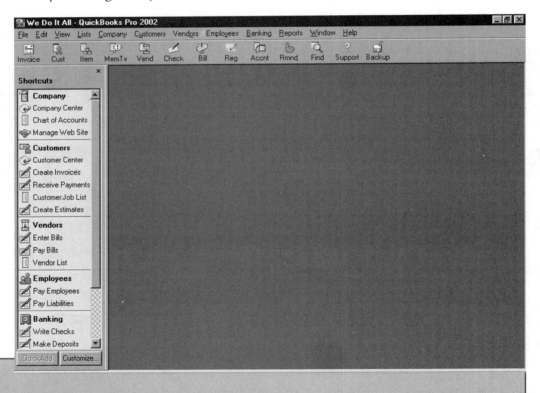

**Figure 21-11 •** Links to navigators and icons for accessing features are grouped by category in the Shortcut list.

**Tip** *If you opt to use the Shortcut list, you should turn off the Navigators list, because having both vertical bars on your screen leaves little room for your QuickBooks windows. You can also turn off the icon bar (you can customize the Shortcut list to add all the icon shortcuts you need).*

## Changing the Appearance of the Shortcut List

By default, the Shortcut list has the following characteristics:

- It's positioned on the left side of your QuickBooks window.
- It displays both icons and text for each listing.

To change those settings, click the Customize button at the bottom of the Shortcut List to open the Customize Shortcut List window shown in Figure 21-12.

- Select Show: Auto Popup to hide the list until you place your mouse pointer over it. At that point, the bar gracefully slides open. This is a way to use all your screen space for QuickBooks windows, opening the Shortcut list only when you need it.
- Select Placed On: Right to move the Navigation bar to the right side of your QuickBooks window. The auto popup feature works the same way.

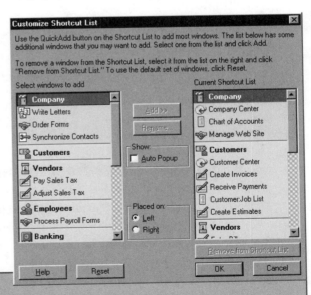

**Figure 21-12 • Change the location and behavior of the Shortcut List by using the options in the center of the Customize Shortcut List window.**

> **Tip** *You can also change the width of the Shortcut list by positioning your mouse pointer over its outside edge. When the mouse pointer turns into a double-arrow, hold down the left mouse button and drag to enlarge or reduce the width of the bar.*

# Customizing the Shortcut List Contents

You can add or remove listings to make the Shortcut list a totally customized tool. You'll probably change your mind a lot, adding and removing listings as you continue to use QuickBooks.

## Adding Listings to the Shortcut List

You can add a QuickBooks feature listing to the Shortcut list in two ways: Add the listing from the Customize Shortcut List window; or add the listing when you're using the window for the task you want to add.

To add listings from the Customize Shortcut List window, select the listing in the left pane and click Add to move the listing to the right pane. The right pane holds the contents of the Shortcut list.

To add a listing for a task you're currently performing, click the QuickAdd button on the bottom of the Shortcut list to add the current window to the listings.

## Renaming Listings on the Shortcut List

You can change the name of any item that is currently on the Shortcut list. Select the item in the right pane and click Rename. Enter the new name in the Rename Shortcut List Item window and click OK.

> **Note** *You can't rename the group headings, only the items.*

## Removing Listings from the Shortcut List

If you decide you don't use an item often enough to let it take up space on your Shortcut list, open the Customize Shortcut List window and select that item in the right pane. Click the Remove From Shortcut List button at the bottom of the right pane. You can restore the item in the future by selecting it from the left pane.

> **Tip** *If you decide you really didn't mean to add items to or delete items from the Shortcut list, click Reset to put everything back the way it was the day you first started using QuickBooks.*

**Caution**    *Watch out! If you remove one of the default items from the right pane, you won't find it later in the left pane. Instead you have to use the Reset option to start over.*

If you log in to QuickBooks, either because a single computer is set up for multiple users or because you're using QuickBooks on a network, the settings you establish are linked to your user name. You are not changing the on/off state or customized appearance of the Shortcut list for other users.

# Managing Your QuickBooks Files

## In this Chapter:

- *Back up and restore company files*

- *Archive and condense data*

- *Import and export data*

- *Update QuickBooks software*

## Chapter 22

In addition to performing bookkeeping chores in QuickBooks, you'll need to take care of some housekeeping tasks. It's important to keep your software up to date, and to make sure your data is accurate. QuickBooks provides some features to help you accomplish these responsibilities.

# Creating Companies in QuickBooks

You can create as many companies in QuickBooks as you wish. You can have your business in one company, your personal finances in another company, volunteer to run the local community association, open a second business, keep your mother-in-law's books, or create companies for any of a zillion reasons.

To create a new company, choose File | New Company from the QuickBooks menu bar. This opens the EasyStep Interview wizard (you saw this wizard the first time you used QuickBooks). You don't have to go through the entire EasyStep Interview, but you should fill out the General sections, which are represented by tabs across the top of the window. The questions are easy to answer, and you just need to keep clicking Next to move through all the sections of the interview.

If you don't want to go through the interview process, the third Welcome screen (click Next twice) has an escape hatch in the form of a button named Skip Interview. Click it to use the shortcut method of creating a company, which begins with the Creating New Company window, shown in Figure 22-1.

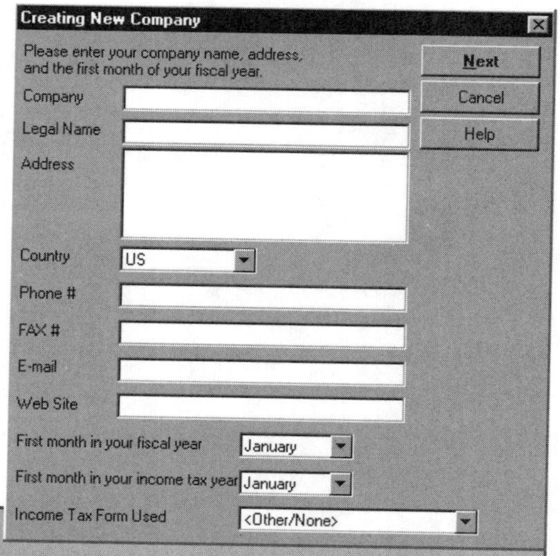

**Figure 22-1 •** Answer a slew of questions in one fell swoop with the Creating New Company window.

Click Next to see a list of company types and select the one that comes closest to this company's mission. QuickBooks uses this information to create a chart of accounts for the company.

Click Next to save the information in a company file. QuickBooks suggests a filename based on your company name, but you can invent your own filename if you wish. Click Save to make this company a file in your QuickBooks system.

QuickBooks loads the new company as the current company, and you can start setting preferences, entering data, and doing all the other tasks involved in creating a company. Read Chapters 1 and 2 for setup help.

# Backing Up and Restoring Files

Backing up your QuickBooks data is an incredibly important task and should be done on a daily basis. If you fail to back up regularly, QuickBooks will remind you periodically. Shame on you if you ever see that reminder—it means you haven't been diligent about performing this important procedure.

## Backing Up

To create a backup of the current company, choose File | Back Up from the menu bar to open the Back Up Company File dialog box.

**Tip**   *The dialog box displays a message explaining that there's an online data storage facility you can use as a repository for your backup files. If you want more information, click Tell Me More, and QuickBooks will launch your Internet connection and travel to the Web where the information resides.*

Choose a location for the backup file. QuickBooks names the backup file for you, which you can change if you wish (but there's rarely a reason to do so). QuickBooks backup files have the file extension .qbb. If you're on a network, you can back up to a remote folder by clicking Browse, selecting Network Neighborhood, and choosing the shared folder that's been set up for your backups.

Never back up onto your local hard drive. Use removable media, such as a floppy drive or a Zip drive, because the point of backing up is to be able to get back to work in case of a hard drive or computer failure.

QuickBooks compresses the data in your files to create the backup file, but if you have a great many transactions, you may be asked to put a second floppy disk in your drive to complete the backup. If so, be sure to label the floppy disks so you know which is the first disk. (You must start with the first disk if you need to restore the backup.)

Don't back up on top of the last backup, because if something happens during the backup procedure, you won't have a good backup file to restore. The best procedure is a backup disk (or set of disks) for each day of the week. If you're using expensive media, such as a Jaz drive, and you don't want to purchase that many disks, have one disk for odd days and another for even days. When you use a disk that's already received a backup file, QuickBooks will ask if you want to replace the existing file with the new one. Click Yes, because the current backup file is newer and has up-to-the-minute data. The old file is at least two days old, and perhaps a week old, depending on the way you're rotating media.

Periodically (once a week is best, but once a month is essential), make a second backup copy on a different disk and store it off-site. Then, if there's a catastrophe at the office, you can buy, rent, or borrow a computer, install QuickBooks, and restore the data.

# Restoring

You just turned on your computer and it sounds different, noisier. In fact, there's a grinding noise. You wait and wait, but the usual startup of the operating system fails to appear. Eventually, an error message about a missing boot sector appears (or some other equally chilling message). Your hard drive has gone to hard-drive heaven. You have invoices to send out, checks to write, and tons of things to do, and if you can't accomplish those tasks, your income suffers.

Don't panic; get another hard drive or another computer (the new one will probably cost less than the one that died because computer prices keep dropping). If you buy a new hard drive, it will take some time to install your operating system. If you buy a new computer, it probably comes with an operating system installed.

Take another few minutes to install your QuickBooks software. Now you're ready to go back to work and make money:

1. Start QuickBooks. The opening window tells you there's no company open and suggests you create one.

2. Ignore that message. Put the disk that contains your last good backup into the floppy (or other removable media) drive.

3. Choose File | Restore from the QuickBooks menu bar.

4. When the Restore From window appears (see Figure 22-2), change any settings that are incorrect.

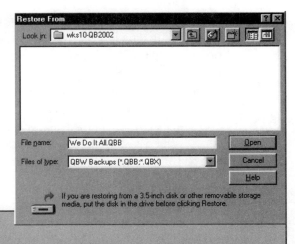

**Figure 22-2 • Use the Look In box to switch to the floppy drive (or a network drive) to locate your backup file.**

5. Click Open. If your backup occupies multiple floppy disks, you'll be prompted to insert disks.

QuickBooks displays a message that your data files have been restored successfully. You did it! Aren't you glad you back up regularly? Click OK and go to work!

> **Tip**   *If this backup wasn't saved yesterday, you must re-create every transaction you made between the time of this backup and the last time you used QuickBooks.*

## Archiving and Condensing Data

QuickBooks provides a feature that enables you to condense certain data in your company file in order to make your file smaller. You can use it to make backing up faster (using fewer disks) or to save room on your hard drive. While this seems to be a handy feature, it carries some significant side effects in the loss of details about transactions. Before using this feature, consider other ways to survive with a very large file.

## Alternatives to Condensing Data

Condensing data is a last-resort solution to a problem that might be resolved by other means. If your intent is to make the backup faster by eliminating the need to insert additional floppy disks, consider getting removable media that is larger in capacity. Drives such as Iomega Zip (the disks hold 100MB or 250MB of data) and Iomega Jaz (the disks hold 1GB or 2GB of data) are terrific for backing up. You can also install a tape backup system that holds gigabytes of data.

**Note** *You can get more information about Jaz and Zip drives at www.iomega.com.*

If your problem is a lack of sufficient hard-drive space, do some housekeeping on your hard drive. Get rid of temporary files, especially those stored by your browser when you visit the Internet. All browsers provide a menu command to empty the temporary files directory (sometimes called the *cache*).

## Understanding the Condensing Procedure

If none of these suggestions is workable, and you feel your file size has gotten out of hand, you should condense your data. Consider this solution only after you've been using QuickBooks for more than a year or so, because you don't want to lose the details for the current year's transactions.

### Choosing a Condensing Date

When you condense your data, QuickBooks asks you for the date you want to use as the cutoff date. Everything you no longer need before that date is condensed. No open transactions are condensed; only those data items that are completed, finished, and safe to condense are targeted. Also, any transactions before the condensing date that affect current transactions are skipped, and the details are maintained in the file.

### Understanding Summary Transactions

The transactions that fall within the parameters of the condensing date are deleted and replaced with summary transactions. Summary transactions are nothing but journal entry transactions that show the totals for the transactions, one for each month that is condensed. The account balances are not changed by condensing data, because the summary transactions maintain those totals.

**Note** *You can also configure the condensing feature to remove list items that have never been used.*

## Understanding the After-Effects

You won't be able to run detail reports for those periods before the condensing date. However, summary reports will be perfectly accurate in their financial totals.

You will be able to recognize the summary transactions in the account registers because they will be marked with a transaction type GENJRNL.

## Condensing Your File

Condensing your QuickBooks file is very simple, because a wizard walks you through the process. To start, choose File | Archive & Condense Data from the menu bar. The Archive & Condense Data window appears, offering two choices for proceeding. You can condense transactions as of a specific date of your choice, or you can remove all transactions.

If you want to choose a date to condense your data, QuickBooks automatically displays the last day of the previous year as the condensing date (see Figure 22-3). You can use this date or choose an earlier date (a date long past, so you won't care if you lose the transaction details). Be sure to choose the last day of a month or year.

Click Next and choose additional criteria for selecting a transaction to be removed. QuickBooks presents transaction types that are not removed by default (see Figure 22-4), and can select any of them to include them in the "to be removed" list.

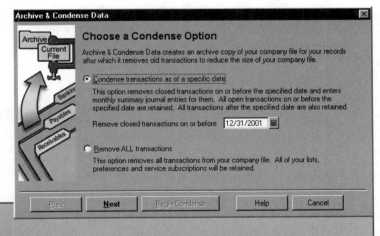

**Figure 22-3 • Select the option you want to use for the condensing feature.**

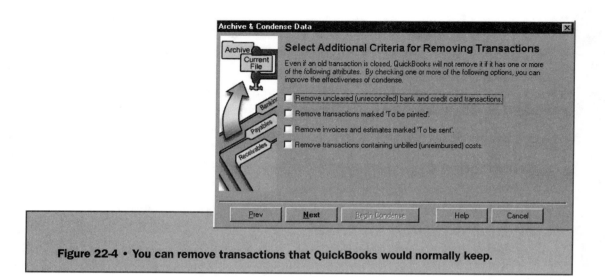

**Figure 22-4 •** You can remove transactions that QuickBooks would normally keep.

Click Next and select the lists (accounts, customers, vendors, etc.) you want QuickBooks to check for unused items that should be removed.

Click Next to see an informational window in which the condense process is explained. Click Begin Condense to start the process. QuickBooks displays a message telling you that first your data file needs to be backed up. This is not an everyday backup, it's the last backup of a full data file before information is removed. Therefore, use new disks for this backup. Click OK to begin the backup.

As soon as QuickBooks finishes backing up it starts condensing data. You'll see progress bars on your screen as each step completes. After a few minutes, you're told that the condensing of your data files is complete, and you're given the name of the archive copy of your data file (which is intact, so you can open it if you need to see transaction details).

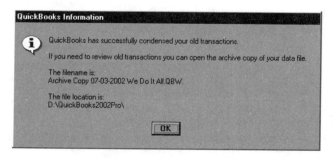

# Updating QuickBooks

QuickBooks provides an automatic update service you can use to make sure your QuickBooks software is up-to-date and trouble-free. This service provides you with any maintenance releases of QuickBooks that have been created since you purchased and installed your copy of the software. A maintenance release is distributed when a problem is discovered and fixed. This is sometimes necessary, because it's almost impossible to distribute a program that is totally bug-free (although my experience has been that QuickBooks generally releases without any major bugs, since Intuit does a thorough job of testing).

The Update QuickBooks service also provides notes and news from Intuit so you can keep up with new features and information for QuickBooks.

**Caution**   *This service does not provide upgrades to a new version; it just provides updates to your current version.*

The Update QuickBooks service is an online service, so you must have configured QuickBooks for online access (see Chapter 16). When you want to check for updated information, choose File | Update QuickBooks from the menu bar to open the Update QuickBooks window shown in Figure 22-5.

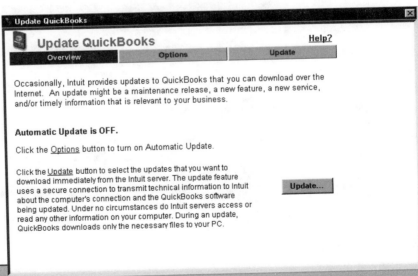

**Figure 22-5 •** In the Update QuickBooks window, you can configure update options or download the latest updates.

> **Note**   *You'll notice in Figure 22-5 that I have the automatic update service turned off. I do this because I don't like the idea of QuickBooks (or any other software, including the operating system) downloading files without my knowing about it. QuickBooks doesn't even have to be running for this function to run.*
>
> *If you have an always-on Internet connection (cable modem or DSL), QuickBooks can be comparing the files on your hard drive to the files on the Intuit Web site constantly. Whenever something new is available, it's downloaded without your knowledge. If you use a modem to connect to the Internet, that behind-the-scenes checkup and subsequent download takes place when you connect, and you don't know it's occurring (you think you're only collecting e-mail or visiting Web pages). When automatic updates are turned off, you not only get to choose when to update, you also can choose what to update.*
>
> *All of this, of course, is a personal philosophy and if you prefer the full automation of automatic updates, don't change the default setting (Automatic Update is ON).*

## Configuring QuickBooks Update Service

Click the Options link to configure the Update feature. As you can see in Figure 22-6, you have several choices for updating your software components. You can freely change any options you set, because nothing is etched in stone.

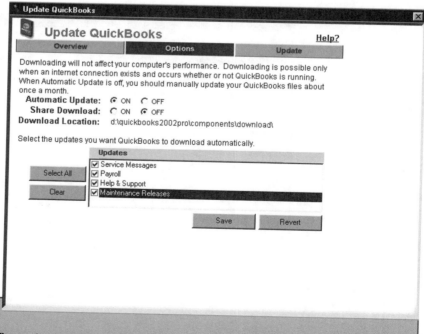

**Figure 22-6 •** Configure the QuickBooks Update services.

## Automatic Updates

You can take advantage of automatic updates, which allow QuickBooks to check the Intuit update site on the Internet periodically while you're connected to the Internet. QuickBooks doesn't have to be running for this function to occur. If new information is found, it's downloaded to your hard drive without notifying you. If you happen to disconnect from the Internet while updates are being downloaded, the next time you connect to the Internet, QuickBooks will pick up where it left off.

## Sharing Updates on a Network

If you're using QuickBooks in multi-user mode, across a network, you must configure the Update QuickBooks service to share downloaded files with other users. The process of updating places the downloaded files on the computer that holds the shared QuickBooks data files. For this to occur, every user on the network must open his or her copy of QuickBooks and configure the Update options for Shared Download.

## Selecting Update Types

Select the types of files you want QuickBooks to download when you update. The most important selection is Maintenance Releases, which fixes problems and adds features.

## Determining Update Status

Click the Update link at the top of the page to open the Update QuickBooks window, which displays information about the current status of the service, including the last date that QuickBooks checked for updates and the names of any files that were downloaded.

Click the check boxes next to each specific type of update to select/deselect those file types. Then click Get Updates to tell QuickBooks to check the Internet immediately and bring back any files. After files are downloaded, click the listing to see more information about that download. Most of the time, the files are automatically integrated into your system. Sometimes the information box tells you that the files will be integrated when you exit QuickBooks.

# Appendices

## Part Five

Technical and instructional books always have at least one appendix. Those of us who write computer books include them so we can organize the books in a way that lets you jump right into the software starting with Chapter 1. However, for most computer software, there's either an installation routine or a configuration routine that must be handled before you dive into using the software, and we use the appendices to instruct you on the appropriate methods for accomplishing these chores.

For accounting software, the installation and setup procedures are far more important than for any other type of software. If the structure isn't right, the numbers won't be right.

You must read Appendix A before you do anything. In fact, you should read it and use the suggestions in it before you even install QuickBooks. That's why I named it "Do This First!" The rest of the appendices can be read as you need them.

# Do This First!

Before you do anything with your QuickBooks software, you have to do three things:

- Decide on the starting date for your QuickBooks records.
- Find all the detailed records, notes, memos, and other items that you've been using to track your financial numbers.
- Create an opening trial balance to enter into QuickBooks.

If you don't prepare your records properly, all the advantages of a computer bookkeeping system will be lost to you. The information you enter when you first start using QuickBooks will follow you forever. If it's accurate, that's great! It means you have the right foundation for all the calculations that QuickBooks will perform for you. If it's not accurate, it will come to haunt you in the worst sense of the word.

It's not that you can't change things in QuickBooks; it's that if you start with bad numbers you frequently can't figure out which numbers were bad. Your inability to trace the origin of a problem is what makes the problem permanent.

So get out that shoebox, manila envelope, or whatever container you've used to keep numbers. We're going to organize your records in a way that makes it easy to get QuickBooks up and running—accurately.

# Deciding on the Start Date

The *start date* is the date on which you begin entering your bookkeeping records into QuickBooks. Think of it as a conversion date. In the computer consulting field, we call this "the date we go live." Things went on before this date (these are historical records and some of them must be entered into QuickBooks), but from this date on, your transactions go through QuickBooks.

This is not a trivial decision. The date you select has an enormous impact on how much work it's going to be to set QuickBooks up. For example, if you choose a starting date in September, everything that went on in your business prior to that date has to be entered into your QuickBooks system before you start entering September transactions. Okay, that's an exaggeration, because you can enter some numbers in bulk instead of entering each individual transaction, but the principle is the same.

If it's March, this decision is a lot easier, because the work attached to your QuickBooks setup is less onerous.

Here's what to think about as you make this decision:

- The best way to start a new computer accounting software system is to have every individual transaction in the system—every invoice you sent to customers, every check you wrote to vendors, every payroll check you gave an employee.

- The second best way to start a new computer accounting software system is to have running totals, plus any open transactions, in the system up to a certain date (your starting date), and then after that every single transaction is in the system. Open transactions are unpaid bills (either customer or vendor).

There is no third best way, because any fudging on either of those choices makes your figures suspect. There's no point in doing all the setup work if it means the foundation of your financial house is shaky.

If it's the first half of the year when you read this, make your start date the first day of the year and enter everything you've done so far this year. It sounds like a lot of work, but it really isn't. When you start entering transactions in QuickBooks, such as customer invoices, you just pick the customer, enter a little information, and move on to the next invoice. Of course, you have to enter all your customers, but you'd have to do that even if you weren't entering every transaction for the current year. (Chapter 2 is all about entering lists: customers, vendors, and so on.)

If it's the middle of the year, toss a coin. Seriously, if you have goo gobs of transactions every month, you might want to enter large opening balances and then enter real transactions as they occur beginning with the start date.

If it's late in the year as you read this, perhaps September or October or later, and you usually send a lot of invoices to customers, write a lot of checks, and do your own payroll, think about waiting until next year to start using QuickBooks.

# Gathering the Information You Need

You have to have quite a bit of information available when you first start to use QuickBooks, and it's ridiculous to hunt it down as each particle of information is needed. It's much better to gather it all together now, before you start working in QuickBooks.

## Cash Balances

You have to tell QuickBooks what the balance is for each bank account you use in your business. Don't glance at the checkbook stubs—that's not the balance I'm talking about. The balance is the reconciled balance. And it has to be a reconciled balance as of the starting date you're using in QuickBooks. So if you haven't balanced your checkbooks against the bank statements for a while, do it now.

Besides the reconciled balance, you need to know the dates and amounts of the transactions that haven't yet cleared.

## Customer Balances

If any customer owes you money as of your starting date, you have to tell QuickBooks about it. You have a couple of ways to do this:

- During the QuickBooks setup procedure (the EasyStep Interview), tell QuickBooks the total amount owed to you by each customer. The amount is treated as one single invoice, and payments are applied to this invoice.
- Skip the customer balance information during the QuickBooks setup procedure. Then enter each unpaid customer invoice yourself, giving the real dates for each invoice. Those dates must be earlier than your QuickBooks start date.

This means you have to assemble all the information about unpaid customer invoices, including such details as how much of each invoice was for services, for items sold, for shipping, and for sales tax.

## Vendor Balances

This is like the customer balances. You have the same chores (and the same decisions) facing you regarding any unpaid bills you owe to vendors. If they're not a lot, it might be easiest to pay them, just to avoid the work.

## Asset Balances

Besides your bank accounts, an asset I've already covered, you have to know the state, as of the starting date, of all your assets. You'll need to know the current value, and also what the accumulated depreciation is.

The open customer balances you enter determine the A/R asset automatically.

## Liability Balances

Get all the information about your liabilities together. The open vendor bills you enter determine your A/P balance automatically.

You'll need to know the current balance of any loans or mortgages. If there are unpaid withholding amounts from payroll, they must be entered. (Now there's an item that's easier to pay instead of entering.)

## Payroll Information

If you do the payroll instead of using a payroll service, you'll need to know everything about each employee: social security number, all the information that goes into determining tax status (federal, state, and local), and which deductions are taken for health or pension. You have all this information, of course; you just have to get it together. If your employees are on salary, you've probably been repeating the check information every payday, with no need to look up these items. Dig up the W-4 forms and all your notes about who's on what deduction plan.

You also need to know which payroll items you have to track: salary, wages, federal deductions, state deductions (tax, SUI, SDI), local income tax deductions, benefits, pension, and any other deductions (garnishments, for example). And that's not all—you also have to know the name of the vendor to whom these withholding amounts are remitted (government tax agencies, insurance companies, and so on).

My advice is that you don't enter a year-to-date amount for your payroll as of your QuickBooks start date. This is one place where you should go back to the beginning of the year and enter each check. If you enter one total amount for each payroll item, and your starting date is July, what will you do when somebody asks, "Can I see your first quarter totals?" If that "somebody" is the IRS, they like a quick, accurate answer.

## Inventory Information

You need to know the name of every inventory item you carry, how much you paid for each item, and how many of each item you have in stock as of the starting date.

## Other Useful Bits of Paper

Find last year's tax return. QuickBooks is going to want to know which tax forms you use. Also, there's usually other information on the tax forms you might need (depreciation schedules, for example).

If you have a loan or mortgage, have the amortization schedule handy. You can figure out the year-to-date (the date is the QuickBooks starting date) principal and interest amounts.

# Opening Trial Balance

Your opening trial balance, which probably should be prepared with the help of your accountant, almost creates itself during the setup process. If your QuickBooks start date is the beginning of the year, it's a snap. The opening trial balance for the first day of the year has no income or expenses. It should look something like this:

| Account Type | Account | Debit | Credit |
|---|---|---|---|
| Assets | Bank | $10,000 | |
| | Fixed Assets | $50,000 | |
| | Accumulated Depreciation/ Fixed Assets | | $5,000 |
| Liabilities | Loan from Corner Bank | | $15,000 |
| Equity | Equity | | $40,000 |

Notice that there is no inventory figure in this opening balance. The reason is that you want to receive the inventory into your system so there's a quantity available for each inventory item. Otherwise, no matter what you want to sell, QuickBooks will think you don't have it in stock. As you bring the inventory in and assign it a value, your inventory asset will build itself.

If your QuickBooks starting date is any other date except for the beginning of the year, your trial balance will also contain information about sales and expenses.

You're now ready to install QuickBooks and fire it up!

# Installing QuickBooks

B efore you begin installing QuickBooks, make sure you have closed any software applications that are running. This includes any virus detection software that's running.

# Starting the Installation Program

To install QuickBooks, put the QuickBooks CD in the CD-ROM drive. The installation program should start automatically. If the CD-ROM doesn't automatically start, click the Start button and choose Settings | Control Panel from the Start menu. When the Control Panel window appears, open the Add/Remove Programs application and click Install. The Install program checks the floppy drive and the CD-ROM drive to find a program named Setup.exe. It will find and start the QuickBooks installation. (If you're using Windows XP, choose Start | Control Panel | Add Or Remove Programs.)

When the QuickBooks setup program launches, you're asked if you want to install QuickBooks. Click Yes to begin installation. The setup program displays a series of windows in which you must enter information or select options.

## Follow the Wizard Windows

The first thing you must do is enter the *installation key code* that came with your software. This code is unique, and you must use it if you ever have to reinstall the software, so put it in a safe place (and remember where you put it).

If you've purchased multiple copies of QuickBooks Pro because you plan to use the network features that are available, you must follow these rules when you enter the key code:

- If you've purchased a five-user value pack, you must use the same key code for each of the five installation procedures.
- If you've purchased a five-user value pack and also purchased additional copies of QuickBooks Pro, you must use the individual key codes for the additional copies.

Choose Express or Custom installation. Custom installation lets you select the installation folder instead of accepting the default location of the Program Files folder.

**Note**   *You must also install Internet Explorer version 5.5 if you don't already have it. The online services in QuickBooks require this version of IE, and if you prefer another browser for your non-QuickBooks work, you can continue to use it.*

You must accept the terms of the license. Then continue with any other information the wizard requires (it changes depending on whether you selected Express or Custom installation).

## Relax While the Files Are Copied

After the setup program shows you a dialog box that confirms the choices you've made, your configuration efforts are complete (click Back to make changes; click Next to continue). It takes a few minutes to copy the software files to your hard drive, and the setup program tracks the progress for you.

When the files are all copied to your hard drive, the setup program asks if you want a shortcut to QuickBooks on your desktop (click Yes), and then it tells you that installation is complete. Click Finish. You must restart your computer before you can begin using the software, and QuickBooks offers to perform this task.

**Note** *If you opt to put a shortcut on your desktop, QuickBooks actually puts three shortcuts on the desktop: a shortcut to QuickBooks, which opens the software; a shortcut to QuickBooks Support and Services, which launches your browser and takes you to the QuickBooks support pages on the Internet (you must be connected to the Internet); and a shortcut to a Web page where you can order a free evaluation copy of TurboTax.*

# Registering QuickBooks

When you first use QuickBooks, you'll be asked to register the software. You can accomplish this by going online or by calling QuickBooks on the telephone. You do not have to register immediately, but QuickBooks will periodically remind you that you haven't completed the registration process.

You will only be able to open QuickBooks 15 times without completing the registration. After that, the software will refuse to run if it's not registered.

You can begin the registration process by responding to the registration reminder notice, or by using the menu items in QuickBooks. To do the latter, choose File | Register QuickBooks from the menu bar. When the Product Registration window opens, choose Online or Phone.

## Register Online

If you choose Online, QuickBooks may walk you through a configuration process for your Internet connection (see Chapter 16 for details about this wizard). If QuickBooks automatically finds your connection, it opens your Web browser and travels to the QuickBooks Online Registration site. A registration form is displayed that you must fill out. Make your selections and click Next to go to the next page. When you have completed all the fields in the registration form, there's a short wait while the QuickBooks registration database collects the information. Then your registration number is inserted into your software.

QuickBooks may also offer to install QuickBooks online services at this time. You can read about those services throughout this book. It's best to wait until you've been using QuickBooks for a while before deciding on adding online features.

## Register by Phone

If you prefer to phone in your registration, choose the Phone option from the Product Registration window. A window opens to show you a group number as well as the serial number that's been assigned to your software. Neither of these numbers matches the key code you entered when you first installed the software (although they're based on that key code).

The window has a field for the registration number. Dial the registration telephone number (it's displayed) and give the serial number and group number to the QuickBooks registration representative. In return, you'll be given the registration number. Write it down so you have a permanent record of it. Then enter it in the field and click OK. Now you won't be nagged about registration anymore.

# Integrating QuickBooks Pro with Other Programs

I f you're using QuickBooks Pro, you can integrate your QuickBooks system with other software you may have installed. This brings more power to both your QuickBooks installation and the other software, including

- Automated integration with Microsoft Excel
- Automated mail merge with Microsoft Word
- Automated synchronization of contact information with Microsoft Outlook and Symantec ACT!
- Integration with third-party software programs that are designed to add features to QuickBooks

# Automated Integration with Excel

Integration with Excel is available automatically in many cases, such as the ability to export reports to Excel. Look for the Excel button on the top of the report window. When you click it, you can choose whether you want to start a new Excel worksheet or integrate this report with an existing Excel worksheet.

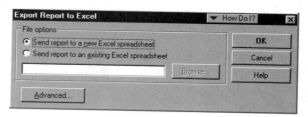

**Caution**   *QuickBooks doesn't check to see if Excel is installed on your computer. If it's not, after you make your choices in the dialog box, QuickBooks will eventually figure it out and display an error message.*

If you select the option to add the contents of this report to an existing worksheet, the Browse button activates so you can locate and select the Excel file.

Click the Advanced button to configure the options and features you want to use for this worksheet.

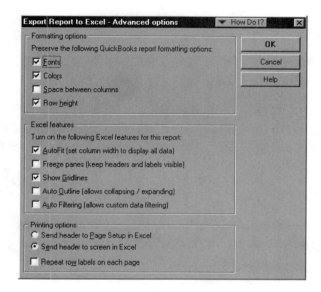

Then click OK to return to the Export Report To Excel dialog box. Click OK again, and Excel opens automatically with the report in the worksheet window. This is a great way to play "what if" games: to see the effect of rising costs, higher salaries, more benefits, or any other change in your finances.

# Mail Merge with Word

Need to send letters to some or all of your customers? Now it's easy, because Quick-Books Pro and Microsoft Word work together to enable this feature. QuickBooks Pro provides a number of prewritten letters for you to use, or you can design your own letter. In fact, you can use an existing Word document for your mail merge activities. To get started, choose Company | Write Letters from the QuickBooks menu bar.

## Using a QuickBooks Pro Letter

When you open the Write Letters window, you see three choices for letter types (see Figure C-1). This is a wizard, so you fill out each window and click the Next button to move along.

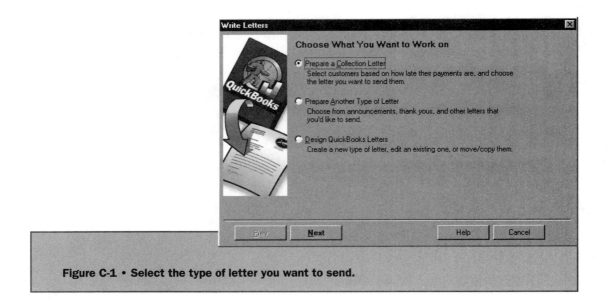

**Figure C-1 • Select the type of letter you want to send.**

If you're sending a collection letter, click Next to define the criteria for adding a customer to the mail merge list (see Figure C-2).

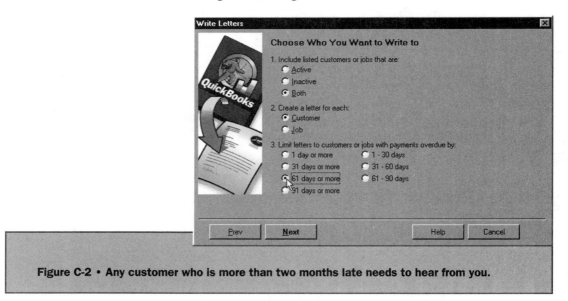

**Figure C-2 • Any customer who is more than two months late needs to hear from you.**

**Note** *If any customers who fall within the criteria have unapplied credits, QuickBooks reminds you of that fact. Cancel the wizard and apply the credits.*

The list of customers who match your criteria appears, along with their balances. You can deselect any customer you don't want to send your letter to.

Click Next to choose the collection letter you want to send. QuickBooks has created a number of different collection letters, as you can see in Figure C-3.

You might want to look at each of the letters before you make your selection, and you can accomplish that with these steps:

1. Open Microsoft Word (you don't have to close QuickBooks).
2. Click the Open icon on the Word toolbar (or choose File | Open).
3. In the Open dialog box, use the Look In text box to move to the folder that holds the QuickBooks letters. You'll find it in a folder named QuickBooks Letters, under the folder in which you installed the QuickBooks software. There's a folder for each type of QuickBooks letter.

4. Open the Collection Letters folder, and then open each letter to see which one you prefer to use.

**Caution** *The letter contains codes for mail merges; don't make any changes to them, or your mail merge may not work properly.*

5. Close Word and return to QuickBooks.

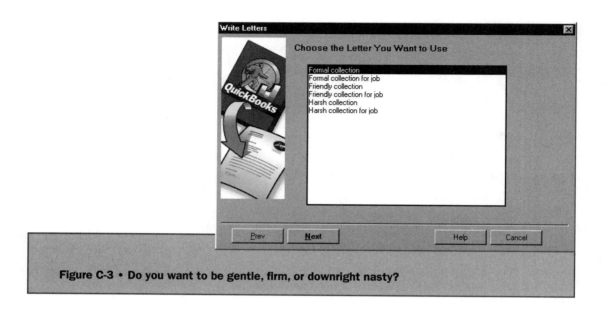

**Figure C-3 • Do you want to be gentle, firm, or downright nasty?**

The next wizard window asks you to fill in your name and title, the way you want it to appear in the letter. After you complete that information, click Create Letters to open Word. (If you haven't completed all the customer fields QuickBooks requires, a dialog box appears, informing you of that fact.)

All of your letters are displayed in the Word window. Here are some guidelines for using this mail merge document:

- There's a page break at the end of each individual letter.
- If you want to make a change in the text, you must change each individual letter.
- Changes you make to the text are not saved back to the original QuickBooks letter.
- You don't have to save the mail merge document unless you think you're going to resend the same letter to the same people (which would be unusual).

When it's all perfect, print the letters.

## Using Your Own Letter

You can use your own text if you don't want to use a QuickBooks form letter, by either writing one from scratch or using an existing QuickBooks letter as the basis of your new document.

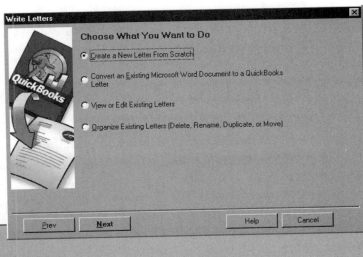

**Figure C-4 • The QuickBooks Write Letters feature offers plenty of options.**

When the first wizard window appears, select Design QuickBooks Letters and choose Next. Then select the method you want to use to create your letter (see Figure C-4).

After you make your selection, choose Next and follow the instructions to complete your task.

## Sending Other Types of Letters

You're not restricted to customers for mail merge; you can send mail to lots of different names in your QuickBooks files (vendors, employees, and others). Just select Prepare Another Type Of Letter in the first wizard window and choose Next. Then select a Name List, choose a type of letter, and specify the names you want to use from the list. The more you use the mail merge feature, the more creative you'll become.

## Synchronizing Contacts

If you use Microsoft Outlook or Symantec ACT! to manage information about business (or personal) contacts, you can synchronize the data in your contact program with QuickBooks. This means you don't have to enter information about customers, vendors, or other contacts in both programs. Synchronization makes even minor changes easier to handle. If a vendor's telephone number changes, you can enter the new information in either program, and then update both programs.

## Understanding Synchronization

You can synchronize the following data:

- Customer contact information, with the QuickBooks Customer:Job List
- Vendor contact information, with the QuickBooks Vendor List
- Other contact information, with the QuickBooks Other Names List

**Caution**     *QuickBooks names that are marked* Inactive *are never involved in the synchronization process (in either direction).*

You can establish synchronization as a one-way process, which is useful when you first begin to use this feature because most of your contact data likely is in one software application. The one-way direction will depend on whether you installed your contact management program before or after you installed QuickBooks.

## Synchronizing the Data

Before you begin, back up your QuickBooks files and your contact software files. Then choose Company | Synchronize Contacts from the QuickBooks menu bar. QuickBooks displays a message urging you to perform a backup before you synchronize. If you've just backed up, click Continue. Otherwise, click Cancel, perform the backup, and then return to the synchronization feature.

**Caution**     *You cannot synchronize contacts if you're working in multi-user mode. Wait until nobody else on the network is working in QuickBooks and switch to single-user mode.*

Synchronization is performed with the help of a wizard, which means you click Next to move through all the windows:

1. The first wizard window asks you to select your contact management program (see Figure C-5). Choose Outlook or ACT!, depending on the software you use.
2. In the next window, select a type of synchronization: Two Way or One Way (if you choose One Way, indicate the direction).

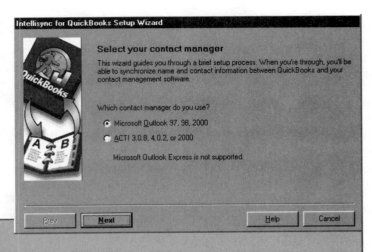

**Figure C-5 • You must have a supported version of your contact software.**

3. The next window asks for the path and name of the database. Unless you have an excellent memory, click the Browse button to navigate through your computer to find and select the database. If you're performing a two-way sync, or a one-way sync into QuickBooks, also select a folder to receive names from QuickBooks.

4. Select the QuickBooks lists you want to synchronize with your database. You may also be asked if you want to exclude any types of names from your contact program (if you perform a two-way synchronization).

5. Tell QuickBooks how to handle conflicts (see Figure C-6).

6. Click Sync Now to perform the synchronization, or click Sync Later to exit the Synchronization Setup Wizard and do the file transfers at a later time.

If you opt to synchronize later, the window that opens when you select Company | Synchronize Contacts offers you a chance to enter the Setup program again (in case you want to change something) or perform the synchronization.

After running the synchronization, QuickBooks displays information about the process. Any data QuickBooks wasn't sure how to handle is presented so you can make a decision (perhaps it isn't clear which type of name the contact is—vendor, other, etc.). When you clear up any confusion, QuickBooks opens a confirmation window showing you all the contacts that will be synchronized. Accept the data if it's correct, and QuickBooks will complete the synchronization. If the data is incorrect, cancel the synchronization and start the process again.

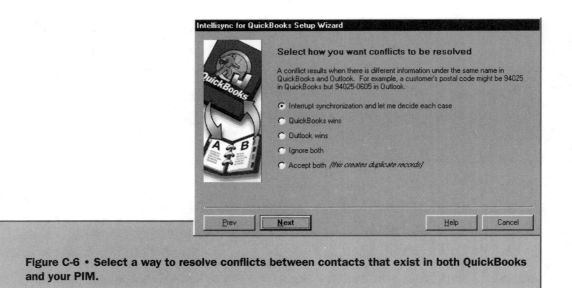

**Figure C-6** • **Select a way to resolve conflicts between contacts that exist in both QuickBooks and your PIM.**

Now you can use your contact program to track conversations and correspondence with your QuickBooks names.

# Integrating QuickBooks with Third-Party Add-on Software

A number of software companies offer programs that work directly with QuickBooks to deliver additional features. You can see what's available by choosing Company | Business Services Navigator to open the Business Services Navigator. In the Technology column, click the link Find Integrated Applications. The Solutions Marketplace window opens, and you can read about the advantages available with integrated software. To see what's available, scroll down to click the link Visit The QuickBooks Solutions Marketplace.

QuickBooks opens your browser and loads the QuickBooks Integrated Applications Web page. Select a business category to see if any software exists that would be useful to your business.

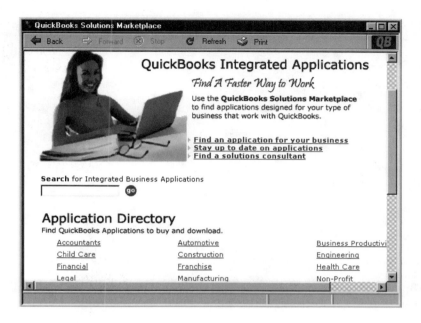

# Using QuickBooks Business Services

uickBooks isn't limited to the dull, number-crunching functions involved with bookkeeping. You have a wide choice of extra goodies you can use to enhance the way you run your business. To see what's available, and to sign up for the business services you need, choose Company | Business Services Navigator. As you can see in Figure D-1, a wide range of extra services is available.

All of the services are fee-based and require Internet access. Many of the services offer a free trial period. After your free period ends, you'll be asked to give QuickBooks a credit card number in order to continue using the service. If you're using QuickBooks Premier, the free trial periods for many of the additional services are longer than they are for QuickBooks Basic and QuickBooks Pro.

In order to access any of the services, QuickBooks opens your browser and authenticates your copy of the software (checks to see that you registered it). You're also asked for an e-mail address so QuickBooks can communicate with you about the services you sign up for.

In this appendix, I'll discuss only some of the services (going over all of them would require a whole 'nother book).

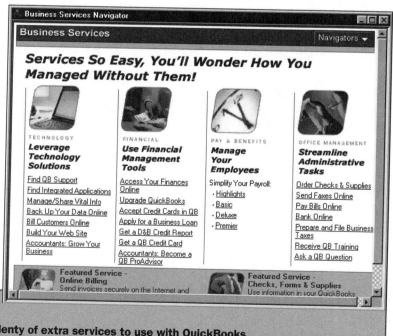

**Figure D-1 • There are plenty of extra services to use with QuickBooks.**

# QuickBooks Site Builder

Add to your sales and marketing toolbox by creating a Web site for your company through QuickBooks. For a small monthly fee (after three free months), you can maintain your own, personalized company Web site. To begin setup, in the Business Services Navigator choose Build Your Web Site (in the Technology column). A wizard takes you through all the steps of the setup process.

Enter information about the type of business you run, so QuickBooks can put relevant information on your Web site. You can change the text and graphics on your site whenever you choose. Supply your e-mail address so QuickBooks knows where to forward messages from people who visit your site and want to contact you. QuickBooks shows you a graphic that illustrates the way your site will look. Depending on the type of business you specified, you may have a choice of graphic styles. If so, pick the one you like best (you can change it later).

The Terms and Conditions under which your Web site is created and maintained are displayed for your approval. Read every word of it so you understand exactly what it is you're agreeing to.

Almost immediately, you receive e-mail from The QuickBooks Team, congratulating you on your new site and explaining how it all works. It takes about 48 hours for information about the location of your site to work its way throughout the Internet. After that, anyone entering your domain name into a browser will reach your site.

When QuickBooks builds your Web site, it uses *placeholder* text—that is, sample text that occupies an area of the page. The placeholder text should be replaced by text related to your company and its services or products. QuickBooks provides an easy-to-use format for editing the content on each page of your Web site.

# QuickBooks Merchant Card Account Services

If you want to accept credit card payments from customers, you can let QuickBooks set up your merchant card account, and then process the credit card sales directly through your QuickBooks software.

To set up credit card services, in the Business Services Navigator, choose Accept Credit Cards In QB. The QuickBooks Merchant Account Service page opens so you can read about the service. To sign up, click Sign Up Now. After you fill out the application, the financial institution QuickBooks uses will review your application and send you an e-mail to tell you how to use the merchant card services.

After you're set up for the QuickBooks merchant account, when you receive a credit payment from a customer select the option Process Credit Card Payment When Saving. Your browser opens and travels to a secure Web site to process the payment.

**Note** *A secure Web site uses encryption to protect data as it travels to and from the Internet.*

# Get Credit Reports on Customers

If you sign up for the QuickBooks Dun & Bradstreet credit report services, you can check your customers' credit status. To sign up, from the Business Services Navigator, click Get A D&B Credit Report in the Financial column.

The Credit Check Services window opens with more information about the service. Click See Pricing Information to examine all the available plans, their features, and their price structures. Besides the monthly fee for a plan, you can purchase extra services for individual fees. If you're interested in subscribing, click the Back button on the Pricing Information page to return to the Credit Check Services window. Then click Sign Up Now.

After you've subscribed to the credit check service, you can check a customer's credit, and you can stay on top of any changes in the customer's credit rating. To perform a credit check, open the Customer:Job List and select the customer. Press CTRL-E to bring up the customer's record. Click the Check Credit button (below the Company Name field).

After you've performed the first credit check for a customer, the Dun & Bradstreet credit meter appears on any Create Invoice or Create Estimates window for this customer, immediately to the right of the Customer: Job field. The credit meter is a semicircle with a color that ranges from green (low credit risk) to red (high credit risk). An arrow points to the portion of the gradient that represents the risk associated with extending credit to that customer. You can click on the credit meter to see credit details or acquire an updated credit report. If you're connected to the Internet, a credit check is performed in the background and the meter adjusts to indicate any changes in the customer's credit status.

# Bill Customers Online and Accept Online Payments

You can conduct business electronically if you sign up for online billing and online payments. To learn about this QuickBooks service, in the Business Services Navigator, select Bill Customers Online (in the Technology Column).

Read the information in the Online Billing window, and if you're interested in this service, click Signing Up For QuickBooks Online Billing. After you've subscribed, you can send customer invoices via e-mail. QuickBooks automatically adds an Internet address (URL) to the e-mail that customers can click to arrange for online payment (either through a credit card or a bank transfer). The payment is deposited into your bank account and QuickBooks automatically enters the payment against the customer's record. Your customers can use a secure Web site to access their invoices, their payment history, and other information about their accounts with your company.

# Index

**G**

**H**

**I**